MW00396008

Belonging without Othering

Belonging without Othering

How We Save Ourselves and the World

john a. powell

and

Stephen Menendian

Stanford University Press

Stanford, California

Stanford University Press
Stanford, California

©2024 by john a. powell and Stephen Menendian. All rights reserved.

No part of this book may be reproduced or transmitted in any form or by any means, electronic or mechanical, including photocopying and recording, or in any information storage or retrieval system, without the prior written permission of Stanford University Press.

Printed in the United States of America on acid-free, archival-quality paper.

Library of Congress Cataloging-in-Publication Data
Names: Powell, John A., author. | Menendian, Stephen, author.
Title: Belonging without othering : how we save ourselves and the world / John A. Powell and Stephen Menendian.
Description: Stanford, California : Stanford University Press, 2024. | Includes bibliographical references and index.
Identifiers: LCCN 2023045496 (print) | LCCN 2023045497 (ebook) | ISBN 9781503638846 (cloth) | ISBN 9781503640092 (ebook)
Subjects: LCSH: Group identity. | Belonging (Social psychology) | Other (Philosophy)—Social aspects. | Other (Philosophy)—Political aspects. | Prejudices. | Intergroup relations.
Classification: LCC HM753 .P698 2024 (print) | LCC HM753 (ebook) | DDC 305—dc23/eng/20231011
LC record available at https://lccn.loc.gov/2023045496
LC ebook record available at https://lccn.loc.gov/2023045497

Cover design: Zoe Norvell
Typeset by Newgen in Garamond Premier Pro 11.25/15

Identity would seem to be the garment with which one covers the nakedness of the self: in which case, it is best that the garment be loose, a little like the robes of the desert, through which one's nakedness can always be felt, and sometimes, discerned.

JAMES BALDWIN[1]

Interdependence and the imagination of others are constitutive features of our humanity. We depend on one another for everything, and remain helpless without the cooperation of others. The development of the capabilities of mankind in every realm and at every level depends on the progress of our cooperative practices and capabilities.

ROBERTO UNGER, *The Religion of the Future*[2]

We must love one another or die.

W. H. AUDEN, September 1, 1939[3]

Contents

Belonging without Othering

ONE

Othering and Belonging

In 1900, the pioneering sociologist W. E. B. Du Bois stood before the first assembled Pan-African Conference in London and boldly declared that "[t]he problem of the twentieth century is the problem of the color line," which he defined as "the question as to how far differences of race—which show themselves chiefly in the color of the skin and the texture of the hair—will hereafter be made the basis of denying to over half the world the right of sharing to utmost ability the opportunities and privileges of modern civilization."[1]

Although Du Bois's memorable phrase tends to strike more contemporary readers, with the benefit of hindsight, as blazingly prophetic, the substance of his brief remarks on this point—and a further elaboration in a better-known published volume a few years later—was more diagnosis than prognosis. Du Bois's commentary was ruminative of recent events and reflective of the state of the world. The imperial powers of Europe were bent on annexing and dividing up Africa in a colonization project historians have dubbed "the scramble for Africa" (1884–1914).[2] After a period of fierce political and legal contestation (which Du Bois brilliantly documented in his magnum opus, *Black Reconstruction*),[3] Jim Crow was hitting its stride in the South. *Plessy v. Ferguson* (1896) was still a recent decision,[4] and southern states were busy calling conventions to draw up new constitutions to disenfranchise Black citizens (1890–1910).[5]

Although the "color line" does not quite capture or anticipate the horror of the Holocaust, the Nazi regime very much understood its genocidal project in racial terms.* Critically, Du Bois stressed the *relations* between different peoples as being a defining challenge for humanity in the twentieth century. Our world today seems engulfed in a variety of overlapping and incessant forms of political and social turmoil. It does not require close inspection to see that "us versus them" dynamics organize, undergird, or are bound up with them.

Although race remains a powerful and enduring cleavage within societies across the globe, not every prominent form of intergroup conflict is based on race or color. Religion, ethnicity, caste, ancestry, language, sexual orientation, gender, and others loom just as large, and in some contexts, much larger. In India, for example, caste and religion undergird a range of much older and far different social divides. In Eastern Europe, language, ethnicity, and religion are conjoined in a different, but equally potent, formula. In the Middle East, religious sects and customs organize deeper social divides. On the Korean peninsula, where race has comparatively little social salience, gender, sex, and class are more prominent social cleavages.

Nonetheless, race and racism provide a readily available framework and common vernacular for thinking about out-group prejudice, discrimination, and intergroup inequality. Social movements, advocacy, legislation, and other interventions designed to promote inclusion and advance equality tend to be modeled on those addressing racism. The functioning of race and racism, particularly in the West, as what psychologists call an "availability heuristic," or a mental shortcut, helps explain the frequent characterization of other forms of out-group bigotry, such as anti-Muslim prejudice, as "racism," even though Islam is a religion, not a race.[6]

---

* Although *color* and *race* are often used interchangeably, they are not the same. This error was the basis of a gaffe by the actor Whoopi Goldberg in which she asserted, incorrectly, that the Holocaust was not about race. Jenny Gross and Neil Vigdor, "ABC Suspends Whoopi Goldberg Over Holocaust Comments," *New York Times*, February 1, 2022, https://www.nytimes.com/2022/02/01/us/whoopi-goldberg-holocaust.html. In Du Bois's usage, it is clear that he is using the term *color* to refer to race.

In addition to racism and antisemitism, hatemongering, demagoguery, ethnic and religious nationalism, polarization and fragmentation, xenophobia, nativism, and anti-immigrant sentiment, confining women into traditional gender roles and restricting reproductive rights, transphobia and LGBTQ bigotry, and Islamophobia are also hallmarks of the current moment, and no populated part of the world is free of these forces.

Given the variety of expressions to this underlying dynamic, it is little wonder that commentators, pundits, scholars, and leaders have struggled to define and characterize events within a pithy, unifying frame or have succumbed to a beguiling conflation. Successful efforts to name or define the dynamics of our current era have proved elusive or misleading, although there have been many attempts.

In this book, we maintain that the problem of the twenty-first century is the problem of "othering." Othering is a persistent and recurring problem in our world that organizes or informs nearly every major problem on the planet, from territorial disputes, sectarian violence, military conflict, the spread of disease, displacement and genocide, to hunger and food insecurity, and even climate change.

———

Far right politicians have become increasingly adept at engaging the anxiety of the "other," stoking fears of demographic change or social incursion. On the left, the myriad of grievances on behalf of oppressed or marginalized people prompt solidaristic expressions and calls for liberation, but the absence of an overarching frame inhibits mobilization of larger sympathetic blocs. Jeremiads against white supremacy, Islamophobia, or xenophobia have not proved galvanizing to the larger public nor prevented further social fragmentation or political polarization. In the center and center-left, there has been a gradual shift away from denialism, with the attendant papering over of social cleavages—by, for example, deemphasizing "identity politics"—to project a unified façade, toward a recognition and deeper understanding of the fragmenting and polarizing social dynamics occurring across the globe, but without an effective organizing framework to counter these dynamics or foster broader solidarity.

One of the avatars of hopeful unity, Barack Obama—as epitomized by his landmark 2004 speech decrying the "slicing and dicing" of Americans into blue or red states—seemed painfully aware of these trends toward the end of his presidency. In an interview with the *Atlantic* late in his second term, President Obama cited "tribalism" and "atavism" as a source of much conflict bubbling over the world. In his view, many of the stresses of globalization, the "collision of cultures brought on by the Internet and social media," and "scarcities," some of which will be exacerbated by climate change and population growth, lead to a "default position" to organize by "tribe—us/them, a hostility toward the unfamiliar or unknown," and to "push back against those who are different."[7]

In an interview shortly after the November 2015 Paris terrorist attacks, in which he refused to use the term *Islamophobia*, French prime minister Manuel Valls explained that "[i]t's difficult to construct a single term that captures the variegated expressions of a broad prejudice."[8] Valls perceptively recognized the need for a nonreductive term that denotes the multidimensional nature of social marginality.

Both President Obama's and the French prime minister's interview commentaries are instances of leaders gesturing in the direction of "othering," grasping for a frame to describe a global phenomenon, but lacking trenchant terminology to characterize it. We make the case for "othering" as a revealing and useful framework that encompasses and pithily describes the dynamics Obama observed, and an answer to Valls's challenge, a single term that captures "variegated expressions" of broad prejudice.

"Othering" is a clarifying frame that reveals a set of common processes, conditions, and dynamics that propagate and maintain social group inequality and marginality. Although specific expressions of othering, such as racism or ethnocentrism, are widely recognized and richly studied, this broader phenomenon is inadequately understood.* Bridging this gap in knowledge is one of the primary purposes of this book.

---

* We may learn a great deal about the dynamics of othering and the othering process by investigating its more prominent expressions, like racism, but it is a mistake to reduce othering as such to one of its many expressions. A related error is presuming

We define othering as a set of dynamics, processes, and structures that, consciously or unconsciously, denies, or fails to accord, full and equal membership in society as well as human dignity on the basis of social group affiliation and identity, and therefore tends to engender marginality and persistent inequality across any of the full range of human differences based on group identities. Dimensions of othering include, but are not limited to, religion, sex, race, ethnicity, socioeconomic status (class), caste, disability, sexual orientation, and skin tone.

Othering is an expansive term that denotes common mechanisms and similar dynamics undergirding many expressions of prejudice and group-based marginalization and subordination without washing out countless critical differences between cases. In the next chapter, we will make the case for "othering" as a framework and term that best characterizes and describes these dynamics by highlighting the limitations of similar terms purporting to denote these phenomena, such a "tribalism," "caste," "chauvinism," and the like. We use the term *othering* as opposed to *otherness*, *otherism*, or *otherized* to show that it is a verb, an ongoing and dynamic set of processes rather than a static condition, fixed attitude, sentiment, or predisposition. With many examples, this book attempts to illuminate the nature of othering, the forces that engender it and the mechanisms that sustain and reinforce it.

In the process, we hope to bring into sharper relief the limitations of many of the commonly advanced solutions to othering. Far from reducing intergroup conflict, repressive responses like assimilation, segregation, and expulsion at best push it temporarily out of sight or bottle it up, leaving grievances to fester until they explode. And while egalitarian and other social justice movements can improve material conditions and the standing of marginalized groups in society, they tend to engender backlash, amplify polarization, and further fragmentation.

This book ultimately argues on behalf of a belonging paradigm and framework as the only one that has the potential to ultimately overcome these dynamics and reweave the social fabric. The problem of nonbelonging

---

that fully addressing one of its more prominent expressions (like racism) will solve all forms of othering.

may be most acutely felt by marginalized and othered groups, but it is experienced by superordinate and high-status groups as well. Across societies, seemingly record numbers of people of all backgrounds report loneliness, despair, and isolation and sense disconnection and dislocation or simply bewilderment. A belonging paradigm is attentive to both the problem of othering and the various crises of identity, resentment, and backlash that exacerbate it.

We regard belonging as both a state of being and a set of processes and interventions that help bring about a more hopeful future. The stakes could not be higher. Building a world of greater belonging is not merely about reducing intergroup inequality and improving conditions for marginalized peoples. It may be necessary to humanity's very survival.

————

Can human beings coexist? This is a deceptively simple question, but in many quarters of society, contemporarily or historically, coexistence among different racial, ethnic, or religious groups seems utterly intolerable, as this book painfully documents. For example, white southerners during Jim Crow found the presence of Black Americans in their schools and neighborhoods just as unacceptable as many Protestants in Northern Ireland found their Catholic neighbors at the height of the "Troubles," or Palestinians and Jewish Israelis may fearfully regard each other in the Middle East today. But separation behind national borders or within ethnic enclaves cannot guarantee security in diverse societies.

Societies that fragment into ever-smaller units multiply the reasons and possibilities for conflict. Smaller and more homogeneous cultural units are more susceptible to insularity and chauvinism. Not only are there more borders and boundaries, but there are more grounds for grievance and potential for provocation.

The question of coexistence is not simply one front in a grand ideological battle between the forces of equity and justice on one side, and intolerance, bigotry, and prejudice on the other. More fundamentally, there is a divide in our world between people who pine to build and inhabit communities organized around a single, primary salient identity and those who desire to live in diverse, pluralistic communities.[9] Unfortunately, the preference for cultural closure that results in balkanization spans all political, ideological, racial, ethnic, religious, and class divisions.

Unless we find ways to challenge these forces, reverse these trends, and build a bigger and more inclusive "we," the future could look more like the bloody past—deepening division, rising hostility, continued fragmentation, nationalistic aggression, and a tragic ledger of ever more deadly and destructive wars and violence. The ultimate outcome would be the end not only of civilization, but potentially of life as we know it on this planet.[10] We must develop and advance a belongingness agenda that embraces all people in order to build a fairer and more just society so that humanity not only survives but flourishes.

————

This is a book about the high price and nature of social group inequality, and how we should address it. Specifically, this book attempts to reveal the contours of the othering process, impress upon readers of the dangers of continued othering, and make the case for belonging as a paradigm that can heal the social fabric and address persistent intergroup inequality. Accordingly, it is organized into two parts. Part I, on othering, encompasses the next three chapters.

We begin our story of othering in Chapter 2 with a tragic and powerful account of othering that illuminates many common elements and key features. From there, we attempt to demonstrate the near universality of the dynamics of othering across quite different societies and over the long course of human history. There appears to be no known human society free from dynamics that marginalize or stigmatize particular social groups. Yet, despite the ubiquity of othering, there is no "natural" or inevitable other. There is no social group that appears marginalized or "othered" in every known society.

The "other" can be a numerical, racial, ethnic, or religious majority *or* minority. An othered group may hold great wealth or be economically precarious. Although numerical advantage, power, and wealth may make it more difficult to "other" a particular group, those advantages cannot completely inoculate against it. One of our key contentions is that any given social "other" is determined by the particularities of the unfolding and

evolving othering process, not by any specific or particular trait, characteristic, chromosome, or condition. In this way, we distinguish between
the concept of "the other" and the actual process of "othering." The social
"other" is constituted through—and as a by-product of—the othering
process.

Different processes of othering yield differently othered social groups,
with correspondingly different forms of treatment, some harsher or more
confining or inhibiting than others. Some groups may be the subject of
opprobrium or disapproval while others are merely pitied or looked down
upon. Others may be viewed as subhuman or with contemptuous disgust
while others are respected but feared and despised.

By examining different accounts and experiences of othering, we can
begin to appreciate that human societies can harbor more than one social
"other." Each of these groups may be differently regarded or positioned in
society relative to dominant or advantaged groups (and each other) because
of the different processes of othering. Misogyny or racism functions differently than Islamophobia or homophobia, constituting differently "othered" social groups and different relative standing and regard in society.
Critically, even members of "othered" groups can participate in the process
of othering various social groups, even their own.

The othering process originates in the process of identity formation
itself, as social distinctions are established and meanings disseminated and
socialized. Chapter 3 reviews theories of identity formation and attempts
to demonstrate that, although social identities are generally experienced
as fixed and stable, they continually evolve. This evolution is occasionally
signaled by shifting terminology or labels, as when terms like "People of
Color" evolve into *BIPOC*, or *Latino* and *Chicano* are propounded as alternatives to *Hispanic*. But these terms reflect changing meanings as well.
This is how *Latinx* becomes a contested identity label, how *Black* evolved
from a term of opprobrium to a widely employed racial category, or *queer*
was "reclaimed" and transformed from a slur to a term of empowerment
and positive identity. These changes are not just differences in nomenclature but also signify a shift in how a group is likely to be seen or regarded,
even if the individual does not similarly experience a shift or decoherence
in identity.

Contrary to the presumption that identities are merely neutral or su-perficial labels rooted in culture, beliefs, traits, or characteristics of the group, social identities, and the range of meanings that attach to them, are by-products of the othering process. For marginalized or subordinate groups, identities are instrumental as a way of fostering solidarity and re-sistance to the othering process. The coherence of marginalized identities, and the attachment individuals place on those identities, tend to corre-spond to the regard or treatment experienced by that group. The more op-pressed or threatened a group feels, the greater the salience and centrality of that identity to members of the group. For superordinate or dominant groups, prevailing identities may be a product of deliberate efforts to re-solve conflicts rooted in prior identities, to create a new and larger "we." The problem arises when this "we" is constructed on an exclusionary basis, defining a clear (although new) "other."

The cornerstone of othering is when a society binds itself to a particular narrow social identity, privileging members of that group or extending spe-cial status and dignity to it above others. The most dangerous expression of this in the modern world is the problem of ethno-nationalism and ethno-states, which tie national identity to ethnic, racial, cultural, or religious identity. Since no human society is entirely homogeneous, such dynamics result in categorical othering.

The problem is not just that some groups have greater material advan-tages or political power; the problem lies with dominance, supremacy, and hegemony. For members of dominant groups, equality feels like oppres-sion. Chapter 4 explores how demagogic identity entrepreneurs organize grievance, spinning insidious conspiracy theories, stoking fear and anxiety of "the other" or fanning animosities that are weaponized into backlash and hatemongering. Although certain conditions, such as rapid environ-mental, economic, or political change, provide fertile soil for demagogues, whether they succeed or not depends upon the norms and institutions in society.

Part II encompassing Chapters 5 through 7, shifts the focus away from the processes that engender othering, and toward the antidote. Al-though not the only conceivable remedy, we argue that a belonging par-adigm is the most promising vehicle for ultimately solving the problem of othering and countering the forces that engender it. Belonging is a powerful aspiration, but we call for a particular kind of belonging required for this purpose. Belonging is a fundamental human need, and that need plays a central role in shaping human societies. When manipulated, the need to belong is actually the source of much othering. One of the powers of othering is that it can forge a sense of social solidarity and belonging. This is community building through exclusion, or belonging based on othering. We reject this type of belonging, and identify the fundamental challenge of how to forge "belonging without othering" instead: how to reject the idea of a categorical other, or "them," and build a bigger and more expansive "we."

Chapter 5 outlines what belonging without othering looks like in theory, policy and practice, law, and then at a deeper spiritual or ontological level. It also calls for moving beyond more limited paradigms, such as "equity," with its emphasis on material resources and tangible outcomes, or "inclusion," in which outsiders are invited, but often treated more as a guest than as a full participant. We present a four-part definition of belonging rooted in inclusion, recognition or visibility, a sense of connection, and empowerment, and share examples how these elements have been realized in practice. We call for a culture that embraces the practice of "bridging," and offer guidance on how to do this effectively.

More than merely a policy-based or practical concept, belongingness introduces difficult philosophical questions about how we develop more inclusive, mutual, interrelated identities, and narratives and stories to support and reinforce belonging practice. Chapter 6 examines how an expansive belonging paradigm requires a better understanding of the self, including its inherent multiplicity and its situated relatedness. It turns out that othering and "selfing" are two sides of the same coin. Identity categories that become deeply rooted are those that provide meaningful social distinctions among people, often through an implicit negation. Thus "white" acquires meaning in relation to "Black," or "Roman" in relation to "Barbarian," or "Christian" in relation to "pagan," "Jew," or "Muslim." In this account, the problem of othering cannot be solved by simply fixing the condition or situation of the marginalized or subordinated group. The othering process creates both the subordinate "other" *and* the dominant or more favored non-other.

One of the practical implications is that we cannot create true belonging in a world in which everyone is clinging to their selves as currently constructed. Nor can we ask people to abandon their existing identities, submitting themselves to an ontological death. We need to lean into our multiplicity and co-create new and varied identities that can knit people together in novel ways, and offer social spaces and experiences that affirm these connections.

How do we build a society and develop a set of narratives and scripts to support and reinforce identities, policies, and practices of belonging? We need new stories and better storytellers. We need stories that leave no one out or behind, and that help re-weave the social fabric while rejecting mythologies of the past.

The call to build belonging without othering should not be viewed as primarily a psychological or interpersonal project. This effort necessarily touches every aspect of our society, including not just what we do but also who we are, and who we are becoming. We need a belonging movement involving all sectors of society. Chapter 7 examines particular moments in history or places where a more broadly inclusive vision of society has been developed and pursued, however imperfectly, and how we might borrow or adapt lessons to advance our own vision of a world of greater belonging.

———

Although the concepts and ideas developed in this book are introduced and progress linearly, this book can be approached or engaged in different ways. For readers primarily concerned with the notion and problem of othering, Part I can function as a book unto itself. We have also provided a supplemental chapter, for readers who want to dive deeper and better understand the specific mechanisms that cause and sustain intergroup inequality, and that therefore tend to be found in various expressions of othering. These mechanisms explain how the social and psychological processes manifest in political and institutional arrangements, and inequitably distribute power and resources across social cleavages. Not every mechanism is evident in each instance of othering, but these mechanisms are common to many expressions of othering. The framework of "othering" helps us see, more clearly, these common features and recognize recurring dynamics across expressions.

For readers primarily interested in belonging, what it means and how to achieve it, it is possible to jump ahead and read Part II for that purpose. For readers who want to understand the principal ideas of "othering" and "belonging" without delving into various details, nuances, or implementation specifics, Chapters 2 and 5 alone can suffice.

We encourage you to follow your interests as you engage this work. But we also invite you to participate in practices that help usher in a world of greater belonging. Our future may depend upon it.

Part I

Othering

TWO

Marginality and the Other

In the early morning hours of August 25, 2017, Myanmar's army and security forces, working in concert with trained civilians, began systematically slaughtering thousands—if not tens of thousands—of Rohingya people, an ethnic and religious minority group, in hundreds of villages throughout three townships in Rakhine state.[1] Rakhine is Myanmar's westernmost state, a long crescent of land roughly the size of Maryland that sits on the Bay of Bengal. Soldiers slit throats, shot victims, burned homes and people alive, and raped and mutilated women and girls. Men and boys were killed first, and infants were thrown into bonfires.[2] Similar stories and scenes of horror played and replayed across the region.

Ultimately, more than two-thirds of Myanmar's estimated 1 million Rohingya peoples fled across the Naf River to the west into neighboring Bangladesh, where they settled in refugee camps of freshly cleared forest. Many hundreds if not thousands of people died during the crossing as boats capsized or from thirst and starvation, or drowned in the rains.[3] Over 700,000 Rohingya escaped to Bangladesh within weeks, the fastest refugee outflow at the time since the Rwandan genocide, according to human rights groups.[4]

Although initially reluctant to characterize the attack as such, by November 22 the U.S. secretary of state, Rex Tillerson, publicly condemned the calamity as "ethnic cleansing."[5] Citing the Genocide Convention and other human rights law, human rights organizations maintained that there were "reasonable grounds" to believe that the "Myanmar Army, Police, and civilian perpetrators acted with genocidal intent to destroy the Rohingya in whole or in part."[6] Subsequently, a United Nations panel called for the UN Security Council to refer Myanmar to the International Criminal Court to investigate generals for the crime of genocide and other human rights violations.[7]

We relay this tragedy as a case study in othering, not for its shocking and culminating violence, but rather the opposite: to pull back the curtain and illustrate how a more banal set of circumstances and common elements preceded and prefigured the events of 2017.

———

Myanmar is a diverse South Asian nation home to more than 50 million people. The majority population is ethnic Bamar, or Burman, who are also predominantly Buddhist. Although ethnic Bamar make up a little more than two-thirds of the population, nearly 90 percent of Myanmar is Buddhist. Ancient monasteries speckle the villages and towns of the nation, and monks are culturally revered.

The Rohingya are predominantly Muslim. Although Rohingya have lived in Rakhine State since at least the seventeenth century, the government has refused to recognize the Rohingya either as an official ethnic minority or as rightful citizens. A 1982 citizenship law stripped most of the Rohingya of their citizenship, while restricting citizenship to officially designated ethnic groups.[8] The basis for this denial was the official government view that the Rohingya were Bengali migrants, or descendants of "agricultural workers imported by British colonial powers that do not belong in Myanmar."[9]

This law preceded a military campaign in 1977–78 known as "Operation Dragon King," which drove more than 200,000 Rohingya into Bangladesh, and in which thousands died.[10] Although the Rohingya were repatriated to Rakhine State the following year, the denial of citizenship made them one of the largest stateless groups in the world,[11] and long a target of discrimination, as noted by President Barack Obama during a Memorial Day presidential speech in 2015.[12]

In 2012, tensions between Rakhine Buddhists and Rohingya escalated, largely driven by a hate-fueled campaign against the Rohingya, culminating in massacres and arson strikes that forced more than 120,000
Rohingya into internment camps.[13] As a result of the conditions in these
camps, which the state still maintains, more than 200,000 Rohingya fled
Myanmar between 2012 and 2015. The attacks escalated in October and
November 2016 when state security forces targeted the Rohingya villages again, and displaced more than 94,000 Rohingya, causing another
74,000 to flee to Bangladesh. It was during this time that the state began
to train local Buddhist citizens for the attacks the following year, culminating in the 2017 episode—and perhaps the most egregious—of ethnic
cleansing.

The "othering" of the Rohingya is not simply a matter of law or accident of history. The Buddhist majority regards the Rohingya with fear
and suspicion. Dehumanizing rhetoric and inflammatory language from
media sources and Myanmar elites fostered a hostile environment and
fanned fears of a perceived threat. The headline to an opinion piece in a
state-run newspaper on November 1, 2016, described the Rohingya as "The
Thorn Needs Removing If It Pierces!"[14] Another piece a few weeks later
described the Rohingya as "detestable human fleas" that "we greatly loathe
for their stench and for sucking our blood."[15] The home affairs minister,
Kyaw Swe, described the Rohingya presence as "an invasion" of "rapid Bengali breeders."[16]

In addition to characterizing the Rohingya as both outsiders and
animal vermin, Buddhist nationalists stoked fears of demographic change.
Although Muslims were no more than 4 percent of the Myanmar population, an editor for a newsweekly said that "we don't want Muslims to
swallow our country," and if something is not done about them, "[t]hen
this country will be a Muslim country. It is such a shame for us that the
land we inherited from our former generations will be lost in our time."[17]

These fears were neither new nor simply a by-product of global post-9/11
Islamophobia.[18] In 1988, army colonel Tha Kyaw issued a directive "to strive
to increase Buddhist population to be more than the number of Muslim
people by way of establishing Natala villages in Arakan [Rakhine] with
Buddhist settlers from different townships and from out of the country."[19]

This resulted in the transplanting of Buddhist settlers into areas of Rakhine State with predominantly Rohingya Muslim populations.

The denials of recognition and citizenship continued across regimes. The 2014 Myanmar census, the first in nearly thirty years, explicitly refused to count the Rohingya because the Rohingya ethnicity was not officially recognized by the government. In fact, Nobel laureate Aung San Suu Kyi, the de facto leader of Myanmar following the nation's transition to democracy in 2015, asked the United States to stop referring to the "Rohingya" by that label, denying their very identity as well as their citizenship.[20] The conditions for the violence of 2017 were decades in the making.

What Is Othering?

Many of the critical and common elements of othering are evident in the plight of the Rohingya: a persecuted religious and ethnic minority in a country with a very large different-faith majority; dehumanizing rhetoric; a fear of demographic, social, and cultural change or incursion projected onto the minority group; demagogic leaders and media vilifying this group; legalized discrimination, including the denial of citizenship; and ultimately targeted violence and expulsion by both private and state actors. Thus this story begins our investigation of the concept of othering with a set of common dynamics: the organized and brutal treatment of a dual minority group, precipitated by local and national leaders against a backdrop of broad prejudice and manufactured fear.

Although some human rights advocates described the Rohingya as the "most persecuted minority in the world,"[21] we suspect that many of our readers are probably unfamiliar with this episode or even the existence of the Rohingya. This lack of familiarity can help us see the elements of othering more clearly than for cases that are closer to home. It is also a reminder that in virtually every known human society over the millennia of human civilization there can be found groupings of people who experience oppression, and face prejudice or even hatred on the basis of some dimension of social significance, and who are treated differently on the basis of being viewed as "less than" or a perceived threat.[22]

The range of social distinctions that might serve as the basis for hierarchical distinctions among peoples is as diverse as human societies. The hierarchies that principally concern us are those that arise between groups or social categories rather than individuals, and then fix the position of those groups in ways that maintain categorical inequality and enable dehumanization. Although individuals can engage in othering practices, our focus is on larger social forces and structures. Accordingly, othering is more than interpersonal bigotry; it is the expression of broad prejudice in law, culture, and norms, and the condition of group subordination and marginality. Nonetheless, pervasive prejudice, stigmatization, and bigotry affixed to a particular social group is an indicator (and by-product) of othering. Significant and durable intergroup disparities are the principal effect of othering.*

When entire groups of people are treated or regarded differently, by law or custom, on the basis of a socially constructed marker of difference, the ideological belief systems that render such differences significant engenders group-based marginality relative to the larger society.† That is, members of

---

* Othering, however, can also exist in the absence of visible disparities along key dimensions of well-being. In fact, some marginalized groups may even perform "better" on some dimensions (for example, women and life expectancy or educational attainment). Another reason that a marginalized or disfavored group may not suffer visible inequities is that they may lie beyond the reach of the systems that are instituted for that purpose. Thus, narratives about the subhumanity of a particular group may be propagated even as that group remains safely removed from processes that would engender inequality or instrumentalities of violence and domination.

† As we describe in more detail later this chapter and the next, the sequencing implied by this phrasing is slightly misleading to avoid overcomplicating matters. This phrasing suggests that identities develop and emerge first, and then society consigns a group to lower status or discriminatory treatment based upon that identity. Although that is generally how the marginalization of social groups is understood, we contend that this causal sequence is erroneous. Group-based identities themselves and corresponding forms of treatment are often co-emergent and sometimes co-constitutive. In other cases, the casual arrow runs in the opposite direction: the disparate forms of treatment and status-making actually *create* or help create the social group.

the group become marginalized on the basis of their group membership, and are denied access to resources, benefits, respect, and rights. This can occur on a broad scale, such as the denial of education, the right to work or participate in the public sphere, or the right to own and dispose of property, or arise in discrete and narrow circumstances, such as limiting access to private clubs and membership organizations, specific occupations, or certain privileges or opportunities.

Readers are probably able to point to many expressions of othering from their own societies, from anti-Black racism to Islamophobia to misogyny, or are aware of global "hot spots," intergroup conflicts underwritten by escalating hatred and embittered animosities, from the Sunni and Shia of Iraq to the Protestant and Catholic "Troubles" of Northern Ireland. In addition to the plight of the Rohingya in Myanmar, there are just as many cases of intergroup conflict shaped by othering that readers are probably less familiar with. To name a few examples of groups "othered" in recent years, we can point to the Tigrayans of Ethiopia, the Uighurs in western China, the Kukis of northeastern India, the Muhammasheen of Yemen, or the Kurds in southeastern Turkey.

Our purpose here, however, is not to comprehensively survey and enumerate examples of othering, but to make the case for othering as a more revealing and insightful framework capable of describing and denoting these multitudinous expressions. In this regard, the case for othering as an explanatory and revealing framework has two parts. Part of what makes othering a useful and illuminating frame is that it helps us recognize key features, patterns, and recurring mechanisms that underlie the myriad expressions of group-based marginality. This is the focus of the supplemental chapter to this book, which attempts to delineate and explicate many of the principal mechanisms and prevailing forces that undergird most expressions of othering. In this sense, the lens of othering helps us see the commonalities among the tropes, laws, customs, and stories that all convey a message about who belongs, who doesn't, and the grounds for such claims. For example, we see tropes about the "filthiness" of the other, or demands or expectations for specials rights or privileges based upon a claim of "settling a place first" or being a chosen people.

But the second part of the argument for othering is that it is pithier, a more descriptively accurate and trenchant characterization of the underlying dynamics, and ultimately more revealing framework than available alternatives. This is our next subject, where we canvass and compare othering with alternative accounts of differentiation and group inequality that attempt to describe similar phenomena.

Why "Othering"?

Despite Manuel Valls's complaint, there is hardly a dearth of frameworks or even simple terms to describe and characterize multiple varying forms of social group inequality and prejudice. The problem is not the lack of such terms, but the limitations and imprecisions of prevailing frameworks or accounts of differentiation these terms characterize or denote. This is the real source of Valls's complaint, and also the source of confusion and conflation, also noted in our introductory chapter, including the tendency to reduce a variety of expressions of othering to a few prominent forms, like racism or ethnocentrism. This tendency not only results in category errors, like conflating religion and race, but it is reductive, denuding the experiences of these social groups to flattening narratives.

To make the case for othering, we compare it with commonly used terms or frames propounded for similar purposes and to describe the same phenomena, beginning with "tribalism." "Tribalism" is frequently invoked to describe or characterize intergroup conflict.[23] The invocation of tribalism is used to suggest some deep anthropological and social-psychological processes essential to the human condition, as if it were a natural, evolutionary, or hardwired tendency. In particular, tribalism is often used to suggest that human beings have an innate tendency to view in-groups favorably and out-groups less so, and perhaps a propensity for violence and conflict that can flow therefrom.

The use of this frame, however, is generally inaccurate and misleading. In contemporary anthropological and historical research, tribes are mostly composed of relatively small bands of people that interacted daily over relatively small geographic areas during their entire lifetimes.[24] Trust was developed on the basis of routine direct contact and intimate relations. Even as a metaphorical frame, tribalism cannot adequately capture the dynamic relations of thousands, if not millions of people. Most Democrats and Republicans, for example, will never experience physical contact with most members of their own party.

The modern world is so unlike premodern "traditional societies" or contemporary tribal ones that this framing ultimately obscures, rather than reveals, the actual othering processes that are central to maintaining in- and out-group relations.[25] As an explanatory framework, "tribalism" flattens groups in terms of position and status in society and simultaneously fails to characterize the uneven power and resource advantages across social groups that othering denotes. It provides little insight into the dynamics of how contemporary societies institutionalize and weaponize group-based marginality or sustain large disparities between groups.[26] Nor does it help us understand how such identities emerge in the first place.

Moreover, the invocation of "tribalism" to suggest innate tendencies regarding treatment of in- and out-groups also turns out to be fallacious. Premodern human behavior and contemporary tribal culture are far more contingent than claims about rampant "tribalism" in contemporary social life suggest.[27] Researchers studying tribal societies have discovered that, far from being inevitable, differential or unequal treatment of other social groups is highly dependent upon the dynamics *within* the tribal group.[28] Specifically, whether a group treats another social group better or worse largely depends upon how it sees the world and its social norms rather than an inevitable by-product of human relations. Some tribal groups are highly egalitarian with respect to outsiders while others are suspicious and fearful.

Also widely used, the frame of "us versus them" to describe psychological and social dynamics suffers similar problems.[29] "Us versus them" framing is descriptively neutral. The "us" is always from the subjective perspective of the speaker, which can be either a marginalized or nonmarginalized perspective. In that way, this framing fails to indicate which group is the marginalized or "othered" group and which is the advantaged or privileged non-other. In contrast, othering implicitly describes imbalances in power and group status in society and indicates the power and positional relations between groups.

Prejudice, chauvinism, and *bigotry* would appear to be terms that address these flaws and helpfully characterize and differentiate between marginalized and higher status groups, assuming that the general direction of such prejudice and bigotry is downward. To the extent that this is true, societal discrimination caused by broad prejudice may strongly correlate othering, but it should not be mistaken for the same thing. There can be prejudice without othering and othering without prejudice. Othering occurs when prejudice becomes culturally or institutionally embedded.

Prejudice, more precisely, is a *by-product* of the othering process, rather than a corresponding dynamic or the source of othering. It is a symptom, not the cause. This is one of the chief insights of Ibram X. Kendi's magisterial presentation on the history of racist ideas in his award-winning book, *Stamped from the Beginning.*[30] In canvassing the historical record, Kendi discovered that racism was used to *justify* policies that produced racial inequality, rather than the source of either those inequalities or the policies and practices that created them.[31] This insight is true more broadly: bigotry and prejudice provide the justification for unfair and unjust arrangements that generate intergroup inequities, and which in turn sustains and reinforces them.

Given the inverted relationship between prejudice and othering, would *stigma* and *stigmatization* serve as terms and a framework that describe the same phenomenon but get the sequencing right? Stigmatization and othering are closely related processes, for reasons that will be explored in more detail next chapter. However, *stigma* and *stigmatization* are both over- and under-inclusive in denoting othering processes and the "other."

In a classic formulation by the great sociologist Erving Goffman, stigma is an "attribute that is deeply discrediting."[32] When affixed to a group, it can correspond to and with dehumanization. According to the Bible, Hebrews were stigmatized in ancient Egypt (or at least, the act of eating with them) just as lower-caste Dalits are stigmatized as "unclean" in ancient and contemporary India.[33] While some forms of stigma may apply to social groups, not all do. In the 1980s, HIV stigma, prejudice against people with HIV, was associated with gay men.[34] However, other highly stigmatized diseases, such as Hansen's disease (also known as leprosy), are not associated with a contemporary social group. Stigma may form around and apply to an inherited trait (such as racial or ethnic identity), an acquired trait, a condition, behavior, or cultural practice. Thus there can be othering without stigma and stigma without othering.

A form of othering without stigma would be pity and condescension. This occurs when a group or community is treated differently and broadly marginalized, but neither the group nor their behavior or cultural practices are stigmatized as offensive, dirty, or a taboo. Rather, the group is simply viewed as less capable, competent, or intelligent, which is then a justification for differential treatment. An example might be people with extreme mental or physical disabilities.

An example of stigma without othering would be when a behavior (like eating certain foods) is viewed as culturally verboten by the broader society or community, but it is not necessarily associated with a particular social group. Consider the broad and complex set of rules for preparing food and slaughtering animals ancient Jewish communities promulgated under the heading of "kosher."[35] In such cases, a behavior or set of behaviors is viewed as taboo (such as eating shellfish), but it is not necessarily encoded as a particular outgroup stigma. Stigmas, however, like prejudice, may be a common result or product of the othering process.

Dehumanization, the "act of conceiving of people as subhuman creatures rather than human beings," is a term that would seem to address the problem of stigmatization as a way to denote othering.[36] When applied to other people, it is difficult to imagine how it could characterize dynamics that are anything but othering. The problem with dehumanization is that it is under-inclusive. Although all cases of dehumanization are probably expressions of othering, not every case of othering involves dehumanization. Groups that are regarded with pity or condescension, rather than hatred or opprobrium, are othered, but not generally dehumanized. Dehumanization, instead, is best understood as a *mechanism* of othering, as described in our supplemental chapter.

To take another label, the acclaimed author Isabel Wilkerson has powerfully made the case for "caste" as a framework that helps us see the similarities of expression and undergirded conditions of group-based marginalization.[37] In this regard, caste would seem to solve the symmetrical connotation of more superficially neutral frames. Yet, in trying to capture the disparate dynamics of caste in India, race in the United States, and antisemitic ethnocentrism in Europe, Wilkerson ultimately reinforces the aforementioned confusion that results from the lack of a pithy available frame, which she hopes to supply.

To begin, caste hierarchies are too limited and rigid to fully encompass most forms of othering. Either as an analytic framework or as a metaphor, caste, unlike "othering" or "otherness," covers a much smaller range. In particular, true caste systems have a rigidity and boundary coherence that most forms or types of othering lack, which can be more porous, fluid, and dynamic, and yet just as pernicious.

Moreover, caste is a unidimensional framework (with groups ranked higher or lower on the caste hierarchy), but group-based marginality (othering) is quite often multidimensional. This is not a minor flaw. In most contemporary societies, there are multiple others, and multiple processes by which groups are rendered as a social other, as we shall see shortly. Not only this, but group-based marginality—denoted by othering—tends to be more intense or extreme when it is experienced through multiple stacked or overlaying identities. The plight of the Rohingya is such a case: an ethnic and religious minority—a twice-over out-group.

Another contemporary example of a group marginalized in this way are ethnic Uighurs in western China.[38] This group is both an ethnic minority and a religious minority in a state that is officially atheist but unofficially dominated by the Han ethnic majority. Yet another example is the recent conflict between the ethnic Meteis and Kukis of India. The Meteis are mostly Hindu and the Kukis are mostly Christian.[39] A judicial ruling giving the numerically greater Meteis access to certain land and privileges in the northeastern state of Manipur enraged the Kukis and set off a violent intergroup conflict, resulting in dozens of deaths and tens of thousands of refugees. Members of these marginalized groups do not simply experience persecution on the basis of their ethnicity or religion, but the compound discrimination of both, and the unique position that this convergence creates. Indeed, this is one of the chief insights of the notion of "intersectionality."[40]

Intersectionality posits that certain stacked or compounded marginalized identities, such as those of race, gender, and sexual orientation, do more than simply add to the burden of people inhabiting those identities, but actually create a unique (and uniquely vulnerable or marginal) socie-tal position.[41] In the classic formulation by Kimberlé Crenshaw, a Black woman was not simply positioned as marginalized on the sum basis of her gender and her race, but in a unique intersectional position that neither Black men nor white women fully experienced, even if their experiences could be combined.[42] Thus, if Black women are systematically denied access to an employment opportunity, antidiscrimination measures that protect her racial identity or gender identity independently may prove insufficient to ensure equal opportunity.

There are ample historical and contemporary world examples that il-lustrate the unique vulnerability or marginality of an intersectional posi-tion.[43] For example, during the Salem Witch Trials in colonial America, hundreds of people were arrested, and twenty were ultimately executed. Age and gender were the salient social nexus in the hysteria. Half of the victims were women in their fifties or older.[44] Similarly, caste and gender seem to play a significant role in the rampant gender violence pandemic in India, where lower-caste Dalit women are far more frequently victims of assault and rape.[45] In both cases, neither age, race, or caste position alone created the unique vulnerability, but the intersection did.

Indeed, this is one of the chief dangers arising in contexts in which social groups have stacked marginalized identities. When society is di-vided between groups that have stacked, non-overlapping identities, then the marginality experienced by the most othered group tends to be more intense and brutal (and, correspondingly, the power and influence of the dominant group is proportionately greater). In such cases the intersec-tional position is, in a sense, the norm for members of that group, rather than a unique or exceptional position.

It is not unusual for multiple identity categories to stack or correspond. People who identify as gender nonconforming or nonbinary are probably more likely to identify as queer or transgender. National identities some-times have strong correlations with certain religious denominations or lin-guistic and cultural practices. In a 2018 survey, over 92 percent of Polish people identified as Catholic.[46] Spanish and Italian national identity are also highly correlated with Catholicism. About 80 percent of India's pop-ulation is Hindu.[47]

Ethnic and religious identities also frequently correspond, particularly in ways that exacerbate marginality and heighten vulnerability. Recall that the ethnic Rohingya were also Muslims in a predominantly Bamar and Buddhist society. Thus the ethnic and religious identities of the Rohingya were stacked at the margins of Burmese society. So too was the case of ethnic Armenians, a predominantly Christian group, who were purged from the new Turkish state during World War I in a genocide tallied at upwards of 1.5 million deaths.[48] Similarly, the Yazidis, an ethnic and Christian sect in Iraq, were targeted for extermination and extreme sexual violence by ISIS.[49] While ISIS murdered the men, they raped and sold thousands of Yazidi women into slavery. When two identities overlay, and both identities are minoritized out-groups, then genocide and other extreme forms of othering may intensify or become more virulent.

The special dangers and risks of stacked marginalized identities perhaps explains the salience of both historical and contemporary antisemitism and Islamophobia as expressions of othering.[50] Many minority Muslim or Jewish populations also share minority or marginalized ethnic identities simultaneously. The case of antisemitism can be particularly confusing because Jewish identity can signify a religious, ethnic, racial, or even national identity. It is not always clear which category of identity is being targeted, especially when these dimensions are so tightly bound.

In a comparison of various cases of othering, one scholar notes that the "persecution of Armenians and Greeks in Bulgaria usually revolved around economic fears, and antipathy toward Irish Catholics or Italian Catholics in the USA during the 19th century largely took a form of religious hatred."[51] Similarly, race prejudice in the United States manifested as racial dislike, concerns about miscegenation, and anxieties around labor competition. Antisemitism in Europe, in contrast, "incorporated religious, economic, racial, and political prejudice. Consequently, Jews were disliked and feared for their religious beliefs and attitudes, their so-called racial characteristics, perceived economic behavior and power, and their assumed leadership or support of subversive political and social movements."[52] This may help explain why Jews, rather than other groups, were so frequently used as scapegoats, and so vulnerable to out-group violence. The more insular the social group along multiple major dimensions of identity, the easier it is to target that group without catching members of dominant or higher status groups.

Not all stacked, corresponding, or compound identities create intersectional vulnerability or marginality; some amplify power or dominance. But in general, the more that certain sets of stigmatized or marginalized traits, characteristics, and identities correspond, the greater the overall danger a marginalized group may face, and the more intense the process of othering will prove to be.

Islamophobia typically combines religious differences with cultural, linguistic, racial, or ethnic differences. In Europe, for example, Islamophobia frequently targets immigrants or refugees from the Middle East or North Africa, and is institutionalized in the form of ordinances prohibiting face covers in public.[53] Thus, it is not simply that Islamophobia targets a religious minority, but a minority several times over.

―――――――

To return to the main point, caste, like race or religion, is a broad category that contains identities that describe certain social positions and characteristics. As such, it is a *basis* for othering, not othering *as such* or a meta-category for othering. Whereas caste is rigid and narrow, othering is supple enough to encompass a wider range of social group marginality and yet specific enough to draw attention to common features and processes. Wilkerson's attempts to position caste as a wider and more encompassing frame reflects the need for a pithy and accessible frame while also falling into the trap that is the source of this need.

Finally, the frame of "insider and outsiders" would seem to address most if not all of the concerns regarding the other frames.[54] It takes cognizance of the existence of social divides; it denotes the groups that lack belonging and those that enjoy it on either side of those divides; and, it is fluid and open enough to encompass varying forms or expressions of nonbelonging, meaning that there can be multiple groups of outsiders (or insiders). To that extent, it would seem to be a close proxy for othering, with outsiders corresponding to "the other."

This frame is still lacking in a few crucial particulars, not least of which is the fact that it a mouthful. Critically, the "insider/outsider" frame implies a simple gradient with a binary position: a group is either "in" or it is "out." We have already noted, and will more fully explore below, that different othering processes can create multiple others. To wit, there are multiple out-groups. But the position of outsiders can also vary tremendously in relation to the dominant group(s) (that is, the "insiders"), and even to each other. This is a nuance that the "insider/outsider" frame is blind to, which smooshes together all groups on either side of the divide. There may be similar mechanisms and common elements among othering processes, but the "other" is not a categorical position. Instead, as we will explore in the next section, the "other" is a specific result of the particularities of any given othering process.

To summarize, "othering" is a term that is supple enough to capture multidimensional and intersectional marginality in ways that more simplistic alternatives, like "tribalism" or "caste," fail to capture. Some terms, like stigma, are overinclusive, denoting phenomena that is not properly othering; while others, like caste, are underinclusive, failing to encompass forms of othering that are multidimensional, intersectional, and more fluid. Othering also connotes the relative position of groups in society, which more superficial frameworks like "us versus them" and tribalism fail to do. Better still, othering can differentiate between the relative positions of different and various *othered* groups, which "insiders versus outsiders" fails to do.

Othering does real work and generates meaningful insights: it helps us classify and recognize both the dynamics and outcomes of processes that drive intergroup inequality and marginality. Moreover, it is also more encompassing and accurate as a description of the underlying phenomena. Now that we have a deeper sense of what othering is, we can begin to specify what we mean by "the other."

Who Is "the Other"?

As noted, every human society has in-groups and out-groups, social groupings of people who tend to enjoy a more privileged perch in society and, conversely, people who live precariously at the margins or in a more vulnerable condition, objects of fear, stigma, bigotry, or persecution. On what basis are such distinctions made?

The most obvious and perhaps intuitive answer is to assert that these distinctions are based upon critical or profound human differences, such as religious belief, skin color, cultural practices, sexuality, or disability. The problem with this answer is that there are infinite differences between people. Clones and twins may be, in some regards. Similarly, the possible groupings of people based upon observed differences is also infinite. The claim that in-group and out-group dynamics appear to be based upon critical or profound human differences is essentially tautological: it assumes which differences are critical or profound.

Scanning the world today, one might be tempted to conclude that a certain set of differences among people (such as ethnicity, race, and religion) are the critical human differences that form the basis for othering. Yet, if these differences are "critical," then why, in some contexts or societies, are these differences essentially irrelevant to the formation of in- and out-groups? Why is homosexuality stigmatized in certain (often contemporary) societies but not in others, like ancient Greece? Why weren't racial distinctions made before the sixteenth century? Why are some societies patriarchal (or patrilineal) while others are matriarchal (or matrilineal)? Why were religious and ethnic differences far more socially salient after the fall of the Soviet Union? Why do some societies revere the elderly and others valorize youth?

For every example of a group that appears to be "othered," or a categorical distinction that seems to provide a basis upon which othering occurs, a counterexample can be found in which that group is not an "other," or, perhaps more importantly, upon which that categorical distinction does not exist. To draw an inference, based upon the prevalence of common expressions of othering across cultural contexts, that certain human differences form the basis for othering is to overlook the contingencies that led to these outcomes.

Another possible answer is that it is not difference per se, but perhaps proximity or familiarity. After all, people who are different may not be viewed as an "other" if they are so distant as to essentially reside in a different world. This answer seems to draw on the same type of anthropological evidence about human evolution occurring over hundreds of thousands of years of life in relatively small bands as those who emphasize tribalism as the overarching dynamic which we call "othering." It may seem reasonable to conclude, based upon this evidence, that familiarity render certain observed differences or cultural practices less fearful, alien, or threatening, and therefore the differences that form the basis of othering would tend to become more significant when a group is more distant.

Although this answer would help explain how a particular social group could be "othered" in one society, while in another they may be highly ranked in social status, this explanation is even less tenable based on available evidence than claims about tribalism. Some of the most extreme forms of othering occur within societies in which proximity and familiarity between groups are greatest. Proximity does not ameliorate hatred; in fact, it can inflame it.

To be clear: difference, alone, is *not* a basis for othering. There are simply too many possible differences between people, and very few human differences are ever used as basis for othering, the drawing of in- and out-groups.[55] Nor are certain categorical distinctions (like racial or religious differences) necessarily a basis for othering. Some are, but others aren't. Moreover, there is virtually no category or categorical distinction that exists across every known society; even if one can be found, there is no universal valence or social meaning given to groups on either side of that categorical boundary.

What this means is simple yet profound: there is no natural, inevitable, or universal "other." Across societies and over time, there is no group that is universally stigmatized, marginalized, or othered, as a product of history, evolution, or otherwise.[56] Nor is there a particular trait or combination of traits that inevitably results in othering or being othered. There is no cultural characteristic, practice, or belief that inevitably results in marginalization. And there is no category supplying a distinction upon which othering universally occurs. As the scientist Robert Sapolsky keenly observes, "[h]umans may be hard-wired to get edgy around the Other, but our views on who falls into that category are surprisingly malleable."[57]

The *apparent* basis of demarcation or difference between social groups upon which othering occurs may be any socially identifiable distinctions or markers, from forehead markers called "bindi" to skin color to garb to behaviors to creeds of worship and beliefs. These differences may signify in-groups and out-groups but they are not in fact the basis for othering. The social distinctions and the social groups associated with those distinctions that are ultimately marginalized through the othering processes (and conversely, those that are valorized) can be signified by virtually anything society imbues with social meaning or significance. What matters is not the signifier but the meaning or significance it is imbued with.

This is not to deny that, in certain periods or over certain geographic areas, particular expressions of othering are more widespread and therefore that certain identities or social groups are more stigmatized or oppressed than others. There are certain dynamics associated with identity categories that become signs of pathology in the social fabric, proverbial "canaries in the coal mine." As already noted, a prominent expression of othering in the Western context is antisemitism.

Antisemitism is not simply an illness that infected a few societies like Germany or even Western Europe, but has flared up over centuries all over the West.[58] Jews in Europe were subject to pogroms, segregation, and discrimination in Italy, Spain, Russia, and other place in Europe from the late medieval period onward.[59] In fact, the term *pogrom* arose to describe anti-Jewish riots that swept the Russian Empire in the nineteenth century.[60]

Islamophobia appears to be functioning similarly today as a leading indicator of othering in its global ubiquity, flaring up most acutely in places where other expressions of othering are especially intense.[61] A similar observation might be made for certain regressive, patriarchal attitudes and policies, or at least antifeminist ones, as another leading indicator, along with anti-LGBTQ animus.

———

One of the main arguments of this book is that, while differing in the particulars, each of the various expressions of group-based marginality is part of a more general phenomenon we call "othering." In our lexicon, *othering* refers to the process by which social groups become marginalized or subordinated, and "the other" refers to the groups that are marginalized and constituted as such through and, as a result of, the othering process. Although already alluded to, what this process looks like will become clearer in the next few chapters. For now, it should suffice to note that the group that is ultimately constituted as an "other" through the othering process is highly contingent based upon the stories, beliefs, and actions of a society and its leaders.

In fact, to be an "other" is not a label applied or position imposed only after social groups have formed, and after social interactions generate a subordinate status for a particular group. On the contrary, the social group that becomes "the other" is, prior to the othering process, likely not even regarded as a distinct social group or cultural unit. The othering process itself constitutes both the group as a socially meaningful identity category and the group as "the other." Once a group is formed as the other, then its social position is normalized to seem natural and inevitable. As noted above, prejudice and stigma are the by-product, not the source, of this process.

The process of othering refers both to the generalizable mechanisms that are common to most cases of othering as well as the specific actions, laws, and norms that embody those mechanisms and the narratives that undergird them. In short, othering is both general and specific. The critical point here is that specific groups designated as "the other" are marginalized relative to the societies they inhabit, and that the process of marginalization is what makes them an "other," not any particular trait or characteristic.

This does not mean that "othered" groups are marginalized in every sphere or area of relations. For example, egalitarian norms across group differences in the workplace or public sphere may be more strongly held than in private spaces, such as the home, social clubs, or places of worship.[62] Marginality in one domain need not entail marginality in another, but it makes such marginality more likely, and in fact, simultaneous marginalization across domains is strong evidence of othering.

Also, as alluded to already, othering is not simply about the distribution of power, social relations, or material resources, but about the constitution of those groups and society itself. Social groups do not simply exist, waiting to be positioned as in- or out-groups by larger forces. Rather, most often these groups are fabricated and imbued with social meaning as part of the process of othering itself. The formation of in- and out-groups occurs simultaneously with the ideological and material bases for which such meanings emerge and group distinctions acquire significance. In other words, the process of othering is not just a set of mechanisms that control the distribution of resources; it is also a process of identity- and meaning-making.

The important point is that *the "other" is defined as a result of, and through, the othering process.* Although this process contains mechanisms that are generalizable across time and space, neither the categorical distinctions upon which othering occurs nor the content of those categories is universal.

––––––

It follows from the preceding discussion but deserves emphasis that the "other" is a group-based designation, not the individual feeling of alienation from society or not belonging in a particular environment, such as a dinner party, work setting, or college campus, due to interpersonal dynamics. Although feelings of anomie or not belonging may be a product of the experience of membership in a social group, othering and alienation are not the same phenomena.

The relationship between alienation and othering is complicated.[63] Alienation has been more commonly observed in societies that are less communal or featuring industrial or postindustrial economies, as opposed to more traditional or agricultural economies.[64] More intense and punitive forms of othering may arise in more traditional or communal societies, since the boundaries between in-groups and out-groups can be sharper and more forcefully guarded. At the same time, less communal societies may have more expressions of othering, even if most particular expressions are less intense than those found in traditional societies, because they tend to be larger, more diverse and complex.

The critical point here is that the "other," in our lexicon, is a categorical label tied to a group-based identity, not merely individual experiences, even those of exclusion or poor treatment. While othering may happen between individuals, we are primarily concerned with the types of othering that are experienced by groups as such or individuals as members of social groups, and less concerned with what individuals experience on an interpersonal or individual basis.

Nor does othering occur as a necessary by-product of the creation of social hierarchies and status rankings. Although othering depends on status hierarchies, not all such hierarchies organize the position of social group identities. Instead, they may be based on occupations, achievements, public virtue, or other traits, characteristics, and activities. In our lexicon, the "other" is not merely a description of *people* who are low-status; it is a description of *social groups* that are regarded as low-status, particularly when that status is largely fixed by society.

Let us be clear what we mean by social groups in this context. In cases of othering, individuals cannot voluntarily and independently shed the "othered" social group identity or the set of meanings or associations that attach to a presumed identity. A sign of othering is when the social hierarchy's status ranking attaches to the social group's members based upon seemingly inherent or immutable identities, like race and ethnicity.* Thus stigmas associated with certain behaviors (like eating pork or beef) or professions (like prostitution or trash collection) are not cases of othering, even if meaningful identities attach to those behaviors or professions, because they do not constitute a social group. As long as individuals are free to engage or not engage in those behaviors or serve in those professions or not, then they can shed any stigma associated with them. In cases of othering, individuals who are considered members of a social group are not so free in that regard, even if they seek to contest the presumed identity label or the set of meanings and associations that attach to it.

There may be cases in which members of a group are consigned by force or necessity to certain stigmatized professions or conditions, and therefore the behavioral or professional stigma attaches to the group as a consequence. We wish to make clear that any "othering" in such cases is a result of the association of the stigma with the group, not the linked condition or behavior. Similarly, if certain stigmatized behaviors are culturally connected to a social group identity, say, because it is part of an ancient

---

* We recognize the complexity of determining whether a characteristic or trait is inherent or immutable, as our discussion of gender in Part II suggests. Similar points could be made regarding disability or many other identities. Without resolving whether an identity is "inherent" or "immutable," we simply wish to point out that the more that a society regards a particular identity as such, and assigns it a lower status rank in the social hierarchy, the more likely this is a case of othering,

religious practice (like circumcision), then it is the stigmatic meaning associated with the group, not the practice itself, that constitutes othering. When practiced by members outside of that group, it is merely stigmatic, not othering.

Experiences of Othering

Now that we have explained the broad features of othering, contrasting it with terms and frameworks that characterize similar or related phenomena, and defined the relation between the othering process and the other, we must descend from the level of theory to show how othering is experienced in the real world. There are several frameworks and models, some of them empirically rigorous, that are helpful in this regard, developed by brilliant minds in a variety of fields.

One of the most important frameworks that help distinguish between different types of "others" is the Stereotype Content Model (SCM) developed principally by social psychologist Susan Fiske.[65] This model can help us recognize the differences in the perception of, and othering experienced, by different groups inhabiting the same society, such as the elderly or the disabled compared to transgender people or racial outgroups.

The SCM locates different expressions of othering along the two dimensions, "warmth" and "competence." *Warmth* refers to the degree of closeness and good feeling that exists in surveys regarding the target group ("including friendliness, helpfulness, sincerity, trustworthiness and morality").[66] *Competence* refers to the degree that the target group is regarded as smart and capable (for example, "intelligence, skill, creativity and efficacy").[67]

These two dimensions form of a matrix of four quadrants demarcating "in-groups" from different "out-groups" falling into three broad categories (see Figure 1). In-groups—or non-othered groups—reside in the upper-right-hand quadrant, and are admired. Various out-groups and othered groups reside in the other three quadrants. But the differences between the quadrants begin to illustrate different forms of othering. The most dehumanized and stigmatized status groups are despised, and are located in the first quadrant or lower left hand, where MRI scans indicate that members

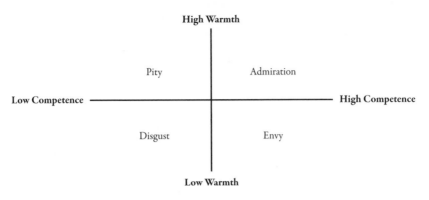

FIGURE 1. The Stereotype Content Model.
Source: powell and Menendian, after Susan Fiske.

of those groups are often not even viewed as human, or more associated with disease or filth.[68] In the other two quadrants of the matrix, an othered group might be esteemed, but envied, or pitied, but not esteemed. Thus different out-groups may be regarded and treated differently depending upon their location within the matrix.

In their research, Susan Fiske and her collaborators found that in the United States the elderly and disabled were viewed as low competence, but high warmth, and thus regarded with pity and condescension.[69] Asians and Jewish people were regarded as high competence, but low warmth, and thus regarded with envy.[70] These differences in regard and social status accompany different othering processes and experiences of othering.

The homeless were regarded in extremes of the low warmth and low competence, but welfare recipients, feminists, Arabs, and the poor generally also inhabited this quadrant, and received a share of disgust. The fourth quadrant, high competence and high warmth, was extended to housewives, the middle class, the Irish, Christians, and, notably, Black professionals (although they were noticeably lower in the warmth scale than the others, they still fall into this quadrant).[71]

In a cross-cultural study of gender attitudes, Fiske observed that women were often "loved" yet broadly disadvantaged in most societies.[72] One explanation for this was the theory of "benevolent prejudice," the idea that prejudice could function in a caring, paternalistic mode (rather than a hostile, antagonistic one) that both justified and reinforced gender inequality.

The SCM then helps us see these nuanced differences in categories of the "other." Not all categories of the "other" fall into the lower-left-hand quadrant. The SCM can be applied to social groups or any other grouping in almost any context. In further research, Fiske and her colleagues applied the model to discover how citizens of the European Union view member states, mapping each state into different quadrants (Germany and the United Kingdom were viewed as high competent and low warmth, while Spain, Portugal, Greece, and Italy were viewed as low competence but high warmth).[73] The same approach was used by survey respondents in Hong Kong and Israel to various social groupings.[74]

One of the key insights suggested by the SCM is the centrality of the role of emotions in mediating and conditioning both cognition and behavior, how we think and how we act.[75] The SCM helps us draw meaningful distinctions between different out-groups in terms of social opinion or feeling. It also illustrates the complexity of these feelings, demonstrating that groups can be regarded as low on one dimension and high on another, or treated differently depending on extant conditions. For example, Fiske and her colleagues show how envied groups can be treated decently under normal conditions, but quite badly in high-pressure situations, giving the examples of Koreans in Los Angeles, Tutsis in Rwanda, Chinese in Indonesia, and Jews in Europe.[76] The SCM mapping then helps us see which groups may be most at risk when such conditions arise.

We note, however, that there may be other dimensions that are not captured by the SCM. The SCM is merely a two-dimensional matrix when social regard is perhaps a constellation of dimensions. Nonetheless, the SCM illustrates the multidimensional nature of othering and different expressions of "the other." In this way the SCM suggests a continuum of othering from milder variants to more extreme. While in-groups lay within the high-warmth and high-competence quadrant, residing in the low-warmth and low-competence quadrant is qualitatively worse than residing in the other two. In this sense, it is not simply that these groups are regarded differently; they are in a more precarious position. Those groups are generally worse off than other out-groups. Accordingly, their treatment regime can follow a continuum that is worse as well. In short, the SCM can help nuance the perception or regard for different othered groups, and

TABLE 1. The Five Faces of Oppression.

Five Faces of Oppression	Examples
Exploitation	Class, gender, race
Marginalization	Race and ethnicity, lack of citizenship
Powerlessness	Labor market, race, gender, class, education
Cultural Imperialism	Race, gender, LGBTQ
Violence	Gender, LGBTQ, race, ethnicity, religion

Source: powell and Menendian, after Iris Marion Young.

their corresponding—and varying—treatment. This suggests important differences, not just between others, but between othering processes.

Another useful taxonomy, but for differentiating between othering processes rather than categories of "other," is Iris Marion Young's five "faces of oppression."[77] A renowned political theorist, Young expended considerable effort studying social difference and theories of justice in landmark scholarly works.[78] In one of her major works, Young distinguished between two forms of "disabling constraints" that afflict disadvantaged or "othered" peoples, oppression and domination.* Under the header of "oppression," she further identified five different forms or "faces," each with its own particularities and characteristics: exploitation, marginalization, powerlessness, cultural imperialism, and violence. A brief review of the "faces" of oppression sheds considerable light on differences between experiences and processes of othering.

In her formulation, exploitation refers to "social processes that bring about a transfer of energies from one group to another to produce unequal distributions, and the way in which social institutions enable a few to

---

*Given the elaborate discussion of different accounts of differentiation, and our argument for the advantages of *othering* over the alternatives, some readers may wonder if these two terms can perform the same work. As Young's own work demonstrates, these terms have critical differences between them, yet both are types of othering. Once again, *othering* has the advantage of encompassing each of these forms without washing out critical differences between them and yet others still.

accumulate while they constrain many more."[79] The second clause clarifies that the harm of exploitation is more than the inequitable distribution of resources, but the structural relations that underpin them. Young sees exploitation in the relations of the wealthy to the poor or working classes, of men to women, and whites to Blacks and Hispanics. For example, when women provide "emotional care" to children and "sexual satisfaction" to men, and "as a group receive relatively little of either from men."[80] Or, to take another example, racial exploitation—as an expression of oppression—arises through a "segmented labor market that tends to reserve skilled, high-paying, unionized jobs for whites."[81]

Second, Young points to "marginalization,"* which she defines as being "expelled from useful participation in social life and thus potentially subjected to severe material deprivation and even extermination."[82] Thus, marginalization, in her framework, arises when, for example, people are denied citizenship or stripped of citizenship.[83] She notes that it is most visible among the "growing underclass of people permanently confined to lives of social marginality, and most of whom are racially marked—blacks and Indians in Latin America, and blacks, East Indians, Eastern Europeans, and North Africans in Europe." In her view, "marginalization is perhaps the most dangerous form of oppression," as at least exploited people are viewed as having value by the powerful. In that sense, exploited people are rarely exterminated, even if they are treated unjustly.

Critically, in her conception, the harm of marginality is not the deprivation of material conditions, but in the lack of belonging: "Even if marginal[ized people] were provided a comfortable material life within institutions that respected their freedom and dignity, injustices of marginality would remain in the form of uselessness, boredom, and lack of self-respect."[84] In this way, marginality is a form of harm and an expression of oppression that touches the core of human dignity.

Third, Young identifies "powerlessness" as a distinctive expression of oppression. In this conception, she refers to individuals who have little or

---

* Note that our definition of *marginalization* and use of that term is more expansive than hers, and encompasses other "faces" of oppression as well as milder conditions than those that fit her definition.

no work autonomy.[85] This extends to those who "execute" versus those who plan, and the use of creativity or judgment in their work versus those who do not. The reason this powerlessness becomes a form of oppression is that it denies dignity and respect to those who inhabit those positions. It denies them the power to co-create and mutuality.

The fourth "face" of oppression is cultural imperialism. While the first three relate most directly to social divisions of labor, the fourth is perhaps the most pertinent to our inquiry. Young defines cultural imperialism as "how the dominant meanings of a society render the particular perspective of one's own group invisible at the same time as they stereotype one's group and mark it out as the Other."[86] In other words, it is the universalization of the dominant group's culture and experience as the norm. In this way, experiences that deviate or differ from the presumed norm are treated as inferior or deficient or simply rendered invisible. Cultural imperialism is the source of what is sometimes called "double consciousness," since it creates a perception of individual and group identity through the dominant culture's lens, as well as the sense from one's own or group's perspective.

Finally, the fifth face of oppression is violence, and systematic violence. As we will argue in more detail in the supplemental chapter, violence is the most prominent and common mechanism of othering, and occurs in many modes and at different registers of power and oppressiveness. For example, communal violence, such as a lynch mob, has long been a tool of oppression, but organized and systematic violence—especially state violence—is a more powerful tool of othering. In any case, state-based and vigilante violence is meted out unevenly in American society, as the Black Lives Matter movement continues to protest. In most societies, marginalized groups are both at greater risk for suffering violence and more frequently its victims. The gendered prevalence of sexual assault and rape is an expression of this face, and lack of accountability was highlighted by the #MeToo movement.

Each of these forms of oppression not only suggests differential forms of treatment, with some being objectively worse than others, but also helps us see how different groups are "othered" differently. These forms of oppression imply distinctive othering processes with different consequences. Thus, in Young's schema, being exploited may be "better" than being marginalized, as exploitation requires some level of minimal concern or care, or perhaps reliance. Note that no known society has ever embarked on a genocidal project on the basis of gender alone, despite the persecution and killing of accused witches.[87] A social group may face greater existential danger if the society can discard them.

While Young's "five faces" classification scheme implies a spectrum of oppression, the differences are not neatly linear along a continuum. While some forms of oppression may be worse than others in some respects, they may be better in other cases, depending on the circumstances.

While these schema may be helpful for delineating among different forms of othering, our main purpose in presenting them is to underscore the complexity of othering, to illustrate that there can be many different types or forms of othering, with correspondingly different social "others."

Multiple Others

In our conceptualization, the categorical "other" is a social group that has been marginalized through a particular "othering" process. The preceding discussion of the Stereotype Content Model and the "five faces of oppression" illustrates how different groups may be positioned as "others" in society, and yet differently positioned in the social hierachy or regarded on account of different processes of othering. Although the othering process has generalizable features and certain commonly found elements or forces that underlie most expressions of othering, this process is not uniform. Different othering processes generate different groups of othered peoples.

The othering process that rendered American Indians "savage" was different from the othering process that subjugated Africans in colonial America as "slaves." Although both were regarded as categorical out-groups, the constellations of meanings that designated each group the "other" differed greatly, as did their corresponding treatment. Although both Africans and Native Americans were viewed as "savages" from the prism of Western civilization,[88] Native Americans were cast in a more noble light, even as they were targeted for long-term extermination.

Gender designations in Western thought have often cast women as "closer to nature."[89] In this formulation, women were believed less capable of rational thinking, more "emotional," and therefore unfit for professional and political spheres. Although citizens, their rights were accordingly restricted in conformity with a patriarchy that was regarded by the dominant group as a benign or benevolent paternalism, requiring the care and support of men, even as they were regarded as the weaker sex. This kind of othering produces a type of treatment and set of rights and privileges distinct from those applying to Black slaves or Native Americans.

A unique expression of the othering process is when an identity, or trait linked to an identity, is viewed as a flaw, illness, or defect. Identities associated with LGBTQ status and disability, for example, are often characterized by societies and institutions as "defects," "conditions," or "illnesses."[90] The treatment regimen accordingly prescribed for individuals with such identities is frequently to try to "correct" or expunge the identity and its corresponding "illness" rather than create a regime that restructures society to accommodate the identity.

A related distinction that may hint at which identities are more susceptible to othering processes is what Andrew Solomon calls "horizontal identities."[91] Unlike "vertical" identities, which are identities that are "passed down from parent to child across the generations," such as ethnicity, race, language, horizontal identities are identities that are "foreign to his or her parents" and are therefore generally acquired from a peer group.[92] For example, most gay and lesbian children are born to straight parents.

Thus, in Solomon's taxonomy, deafness, homosexuality, and dwarfism are horizontal identities that were and continue to be treated as defects or illnesses in many times and places. The important insight derived from the distinction between horizontal and vertical identities is that families and clans tend to welcome and reinforce vertical identities, generally as part of the childrearing and socialization process, while opposing or remaining fearful, circumspect, or anxious of horizontal ones.[93] And by extension, this applies to communities and even nations. Thus, if a religious community treats an identity as "sinful" or "unclean," as has been the case with lower-caste Dalits as in some Hindu traditions or LGBTQ persons in the Abrahamic religions, and a nation treats an identity as a "criminal," then we can begin to see two different ways of being othered, even if these treatments occasionally overlap. Some identities, like homosexuality, have been regarded in some societies, like postwar America, as a "crime, an illness, and a sin."[94]

To the extent that some traits or customs associated with a social group are regarded as either unclean or immoral, then we may regard them as a form of stigma attached to the "other."[95] In his study of stigma, the sociologist Gerhard Falk concluded that there were two broad forms of stigma: "existential" and "achieved." Existential stigma refers to groups who are stigmatized because of their traits or identity, whereas achieved stigma refers to people who are stigmatized by actions or life conditions.[96] Falk also observed that many societies harbored stigmas of both types. We extend this observation to note that many societies harbor multiple stigmas of *each* type (that is, multiple "existential" stigmatized groups).

This is also true of othering and othered groups. Most modern complex societies harbor multiple others, and therefore multiple othering processes yielding those others. The processes that "other" marginalized groups like African Americans or Chinese Americans are different from those that "other" people with disabilities or LGBTQ persons. More deeply, differences between othering processes can exist even between groups within the same category of othering. For example, the processes that render Asians as a racial "other" are different in certain particulars from those that marginalize Black people.

But just as each society can have multiple stigmatized groups, it is also true that the stigmas that exist in one society may have no social salience or significance whatsoever in another. Tax collection may be a stigmatized profession in one society and not in another. The taboo on slaughtering and eating cows in Hindu culture has little weight or influence in the United States, as the proliferation of beef hamburger establishments readily attests.[97] Kosher rules frown upon consumption of shellfish, which are delicacies among innumerable contemporary and ancient societies. Some taboos may seem so deeply ingrained as to be natural or universal, but a cursory review shows that they are not. Very few, if any, human taboos are universal, even behaviors such as incest or homicide.[98]

Generally speaking, the same is true of othering: each society can have multiple othered groups, and groups that are othered in one society may not be in another, especially if it is more temporally and geographically distant. Thus, although LGBTQ persons may be viewed as a categorical "other" in many relatively modern societies, that was not necessarily true of, say, all societies in every time and place. In ancient Greece, homosexuality and bisexuality were not socially stigmatized or viewed as categorically distinct in the way that they tend to be viewed today in many Catholic societies.[99] In both the cases of stigmatization and the othering process, the differences that become socially or culturally relevant depends upon the meaning ascribed to those differences by the dominant or hegemonic group.

More deeply, it is not just that othering processes, like stigmatization, vary in their particulars from society to society, but groups that are rendered as an "other" may not even be regarded as a separate and distinct social group at all! Caste stigmas that regard Dalits as "untouchable" within Hindu cultures have little salience or social significance in Western societies, which, until recently, were largely unfamiliar with Hindu faith and customs. Similarly, more contemporary stigmas on interracial or interfaith marriage would have seemed utterly incomprehensible to ancient civilizations that had no concept of race or the religions at issue to base such taboos or stigmas on.[100]

At bottom, however, social stigmas and horizontal identities are generally a cue toward an othered group. This does not mean that all othering reduces to these dimensions of difference. The universe of "othered" groups extends beyond social stigma and horizontal identities. But these concepts are useful indicators of othering or vulnerability to othering, helping us identify othered groups. At the same time, they can help us understand how multiple, different "others" can arise simultaneously within a society.

The multiplicity of "othered" groups, however, does not mean that the othering processes that produce them are always or entirely distinct or unrelated. We have emphasized the fact that the "other," in our analysis, may vary from context to context, as a way of rebutting the presumption that certain traits or social groups are a universal or natural other. But some othering processes may undergird multiple expressions of othering. For example, certain traditional religious doctrines or cultural formations can simultaneously undergird both patriarchal or sexist gender norms and the repression of sexual minorities. In that way, a strong preference for tradition gender relations, such as a preference that women work primarily in the home, and perform disproportionate childrearing and domestic chores, may be a predictor of hostility to same-sex marriage. If so, then the process that results in the othering of both women and LGBTQ person may be conjoined, even if the resulting "others" are socially distinct.[101]

Othering by Others

If there can be multiple groups that are othered in a society—multiple "others"—then can one of those groups contribute to the othering of another? The answer, unfortunately, is yes. While some definitions of racism would make it impossible for a racially marginalized group to engage in racist practices against a dominant group,[102] that is definitively not the case for othering processes.

Othering processes are any mechanisms that engender or reinforce social group stigma, dehumanization, inequality, or marginality. In any society with multiple others, members of marginalized groups can become active participants in the process of othering different social groups. There are ample documented cases, for example, of Native American tribes and individuals owning African slaves in the Americas, establishing or enforcing anti-Black codes and adopting discriminatory practices, or denying Black tribal members equal status and rights, even to this day.[103] In 2000, the Seminole Nation voted to strip tribal membership from many Black descendants of slaves held by the tribe.[104] As recently as 2021, several large Native tribes denied many of the same people access to health care.[105]

This is not just a case of individual Native Americans or tribes participating in a structure of white supremacy; Native American tribes generally sided with the Confederacy in the Civil War against the Union.[106] Similarly, in South Africa, there are documented cases of Indians, classified as "colored" in the apartheid and pre-apartheid racial schema, supporting laws that promoted racial segregation, and other discriminatory laws.[107]

To take another example, the Black comedian Jerrod Carmichael recently came out of the closet as a gay man. By his own account, his religious southern family has struggled to accept his sexuality, and prefers not even to acknowledge it.[108] His mother regards his sexual orientation as a "lifestyle" choice, and against her Christian values and God. His father asked him to avoid publicly discussing it. Carmichael notes that acceding to his family's preferences, and simply remaining silent about it or avoiding the subject, entails a heavy cost: "if I accept the quiet, it makes me hate myself."[109]

Many marginalized groups hold views or engage in practices that engender or sustain the marginality of other social groups, especially sexual minorities. Southern Black Christians may tend to be more socially conservative when it comes to sexual orientation and gender identity than is generally known, but that is not unusual. Many Latinos—who tend to be disproportionately Catholic—are more likely to be anti-abortion and supportive of more traditional gender roles than white Americans.[110] Many formerly colonized African countries have anti-LGBTQ laws, including some of the harshest penalties in the world.[111]

To the alarm of some commentators and observers, some prominent Muslim American policy makers have sided with social conservatives on LGBTQ issues.[112] In Hamtramck, Michigan, where voters in 2015 elected one of the country's first majority-Muslim city councils, the city voted in 2023 to ban Pride flags on city property, a symbol of LGBTQ inclusion and acceptance.[113] In Montgomery, Maryland, the right-wing "Moms of Liberty" joined with some Muslim parents to protest curricula and reading material on LGBTQ people.[114]

Members of marginalized groups may contribute to othering processes by circulating narratives or dehumanizing rhetoric regarding other marginalized groups. In late 2022, both Kanye West, the eccentric entertainer and artist, and Kyrie Irving, a mercurial professional basketball player, circulated antisemitic messages and promoted a documentary widely condemned for its antisemitic tropes.[115]

There are also ample cases of members of a marginalized group discriminating against members of another group. There are cases of abuse and use of anti-Black epithets by Latino workers in California.[116] But there are also many commonly used anti-Asian slurs used by Black Americans.[117] Such dynamics are not new. Even as they were being systematically discriminated against, many nineteenth-century Irish immigrants quickly adopted anti-Black views and prejudices.[118]

And these dynamics may intersect. One of the most shocking and recent examples was a secretly recorded conversation of three Latinx members of the Los Angeles City Council.[119] In a discussion of city redistricting processes, the three denigrated Black and indigenous people.[120] Here political discrimination was undergirded by noxious racist ideas about other marginalized groups, even as they publicly signaled racial solidarity in the past.

Perhaps most disconcertingly, like Harriet Beecher Stowe's "Uncle Tom," members of marginalized groups can play a critical role in upholding systems and structures of power or cultural arrangements that maintain their own group's marginality.[121] One reason for this might be to attain relative material advantages. Candace Owens is a Black right-wing pundit who has built a lucrative career critiquing the Black Lives Matter movement and denigrating victims of police brutality and violence, like George Floyd.[122] Kanye West was photographed at a fashion show in Paris standing next to Owens wearing a "white lives matter" hoodie.[123]

This oppression even extends to inciting violence. An angry mob attacked and brutalized a young woman in Delhi, India, in January 2022, not necessarily a rare occurrence in a country with a patriarchal culture and an endemic pattern of gender violence.[124] What was shocking about this attack, however, was that the video revealed that most of the "baying mob" were women, many of whom called for the victim to be raped.[125] Some observers described this as "internalized patriarchy."

While a shocking expression, feminist scholars have long observed the role that women play in accepting or internalizing sexist ideologies. Although so-called "hostile" prejudice is the more familiar form, some scholars regard "benevolent" prejudice as more insidious for legitimating and "help[ing] to justify and maintain inequality between groups."[126] As Susan Fiske and her colleagues observe, "dominant groups prefer to act warmly towards subordinates, offering them patronizing affection as a reward for 'knowing their place' rather than rebelling."[127] She found that in about half the countries surveyed, women endorsed benevolent sexism as much as men, but in countries with the highest sexism scores, women endorsed it more strongly than men.[128]

Although it may be the exception rather than the norm, we must recognize that othered groups may participate in and contribute to the othering of other marginalized groups, including their own.

———————

Any given society can have more than one othered group, and modern ones are likely to have many. The experience of the othered group, especially the type of treatment they are subjected to, will vary based upon the nature of the othering process. But how are such groups constituted in the first place? How do the social identities that attach to such groups emerge? The next chapter will attempt to answer those questions, with a deeper look at the othering process.

THREE

From Us to Them

To anchor our discussion, take reflective pause from this text, and consider for a moment the matter of identity in personal terms. How do you identify? What are the identities that are most significant to you? To which social groups do you affiliate? We have found that asking students to list meaningful identities is a powerful pedagogical classroom technique, helping students build community and trust by sharing their stories and discovering commonalities while learning about difference.[1]

One of the most important insights from this exercise is that we each have many simultaneous identities. We have religious, gender, racial, professional, and relational identities. We have identities that characterize our sexual orientation and those that reflect our education and occupation. We have identities that describe the bonds of kinship and family roles and those that express our national origin and social affiliations.

While some of the identities we hold relate to the choices we make in life, such as our chosen profession or procreative decisions (that is, becoming a parent), many others appear to be imposed upon us, determined from without. In either case, many of our identities conform to a public and shared taxonomy, like entries in a dictionary, which are, if not natural and immutable, at least well settled, seemingly beyond the reach of popular debate or individual contestation. As a result, our identities can be simultaneously intimate, appearing to emanate from the deepest parts

50

of ourselves, but also remote and coolly distant categorical classifications imposed by society. Upon closer inspection, many of the identities we hold, much like definitions found in the dictionary, are less rigid and fixed than we tend to perceive or appreciate.[2]

One of us is a baby boomer from Detroit. When he was born, the government census takers regarded him as a "colored boy." By the time he went to college in the 1960s, he was counted as African American. Today he is probably regarded by many as a Black man.

This story is remarkable, in the sense that one's racial identity could change so much over time, and yet it is also conventional and easily understood. One interpretation of this story is that the differential racial labels are merely changing terms, but denote the same, underlying identity. From that perspective, these terms are largely synonymous, each describing people of African descent residing in America. In this sense, the shifting terminology is largely semantic, and reflects little about differences in meaning, Consider another story then:

The other one of us is a child of baby boomers. His paternal great-grandfather was an Armenian refugee from the Ottoman Empire in 1895, fleeing territory that is now part of Turkey. At that time, the prevailing consensus was that ethnic Armenians were West Asian.[3] In 1909, a federal circuit judge overruled an immigration officer, and held that Armenians were "Caucasian," as they had migrated to Asia Minor from the Caucasus region.[4] By 1925, prevailing law held that Armenians were considered part of the "white race."[5]

One way of interpreting this story is that a prevailing classification was replaced by a different, but more accurate one, just as, in the natural sciences, one prevailing (but mistaken) paradigm (say, the Ptolemaic view of the solar system) was replaced with another (Copernican/heliocentric), found to be more accurate. Applied to this case, that interpretation suggests that the previous consensus was wrong, and Armenians were always white, but were incorrectly classified before as Asian.

As you probably surmised, we presented these stories to suggest something more complicated at work than recounting a semantic evolution toward more "accurate" identity classifications. The second story begins to illuminate the first story. To unpack that story further, we must cast ourselves back to the early 1960s. In that time, to call a person of African descent "Black" was widely regarded as an epithet, or proverbial "fighting words."

To understand why, we have to recall that, in English vernacular, *black* is freighted with an array of negative connotations: *black magic, black sheep, black death*, and so on, indicating or connoting evil, malice, or death and decay.[6] There was an active and deliberate effort, led by Stokely Carmichael, Charles V. Hamilton, and Malcolm X, among others, to reclaim *Black* as a positive identity marker, with a different set of meanings than *Negro, colored*, or even *African American*.[7] James Brown's anthem "Say It Loud—I'm Black and I'm Proud" was on the crest of a wave in the late 1960s and '70s to redefine Blackness in ways that rejected those prior meanings.[8] These narratives did more than simply assert Black pride; they sought to commend Black beauty, accomplishments, and intelligence and recenter Black history, including African history.[9]

This was hardly an easy, straightforward, or uncontested process. At the time, *Negro* was far more widely used and broadly accepted as an identity label. Martin Luther King Jr., for example, spoke and wrote in terms of the "Negro" and the "Negro people." In "I Have a Dream," his most famous speech, he repeatedly invoked the term *Negro* to refer to the African American community, stating, to take one of many instances, that "[o]ne hundred years later, the Negro lives on a lonely island of poverty in the midst of a vast ocean of material prosperity."[10]

This was not simply the peculiar usage of Black southern preachers. One of the most famous and well-known contemporaneous books covering the civil rights movement in its heyday was Robert Penn Warren's *Who Speaks for the Negro?*[11] Similarly, the federal government's Kerner Commission report of 1968 spoke almost entirely in terms of "Negro" neighborhoods and communities.[12]

Moreover, prominent African American figures opposed the term *Black*. Thurgood Marshall, the first African American United States Supreme Court justice and one of the principal architects of the litigation that led to *Brown v. Board of Education*, as well as one of the nation's most accomplished lawyers, resisted, up until the end of his life (he died in January 1993), the term *Black*. As one of his law clerks recounted, "He hated the term '[B]lack'—which had been an opprobrious way of talking about the people to whose fight for equality he'd devoted his life . . . he wasn't going to let 'a bunch of kids' (sometimes put more strongly) tell him what he should call himself."[13] *Negro* remained his "descriptor of choice."[14]

Regardless of the interpretation applied to our brief vignettes, whether you regard these terms as simple synonyms or containing subtle or not-so-subtle shifts in meaning, it is undeniable that identity categories—including those that seem immutable—shift and evolve over time. It may also be true that the evolving terms and labels can be used as synonyms, but to regard such changes as merely semantic overlooks deeper forces at work and the inherently unstable nature of identity itself.

Within a single lifetime—even a generation—racial, ethnic, gender, and many other identities have been dramatically reconstituted and redefined. Popular identities exist today that were virtually unimaginable a generation ago in terms of gender, sexual orientation, and even race, and undoubtedly will continue to evolve well into the future.

Governments race to keep up. The United States decennial census has rarely maintained a consistent racial and ethnic classification scheme between consecutive censuses.[15] In the last decade, the Census Bureau considered, but ultimately did not adopt, a proposal to reclassify "Hispanic" from an ethnic category on the 2010 census to a racial category on the 2020 census. How can something as seemingly fixed and immutable as a racial or ethnic identity change over time, as from one census to another, let alone from one category to another?

This chapter will try to answer this question, beginning with an investigation of identity formation. Group identity formation is a complex process—far more than is generally appreciated. This chapter will examine theories explaining how such identities arise and secure affiliation. From there, this chapter will turn to the constellation of meanings and associations that arise in connection with identities. Identities are more than empty or neutral categories that signal superficial characteristics. They are imbued with socially relevant information that impart assumptions about characteristics of people with those identities.

As we will show, and as you may already suspect, the meanings that identities impart—especially identities such as gender, race, and

ethnicity—signal and ultimately imply not only characteristics about individuals sorted into those categories, but also their position in a society.
In other words, as we will see, identity plays a role in determining what is
called "group positionality." These individual and group meanings and the
categories themselves do not arise in an orderly sequence, but are bound
up with one another, and emerge together. In fact, the socially significant
meanings and various associations tethered to particular group identities
are in part the impetus for identity formation in the first place.

———

There are nearly as many theories about the origins of identities as there
are identities that have emerged. A broad and diverse literature on identity spans multiple disciplines, with very different points of emphasis and
conclusions.[16] A comprehensive evaluation of that literature is beyond
the scope of this book. Our focus here is on the development and emergence of *group*-based identities, not individual identity development. The
latter is mostly the province of psychology, and is well covered in that
literature.[17]

Our interest here is not so much in the origin of identities per se, but on
the ways in which identities acquire social currency, meaning, and significance, securing the affiliation of individuals. Thus our focus is not so much
identity *formation*, as it is identity *affiliation*. In addition, we wish to understand how such identities became coded as "us" or "them," as in-groups
or out-groups, the essence of the othering process.

One of the longest-running (though now largely settled) debates was
over whether identities—especially racial and gender identities—are bio-
logically determined, socially constructed, or both. The concept of race,
for example, was long thought to be a genetic or biological distinction, determined by blood (at least in the United States).[18] In this way, race was
thought (and may still be continued to be viewed) as immutable, inherent,
and categorical.

What about mixed-race people? Mixed-race identities complicate racial
classification taxonomies, but the one-drop rule, along with supplementary
classification schemes that delineated racial proportions (for example, "oc-
toroon" and "quadroon") was an attempt to manage that.[19] It is unresolved

to what extent contemporary legal codes regard race as immutable (or as categorically distinct from "color," "ancestry," or "ethnicity"), but it is clear that race is largely viewed as inherent or inherited based on how most countries regard racial identity.[20]

Transgender identities and gender fluidity perhaps most vividly illustrate the limits of the biological model. Here gender identity is partially or entirely decoupled from sex and biology. There is no accommodation for gender fluidity under a biological model. And under a simple binary model, neither intersex nor trans identities are cognizable. To be clear, we are not claiming that biology plays no role in informing gender identity, but that a biological approach to race, gender, and any group identity is woefully inadequate to describe the social reality of that identity.

Indeed, this is the scientific consensus. After World War II, which was in part spurred by a variety of pernicious racial ideologies, the scientific community reached a consensus that race lacked a scientific basis.[21] More recent developments in human genetics, including the breakthrough decoding of the human genome at the turn of this century, seemed to support this conclusion, by failing to find any broad genetic differences between racial groups as such.[22] Although there are tremendous genetic variability among people and populations, geneticists found that "any two individuals within a particular population are as different genetically as any two people selected from any two populations in the world."[23]

It would seem that the strongest case for a biological basis to identity is in the domain of gender. After all, there are obvious biological, physical, and hormonal differences between sexes. Men are taller on average, for example.[24] Yet research shows that categorical differences between the sexes beyond genitalia and reproductive organs are elusive. A large MRI study of over 1,400 brains found that sex and gender identities showed that the human brain cannot be cleanly sorted into male or female classes.[25] And, in practice, gender identity appears more expansive and dynamic than simple sex differences or biological reductionism would suggest.[26]

If biology cannot explain identity, even the those that would seem to be genetically endowed or inherited, then what is the alternative? The alternative to a biological deterministic model is that race, gender, and other identities assumed to be "natural" or "biological" are in fact socially constructed.

But it is a superficial cliché to assert that race—or any identity—is socially constructed. The more important questions are how and why.

The Social Construction of Identity

Some group-based identities are ancient, while others are comparatively recent. Although variable in many particulars across cultures and time, gender appears to be a social construction of ancient origin.[27] Feminist scholars and feminist theory have contributed enormously to the now-commonplace understanding of gender as a social construction rather than biological differences attributed to sex, and the corresponding recognition that many differences traditionally regarded as sex-based are now understood as socially produced and maintained.[28]

One strand of this scholarship emphasizes the powerful role of the family as an institution, and the social expectations, work, and norms that arise and exist within the family, which ultimately permeate the rest of society.[29] Other feminist scholars emphasize various forms of gender-based prejudice or discrimination that afflict political and cultural institutions and the marketplace, and thereby structure gender inequality.[30] Still others, such as Judith Butler, have revealed how gender identities are powerfully shaped by countless iterative interactions and performative scripts that people adopt and follow.[31]

Adherents to ancient religions engage in practices, customs, and communities that generate and sustain identities that are also long-standing, although continually evolving. In contrast, national identities tend to be recent in origin. American or German nationalities only emerged with the creation of those respective nation-states, yet powerfully shape our self-conceptions. For example, American colonists would have identified as British subjects in most cases before the American Revolution. Or, in the early nation, they would have identified—and saw themselves primarily—as Virginians, New Yorkers, Rhode Islanders, and the like—not as Americans.[32]

The German nation-state was constructed out of myriad of German-speaking kingdoms, principalities, duchies, and free cities during the nineteenth century, resulting in the German confederation in 1815, and ultimately the German nation-state, initially known as the "German

Empire," in 1871.[33] Similarly, the modern Italian state followed the unification of kingdoms, republics, and separate states, a process that culminated, perhaps not coincidentally, also in 1871.[34] But as the Piedmont statesman Massimo d'Azeglio declared, "We have made Italy. Now we have to make Italians."[35]

In fact, although nations and states are ancient political entities, the modern nation-state is generally traced to the Treaty of Westphalia of 1648.[36] Similarly, there is a general historical understanding that the concept of race, as such, did not exist before the seventeenth century.[37] Although it may be possible to read differences about humans into ancient observations, there is no mention or even suggested conception of "race" as it is understood today, until roughly the seventeenth and eighteenth centuries.[38] In that sense, from a historical vantage point, race is a relatively recent concept, and certainly more recent than ethnicity or tribe.[39]

Given that the concept of race as a social category dividing humans into branches emerged at the same time as the creation of a large-scale slave labor system primarily featuring Africans, some scholars claim that race was *created* as a category to justify an exploitative and capitalistic economic system based on slave labor. That is, the assumed or claimed "inferiority" of African slaves by race was viewed as a justification for slavery.[40] A version of this theory is prevalent in Marxist and neo-Marxist theories regarding the social construction of race, that race was and continues to be used as a way to divide white and Black labor from organizing for common interests.[41]

Another theory ties the construction of racial identities to the project of constructing the modern nation-state.[42] In his comparative study of the histories of the United States, Brazil, and South Africa, the political scientist Anthony Marx argued that "states made race," in the sense that official actions enforced distinctions that became known as racial. Specifically, he argues that racial identities were devised and propounded as part of a strategy by political elites to resolve internal conflict by consolidating several previously held oppositional identities into new national identities. The key to this strategy was exclusion. Thus, in the case of South Africa and the United States, political elites forged nation-states by excluding and marginalizing Black people.

In his case studies, racial (and other) identities were the driving force used to "integrate populations otherwise at war and engaged in ongoing competition."[43] In South Africa, the central conflict was between the Dutch Afrikaners and the British, where the unifying philosophy that brought them into alliance was the subjection of indigenous Africans, ultimately settled by the Afrikaner-controlled state of 1948, which imposed apartheid. Similarly, in the United States the lines of conflict were between workers, including indentured servants and laborers, as well as between northern industrialists and southern planters. These conflicts, Marx argues, were managed through the imposition of racial hierarchies. Thus conflicts like Bacon's Rebellion and other cross-racial alliances were stymied through a project of racial nation-state building.* Similarly, bloody conflicts including the American Civil War were managed through a Reconstruction that ultimately abandoned the pretense of protecting freedman in favor of the national reconciliation.[44] In Marx's formulation, race was the glue to nation-state building or maintenance. In each case, political elites used identity—religious and racial identities, among others—to unify disharmonious groups by excluding still others.

In the United States, this dynamic suggests how so many diverse peoples from unrelated tribes or ethnic groups were constituted into racial categories, particularly through the nineteenth century and early twentieth century.[45] This is how the "Irish," like many other European ethnic categories, was once a distinct racialized category but is now firmly encompassed within "white."[46] "Race-making" was a process connected to the project of nation-state identity consolidation.[47]

History supplies many examples of how social group identities were consolidated or formed along lines far beyond those in Anthony Marx's case studies. Religious identities were forged in a similar manner. When Pope Urban II urged Christians of Western Europe to undertake the First Crusade in the eleventh century, he well understood that binding European knights and nobles into a single military force would dampen the incessant wars that they had been waging among themselves.[48] Under a

---

* Since race was not a fully formed concept, this is a post hoc description.

single banner, these forces would bond with each other and imagine a new external foe, largely Muslim and Jewish peoples they encountered along the way. One of the enduring effects of these efforts was to redefine what it meant to be a Christian, and to tamp down (at least temporarily) incessant warfare between kingdoms and principalities of Christian Europe. As the American philosopher Eric Hoffer observed, "hatred is the most accessible and comprehensive of all unifying agents."[49]

The sociologist Gerhard Falk claims that every society stigmatizes some conditions and behaviors because doing so provides a basis for group solidarity by delineating "outsiders" from "insiders."[50] In this regard, stigma plays a constitutive role—it specifies the trait, behaviors, or characteristics that delineate insiders and outsiders, while denigrating the now-stigmatized element and simultaneously binding the dominant group together. This theory of stigma is essentially a description of the othering process and suggests the reasons for it, particularly the need to bind together formerly antagonistic peoples and socially delineate who belongs and who does not. If Falk's theory of stigma is to be credited, then this dynamic extends beyond the social construction of race to that of all identities bound up with the othering process. This is not an overstatement: the othering process constructs both the identities of the dominant and favored groups as well as the socially excluded and marginalized peoples.

The process of exclusion produces new shared interests and experiences among the excluded, and thereby contributes to the project of identity formation for those people. Thus the processes that Anthony Marx describes as "making race and making states" helped constitute both whiteness *and* Blackness. The difference is that the *marginalized* group is both formed and activated to solidaristic resistance by the processes of othering while the dominant group is the forged alloy of previously independent, and often adversely competitive, groups.

Group Formation Through Resistance to Othering

It is not a small thing to point out that the construction of many prevailing identities emerged hand-in-hand with the process of nation and state building. Indeed, the concept of nation depends on some notion of identity. But the coherence of a nation-state depends upon the presence of a nation, an identity that can demand and expect some allegiance beyond mere residence. As this brief survey suggests, leaders of all kinds, including national builders, emperors, capitalists, and religious leaders, play a role in identity formation and emergence. Political and social leaders play an important role in this process by articulating these identities and giving them content and meaning, and in promoting and using certain labels in ways that become widespread.

But these identities wouldn't stick unless they served a practical function for ordinary people. Even beyond leaders and elites, large-scale social, political, economic, and religious forces play a role in forging identities that become relevant to us, making some social groupings more obvious, functional, and useful as an organizing framework. This is not only how disparate white ethnics (Anglo-Saxons, Germans, Polish, Irish, and Italians alike) become raced "white," but also how diverse peoples become raced as "Asian," "Hispanic," or "Native American."

The effort to organize a nation or state around a particular identity or set of identities creates a correspondence: the group who is *not* designated as part of the nation, or upon which a dominant group's identity is centered, is othered. If a nation's identity is rooted in a particular religious, ethnic, or racial group, as many leaders around the world today claim (for example, Hinduism in India, Christianity in Europe and the United States, or Jewish identity in Israel), then anyone who is not a member of that group or does not share that identity is tacitly or visibly excluded or marginalized.[51] This is the problem of ethno-nationalism discussed later in this chapter. The valorization of one set of identities creates an implicit correspondence that denigrates, devalues, or disadvantages people outside of that group.

In short, the othering process plays an outsize role in identity formation itself. Not only does the othering process constitute "the other," but it also (and simultaneously) constitutes the meanings associated with the identity that is so characterized. Such forms of othering will engender identity claims as an oppositional force—a way of contesting oppressive and unjust arrangements.

In other words, disparate peoples can be united into a social group as a result of, and in response to, various forms of othering.[52] The Russian invasion of Ukraine—ostensibly intended to split the Ukrainian people and reunite the Russian-speaking portion with their Russian neighbors, paradoxically had the opposite effect.[53] The Kremlin characterized Ukraine as a fabricated nation,[54] but the Russian invasion helped foment an embattled solidarity between the Ukrainian-speaking and Russian-speaking citizens of Ukraine, and thereby helped solidify a national consciousness. The Russian invasion may have been the cement for Ukrainian national identity.[55] The invaders failed to appreciate that all identities are fabricated, and that their attack could help create the thing they denied existed: a Ukrainian nation.

This insight is generalizable: countless peoples have been formed or organized into meaningful social and cultural units through processes of othering, and their corresponding efforts to resist being othered, whether that means being enslaved, attacked, excluded, exploited, or otherwise marginalized.[56] Without an identity to secure commitments and latch coordination around, mobilization is more difficult.[57] As the Occupy Wall Street veteran Jonathan Smucker observes, "there can be no serious social movement—the kind that challenges the powerful and the privileged—without a corresponding serious group identity; a sense of solidarity and cohesion that encourages core members to contribute an exceptional level of commitment, sacrifice, and heroics over the course of a prolonged struggle."[58]

Once consolidated into a group through a shared identity, people can then more easily organize in solidarity to protect their interests, well-being, and safety. In that sense, identities provide a vehicle to organize and coordinate calls for justice, equity, and inclusion. This is one of the paradoxes of exclusion: its purpose is to create solidarity within the dominant or favored group, but it also helps fabricate and strengthen the identity of the excluded.[59]

This helps explain how terms like *Latino*, *Asian American*, or even *Native American* become socially salient and functional. The labels *Native American* or *American Indian* describe a vast and often vastly diverse groupings of peoples, including the Lakota, the Sioux, Navajo, Cherokee, and Iroquois, to name but a few. These are peoples with notably different cultures, languages, customs, and traditions, linked largely by the fact that they are indigenous to North America, and by a shared or similar historical experience of being forcibly removed from their lands and broken treaties with the United States. These peoples are a constitutive "other" to the construction of the United States as a nation-state, and as such, the broad identity of Native American, however imperfect, performs critical work.

Many of these labels describe large, heterogeneous groupings of people. As with *Native American*, both *Latino* and *Asian American* denote peoples from vastly different national, cultural, and linguistic backgrounds. One need only interview Cuban Americans in Miami on their political views as compared to people whose ancestors are from El Salvador, Colombia, or Mexico to recognize the gulf of difference. Or remember that Japanese, Chinese, Korean, and Vietnamese-descended peoples in the United States have vastly different experiences of oppression (Chinese exclusion and labor versus Japanese interment) in the United States, not just from their places of national origin.

And yet these broad labels have found a foothold because they provide some social taxonomic function. In fact, there was a deliberate political movement behind the advent of the term *Asian American* to describe these groups from the late 1960s.[60] It was, in part, a movement away from the term *Oriental*, with its varied and pejorative connotations, as famously deconstructed by Edward Said.* The spate of "anti-Asian" violent attacks in 2020 and 2021 may have played a role in making the label *Asian American* more socially relevant by helping identify the group that is being targeted and victimized.[61]

The emergence and then broad consolidation and wide (although certainly not universal) acceptance of certain identity labels and categories cannot be explained on the basis of descriptive precision. The groupings of peoples are simply too diverse to denote or convey any specific meaning reflective of those peoples as a cultural unit. Instead, these identities acquire salience as a result of some prevailing imperative or overriding need. One of those imperatives is clear: resisting and contesting processes of othering.

---

*We also wish to note—and properly credit—that Said was one of the earliest exponents of the notion of the "Other" as a formal category, a notion explicated as part of his deconstruction of Orientalism. See Edward W. Said, *Orientalism* (New York: Vintage Books, 1979), 25.

In short, group identities emerge and take root when there is a common story, experience, or pattern that emerges across a population or population segment. In many cases, previously unrelated peoples then become linked through this shared experience. This is one meaning of the feminist notion that "the personal is political."[62] Many seemingly personal experiences may be a result of large-scale social forces, structures, and dynamics. Moreover, any effective remedial action requires coordinated action in the public sphere. The formulation of a narrative that both describes these shared experiences and the identity that undergirds them is what philosophers call "articulation."[63] These are by-products of the othering process.

Contested and Reclaimed Identities

Identities emerge to solve different problems. And in solving one set of problems, they create new ones. As a vivid illustration of this dynamic, compare our brief personal vignettes that opened this chapter with the evolving labels used to describe Hispanic peoples or people of Latin descent.

In the 1990s and 2000s, *Latino* was embraced as a more inclusive term (over *Hispanic*) for encompassing non-Spanish-speaking peoples and nations, including Brazilians.[64] Proponents felt that this term might help weave a common political identity among Latin peoples, especially those in the United States, and promote group solidarity. Conversely, *Chicano* was embraced in the 1960s for the opposite reason as *Latino*: it was an attempt to specify and differentiate between certain Spanish-speaking peoples.[65] In particular, it was meant to specify people of Mexican ancestry (as contrasted with, say, Cuban) and also connote mestizo or indigenous heritage, which is not captured by the term *Hispanic*.[66]

More recently, *Latinx* has been widely propounded as a gender-neutral noun for people of Latin or Hispanic descent, but this effort has been contentious. It has been mocked by some non-Hispanic people as peculiar and unpronounceable, but it has also been critiqued by people of Latin descent themselves as esoteric and something that emerged from the academy rather than organically. The even more obscure *Latiné* has been circulated as a term that better reflects the Spanish language while remaining gender neutral.[67] As the first Hispanic United States senator from California,

Alex Padilla observed that these debates are not new but are merely the most recent iteration of the debate "of Hispanic versus Latino versus Chicano versus Mexican American."[68]

This dynamic is generalizable. There is no uncontested, natural, or universal label. Some terms and labels acquire greater social salience and political utility while others fade. The use of *Indian* to denote peoples indigenous to the Americas was originally a mistake, due to the confusion of European explorers. Yet it is often preferred by indigenous peoples over the alternatives, except in Canada. Native American peoples in Canada prefer the term *First Nations*, which acquired greater salience and use starting in the 1970s.[69] Others in South American prefer the term *Amerindian*. And groups in Alaska often prefer *Alaskan Natives*. The group-based taxonomies we live with, and the labels used to demarcate among them, may appear natural, stable, and consensual because they are inherited or adopted by convention and broad usage. But they are usually fraught to begin with, and their adoption is based upon certain exigencies, settlements, or conditions.

What work, for example, is *Latinx* trying to do, and for whom? As Senator Padilla notes, much like *Negro, colored, Black,* and *African American, Latinx* "comes across in different ways to different people in different parts of the country." He elaborates: "Latinx . . . for the younger generation especially, it is purposeful. It is more than just symbolic. In the Spanish language, you have feminine versus masculine nouns, and the move to Latinx is one way of saying, 'You know what, if we're all equal, let's let our language reflect that.'"[70] Survey research affirms this claim. A Pew survey found, for example, that six times as many 18–29-year-olds have heard of the term as those 65 or older, and nearly three times as many use the term.[71] There is a similar generational (and geographic) divide in census respondent use of *Negro* compared to *Black* or *African American*.

———

In most cases, identities we live with appear stable and fixed because the period of contestation and evolution occurred before our time, or because the outcome appears inevitable afterward, even if it felt fraught during the contestation period. In our time, many identity categories are undergoing dramatic and rapid evolution. There is probably no supertype of identity that has evolved as much or as quickly as those describing gender and sexual orientation in the past few decades.

The first initialism to describe non-hetero peoples was *LGB* in the 1990s (prior to that, "gay and lesbian" was the predominant label). Gradually, new initials were added. By the twenty-first century, *LGBT* became an umbrella term that is often used to refer to the community as a whole.[72] Today the initialism has become more extensive (LGBTQIAA), as have the pronouns used to describe people of that community (including *they, their, them*) and the concept of nonbinary. This evolution of preferred terms, pronouns, and acronyms has hardly been uncontested, but it has found wider acceptance.

Even the term *trans* has evolved. *Transsexual* was a term used widely in the 1970s to describe people with gender dysphoria, including those who sought gender reassignment surgery. Today many transgender people reject that term, partly because of concerns that its past use by the medical and psychological community was overly pathological.[73]

It is not only the case that terms used to describe or denote identity evolve over time, through debate and contestation, but many formerly mistaken or pejorative terms have been embraced. Recall how the othering process has a tendency to engender solidarity and greater cohesion among the people othered. This helps explain how terms of marginalization or oppression are reappropriated, or, more precisely, "reclaimed," as *Black* and *queer*, among many others, have been. Reflecting on his life as a gay man, Andrew Solomon describes how "years of self-loathing as a yawning void" can only be compensated when "celebration needs to fill and overflow it."[74] One of the ways this happens is through the valorization of marginalized or stigmatized identities, perhaps best illustrated by the mantra "I'm Black and I'm Proud."

The term *queer* itself was long an epithet—a slur used to marginalize gay people as unnatural or subversive.[75] Its first known usage, around 1513, indicated something not-normal, peculiar, or odd.[76] The first reference of the word in relation to homosexuality was in the late nineteenth century, and the term was entered into the dictionary a few decades later.[77]

Yet *queer* has been redefined and reclaimed to empower in similar ways to how, especially among younger Black people, the n-word is sometimes used as a term of familiarity (although many older Black people, especially civil rights movement veterans, prefer not to use it, and some strongly condemn such use).* The word *queer* now adjoins or modifies many descriptive labels, from queer studies to queer love.[78] This is not to say that this process is seamless. The Association for LGBTQ Journalists advises that the term should be used with caution, and that it is "still extremely offensive when used as an epithet and still offensive to many L.G.B.T.Q. people regardless of intent."[79] It is not hard to imagine that Thurgood Marshall felt the same about *Black*.

———

All identities are probably contested, but only reclaimed identities are obviously so. In those cases, the project of reclamation is essentially overcoming or erasing stigma. And the participants and intended audience for such projects is not just the larger society. In many cases, members of the marginalized group may accept or internalize that stigma, as epitomized by the famous doll study by Kenneth Clark, where Black children preferred to play with white dolls.[80] In this regard, *Black* was not just a racial epithet, but an expression of colorism as well. One of us recalls the rejection and sting of being labeled "Black." Thus, Black pride or gay pride is a message intended as an antidote to a prevailing view that such identities are not something to be proud of.†

The work of identity formation for social groups is both top-down and bottom-up, but above all it is highly interactive. Efforts to create new identities or reclaim pejorative labels are often driven by elites or cultural influencers, but they only work if they are responsive to some need that allows them to resonate, take root, and spread. This, in turn, has unpredictable effects on the constitution of identity for other groups. Consider how as

———

* While the appropriate use of the n-word continues to be deeply contested, there is general agreement that the term remains off-limits to non-Black people.

† Such efforts are ongoing. Colorism has and continues to operate in many Black communities. This is another example of how "othered" groups participate in the othering process.

African American entered mainstream parlance, some whites started to use *European American* as an identity label.

Boundary Work

Having seen how large-scale forces (particularly the othering process) shape identity formation (and that this formation is ongoing), we need to dig deeper to understand how this works at a granular level. Social scientists have made headway into the mystery of identity formation, by outlining the mechanisms and processes by which categorical social boundaries arise and become salient.[81] Sociologists call this "boundary work."[82] The boundary is the line of demarcation that helps organize relations between people on either side of the boundary, between people across the boundary, and "shared representations" of the zone itself.[83]

The late, great sociologist Charles Tilly theorized a limited number of mechanisms to explain this.[84] His theories, considered in whole or in part, help us better understand how group identities arise and are institutionalized, and how this institutionalization reinforces group inequality. When the Nazis enacted the Nuremberg Laws, for example, identifying anyone with at least 25 percent Jewish ancestry as a Jew, and then deprived them of German citizenship, they "activated a Jewish/non-Jewish boundary in a thousand demeaning and costly ways."[85]

According to Tilly, "public politics invariably involves the creation, activation, and transformation of visible us-them boundaries."[86] In Tilly's understanding, a large part of this process involves the *shared* representations of groups across a boundary. The boundary delineates not only the identities and relationships between groups on either side, but also the stories and social meanings that each group has about itself and the other. Thus the boundary entails representations concerning the differences between both groups held by either group on either side of the boundary. For example, it includes the "representations concerning [Jewish and Palestinian] differences by [Israelis]," as well as "representations concern[ing] [Jewish and Palestinian] differences by [Palestinians]."

One of the most important boundaries that have been recurringly invoked and repeatedly activated is that of "savage." Since ancient Greece, this boundary has played a critical role in policing religious and cultural belonging. This foundational boundary has been a through-line in Western civilization.[87] It has shaped the identity and content of the identities of many Western societies over the ensuing millennia. Although the content of the category has mutated many times, the category itself has been deployed to distinguish between people who belong and people who do not, and are therefore marked as the other.

Although the views of all involved matter, there is usually an asymmetry across the boundary. Representations, beliefs, or views held by one group may have more power and potential for harm than the views of another group regarding the first. This is not to diminish the harm created by representations held by a marginalized group regarding another marginalized group, but it is important that we recognize that such harms are not all the same or equal in potency or power and not flatten them into false equivalencies.[88]

Some mechanisms of boundary work reinforce existing identities by institutionalizing them. Thus the Coalition Provisional Authority—the transitional government installed after the 2003 invasion of Iraq—reinforced existing social cleavages by requiring religious identification (Shia, Sunni, or Kurd) within Baghdad's Green Zone and other parts of Iraq.[89] Instead of deactivating a social boundary, the CPA made the mistake of heightening an existing one. This error was unfortunately reminiscent of how European colonial powers reinforced tribal and ethnic delineations in Africa as a way to maximize their power and control ("divide and conquer").[90]

While some mechanisms of boundary work reinforce existing identities, others create them, cleaving them out of existing formulations and producing massive societal convulsions in the process. Perhaps one of the clearest and most widely dramatized examples in history is England's King Henry VIII's schism with the Catholic Church in 1534. By forming the Anglican Church, and declaring himself the head of it, he not only broke with the Catholic Church, but demanded that his subjects break as well. On account of his refusal to take an oath to his king's supremacy, and unwillingness to acknowledge the validity of Henry's marriage to Anne Boleyn, the statesmen and noted author Sir Thomas More was tried for treason and executed.[91]

The ultimate significance of the schism, however, lies in the fact that, within a generation, the larger part of a nation changed their religious fealty and allegiance, and thereby a significant part of their identity, from Catholic to Anglican, and adopted this entirely new religious identity. This illustrates how new identities form, the swiftness with which it can occur, and the consequences that flow from it, as well the role that elites and power often play.

A formative but underappreciated example of boundary work in the American context was the adoption of antimiscegenation statutes by colonial authorities. These laws prohibited free Black persons from marrying white colonists.[92] Virginia, the largest colony, enacted the first such law in 1691, and Maryland followed suit a year later in 1692. The colonies began to consider such measures in the aftermath of Bacon's Rebellion in 1676. Intermarriage threatened the ability of colonial leaders to maintain a pliant labor force. Previous laws had simply prohibited marriage based upon class or condition of servitude, but these were the first formal laws that created an explicit race line, and thereby represented multiple boundary work mechanisms theorized by Tilly. Their significance to the creation of race in Americas as we know it is hard to overstate. The norms these laws help engender and entrench racial identities and the stigma against inter-racial marriage they instilled endured for centuries. Some version of these laws remained in effect in the United States until 1967.[93] And it was not until 1993 that a majority of Americans indicated support for interracial marriage.[94]

In many cases of othering, mechanisms of boundary work in one social cleavage become a template for othering in other domains or contexts. Distinctions made in one context can be directly applied to another. So, for example, if discriminatory laws are adopted in voting or military service, then they may be more easily applied to employment or educational contexts. This is how Jim Crow and apartheid regimes operated: they were rarely confined to one small sphere of public life, although they started off one step at a time, rather than as an initial comprehensive regime of racial control.

The creation of a discriminatory or invidious distinction in a single arena—such as military service or marriage laws—may seem insufficient to suffuse a broader society with prejudice. One of Tilly's theorized mechanisms of boundary work, "borrowing," plays a critical role in the spread of private or public prejudice. Tilly cites the case of how business managers reinforced occupational gender segregation through borrowing: "a good deal of sex segregation results . . . from borrowing, as managers set up new offices and firms on existing models, including the assignment of men to higher-paid job categories."[95] In short, the division of labor and norms in one branch or company spread to others, resulting in a stifling uniformity of practices and occupational gender segregation, as might be seen in a 1960s sitcom or the prestige drama *Mad Men*, where women are generally relegated to secretaries or assistants.

To take another example, President Woodrow Wilson incorporated Jim Crow–style segregation in the federal government when he segregated federal agencies, extending a regional state-level practice nationally.[96] In this way, private discrimination can be adopted by public authorities, or vice versa through such borrowing and emulation. The spread of such practices plays a critical role in giving these identities social, economic, and political significance. It is these practices and norms, as much as anything "natural," that not only gives rise to social meanings ascribed to gender identity, but actually helps constitute the categorical boundary itself.

The templating function of boundary work provides an important insight into how othering proliferates while evolving: the experience of othering in one case may make it easier to other in another case. Thus the experience of institutionalizing racism in the United States helped provide a template for other forms of discrimination, exclusion, and oppression. This is why Michael Omi and Howard Winant refer to race in the United States as the "master category." Such a category does work in shaping culture and structures as well as how other marginalized groups are seen.[97]

There are also costs to maintain such boundaries. Just as enforcement of physical boundaries—erecting and maintaining walls—entails infrastructure, monitoring, and patrol and policing costs—so too does the cost of maintaining group boundaries through boundary work. Thus, in economic terms, the "returns" on such boundaries must exceed the costs of sustaining and monitoring such boundaries. The rewards to dominant or advantaged groups for creating and enforcing such boundaries must be great.

Through the Looking Glass

Understanding that identities are themselves a product of large-scale highly interactive social forces does not tell us everything we need to know about how they arise and how they are adopted, especially at the individual level. Are they slipped on like an article of clothing or always imposed by forces beyond our control? How do individuals navigate the constellation of identities imposed upon them or available to them?

Nor does it answer the question of how individuals and groups determine which identities are salient and which are less significant or meaningful. The discussion thus far suggests answers to these questions, showing how, for example, nation-state building has a profound impact on identity formation. But that discussion is incomplete. We need to better understand how the contestation over such identities plays out.

Identities matter—they shape our lives and how we are treated—but that does not mean that they are fixed or uncontested. On the contrary, they are often deeply contested, as the examples of "queer," "Latinx," "BIPOC," and "Black" illustrate. To begin, as Charles Tilly observes, identities are "always assertions, always contingent, always negotiable, but also always consequential."[98]

Group identities are created, formed, and become markers of social significance before individuals adopt them. Yet individuals play a role by interacting repeatedly with others, and thereby "renegotiating who they are, adjusting the boundaries they occupy, modifying their actions in rapid response to other people's reactions, selecting among and alternating available scripts."[99] The contestation process is enormously consequential. It affects not only the target group, but also nontargeted groups, institutional arrangements, and broad social structures and meanings.

We take the position that identity formation is primarily the by-product of a social, "inter-subjective" process.[100] This is a baroque term to describe a simple concept: neither individuals nor society fully determine the boundaries that dictate or give meaning and significance to an identity. Rather, identities and the content and meaning they acquire are determined by the jostling and interplay of individual assertions against other people's acceptance or denial of those assertions. As Kwame Anthony Appiah explains, "an identity cannot simply be imposed upon me, willy-nilly, but neither is an identity up to me, a contrivance that I can shape any way I please."[101]

Consider for example, the self-identification of Barack Obama as a Black man. In his campaign for president, some Black commentators openly questioned if he was "Black enough," on account of having a white mother and being raised by white grandparents.[102] Some commentators put considerable weight on the fact that Obama, although not a descendant of American slaves, married Michelle Robinson, a woman who hailed from the south side of a Chicago, a narrative that some felt was more "authentic" in some sense to the Black American experience. On the other hand, some commentators even wondered whether Obama was "too Black."[103] Clearly, there is considerable complexity at play.[104]

Identity formation is more complex than simply an assertion of identity by either a dominant or a marginalized group. Social psychologists studying identity formation have developed elaborate theories to explain these processes. For example, the "interactive model of identity formation" describes how social interactions create emergent identities.[105] This and other models emphasize the interactive and social dimensions of identity development.

The notion of intersubjectivity also informs W. E. B. Du Bois's notion of "double consciousness."[106] This is a lens that members of marginalized groups experience when viewing the world as a member of a marginalized group, but also in regarding their group from the lens of the dominant group. The sense of dissonance is more acute when the divergence between the two views is widest, and when the othering process is most intense.

———

This interplay between individual assertion of identity and the reaction or counterassertions of others also helps explain a concept like "passing." In sociological terms, passing is the ability of a person to be regarded as a member of an identity group or category different from their own.[107] In its original form, passing is the idea that individuals of one race, typically Black, who are especially light-skinned or fair-complexioned, may present themselves as white and find that other people accept or do not question that identity assertion.[108] The motive for passing may be to access privileges or benefits that do not exist for their inherited identity or to cope with or avoid stigma. Thus many Black people in the antebellum and Jim Crow periods who presented as white may have done so to access privileges denied members of their group. Doing so does not disturb the boundary, but allows individuals to cross it.

There are many examples of members of marginalized ethnic or religious groups converting or "passing" in terms of espousing adherence to a particular religious faith to avoid becoming victims of violence. During the Armenian genocide, many (although not all) ethnic Armenian Christians avoided being killed if they converted to Islam.[109] Similarly, Jewish people during European pogroms have avoided similar results by converting or pretending to convert to Christianity.

LGBTQ people may occasionally engage in passing for similar reasons. For example, the "Don't Ask, Don't Tell" doctrine was a rule that allowed LGBTQ persons to serve in the US military so long as they concealed their sexual orientation. Thus LGBTQ persons had to pass in order to preserve their military careers.

Not all "passing" is deliberate or motivated; it may be inadvertent or situational. Many bisexual persons are married into relationships that, to outward appearances, present them as heterosexual (or strictly homosexual).[110] In this case, there may be a difference between a disposition, personal identity, and social identities. A person's disposition in terms of sexuality, for example, may be consistent with their averred identity, but may be inconsistent with their social identity, how they present or appear to friends, family, and colleagues.

In the United States, evolving norms tend—although some states currently deny this—to grant the individual the right to identify the gender of their choice. Although not every institution or social setting will accept an individual's personal assertion of their own identity, many will, especially in regard to gender identity.[111] Most states allow people to change their gender on their birth certificates in this regard, for example.

The intersubjectivity of gender identity becomes most evident when personal assertions are contested. Transgender people encounter such dilemmas regularly—with some quarters of society readily recognizing the transgender person's asserted identity while others seeing only through the narrow lens of biological sex, unwilling to recognize the social construction of gender, recognize their gender identity, or employ the person's preferred pronouns. This is the tension between assumed gender identity playing against asserted. In this sense, peer "policing" plays an active role in identity.[112] The push and pull of identity assertion against identity contestation shapes intersubjectivity.[113]

Intersubjectivity as the central dynamic of identity formation means that the subjectivity of the individual does not automatically or even usually trump the subjective views of peers or larger social relations. Indeed, more often than not, the opposite is true. Although individual assertions matter, larger social perceptions will trump individual subjectivity, as Rachel Dolezal discovered. A white woman of Italian heritage, Dolezal presents herself as and asserted Black identity, even chairing a local NAACP branch.[114] Her subjective identity was questioned by others holding the same identity, resulting in considerable social and professional penalties and raising questions about the fluidity and fixity of racial identities.[115] When Barack Obama was asked on the CBS News show *60 Minutes* if he was "Black enough," he explained that "if you look African-American in this society, you're treated as an African-American."[116]

It is not just the identity category itself that is shaped through the intersubjective process, but the content or meaning of that identity as well. Every identity category has a fraught and contested set of meanings. Queer peoples have engaged in vigorous debates within the LGBTQ community, for example, about the meaning of that label, and whether LGBTQ peoples should strive for assimilation into a "normal" American life, or retain some differentiating—and perhaps oppositional—identity.[117]

———

It is important to emphasize that the intersubjectivity is not simply about the interplay of subjectivities—between the self and others. It is also an interplay of the assertion of the self against the *internalized* subjectivity of peers, acquaintances, and the larger social world. In other words, there is an interplay in our own minds, not just in social terms. This can result in an uncomfortable cognitive dissonance.

This dissonance can sometimes show up as denial. Andrew Solomon recounts his difficulty accepting his homosexuality.[118] If someone regards themselves as a "jock," but realizes that the larger world views them as a "nerd," there will be not simply cognitive dissonance, but some internal negotiation that occurs as the assertion of self runs up against an undeniable set of external—but also internal—assumptions. In 1902, a sociologist labeled this underlying the dynamic "The Looking Glass Self," a metaphor that captures the idea that part of the constitution of our identity is based upon how we think others see us.[119]

The view that identities are socially constructed, counterintuitively, does not entail the conclusion that such identities are not inherited. As suggested before, even if undergirded by certain psychological, physiological, or otherwise phenotypical features, all identities are nonetheless socially constructed. The categories, content of the categories, and the meanings that give them life are all undetermined by biology.

Nonetheless, inheritance is an identity template. Recall the distinction between vertical and horizontal identities propounded by Solomon. Vertical identities are those that we "inherit," like race, religion, or ethnicity. These inheritances are not merely biological. Consider, for example, the case of someone adopted at birth by different-race parents or a different-race egg donor.[120] Is a child born and raised by two white parents through a Latin American egg donor Latino? As Appiah explains, the answer is "a matter both of how you identify yourself and of how others identify you."[121] In this process, appearance matters to some extent, because appearance can shape the response or assumptions of others, which people who "pass" have exploited. But the "brute force of ancestry" alone cannot answer the question, as it will depend upon the child's assertion of identity and the acceptance or contestation they encounter.

The distinction between vertical and horizontal identities demonstrates that humans have some agency in terms of identity. We inherit some identities, but others we enter into more fully and willingly, looking for a community to belong to. Different social groups establish different cultures, norms, and outlooks, and these can be entered into under certain conditions and not under others.

While it may seem to us that identities are aspects of ourselves that we select or choose, it turns out that identity formation is a complicated process that is primarily social. Identity formation is neither a top-down nor entirely individual process, but rather collective, mutual, and horizontal as well. The key is understanding its social terms. Identity begins with social processes.

As Tilly put it, "interpersonal transactions compound into identities, create and transform social boundaries, and accumulate into durable social ties."[122] In his view, social processes—above all—determine which identities become salient, and which remain subordinate. He continues: "if social construction occurs, it happens socially, not in the isolated recesses of individual minds."[123] The identities we adopt are generally produced by social interaction and social forces. Even when asserting gender identity, we rarely pull our averred identity out of the ether, but out of a social milieu that offers a range of options to select among.

On the other hand, identity formation is not entirely predetermined externally either. Individuals—especially in concert with others—can push to assert new identities or against conventional meanings. Social categories are shaped, manifested, and entrenched through large-scale social forces, even law, but they aren't entirely created by states or societies.[124] States may use available identities to advance their goals, but it matters why some social distinctions become salient and others don't. Identities and the meanings they produce must have some utility or function—some hook to latch on to—in order to become widespread.

People of color, for example, was a term that emerged in the 1990s to decenter whiteness, and to reflect the fact that in some places and states, people of color were not actually "minorities."[125] A more recent example of an initial-based neo-identity category is *BIPOC*, an acronym that stands for Black, Indigenous, and People of Color. *BIPOC* incorporates the earlier concept of "people of color" and attempts to recognize indigenous peoples and the unique and specific experiences of Black peoples.

On the other hand, this acronym is not without problems. By providing a separate initial for Black people and people of color, the term potentially implies that Black people are somehow not people of color. Some critics claim that by separating out Black, but not explicitly mentioning Asian or Latino, who are foundational "others" in the Southwest and West Coast of the United States, the term creates a "hierarchy of oppression."[126] Nonetheless, this imperfect term has found wide purchase and more popular usage.

This is not to suggest that there is a perfect label or precise term. There never will be. Our point is rather to illustrate how language, identity, identity categories, and meanings evolve, serving some purposes and becoming adopted, while others lose their purchase as they become less useful. To return to the question that started us off: Is identity like an article of clothing to be put on or taken off? Identity is both like and unlike that. It is an assertion, but it is also contested, changing, evolving, sometimes thrusted onto people, sometimes embraced, sometimes reclaimed, and sometimes co-opted. If we fail to embrace the reality that identity isn't fixed, just like rivers and mountains, we are in resistance to life itself.

Classifying and Categorizing

Contrary to the presumption that identities initially emerge either as neutral or largely empty superficial signifiers, and are only subsequently imbued with a range of social meanings, we maintain that identities *are created to provide* socially significant cues and convey particular meanings. Social group identities and the social meanings that are associated with those identities are, in a sense, co-constitutive, and co-emergent. This process helps reveal how othering occurs because the content of these meanings shapes the perception, treatment, and social regard for members of each group. They tell us whether to fear, hate, pity, or respect members of that group.

Scholars have long observed patterns within human societies where people organize and collectively define themselves along dimensions of difference and sameness. Studies since the 1950s demonstrate the tendency of people to identify with whom they are grouped, no matter how arbitrary or even silly the group boundaries may be, and to judge members of their own group as superior. One of the most famous experiments on the power of identity to shape perceptions and import social significance is the

Robbers Cave Experiment, carried out by Muzafer Sherif and colleagues in 1954.[127] This experiment also underscores the socially constructed nature of identity and sheds light on the contextual factors that make identity meaningful.

In this experiment, nearly two dozen teenage boys of the same religious affiliation and class were assigned to one of two groups in a park in Oklahoma. They were then asked to engage in activities involving common goals and required group cooperation with prizes for the winning group. In addition to the emergence of group-based dynamics, such as norms, behaviors, and hierarchies within each group, the researchers found that each group developed aggressive in-group and out-group dynamics, including "burning the flag of the other group, refusing to eat together, singing derogatory songs about the other group, etc."[128] These behaviors abated when the groups were intermingled and assigned cross-group cooperative tasks. But the experiment is important for underscoring how quickly in-group preferences and assumptions arise even in contexts in which group identities are quickly fabricated for experimental purposes.

While these studies, and others like them, fuel assumptions about human tribalism and a suspicion that humans naturally organize into us-versus-them social groupings, it is important to emphasize that the content of those categories is not predetermined, but socially constructed and contextually influenced. There may be a human tendency to impose classifications and taxonomies on social life (to create categories and sort objects into them), but that does not necessarily entail a particular set of meanings, let alone extremely stigmatic or hierarchical ones.

Classification schemes are now understood as necessary to both survival and intelligence, and human beings appear hardwired to make categorical distinctions. Without mental categories to differentiate between objects and concepts, the world would appear like a Jackson Pollock painting, or as a "blooming, buzzing, confusion."[129]

In fact, this memorable phrase was used by William James, the father of psychology, to describe the world as infants encounter it. By this he meant that infants do not experience the world as non-infants do, populated with readily identifiable objects that possess features such as size, color, shape, and meaning.[130] When an infant sees a "chair" or a "spoon," they don't recognize it as such, but as a unique object, perhaps even as something without anything in common with anything else.

Although the science of infant psychology has come a long way in the century and more since James's observation, the underlying point—that humans rely on taxonomies and classification schemes to make sense of the world—remains true. We can see a spoon that we've never seen before—one that is unique in terms of its contours, material, size, or color—and still recognize it and correctly classify it as such. This is the power of categorical reasoning. The capacity to perceive objects or patterns in seemingly any visual field is what gives rise to star constellations, cloud watching, Rorschach tests, and even many optical illusions. This tendency, called pareidolia, was once thought to be a symptom of psychosis or mental illness but is now understood to be a normal and ordinary part of human cognition.[131]

The human tendency to make categories and to sort objects into one category or another is not simply a by-product of our intellect; it may have an evolutionary basis: the ability to distinguish between an edible fruit and a poisonous one enhanced survival. As one scholar concluded, "If our species were 'programmed' to refrain from drawing inferences or taking action until we had complete, situation-specific data about each person or object we encountered, we would have died out long ago."[132] To function efficiently, our brains have evolved processes for simplifying the perceptual environment and acting on less-than-perfect information. The mechanism for accomplishing both goals is the use of categories. Associations between color and poisonous berries or appearance and venomous snakes are examples of such categorical reasoning, but they extend to everything in the world, including other people. We make distinctions between things as a way of making sense and meaning of the world.

Although we are hardwired to make categorical distinctions, neither the categories nor the content of those categories nor the meanings associated with them are predetermined or natural. How then, are these categories created and distinctions drawn? Our environments and social contexts, which include families, community leaders, and friends, tell us which distinctions matter and which associations, stereotypes, and meanings map to those categories.

Human beings, even young ones, are quick to make connections, observe patterns and correspondences, and draw broad inferences based upon such covariations. When we see people of a certain gender or people of certain races or ethnicities in certain jobs or occupations or living in certain neighborhoods, we are quick to encode those connections. In that way, our environments prime us to observe particular differences and instruct us on which differences are relevant.

These associations are not only descriptive or neutral; they are loaded with meanings that help us navigate our social worlds. Thus, both the construction of categories and the meanings that attach to them are a social process. It happens at a larger scale and a faster speed than any of us can individually control or can even fully become aware of.

There is a fascinating literature on race classification that demonstrates the power of meaning to shape our classification process. Research by Aliya Saperstein and Jennifer Eberhard illuminates how people differently perceive individual identities in different contexts or with different contextual cues.[133] They found, for example, that medical examiners and funeral directors' racial classification decisions are influenced by the cause of death, showing that racial stereotypes shape how people are perceived and classified by others.[134] In particular, an ambiguously raced deceased person may be more likely to be labeled "Black" if they died as a result of violence.

These findings are part of a rapidly growing body of research on what is called "mind science" research or, more narrowly, implicit social cognition. This research has uncovered many of the unconscious processes and mechanisms undergirding social judgments, especially the associations that become installed and triggered beyond our conscious awareness.[135] The speed with which these associations can be drawn is a test of their strength, and the basis for the implicit association test (known as the IAT), a gauge of unconscious bias.[136]

None of our social identity categories, race included, are naturally seen or noticed. They only seem natural in a society that has already decided, in practice if not by explicit convention, that race matters, and carries social if not political or legal significance. This insight would apply to most identity categories. We absorb the categories, the content, and the meanings socially and largely into our unconscious. Thus, the effort not to "see" or notice race is all but impossible in a society where race is a salient social identity that conveys relevant social meanings. To repress the categories would be to deny ourselves access to these meanings and inhibit our ability to navigate the complex social worlds we are embedded within.

Dominance and Group Position Theory

Now that we have a sense of how group identities emerge and various meanings and associations attach to them, we can apply these principles to the construction of social hierarchies. We emphasized in the last chapter that the "other" is a group constituted by and through the othering process. What we mean by this should now be clearer.

Although it is possible that a previously nonmarginal social group becomes marginalized through the othering process, it is far more likely that the "othered" social group itself is fabricated or constituted by the othering process. Prior to the othering process, the othered group is generally not regarded as a distinct social group at all. In other words, the othering process renders both the social group and its marginalized status or stigmatized condition simultaneously. The othering process does the boundary work of creating a new category or relevant social distinction as well as a set of negative or at best ambivalent social meanings that now attach to that group.

As an example of this, we saw how processes of nation-state building consolidate prior, diverse identities into new racial identities. All new identities necessarily draw people with prior identities into them. Thus the categories of "Dalit" or "Native American" or "queer" were created and applied to people not necessarily constituting a distinctive social group prior to the imposition of those identities. The othering process both created the identity (as well as the contrasting ones) and fixed the social position of those groups in relation to each other.

The meanings that attach to each social group emerge from society's social practices and norms, and not from the characteristics of the othered group. Once a group is othered, then its social ranking position is normalized to seem natural and inevitable. Caste systems, for example, do not generally differentiate between previously established social groupings, but actually create new groupings, and simultaneously provide the justification for differential treatment and the subordination of lower-caste groups and the dominance of upper-caste groups within that system. Human beings are not just categorizing creatures; we are symbolic and meaning-making animals. We form rich, complex, and vivid social worlds that exist principally in our minds and then become institutionalized in the world through our policies and practices.

The relation of identity and characteristics to the othering process illustrates why it is a mistake, however common the trope, to assert that people are discriminated against on the basis of their traits, beliefs, or characteristics. So, for example, in a racist society, the claim is that people are discriminated against on the basis of their skin color. Such an assertion implies that skin color is both the ground and the reason for racial discrimination. On the contrary, skin color is rendered socially salient through the institution of racist ideas and racist structural arrangements. It is the belief in different races and the superiority or inferiority of traits of some of them that is the ground. The practices and institutionalization of those beliefs then foster conditions that serve as the justification. One cannot be racist until the racial groups, and the corresponding array of meanings, have been socially constructed. This dynamic is generalizable. Discrimination occurs on the basis of an othering process that renders certain traits, beliefs, or characteristics socially opprobrious.

The othering process constitutes both the "other" and the more favored non-other in categorical terms and in terms of social meanings that attach to those categories. Group position theory helps us understand how this occurs by focusing our attention on the specific processes that engender both the constitution and the relative positioning of social groups.[137] According to this theory, group definitions, boundaries, and meanings are the product of complex collective and social processes rather than a result of individual interactions or bias. As one of the earliest expressions of this theory by Herbert Blumer describes:

> Through talk, tales, stories, gossip, anecdotes, pronouncements, news accounts, orations, sermons, preachments, and the like, definitions are presented and feelings expressed.... If the interaction becomes increasingly circular and reinforcing, devoid of serious inner opposition, such

currents grow, fuse, and become strengthened. It is through such a process that a collective image of a subordinate group is formed, and a sense of group position is set.[138]

Group position theory not only suggests how group-based identities become socially constructed, but how they become relationally fixed. The boundaries of group definition and the constellation of meanings and associations that map to those categories emerge simultaneously. The novel element this theory interposes, however, is that these meanings and the identities they inform are positioned hierarchically in society. Group positionality gives social meaning, significance, and content to group identity. To dominant groups, it signifies power, prestige, and status, irrespective of income, education, or wealth.

Status and group position is a bit different from resources and power, the instruments of group-based inequality. Instead, status and group position "is based on cultural beliefs rather than directly on material arrangements."[139] A low-income but high-caste Brahmin may still enjoy certain status prerogatives over a wealthy and highly educated low-caste Dalit. The aristocratic and much wealthier Tutsis were the primary victims in the Rwandan genocide, perpetrated by the much poorer but more populous Hutus.[140] Or, in the American context, a poor white farmer was viewed in the Jim Crow South as having a higher social standing than a well-educated middle-class Black professional.

As these examples suggest, group position theory depends upon the existence of social hierarchies. Traditional identity hierarchies figure prominently into the social meanings ascribed to identity. The competition for status matters immensely to humans, and it plays a significant role in the production and evolution of group-based identities.[141] Some scholars assert that all human societies and cultures have social hierarchies.[142] Such hierarchies are a source of much intergroup conflict. But the most intense conflicts arise when group boundaries are generally fixed and enforced, and when one group tries to dominate another.

This problem has innumerable expressions: Hindu hegemony, Zulu nationalism, Han chauvinism, and yes, white supremacy. After all, another word for dominance is *supremacy*. Hegemony, ethno-nationalism, chauvinism, and ethnic, racial, or religious supremacy is nothing less than an assertion that one group has or should occupy a privileged and superior position in society. It is a license to other.

Dominance and supremacy does not necessarily require or entail greater wealth or even superior numbers, but it does imply special status, power, privileges and prerogatives. There are many examples of minority groups exercising social dominance. Relatively tiny numbers of white Europeans dominated nations like South Africa, India, or parts of China. Ethnic Sunnis dominated the Iraqi state until the American invasion in 2003, despite their far smaller numbers.[143] One of the most recent groups victimized by ethnic cleansing are the minority Tigrayans of Ethiopia, an ethnic group that ran the government in the 1990s.[144]

In the West, it is fashionable to ascribe many social ills to white supremacy. In many cases, this is a misdiagnosis of the problem. The problem isn't *white* supremacy; it is supremacy. White supremacy is merely an expression of a much broader phenomenon. The details may vary, but the key features are strikingly similar. A global perspective reveals this clearly, as many other forms of ethnic and racial chauvinism are on the rise or threatening. After all, neither Hindu or Houthi supremacy, Sinhalese Buddhist, or Zulu nationalism can be characterized as "white."[145]

In our view, a desire or push for dominance is no more justified when it is advanced by a previously marginalized or subordinated social group than when it is propounded by a traditionally high-status or dominant group.* Either case breeds othering, with its many attendant harms. The problem of othering is tightly connected to the problem of dominance and domination. Although not all expressions of othering feature a dominant

---

*This particular dilemma has occasionally arisen in the context of anticolonial movements, which seek to remove an external political entity that controlled the resources and dominated the indigenous people, such as the British in India. The dilemma, as we will show in the next section, arises when that power has been cast off. Specifically, how should non-indigenous settlers and their descendants be treated? As full citizens with equal rights, as subordinates in the postcolonial society, or perhaps removed, as in the expulsion of Indians and Asians from Uganda in 1972?

group (not all high-status social groups achieve dominance), a desire for or pursuit of dominance itself can cause othering. To some extent, it may be impossible to erase deeply embedded social hierarchies let alone reposition groups relative to each other in society. But what can be addressed or curbed is dominance and supremacy.

Ethno-Nationalism

All societies feature an array of social groups, those categories or configurations of socially meaningful units to which people affiliate. As we have seen, those groupings are not defined independently or in some entirely abstracted manner, but in relation to each other, often through the othering process. Thus all societies not only have social groups, but those social groups are differently positioned in society relative to each other. Some are thought of more warmly, while others are viewed with suspicion or pity. To a large extent, this is inevitable. Human beings are taxonomic creatures, who imbue our social worlds with rich and varied meanings.

But what is not inevitable is either *which* peoples are treated differently or the degree or extent to which such hierarchies become institutionally reinforced or culturally affixed. There are many modes or forms in which such hierarchies become institutionalized, but the umbrella term often used to describe contemporary forms is *ethno-nationalism*. In this way, ethno-nationalism is one of the most common expressions of institutional othering and the contemporary othering process.

Like many of the other terms used to denote or signify expressions of othering, the term is somewhat imprecise as a descriptor. Ethno-nationalism is a movement or push to tie a particular set of identities, whether they are ethnic, racial, religious, cultural, linguistic, or a fuzzy notion of ancestry, to the nation-state, either in terms of citizenship or legacy citizenship, and often a corollary set of rights or privileges. So-called "ethno-states" are states that codify these relationships in laws and constitutions or simply recognize them as a matter of tacit practice and symbolic expression. In short, ethno-states institutionalize social group position in relation to the state.

Examples are plentiful. In his infamous "Cornerstone Speech" in 1861, the vice president of the Confederate States of America, Alexander H.

Stephens, declared that "our new government, is the first, in the history of the world, based upon th[e] great physical, philosophical, and moral truth [that] the negro is not equal to the white man."[146] He called this the "cornerstone" of the new government. But it was far from the last. The Afrikaner government of South Africa and Rhodesian governments were all erected upon the same "cornerstone."[147] It goes without saying, but is worth reminding, that the Nazi state of Germany was similarly (re)-founded, although upon Aryan/Nordic racial and ethnic identity.

More recently, in 2022, the Hungarian prime minister Viktor Orbán gave a major speech in which he largely defined Europe, and to a larger extent the West, and by direct inference his own country, in terms of race.[148] In his formulation, countries with mixed-race populations are no longer "nations" as such. It is worth emphasizing that he specified race, not culture or even ethnicity or religion, as the ground for defining the nation. In addition to race, it is not uncommon for ethno-nationalist movements to emphasize culture, ethnicity, or religion as the binding agent of a nation, and thereby the nation-state.

Not every state that binds a particular social identity to its national identity, or ethno-nationalist movement that seeks to do so, has done so on the basis of whiteness or even Christianity. Hindu hegemony, or the political ideology denoted as "Hindutva," is an assertion that India is or should be a Hindu-centric nation-state rather than a democratic, pluralistic one, and that Hindus should enjoy pride of place within the nation-state.[149] The BJP (described in more detail next chapter) and the RSS are political organizations in India seemingly aimed at making India a Hindu state and its ethnic and religious minorities second-class citizens.[150]

A similar dynamic is observed in Sri Lanka. The Sinhalese Buddhist majority long dominated the state. They succeeded in adopting a constitutional provision, Chapter II, Article 9, which states, "The Republic of Sri Lanka shall give to Buddhism the high place in hierarchy and accordingly it shall be the duty of the Head of State and Head of Government to protect and foster the Buddha Sasana."[151] After decades of civil war between the Sinhalese Buddhist majority and the Tamil minorities, various political movements seek to extend or further Buddhist dominance. The Bodu Bala Sena (known as BBS) is an ultranationalist movement that has been accused of heinous violence against the Tamil minorities as well as anti-Muslim fearmongering.[152]

In the transitional period following the end of apartheid, there was a potent although unsuccessful push to reimagine South Africa as a Zulu nation, including the restoration of the Zulu king.[153] It was not only South Africa's white Afrikaners that opposed this possibility; the country's other Black ethnic groups opposed the substitution of white dominance with Zulu dominance in the new democratic nation-state as well. Although the African National Congress (ANC) party, under the leadership of Nelson Mandela, who was Xhosa, not Zulu, embraced the "rainbow nation" concept (and was founded to unite Black South Africans across tribal, ethnic, and linguistic identity), one of Mandela's successors, Jacob Zuma, has been credibly accused of stoking Zulu nationalist sentiment.[154] Zulu nationalism was an understandable but unfortunate response to the oppression of apartheid.

So, too, is Hawaiian nationalism—the view among indigenous and legacy Hawaiians that the state of Hawaii should not only secede from the United States, but that political, social, and economic control should be returned to them as well, as reparations for claim that the archipelago was invaded and forcibly annexed in the late nineteenth century.[155] Under this vision, Native and indigenous Hawaiians would presumably be given privileges and status above those of the non-Native residents. Some even call for a restoration of the Hawaiian monarchy.[156]

As one of the foregoing examples illustrates, ethno-states can be erected on the basis of religion, not just race or ethnicity. Forms of national political statehood organized in this way are sometimes described using the anodyne term *confessional state*, a state that not only officially recognizes and even practices a particular religion, but encourages its practice in a variety of ways.[157]

States with official religions are far more common than bald ethno-states, and there are several dozen on the globe today. We already noted Sri Lanka's. Saudi Arabia's "Basic Law" states, "The Kingdom of Saudi Arabia is a sovereign Arab Islamic State. Its religion is Islam."[158] The unrecognized and short-lived Islamic State of Iraq and Syria (ISIS) is obviously another example of a state deliberately organized on a religious basis, with an official state religion. Even progressive Costa Rica declares that the Catholic Church is the official state religion. And, in surveys, nearly a third of Americans are supportive of a constitutional amendment declaring Christianity the national religion.[159]

Although the trend is away from state-based religion, even states that have officially abolished it will often replace it with a symbolic statement that recognizes the role of a particular religion in society, as Spain does for the Catholic Church.[160] Similarly, without denying equal rights or freedom of religion to any particular group within a state, some states are what one author calls "kin states," states that offer certain privileges to ethnic or religious groups such as a priority in immigration laws. Although such "right of return" laws are most visible in the cases of states like Russia, Armenia, and Israel, they also exist in stable liberal democracies like Canada and Germany.[161]

Although a sharply contested term, *Zionism* is sometimes interpreted as an ethno-nationalist claim that Israel is foremost a Jewish state, providing special privileges for Jewish citizens of Israel relative to their Arab counterparts.[162] Although Israel was ostensibly founded on more universalistic terms, to some extent, this interpretation has been codified. A 2018 law passed narrowly by the Israeli Knesset declared the ethnic-religious identity of the state as exclusively Jewish.[163] The symbols of the state, for example, are exclusively Jewish in character. This was more than an ordinary piece of legislation: it is a "basic law" that functions at a constitutional level. It is little wonder that Arab "citizens" of Israel often feel that their status is of a second-class order.[164]

Some defenders of ethno-states, or the "particularistic nationalism" that undergirds them, refer to them as "ethnic democracies."[165] In a classic liberal democracy, all citizens are treated alike, forging the many into one political community. In contrast, an ethnic democracy, according to its defenders, is "a refuge for people hounded on account of their ethnic identity," as well as to restore to them "the cultural richness that a people have when they live in their ancestral homeland, speak their own language, and chart the course of their own future."[166] In this mode, it is argued, ethnic democracies are both common and nonproblematic, consistent with international norms and law.

Others, perhaps more stridently, claim that "ethno-states" are the natural organizing principle of nation-states prior to the advent of nondiscrimination and widespread equal protection laws. While this claim has some evidentiary support if viewed narrowly through the lens of modern nation-states, it is certainly not true of most forms of human civilization, as virtually every known major empire had few qualms about extending citizenship across lines of group difference.

Moreover, migration, war, and conquest are perennial forces in human history. Over centuries and millennia, people, languages, and cultures have mingled while borders have shifted over and over again as cultures evolved and mutated. Seen from a long enough time horizon, there is probably no place on earth that can be undeniably connected to a single, stable group, with perfectly overlapping culture, language, ethnic identity, and religious traditions.

Ethno-states and ethno-nationalist movements leverage the prevailing political formation, the nation-state, to institutionalize group positionality in societies. Despite what defenders of ethno-states may assert, the idea that a particular group within society should be accorded special privileges, status, or prerogatives, except as remedy for past harm, is utterly inconsistent with the idea of political equality at the heart of democratic societies, let alone the liberties and freedoms they require. It is nothing less than institutionalized othering by affixing group positions in law. Ethno-states and ethno-nationalist movements are one of our most significant challenges.

―――――――

Our identities are important to us. They define who we are. We each hold a constellation of identities: occupational and professional, familial and relational (mother/brother, etc.), religious, ethnic/racial, gender, sexual, and much more. Unbeknownst to most of us, the othering process plays an outsize role in fashioning these identities and the meanings that attach to them. The othering process constitutes identities through the forming of categories and the institutionalization of relations, resources, and power that give meaning to those identities. Group position theory helps us understand how such meanings are developed and become culturally coded and socially embedded.

In a larger sense, however, the othering process is not just a force that determines the identities and distribution of resources in society; it is also constitutive of that society through symbolic interaction and meaning generation. The full ramifications of this insight are beyond the scope of this book except for a few brief remarks here.

The systems of formalized human hierarchy that are developed and instituted through the othering process play an outsize role in defining the institutions and structures that govern and organize that society. Slave societies, for example, from the most ancient to antebellum America, are profoundly shaped by the fact of slavery. The existence of slavery becomes constitutive of the concept of freedom itself (which is tangibly defined in reference to the condition of slavery), but also a wide range of societal features such as citizenship, occupational possibilities, property relations, criminal justice, and law itself.[167] In the antebellum American context specifically, racial slavery played an outsize role in defining not only concepts of liberty and freedom, but also equality and encoding various racial meanings. Similar observations could be made for how group hierarchies and othering processes shape the institutions, culture, and social fabric of other societies.

Otherness is a *description* of being an outgroup. Othering is a description of the *process* of being marginalized by dominant groups and society. This chapter helped us understand the nexus of identity formation and the othering process. Now it is time to specify the conditions under which processes of othering seem to arise and in which specific group-based identities become socially significant. As we will see, othering processes are driven by the interaction of large-scale social forces and the behavior of elites.

FOUR

Fear of the Other, Rise of the Demagogue

A series of stunning political developments sent shock waves through the corridors of power in 2016. Not the first, but one of the most significant events was the so-called "Brexit" vote. This nonbinding referendum, held on June 23, 2016, asked the electorate of the United Kingdom the simple question of whether the UK should remain a member of the European Union, a complex legal and economic union of nation-states committed to the free movement of labor and goods, and to applying a set of laws and rights protected by EU treaties. Deciding to end a forty-four-year relationship with the EU, a slim majority of the referendum voters ultimately elected to leave.[1]

Superficially, this vote had little to do with the themes of othering, as it pertained to a specific political and economic arrangement. Yet, as the circumstances and cultural context behind Brexit have been more deeply analyzed, the Brexit vote now appears as one point in a constellation of larger forces and issues that lay at the heart of this book.

The Brexit vote was polarized along lines of race, age, and social and economic class. "Leavers" tended to be older, white, Christian, and more working-class.[2] Those that opposed the Brexit, the "remain" camp, were younger, more racially, ethnically, and religiously diverse, and more urban and cosmopolitan. Pollsters found that high turnout among older white, working-class people residing in disadvantaged communities partly explained the result.[3] Education was one of the most powerful predictors of the Leave vote, with higher educated and more highly skilled voters voting to remain, and lower-skilled, lower-income areas more likely to vote to leave.[4]

Although mistrust of EU institutions and conventional politicians appears to have played a role, studies have shown that concerns over immigration played a larger role in motivating "leave" voters.[5] Indeed, one of the messages of the pro-Brexit supporters was to "take back control of our borders."[6] It appears that anti-immigrant sentiment may have been especially appealing to communities that have been further and further disadvantaged in the postindustrial economy, and that these communities are both older and whiter, but also more resentful of immigration, both for economic and cultural reasons.

Another element appeared to be Islamophobia. A spate of anti-Muslim incidents studied after the vote also suggests that bigotry and fears of a cultural, racial, or religious "other" were motivating factors among the electorate.[7] In short, immigration, fears of cultural change and incursion, nativism, Islamophobia, anti-elite sentiment, deindustrialization, and education were all bound up in the riptide currents beneath a seemingly simple and placid question about the future of the UK.

These currents were successfully manipulated by a skilled political entrepreneur to achieve the desired results. The pro-Brexit vote was primarily led by the United Kingdom Independence Party, and its controversial leader, Nigel Farage, who achieved enduring notoriety and political visibility as a result of the campaign.[8]

Trump and Wallace

Although Brexit was a foreshock, the climactic political earthquake of 2016 was the ascension of Donald Trump to the US presidency. Trump quickly rose to prominence in a large and crowded Republican Party nominating contest, in which he defeated the brother of a former Republican president armed with a much larger campaign war chest, senators, governors, and other Republican hopefuls, and then stunned prognosticators by eventually defeating former US senator, secretary of state, and first lady Hillary Clinton in the general election that November.

Following the 2012 presidential election, the Republican Party commissioned a report that sought to uncover the reasons for its electoral defeat.[9] In the report, the authors concluded that one reason for the party's loss was the lack of outreach to nonwhite communities. Specifically, it found: "We need to campaign among Hispanic, black, Asian, and gay Americans and demonstrate we care about them, too. We must recruit more candidates who come from minority communities. But it is not just tone that counts. Policy always matters."[10] During the 2016 primary campaign, Donald Trump not only ignored this advice; he veered in the opposite direction.

Well-known to the public as wealthy a real estate developer, Trump crafted a reputation as a serious businessman, an image he had carefully cultivated over decades, mostly as a television celebrity. At some point during the Obama presidency, however, Trump began using social media, most notably Twitter, to criticize the administration, and even propounded an unfounded theory that Obama was not an American citizen and had a fraudulent birth certificate.[11] By dabbling in such conspiracy theories, Trump not only became one of the leading advocates of "birtherism," but found himself as a popular muse at the center of an emerging right-wing social media ecosystem.[12] This ecosystem was defined by the shameless and relentless circulation of conspiracy theories, baseless accusations, and salacious stories, all insulated by First Amendment protections.[13]

Trump's identity as a right-wing provocateur was affirmed with the launch of his campaign. In announcing his presidential bid on June 16, 2015, Donald Trump asserted that many immigrants from Latin American, and Mexico in particular, were criminals and drug pushers, and were invading the country.[14] To solve this problem, he promised to "build a wall" on the Mexican border of the United States to deter and prevent unauthorized immigration from Mexico and Latin America. Similarly, in December of that year, he called for a "total and complete shutdown of Muslims entering the United States."[15] This was on top of calling for greater surveillance of mosques, barring Syrian refugees from entering the country, and the possible creation of a database to track all Muslims in the country.[16]

Despite many denunciations from his own party, Donald Trump secured the Republican Party nominations and won the presidency. Critically, he garnered extraordinary support from white voters and rural and exurban electorates in key midwestern swing states of Pennsylvania, Ohio, Michigan, and Wisconsin, states hardest hit by deindustrialization and brain drain.[17] He broke through the Democratic "blue wall" in the Midwest and flipped a small number of states by narrow margins that carried him to an Electoral College victory, despite a massive defeat in the popular vote.

Shortly after the election, "alt-right" leader Richard Spencer spoke at a conference of several hundred in Washington, DC, celebrating the election result with a Nazi salute to President Trump:[18] "Hail Trump, hail our people, hail victory!" Spencer explained that his goal is "a new society, an ethno-state that would be a gathering point for all Europeans," and has called for "peaceful ethnic cleansing."[19] President-elect Trump was criticized for giving an equivocal response, just as he had been for failing to distance himself from comments made by Ku Klux Klan leader David Duke some months before.[20]

Styling himself as a "nationalist,"[21] and explicitly drawing comparisons between himself and the populist president Andrew Jackson (who, not incidentally, propounded the federal Indian removal policy),[22] Donald Trump was in fact a different type of political actor altogether. Trump was the first demagogue elevated to the United States presidency, although he was not the first to run for that office.

The most recent figure of note in that regard was Patrick Buchanan, whose quixotic 1992 and 1996 Republican primary campaigns had many striking similarities to Trump's, including railing against free trade agreements and restricting immigration.[23] Buchanan didn't come close to winning the nomination, but he won nearly 23 percent of the primary vote in 1992 and nearly 21 percent in 1996, including a stunning upset in New Hampshire against Bob Dole.[24] Given the policy similarities, it is understandable why Buchanan is compared to Trump.

But the closest modern template for Trump in terms of policy, style, and temperament is the late Alabama governor George Wallace. Although notorious as a staunch segregationist and, most infamously, for a fiery speech in 1963 that pledged to support segregation "forever" in defiance of federal law,[25] Wallace tempered his rhetoric by the time he ran for the Democratic presidential nomination in 1972 to broaden his appeal beyond the South.

Unquestionably, Wallace ran a campaign that appealed to racial resentment and opposition to civil rights, but his strength was white, blue-collar, union workers in the industrial heartland. Although Wallace won five former Confederate states in a quixotic third-party campaign in 1968, he won five very different states in the 1972 Democratic primary before his campaign effectively ended when he was shot and paralyzed by a would-be assassin mid-campaign. He won Florida, Tennessee, Maryland, and North Carolina, but his most impressive and second-strongest showing was Michigan, where he won nearly 51 percent of the vote, at a time when blue-collar union strength was near its apex.[26] Additionally, he finished a close second in Indiana, New Mexico, and Wisconsin, and a distant second in Pennsylvania. In short, Wallace competed strongly in—and won—border states and in the industrial heartland.

That is only where the similarities to Trump begin. *Rolling Stone* magazine's "gonzo" journalist Hunter S. Thompson's campaign reporting, later compiled into a landmark campaign account, conveys both a sense of Wallace's appeal in the industrialized North, especially the Midwest, and Wallace's campaign style. Although he finished in second place (behind George McGovern), Wallace was so popular in Wisconsin that "every one of his rallies attracted more people than the halls could hold," Thompson observed.[27] Thompson attended a rally on the south side of Milwaukee and recounted one enthusiastic supporter saying that Wallace "ain't the same as the others. He don't sneak around the bush. He just come right out and *says* it."

In addition to his candor and willingness to make politically incorrect remarks, Wallace's style was viscerally entertaining to his audience. Thompson's reporting captured the essence of his appeal:

> The air was electric even before he started talking, and by the time he was five or six minutes into his spiel I had a sense that the bastard had

somehow levitated himself and was hovering over us. It reminded me of a Janis Joplin concert. Anybody who doubts the Wallace appeal should go out and catch his act sometime. He jerked this crowd in Serb Hall around like he had them all on wires. They were laughing, shouting, whacking each other on the back . . . it was a flat-out fire and brimstone performance.

It is difficult to avoid seeing the analogies to Trump, known for his dynamic ability to work a crowd, using large stadium rallies to energize his base and rouse himself, all the while railing against the "boring" style of conventional politicians. But the parallels extend beyond personal style to campaign mode. In another passage, Thompson analyzes Wallace's campaign tactics:

> The only one of the candidates this year who has consistently ignored and broken every rule in the Traditional Politicians Handbook is George Wallace. He doesn't do plant gates and coffee klatches. Wallace is a performer, not a mingler. He campaigns like a rock star, working always on the theory that one really big crowd is better than forty small ones.[28]

A contemporary political journalist could say the same of Trump, whose boisterous "Make American Great Again" campaign rallies are as much of an entertainment spectacle and community event as a political rally, replete with "superfans who follow Trump from rally to rally" like the Deadheads who followed the Grateful Dead tour.[29] The "thrilling" personal style and political stagecraft of Trump and Wallace, mapped onto the strategic appeal to resentments and fear of the "other," are textbook traits of a demagogue.

Political Demagoguery

There is no single definition of *demagogue*, but one of the most insightful, although incomplete, was propounded by the nineteenth-century American author James Fenimore Cooper. According to Cooper, to qualify as a demagogue, a politician had to satisfy four elements:[30]

1. They fashion themselves as a man or woman of the common people, as opposed to the elites;

2. Their politics depends upon a powerful, visceral connection with the people that dramatically transcends ordinary political popularity;

3. They manipulate this connection, and the raging popularity it affords, for their own benefit and ambition; and

4. They threaten or outright break established rules of conduct, institutions, and even law.

According to Cooper, this last element distinguishes a mere populist from a true demagogue. Applying this definition, Andrew Jackson, no matter how much he appealed to a certain demographic or notorious his policies, acted within the bounds of constitutional law—a committed institutionalist—whereas Senator Joseph McCarthy, the infamous anti-communist red-baiter, traduced those institutions and customs, becoming America's most infamous demagogue of the twentieth century.[31]

The term originates in ancient Greek political thought, based on figures that the ancients were well acquainted with. Meaning "leader of the rabble" or "rabble-rouser," ancient Greek writers described demagogues as leaders who used rhetoric to incite followers and stoke fears for political gain. These writers usually cited demagogues as leaders who threatened the stability of fragile ancient democracies by exploiting the passions of the people to gain power.

Thucydides and Aristophanes both described the Athenian leader Cleon as an archetypal example.[32] Cleon was responsible for the overthrow of the great Athenian leader Pericles. Cleon engineered his defeat with a series of lies, accusing Pericles of misusing public money and being too soft on their enemies (especially Sparta). In contrast to Pericles's manner of great dignity and "cool statesmanship," Cleon was described as having a "vulgar style" and a manner that was "thrilling" to the people (making for an obvious comparison to Obama and Trump). It was the popular playwright Aristophanes who eventually exposed Cleon's nature to the public, which ultimately led to his downfall.

Because democracies rely on the will of the people, both ancient writers and the founding fathers of the American republic greatly feared demagogues. Drawing on the warnings of the ancients, the framers of the US Constitution were acutely aware of the dangers that demagogues posed to republics. The first and last of the Federalist Papers, a series of essays anonymously published in leading newspapers promoting and defending the Constitution of 1787, addressed this dilemma.

In the Federalist 1, Alexander Hamilton observed, "History will teach us that . . . of those men who have overturned the liberties of republics, the greatest number have begun their career by paying an obsequious court to the people; commencing demagogues, and ending tyrants."[33] Hamilton and his colleagues felt that the new Constitution provided the greatest safeguards against this threat by distributing power across branches and across institutions. Until Trump, these measures proved to be an effective bulwark.

This is not to say that there are no other notable demagogues in American political history; just that no other ascended to the presidency. Some commentators feel that a New Deal–era southern politician with presidential ambitions, Huey Long, was such a figure, but he was assassinated before his ambitions could be realized. As a governor of Louisiana and United States senator, Long was an early supporter and then a harsh critic of the New Deal. Historians have frequently regarded Long as an archetypal demagogue, something his portrayal in films and literature, such as *All the King's Men*, has done little to dissuade.[34]

A more obvious case was Thomas E. Watson, a prominent late-nineteenth and early-twentieth-century politician who was a leader in the populist movement and a vice presidential nominee on the People's Party ticket in 1896 before he transformed into a demagogue stoking racial resentment to revive his flagging political fortunes.[35] As a populist, Watson had waged an inclusive campaign against the robber barons, banks, and railroads, championing the common farmer. Watson abandoned his racially inclusive stances by 1904 and 1908 and launched racist and nativist attacks in speeches and in his writings to gin up public support in statewide elections.[36]

Another obvious case was the San Francisco labor leader Denis Kearney, of the Workingmen's Party of California. Although an Irish immigrant himself, Kearney built a political career attacking Chinese immigrants, many of whom came to California to work on the transcontinental rail-road. Although inveighing against "monopolists," bankers, and railroad tycoons, Kearney aimed most of his fire at Chinese workers, also known derogatorily as "coolie labor," as a race of "cheap working slaves" who un-dercut American living standards, and thus called for them to be expelled from the country.[37] In speeches in 1877 and 1878, Kearney scapegoated Chinese laborers as the reason for low wages among white workers, and led large crowds into race riots (including the 1877 San Francisco riot) that destroyed Chinese laundries, shops, and residents.[38] His ultimate legacy, however, was helping push the federal Chinese Exclusion Act, which he took credit for by making the issue a national concern.[39] This notorious 1882 law prohibited all immigration of Chinese laborers.[40] After a failed attempt to get onto a vice presidential ticket for a third party, by the turn of the century, Kearney's political fortunes faded, and he died in obscurity.

But the world's most infamous demagogue was not an American politi-cian, but a man who brought the world to disaster, Adolf Hitler. With fiery oratory and a charismatic style, Hitler created a visceral connection with his audience, while also railing against a smorgasbord of bogeymen: bank-ers, Jewish people, and people of color.[41] Hitler articulated a vision of racial hierarchy with Aryans at the top, and Jewish people at the very bottom, combined with an ideal of racial purity.[42] He took this rhetoric to extreme application, creating horrors in his wake by removing Jewish people from territory he controlled (often by conquest), engineering the Holocaust, and clearing Eastern European lands for agriculture.[43]

Fear of the Other

Demagoguery is a strategy for using fear of the "other" as a vehicle for po-litical entrepreneurship, to build, consolidate, or maintain political power. Demagogues are opportunistic. They will attack any group they feel is vul-nerable and can scapegoat or vilify to successfully instill fear into their au-dience and draw supporters. A recent example of this was Trump's efforts to rebrand the Covid-19 virus as the "Chinese virus."[44] Researchers found that after Trump tweeted out the slur, there was a sharp rise in anti-Asian sentiment on Twitter.[45]

As the foregoing examples suggest, at the core of a demagogue's appeal and message is fear of the "other," whether the "other" are communists, Chinese, Black people, Mexican laborers, gay people, Muslim "terrorists," or even bankers, capitalists, institutions like the EU, UN, or other "elites."

The demagogue promises to solve complex, often intractable problems or problems beyond their control, by blaming those problems on the "other." Most infamously, Hitler blamed interwar Germany's problems on Jewish people.[46] More recently, a far-right Italian political party, the "Brothers of Italy," argues that the country's economic malaise can be solved through "abjuring of migrants and defense of the traditional family,"[47] which is an implicit attack on LGBTQ people and feminism, or policies and practices that seek equal social, economic, and political rights for women. If successful in achieving political power, the demagogic strategy often results in more othering, through the adoption or pursuit of policies that further marginalize, control, or exclude those groups.

While in some cases demagogues organize fear of the powerful, in most cases that fear is directed downward at the marginalized or less powerful, a critical element Fenimore Cooper's definition overlooks. Elderly women, particularly widows or unmarried women, were especially vulnerable in societies swept up by witchcraft hysteria. In the Philippines, Rodrigo Duterte rode a campaign to the presidency vowing to rid the country of crime, resulting a stunning spate of extrajudicial violence and police-involved killings, mostly falling on marginalized and low-income people.[48] In Trump's case, researchers found that a core part of his appeal was animus against four groups: Black people, Latinos, Muslims, and LGBTQ people. Using a qualitative "feeling thermometer," researchers found that animosity against these four groups strongly predicted support for Trump, but did not extend to support of Republican Party itself.[49]

While the founding fathers and the ancient Greeks were mostly concerned about demagogues for the chaos and disorder they caused, demagogues and demagogic tactics play a critical role in the othering process. Not merely agents of chaos, they organize fear of the other in a way that often initiates or contributes to the othering process, helping create the other. In this regard, our concern is not just with demagogues themselves—charismatic figures who rouse the fears and passions of the people to secure political power and traduce institutions, norms, and laws—but with demagogic movements and tactics more broadly. The use of demagoguery in ways that contribute to the othering process does not depend upon demagogues—it can flow through political movements or be used as a tactic for securing political power in the hands of skilled political strategists, who are not themselves demagogues.

Perhaps the most famous demagogic movement in American history is the Know-Nothing movement, which arose in response to waves of Irish and German immigrants, and enjoyed notable electoral success.[50] Railing against these immigrants not only on the basis of their ethnicity but also their religion, they feared the spread of "papist" designs.[51] For example, in a 1835 sermon "A Plea for the West," Rev. Lyman Beecher described new immigrants as an attempt by the pope to conquer America.[52] The American inventor Samuel F. B. Morse wrote letters to a prominent New York paper warning that "Catholic monarchies of Europe were sending immigrants to take over this country and force it to succumb to the doctrines of despotism and popery."[53] In this way, the Know-Nothing movement was anti-immigrant and anti-Catholic, a fused "other."

———

Demagogic political parties are not difficult to find. Reactionary and far-right parties based on nativism, xenophobia, and other specific fears can be found at the fringes of most modern democratic societies, and not just in the West or global North. They are rising and building power all over the world. One notable case is the Bharatiya Janata Party in India, under the leadership of Narendra Modi. His party has degraded norms of India's liberal democracy as well as undermined its constitution by touting a fusion of Hindu nationalism and political power, with Muslims and lower-caste Hindus as the primary enemy.[54]

Hindu nationalism is associated with many toxic preferences. For example, a Pew survey of India found that Hindu nationalism was associated with greater support for religious residential segregation and opposition to interfaith marriage.[55] And despite India's tremendous ethnic and religious diversity, now two-thirds of Indians, under Modi's leadership, say that is very important to be Hindu to be "truly" Indian. Demagogues not only organize fear of the other; they also foster a sense of community and belonging for their target audience.

Similarly, recall the attack on the Rohingya in Myanmar, and the comments that presaged it. Political and military elites played a critical role in fomenting that crisis. In both that case and in the case of Modi and the BJP, they draw upon an imagined past, when the dominant group—in this case, upper-caste Hindus—were at the pinnacle of their glory. One of the stranger beliefs espoused by Modi is that ancient Indians flew airplanes and even spacecraft seven thousand years ago.[56] This is part of a larger project of projecting past glory, not only trying to revive that glory,[57] but dangerously tapping into a fear that the past is threatened or lost because of the presence of the other. This story of past greatness, revival, and threat need not have any basis in fact to hold sway. Its aim is to use the anxiety being experienced in the present politcal moment and turn it into actionable fear of the other for political power.

Demagogic politicians, political parties, and political movements are critical drivers of othering, but demagoguery can also be purely tactical, a tool of a skillful politician to achieve a narrower aim or goal. Even when used in this way, tactical demagoguery can contribute to othering. In the early nineteenth century, fears of slave revolts in the American South, following the failed uprisings in the early 1800s of Nat Turner, Gabriel Prosser, and Denmark Vesey, were skillfully manipulated by politicians such as John C. Calhoun (who, although a notorious reactionary, was not himself a demagogue) to strengthen and reinforce the ramparts of racial slavery in the South, as well as to reinforce federal proslavery legislation, including the Fugitive Slave Laws.[58]

More recently, Karl Rove, a senior political adviser whom President George W. Bush called the "architect" of his 2004 campaign, credited eleven anti–gay and lesbian marriage ballot initiatives for helping reelect the president that year.[59] Rove and other Republican strategists believed that these ballot initiatives, which all passed with overwhelming support, were instrumental in getting evangelical, rural, and socially conservative voters, a key part of Bush's electoral base, to the polls in record numbers in key battleground states.[60] Not coincidentally, perhaps, this was the only national presidential election since 1992 where the Republican candidate won the national popular vote.

The 1988 presidential campaign of George H. W. Bush, his father, relied upon an advertisement, known as the "Willie Horton" ad, that was designed to appeal to white fears of Black crime.[61] In the thirty-second advertisement, viewers are shown a grainy black-and-white mug shot of a heavily bearded and Afro'd Black man. The ad claimed that Horton committed a series of crimes while on furlough from incarceration based on policies supported by Bush's opponent, Massachusetts governor Michael Dukakis. Dukakis enjoyed a sizable lead in the polls earlier on in the campaign, and the advertisement is considered to have helped Bush win the election, especially after Dukakis flubbed a debate question about the death penalty, which reinforced the perception that he was "soft" on crime.[62]

In all its forms, demagoguery creates, presents, or packages a threat. In stirring up fears of slave rebellions, Black criminals, Islamic terrorists, witchcraft, trans women in school bathrooms, or Mexican gangs, the threat is partly one of security, that of physical and material safety. Yet that is not all these fears are. After all, in many cases, there is no obvious physical danger or material loss, and yet the appeal to fear is just as potent.

Identity Threats

Why would Karl Rove, as a political strategist, push ballot initiatives (and even the federal "Defense of Marriage Act") banning same-sex marriage as a cultural wedge issue? After all, allowing same-sex couples to wed in no obvious way affects the material well-being, economic privileges, tax benefits, or physical safety of heterosexual people, let alone heterosexual married couples. This materialist account misses something quite important. Legalizing gay marriage was seen, in some quarters of society, as an attack on certain religious traditions. More specifically, it was seen as an attack on the pride of place and respect and regard granted to certain religious institutions and religious values in society.

Fears of attack or crime can be powerful drivers of political and social behavior. But this is not the only way in which the fear of the other manifests or is weaponized. While threats to safety or security or material interests can be powerfully motivating, threats to identity are equally gal-vanizing. An identity threat is a real or perceived risk or danger to an indi-vidual's social group or the status of that group in society.

Amartya Sen and others have accurately observed that "identity threat"—when a group feels under attack—is also a way to make certain identities more salient and central to our being.[63] We already noted how the attack on Ukraine by Russian forces may have paradoxically helped cement Ukrainian national identity and deepened solidarity across tradi-tional lines of difference (linguistic, cultural, etc.) through the mobiliza-tion and organized resistance to the invasion.[64] This is true more broadly. When people feel their faith is threatened or that they are threatened be-cause of their faith, then their religious affiliation can seem like their entire identity.

The fact that these threats can be intangible or immaterial is captured by the memorable but ironic phrase "the wages of whiteness," coined by W. E. B. Du Bois.[65] The phrase denotes the psychological "wage" that white people gain from being members of a higher-status racial group. The reason the term is ironic is that DuBois is explicitly observing that this "wage" is non-economic and intangible; it is being paid by elites to poor whites at the *expense* of advancing their actual material benefits.

––––––––

Identity threats arise either when a group's status or position is threatened or simply when a group is being attacked. Identity threats are most obvi-ous in cases where governments, policy makers, or critical institutions or leaders in society engage in broad discrimination or oppression against a particular social group. The more besieged a group feels, the more they may be stimulated to action or organized into solidarity.

Thus, when demagogues scapegoat a group, they intensify the salience of that group identity both in society and among the target group. When policy makers enact anti-LGBTQ legislation, then LGBTQ persons are not only more likely to feel an identity threat, but also to feel that their sexual orientation and/or gender identity is more central to their being and sense of self. For example, the Log Cabin Republicans—an organization of LGBT Republicans—formed in the late 1970s to help organize opposition to a discriminatory California ballot measure known as the "Briggs Initiative" that would have prevented gay people from teaching in public schools.[66] They succeeded, and the organization is now national.

This dynamic is not unusual, and in fact this is how marginalized identities are often formed. Many marginalized social group identities are created, formed, or strengthened in reaction to the othering process. Recall the discussion of how Asian American and AAPI (Asian American and Pacific Islander) identity may have deepened in response to a spate of violence targeting Asian Americans since the onset of the Covid-19 pandemic.[67] Members of a group under threat will often organize in solidarity to protect their interests, well-being, and safety.

Many of the expressions of rising ethnic and religious nationalism across the world, whether it is white, Christian nationalism, Hindu or Zulu nationalism or even Buddhist nationalism or Han nationalism, are animated by perceived identity threats. Thus Hindu nationalism might become activated by a perceived attack on caste hierarchies or interfaith marriages. Or, in the United States, identity threats could be triggered by an attack on heteronormativity or white status.

In this way, it is not just the identities of marginalized groups that are rendered more salient and central when there is a perceived threat, but identities of more favored or higher status social groups are as well. This can help explain why white identity in the United States is becoming more salient, and white racial consciousness more pronounced, than when whites were more predominant numerically.[68] Identity entrepreneurs are inculcating narratives of white loss to foster the perception of identity threats. The most common response to an identity threat is the excessive assertion of the threatened identity, as a defensive measure.

Identity threats are perhaps the most powerful appeal that a demagogue can make. They are not simply saying that a particular group is threatening your safety or security; they are asserting that an enemy group is a danger to your very being. Identity threats are therefore ontological, not simply material. The reason they are so dangerous is that people will sacrifice material interests, their well-being, and even their lives in service of ontological goods. This is perhaps most obvious in the case of sacred symbols.

Sacred Symbols

It cannot be denied that material conditions matter. Wars are undeniably fought over territory, water, trade routes, arable land, and so forth. Political battles are often over inclusion, voting rights, antidiscrimination laws, accommodation, and the like. But we pay insufficient attention to the symbolic realm as a matter of both politics and analyses. Politics is almost always about identity. Even material issues are wrapped up in identity clothing. The fight over welfare reform was racialized because food stamps and employment assistance became coded for Black people.[69] Similarly, the fight over bathrooms in schools is coded as protecting or attacking LGBTQ people.

On occasion, the perceived benefits or harms of othering are largely or entirely symbolic, and nonmarginal groups are willing to sacrifice some degree of material advantage to realize those benefits, as Du Bois recognized. This underlying idea is also embodied in what the Robert Sapolsky calls "sacred symbols."[70] Sapolsky's argument is that human beings fight over symbols just as often as material reality. This helps explain the intensity of the feeling over debates such as whether it should be legal to burn flags, or whether and how to treat religious symbols, and the often-violent reactions that can ensue when certain religious icons or symbols are defaced or degraded.[71]

Specifically, these symbols are "sacred" because they help consolidate identity and bind people together, providing them with enormous meaning and purpose. One illustration of the importance such symbols is the fervent and dangerous effort to protect some early-eighteenth-century artworks from being destroyed or captured during the Russian invasion of Ukraine.[72] These artifacts were valued beyond their religious or historical significance as a source of Ukrainian identity. Why else would Ukrainians risk their lives to protect such inanimate objects?

However, sacred symbols are not just items of patriotic or religious significance, such as flags or religious icons—they can also be things of merely cultural significance, such as guns, or institutions, such as marriage. This helps explain why debates over guns or marriage are so fraught—they are not just about the material instruments or tax benefits associated with each. They are about identity, community, culture, and tradition. Thus some gun rights advocates are fighting about more than the narrow question about constitutional meaning or whether a policy advances public safety or not, but about preserving a certain identity, culture, and even "a way of life."[73]

Similarly the fight over the Confederate flag or Confederate statues is not simply about their expressive aspect but their identity component. After years of debate, in the wake of George Floyd's murder, Confederate statues were taken down across the country, the Confederate battle flag was removed from public icons, and schools bearing the name of Confederate generals were renamed. Although the Confederacy is regarded by many Americans as a traitorous and racist political project, to many southerners those symbols have become sacred, and the push to remove them is an identity threat.

Another example of an identity threat intertwined with sacred symbols is the multigenerational fight over religion in the public square, much of it waged over public schools. In 1962, the United States Supreme Court ruled that public school officials could not coerce schoolchildren into prayer or religious observance.[74] And just two years before that, presidential candidate John F. Kennedy gave a major campaign speech embracing a strong separation of church and state.[75] His speech was designed to deflect anti-Catholic bigotry and fears that, as the nation's first Catholic president, he would allow the institutional Catholic Church some influence over the administration of the government, or possibly let his faith influence his policy decisions. Yet, by emphatically declaring that his faith would play no role in his public duties, he paradoxically engendered a growing fear of creeping secularization in American life. About half of American households in 1960 attended church once a week, but that rate would decline by 10 percent by the end of the decade. A spokesperson for the National Council of American Churches lamented that "[t]here's competition from scientific thought and a materialistic culture."[76]

As an identity threat, these developments helped stimulate the rise of the so-called "religious right" in American politics, the fusion of Christian churches and Republican Party politics. Galvanized in part by this movement, advocates for more than two generations have tried to find ways to create more space for Christian observance in the public square, fighting one case after another.[77] One of their avatars, former Pennsylvania senator

Rick Santorum, also an erstwhile Republican candidate for president, said that JFK's 1960 speech "made him want to throw up."[78]

There were even significant efforts in the 1950s and '60s to try to pass a constitutional amendment that would give Christianity a special role in American society, either as a state religion or otherwise.[79] In 1954, "under God" was added to the Pledge of Allegiance,[80] partly in response to the perceived threat of atheistic Soviet communism, but such efforts intensified in the wake of the Supreme Court's school prayer decision.[81]

Skillful demagogues can turn many issues into apparent identity threats. This is how the pursuit of LGBTQ rights or marriage equality can be viewed as an "attack on traditional marriage" or "Christian values" or even the "Catholic Church." It's not that prohibiting discrimination in public employment against gay people or sanctioning same-sex marriage is an attack as such, but it can be made to *seem* as if it were. Rove sold these ballot initiatives and the federal Defense of Marriage Act as preserving the pride of place that traditional marriage enjoys, along with its religious underpinning, in American society, against the attacks of those who would undermine those institutions and the identities they represent. This explains how Rove was able to leverage anti-marriage-equality ballot measures into a presidential campaign victory.

Against the backdrop of the examples of religion and guns, it is easy to see how Barack Obama could have triggered an identity threat with these infamous remarks in 2008:

> You go into these small towns in Pennsylvania and, like a lot of small towns in the Midwest, the jobs have been gone now for 25 years and nothing's replaced them. And they fell through the Clinton administration, and the Bush administration, and each successive administration has said that somehow these communities are gonna regenerate and they have not. And it's not surprising then they get bitter, they cling to guns or religion or antipathy toward people who aren't like them or anti-immigrant sentiment or anti-trade sentiment as a way to explain their frustrations.[82]

In a crude way, Obama was attempting to show how economic precarity intertwines with identity threats and sacred symbols. Yet, ironically,

Obama's statement was itself an identity threat, or used to make them. Obama's statement was relentlessly quoted and weaponized to humiliate and stoke outrage among millions of Americans who were told that their president thought that they are backward, and that he—and other elites— looked down on them. This happened even though his intent was exactly the opposite—it was intended to empathize with people whom prior policy makers had abandoned or ignored.

Status Threat[83]

Identity threats operate symmetrically, if not universally: they generate solidarity, mobilize, and strengthen identity attachments whether deployed against marginalized groups or advantaged or even dominant social groups. We have noted that identity threats can occur either when a group is attacked on the basis of their identity per se, some set of sacred symbols associated with that identity is threatened, or when the *position* of that group is threatened. It turns out that the latter is a special and very important case of identity threat.

The previous chapter emphasized the role that group positionality plays in shaping the meaning of identity. This is the predicate for a unique form of identity threat. Identity threats that seem to endanger the position, prerogatives, or advantages of a dominant group are not just a threat to identity, they are *status* threats—a threat to the status of that group.[84] Thus status threats are generally not direct attacks on the safety or security of a group, but rather a threat to the group's position in society, its prerogatives, dominance, or privileges.

As long as marginalized or oppressed groups tacitly accept or acquiesce in their subordinate position, dominant or higher-status social groups may often regard them with care or even affection.[85] But if they seek to challenge their station or the legitimacy of their lower status ranking, then this can trigger swift hostility and antagonism, like how a fawning suiter's attention can quickly become angry and abusive if spurned.[86]

Members of dominant groups perceive status threats not directly as efforts to challenge unjust social hierarchies, but as threats to their freedom and security.[87] Status threats are signified by a variety of related symptoms, such as status anxiety, and what Barbara Ehrenreich called a "fear of falling"—the concerns or apprehensions that arise as a result of significant social change, specifically that a previously high-status group may lose additional ground in the social ladder or hierarchy.[88] These fears do not require a rational basis; promoters only need to persuade their audiences that they exist, as by conjuring up conspiracy theories. Thus the desire to preserve social hierarchy or dominance and avoid the fear of falling is a source of immense political power.

These are not speculative observations. A particularly influential paper generated by an American political scientist claims that status threat was the primary explanatory variable for Trump's victory in 2016.[89] Many observers have noted that Trump's greatest support was not among the lower-income people, as would be expected if his appeal was primarily economic, nor in places that had the greatest diversity or demographic change, as would be expected if it was merely raw animus that undergirded his appeal. Rather, he received the greatest support in counties that had lost manufacturing jobs or suffered *relative* economic decline, but his core supporters were not generally poor, but actually rather affluent.[90] These were not people suffering objective deprivation.

This dynamic fits well within a general observation stretching back centuries that "the most politically destabilizing group tends not to be the desperate poor, but rather middle classes who feel they are losing status with respect to other groups."[91] Alexis de Tocqueville noted that the French Revolution, for example, was triggered not by indigent peasants, but by a pressed middle class with declining fortunes.[92]

Critically, status threats are not perceived as a threat from amorphous sources, but from a particular group or set of groups who are striving to improve their condition or fighting for inclusion. Consider Trump's core policy agenda through the lens of status threats and status anxieties: building a wall on the Mexican border, stopping travel from Muslim countries, and slowing the flow of immigration and halting refugee resettlement are all policies that could be seen as actually or symbolically slowing demographic change toward a nonwhite majority in the United States, and preserving—if not strengthening—white majoritarianism. Even his core political slogan, "Make American Great Again," was viewed as a code for

"Make America White Again," harking back to a time before the civil rights movement.

Although some of Trump's defenders regard such glosses as strained interpretations, two of the most salient events of the Trump presidency reinforce this view. The first was in Charlottesville, Virginia, in 2017, and the second was the January 6, 2021, insurrection at the United States Capitol. Both events were replete with symbols of white supremacy, the Confederacy, and neo-Nazi movements.

Trump demonstrated a rare tendency to speak in explicit terms about racial, ethnic, and religious "others" while appealing to a white nationalist base. He did so despite the warnings and protestations of his party elders. Since the 1970s, there have been very few serious candidates for national office who explicitly spoke in such terms, preferring to speak in terms of a "dog whistle."[93]

In August 2017, white nationalists, neo-Nazis, and other alt-right groups converged in a rally called "Unite the Right" in Charlottesville, Virginia, ostensibly to protest the removal of Confederate statues.[94] Hundreds of white nationalist protesters showed up, marching in khakis and carrying tiki torches. Among the chants of the white nationalists were "Jews will not replace us."[95] Eventually the marchers clashed with antifa, Black Lives Matter, and other counterprotesters. The result was a spasm of violence that resulted in the murder of one protester, Heather Heyer, by a white nationalist who rammed his vehicle into the crowd, also resulting in dozens of nonfatal injuries to others.[96]

Following the rally, President Trump, once again gave an equivocal response. Initially, instead of calling out and condemning the white nationalists, he decried "hatred, bigotry, and violence on many sides."[97] This was widely interpreted as creating a false equivalence between bigots and counterprotesters, and Trump was applauded by Richard Spencer and other white supremacists.[98] A day later, the president tried to clarify his views, and explicitly condemned "KKK, neo-Nazis, white supremacists and other hate groups" in a scripted speech.[99] Yet a day after that, he reiterated his initial response that there was "blame on both sides."[100] A week later, he seemed to side with the white nationalists' aim of critiquing the removal of Confederate statues by saying, "They're trying to take away our culture, they're trying to take away our history."[101] The clear impetus was the fear that certain symbols and monuments—no matter how closely linked to white supremacy—were being taken down.

During the invasion of the Capitol on January 6, 2021, thousands of Trump supporters stormed the building, overtaking the Senate chambers, House floor, and even raiding offices of the Speaker.[102] But among the iconography, gear, and imagery of the episode was a Confederate battle flag carried through the main hall of the Capitol, something that had not even occurred during the Civil War. Many white supremacists and neo-fascists were prosecuted for their role and involvement in the events of that day.

Social groups can be mobilized and spurred to action in response to identity threats, and may even react violently in cases of extreme oppression. However, the risk of violence is often greater when a traditionally advantaged or dominant group is presented with a status threat. This risk is greater because of that group's relative power, influence, and intense desire to preserve the status quo ante. In the Jim Crow South, for example, the white power structure often responded to civil rights protests not only with a more strident defense of segregation, but with increasing state violence and extrajudicial murders.[103] Similarly, in South Africa, growing resistance to the apartheid state was met with greater repression.[104] There were credible claims that a different and more vigorous police response was triggered by the Black Lives Matter protests than for various alt-right and white supremacists protests.[105] One possible explanation is that the former triggered a status threat while the latter did not.

Scholars have found that social marginalization, being pushed to the fringes of their national community and deprived of the traditional roles and social respect, for members of formerly or traditionally high-status groups, leads to support for radical, anti-establishment political parties or leadership.[106] A trio of European political scientists call this phenomenon "dominance syndrome," which is extreme political discontent caused by fear of loss of status or status-seeking behaviors, such as efforts to dominate other groups or peoples.[107]

The dynamic by which status threats trigger violence works at the level of nations as well. This insight is the basis for the so-called "Thucydides trap," the observation that hegemonic powers tend to go to war against rising powers.[108] Thus, in the Peloponnesian Wars, Athens and Sparta warred not over territory or trade routes, but a fear of waning prestige, power, and dominance. Russian president Vladimir Putin's grand conquest ambitions are about reuniting the "Russky Mir," or Russian-speaking world (which is why he targeted eastern Ukraine), rebuilding the lost prestige of the Soviet Union, and overcoming the psychic trauma and humiliation of its dissolution. The main point is that the greatest danger to social order is not always from the most powerful or the most oppressed, but from those who feel that they are losing power and prestige or have been humiliated.

Replacement Theory

Status anxiety—the fear of falling and cultural displacement—is the basis for the so-called "replacement theory" conspiracy.[109] Replacement theory does not describe or imply a threat of immediate physical injury, insecurity, or even incursion or invasion per se. Rather, it is a fear of demographic change. Specifically, this is the theory that native-born persons are being deliberately "replaced" by another group, usually a racial, ethnic, or religious "other."[110] Unfortunately, this theory has gained considerable traction in mainstream political discourse in the United States and beyond.

Most Americans first encountered "replacement theory" in the wake of a vicious attack by an eighteen-year-old white man in Buffalo, New York, in May 2022.[111] The shooter targeted an African American neighborhood, killing ten people and injuring three more. Just before committing this heinous crime, the shooter circulated a 180-page "manifesto" that emphasized this theory, and his commitment to white supremacy. This theory had similarly inspired other attacks, including Dylann Roof's attack on South Carolina parishioners in 2015.[112] The most deadly such attack was on a Norwegian youth camp in 2011 that resulted in seventy-seven deaths.[113] The attacker published a compendium or manifesto in which he railed against the "Islamization of Europe" and the European Union project, and called for the deportation of Muslims.[114] But this theory is no longer restricted to the fringe; it has gone mainstream.

In the 2022 campaign for the French presidency, a center-right candidate, Valérie Pécresse, invoked the "great replacement," a variant of

replacement theory attributed to a French writer, but in a manner understood to be referring to fears of immigrants and Muslims.[115] The reason
this was a notable development is that not even Marine Le Pen, the far-
right runner-up in the 2017 presidential campaign, invoked that idea, let
alone uttered that phrase. The use by Pécresse has been interpreted as a
signal of greater political acceptance in the mainstream.

The author for whom this particular variant of replacement theory is
attributed, Renaud Camus, maintained that previous generations of European immigrants had been drawn by "love" for France, but newer arrivals
since the 1970s—mostly from France's former colonies—didn't come "as
friends."[116] Instead, he characterized them as conquerors and colonizers,
motivated by revenge and a desire to punish France.

In the United States, several Republican lawmakers espoused an American version of this theory. A Republican congressman from Pennsylvania
said in a House committee meeting, "For many Americans what seems to be
happening or what they believe right now is happening is, what appears to
them is we're replacing national-born American—native-born Americans
to permanently transform the political landscape of this very nation."[117] A
Republican senator, Ron Johnson, asked if Democrats "really . . . want to
remake the demographics of America to ensure their—that they stay in
power forever? Is that what's happening here?"[118]

The popular then–Fox News host Tucker Carlson also produced a segment on the replacement theory in 2021, arguing that the Biden administration was trying "to change the racial mix of the country."[119] The subsequent wave of Republican politicians espousing this theory appeared to be
taking their cue from Carlson, but the most successful American politician
advancing their career on this idea is undoubtedly Donald Trump.

In the 2016 campaign for the presidency, Trump declared that "this
will be the last election that the Republicans have a chance of winning because you're going to have people flowing across the border, you're going
to have illegal immigrants coming in and they're going to be legalized and
they're going to be able to vote and once that all happens you can forget it.
You're not going to have one Republican vote."[120]

Most of the claims or expressions of replacement theory seem too incredible to be taken literally (for example, not a "single" Republican vote?).

In many contexts in which replacement theories are expressed, the group that is feared to be "taking over" is numerically or proportionally too small to outnumber or even threaten to outnumber the group that is being riled up. Recall that in the case of Myanmar, demagogic elites stoked fears that the Muslim minority Rohingya were "taking over." Similarly, although Muslims are just 15 percent of the population in India, some Hindu nationalists claim that the Muslim minority will take over within a decade.[121] In both cases, the demographic numbers in question—either at present or on a projected growth trajectory—are far too small to plausibly suggest that the ethnic or religious minority would actually become a majority, let alone a dominant electoral force.

The implausibility of the replacement theory claim as a credible quantitative argument belies the essence of the theory: it is not a fear that a group is actually going to be replaced or even eventually outnumbered by another group; rather, it is a feeling of dispossession or loss of status. Thus status threats are not about being replaced or outnumbered. At their core, they are about one group feeling as if it is losing its position in society, particularly if that group is one that enjoys an advantaged place or certain prerogatives or respect in society.

Replacement theories are neither specific to white or Christian supremacy, as some media coverage or commentators often suggest.[122] Another recent expression of replacement theory came from Tunisia's president Kais Saied, who has tried to bolster his flagging political support by vilifying immigrants, particularly from sub-Sahara. He asserted that these migrants were part of a secretive effort to turn Tunisia into "a purely African country with no affiliation to the Arab and Islamic nations."[123]

Nor are such theories of recent origin, the product of postcolonial fears. In fact, such theories are ancient. Perhaps the earliest expression of replacement theory is found in Exodus, the second book of the Bible. The first chapter of that book explains that the new Egyptian pharaoh feared the growth and strength of the Hebrew population within the empire, complaining that the "Israelites have become far too numerous for us," and thereby embarked on a campaign of enslavement.[124] Whether this is an accurate historical account or not, it shows that replacement theories as a status threat are neither specific to white supremacy nor to contemporary societies.

Backlash

One of the paradoxes and fundamental challenges to equity, inclusion, and belonging initiatives is that virtually every effort supportive of those goals will sow the seeds of its own counterattack. The failure to appreciate and grapple with this fundamental fact of social progress has led many social justice movements to falter or succumb to a well-organized backlash. The reasons for this are more easily appreciated in light of the preceding discussion on identity and status threats.

At the heart of every effort to foster greater equity and inclusion in any society is a challenge to or disruption of traditional hierarchies, such as those on the basis of race, religion, ethnicity, gender, or caste. This is the nature of efforts to promote inclusion: inherent in any such project is an attempt to erase, weaken, or demolish group-based hierarchies. In practice, this is felt and experienced as a status threat—a loss of group position, dignity, or privileges.

It is not uncommon for members of traditionally dominant social groups to feel that recent policies designed to promote inclusion or equality are a direct threat to them, and thus a basis for manipulation by politicians to stoking anger and resentment.[125] In South Korea, for example, a strident antifeminist movement has found its footing, mostly among precarious young men who fear that the gradual dismantling of patriarchal norms has undermined opportunity.[126] According to polling, 90 percent of men in South Korea identify as antifeminist or are antifeminist in their sympathies.[127] Gender debates are now roiling the country's politics.

Efforts to promote inclusion and equity easily trigger status anxiety and become status threats when framed through a narrative of dispossession or loss. This is gives rise to backlash. Status anxiety is both a source of opposition to further efforts to promote equity and a font of resentment that can be stoked and manipulated by deft politicians. Remarkably, this backlash arrives even if there is broad support for the moral or ethical imperative of equality. This is because the mechanism of backlash is different than the effort to promote inclusion. One is an abstract principle, while the other is the felt or perceived effect of the implementation or realization of that principle.

Some people may endorse the egalitarian principle in the abstract (appealing to their better angels) but oppose the implementation of the principle in practice or policy, or feel sadness, despair, or anger in its wake, and never notice the cognitive dissonance. For this reason, a particular effort to promote inclusion may enjoy broad support, even among those who become part of the agitated by the demagogue after a successful campaign or policy victory. This helps explain Obama-to-Trump voters. The backlash is triggered through the loss of status, respect, and esteem that is a natural and predicable by-product of attacking traditional or established hierarchies.

One common trope or refrain that can be observed across many cultural contexts where a formerly marginalized social group has made gains is the express fear that that group is "taking over." For example, in the aftermath of the civil rights movement, many white Americans were quoted as saying that Black people were trying to "take over."[128] Recall that in Myanmar, India, and France, fears were expressed that Muslims were trying to "take over."

This is the basis for the "great replacement" theory noted earlier, in France. Although there is absolutely no evidence that Muslims were trying to seize political power as a bloc or planning to outnumber the predominant ethnic, racial, or religious group, simply the loss of dominance is felt as if the marginalized group is taking over. For members of a dominant group, equality can feel like a threat.

Paradoxically, efforts to promote inclusion and celebrate diversity can reduce a sense of belonging for traditionally dominant groups. As inclusion increases, net belonging can actually diminish. This is the basis for Arlie Russell Hochschild's clever title, *Strangers in Their Own Land*, a well-timed and revealing survey of Tea Party supporters in Louisiana.[129] Although it was ostensibly triggered by an economic crisis (and the Obama administration's efforts to respond to that crisis), anthropological studies of the Tea Party movement found that most of the organizers and participants were relatively insulated from the economic downturn, and disproportionately older, white baby boomers and retirees. Rather than organizing around fiscal objectives that motivated CNBC business reporter Rick Santelli's infamous rant,[130] they were primarily triggered by long-simmering cultural grievances and concerns about the multicultural future of the country. As Hochschild's title suggests, a central theme was a feeling of dispossession, of alienation from the younger, diverse Obama coalition. Other accounts of the Tea Party activism and the American right have uncovered similar themes, including forms of conspiratorialism found in replacement theories.[131]

This dynamic helps explain how members of dominant groups can, paradoxically, behave like aggrieved victims. Indeed, claims of victimhood are often how reactionary or hate groups garner support.[132] This is the fertile ground in which replacement theory conspiracies sprout. Such theories simultaneously provide a nefarious target of blame (usually elites) and a group or set of groups that must be opposed in order to maintain hegemony (Muslims, nonwhites, etc.).

———

This also explains the frustrating reality that *both* members of marginalized groups and traditionally higher-status groups can simultaneously feel a lack of belonging in society. Many Black South Africans feel that the post-apartheid governments did not go nearly far enough to redistribute land and economic resources from the white elite, but a sense of alienation, sadness, and nonbelonging associated with life in post-apartheid South Africa is widely detected among the white population.[133] One pithy expression of this sentiment is found in a popular Afrikaner song lyric that complains, "I'm in love with my country, but does my country still love me?"

If, as some claim, happiness is "reality minus expectations,"[134] then it is easier to understand how discontent, despair over the future, and backlash can become a more powerful political force than poor material conditions alone. Researchers found that that despair in America is associated with falling status, not necessarily objective conditions:

> The deepest desperation is among cohorts in the white working class who previously had privileged access to jobs (and places) that guaranteed stable, middle-class lives. Rather ironically, African Americans and Hispanics— the cohorts that historically faced high levels of discrimination—retain higher levels of well-being, especially hope for the future.[135]

The places with the most desperate material conditions are not in the vanguard of populism. Rather, the formerly prosperous places are.[136]

This analysis suggests that one of the challenges for all equity movements is to promote equity without threatening, or appearing to threaten, the status and well-being of previously dominant groups. This doesn't mean such movements should bow to the absurd or sacrifice their principles, but taking steps to reduce unnecessary status anxiety or blunt potential status-threat counterattacks may prove essential to the sustainability of equity efforts. Equity efforts must appear positive-sum rather than zero-sum, and be framed in a narrative of progress and betterment for all.

Conditions for Othering

Some general observations can be made on the conditions that make othering strategies more likely. As Pankaj Mishra observes, "The appeal of the demagogue lies in their ability to take generalized discontent, the mood of drift, resentment, disillusionment, and economic shakiness, and transform them into a plan for doing something."[137] It does not matter whether the course of action is sensible or well calculated to address the underlying discontent.

Demagogic political entrepreneurs and strategists appeal to anxieties or fear of the "other" in order to boost their own political fortunes. What is not entirely clear is the degree to which they *create* and inculcate such prejudices and fears, or *activate* those that were already present.[138] This question is important to understanding the specific role that demagogic forces play in the othering process, and how we respond to or counter such forces.

In the case of fanning a flame, demagogues are spreading a fire that is already burning, suggesting that they are trying to expand the reach and influence of a particular set of pernicious ideas, spreading and deepening othering. Removing the demagogue does not eliminate the tinder fuel. Another spark could start a conflagration. In the case of stoking a fire, demagogues are assumed to activate latent or extremely weak prejudice and passions, making them more intense by giving them more oxygen, turning faint embers into a strong blaze.[139]

Either scenario suggests a different response or understanding of the othering process. If the demagogue is creating such hatred, then the solution is to get rid of the demagogue to stop othering, and the genie can be put back in the bottle. Similarly, if the demagogue is activating latent prejudice, then removing the demagogue eliminates the trigger, and the flame can be suppressed. On the other hand, if the blaze is already out of control, and the demagogue is simply fanning the flames, then you need a fire department to douse the fire. Removing the demagogue will not solve the problem. In that case, the only way to deal with that problem is by addressing such passions and prejudices or by presenting a more compelling alternative vision.

Without resolving the issue of whether demagogues are creating or fanning existing fears and prejudices, there do appear to be certain prevailing conditions that make demagoguery a more successful political strategy. Mishra's observation begins to pinpoint what those might be. Severe economic downturns appear to be particularly fertile ground for rising demagogues. Generalized suffering inclines more moderate sections of the population to take a greater political risk by throwing support for extremist elements in the political sphere, in the hopes that conditions might improve or to shock the establishment out of a stupor. It is not a coincidence, for example, that Adolf Hitler and Huey Long rose to power in the midst of the Great Depression or that Denis Kearney's anti-Chinese demagoguery reaches its zenith in the middle of the "Long Depression," a severe economic contraction of the 1870s.

But demagogues can sprout in other conditions, including periods of economic growth, as the cases of George Wallace and Donald Trump demonstrate. Large-scale social change, along the lines sketched in the previous section, can be a powerful weapon for demagogic politicians. Many observers or commentators have tried to pin part of the success of both Nigel Farage's Brexit campaign and Trump's first presidential campaign on underlying economic forces. But as massive resistance—the immensely potent and organized effort to maintain Jim Crow in the face of the civil rights movement—illustrates, fear of the other and the demagoguery that harnesses it can arise even in the best of economic conditions (the 1960s had some of the highest economic growth rates in American history).[140]

———

It is undoubtedly true that deindustrialization, economic pain in rural areas, and other economic forces were contributory factors, but large-scale demographic change in the United States and the United Kingdom, including fears of Muslims, were just as significant in the political shocks of 2016. Recall that Trump launched his political career on the lie that Barack Obama was a noncitizen, and that he was born in Kenya. That the first demagogue was elevated to the presidency after the nation's first Black president was in office, and when a majority of school-age children in the United States were nonwhite for the first time, is hard to dismiss as a coincidence.

Fears of demographic change is another powerful enabling condition for othering. This becomes an ontological threat that is even more powerful than fears of crime or material or physical insecurity. This dynamic has been observed not just in France and the United States, but all over the globe. Some commentators describe it as a "majority with a minority complex."[141]

This dynamic is also quite prominent in South Asia. It played a powerful role in Myanmar, as we already noted, but also in India and Sri Lanka. Sri Lanka is nearly three-quarters Sinhalese Buddhists, but the proximity to India's large Tamil population, and decades of civil war, contributes to a fear of incursion or losing dominance.[142]

The fear of demographic change need not occur from immigration or external incursion, but potentially from different birth rates between social groups. Some have expressed a fear that Israel might lose its "Jewishness" due to larger birth rates from the Arab minority. Astute observers claim that this was also a contributing factor to the "Troubles" of Northern Ireland: that the Protestant majority (which had won the civil war in 1690 that established Protestant dominance) was being threatened by higher Catholic birth rates.[143] Although a recent census now suggests that Catholics have just become the majority in Northern Ireland,[144] the underlying issue is not fear of that fact alone, but what it means for dominance, power, and position in society. It is the status threat—the fear of "falling" or losing a position of dominance or relative advantage—that is the underlying issue.

———

Fear of large-scale demographic change or of social incursion is very fertile ground for demagoguery, but perhaps the most dangerous ground and conditions in which othering becomes a very potent political strategy is not large-scale social change, but large-scale institutional change. Periods of enormous political disruption, instability, and transformation are often periods in which new forms of othering emerge or processes of othering rapidly intensify. This is especially true in cases where that transformation is a devolution from a larger political structure to a more fragmented one. The end of the Age of Empires during World War I and the end of the Cold War mark two prominent historical junctures in which multiple instances of severe and often violent ethnic conflict (even eruptions of genocide) burst the seams of the social fabric.

Whereas nation-states often manage conflict through the *consolidation* of prior identities into new national identities (as noted in the previous chapter), large-scale empires manage conflict by *accommodating* diversity. Empires such as the Ottoman, Roman, and Byzantine, among others, were built among countless tribal, ethnic, and religious groupings and cultural units. The larger, more diverse empires could not, however, in the same way, build into their heart the same kind of exclusionary racial, ethnic, tribal, or religious identities as nation-states, and therefore managed those conflicts differently, through accommodation and pluralism. Thus the Roman and Ottoman Empires, for example, demanded loyalty and allegiance but afforded rights and privileges to various groupings within them to manage tensions, although not always successfully. This is one of the underpinnings of a famous saying, attributed to Jesus of Nazareth: "Render therefore to Caesar the things that are Caesar's; and to God, the things that are God's."[145] It is a recognition that empires permit multiple loyalties.

So long as citizens accorded loyalty to the empire and paid taxes, those citizens enjoyed certain liberties. The Roman Empire extended citizenship and accompanying rights to conquered peoples, from whom it expected political loyalty in return.[146] The universalist aspirations of imperial projects like the Roman Empire are also exemplified by the fact that one of the Roman emperors was African, Septimius Severus.[147]

Similar dynamics are evident in large empires of the last millennia. The Ottoman Empire's so-called millet system provided nonterritorial, religious autonomy to religious minorities within the empire.[148] Similarly, the Austro-Hungarian Empire, ruled by the Hapsburgs dynasty, was institutionally multi-ethnic and multi-lingual.[149] In these cases, diverse communities were brought together, often through the force of conquest, under a new, salient imperial identity.

This is not to suggest that empires are benign political institutions. They are generally expansionist, colonialist, and brutally violent, especially to the peoples they conquer or attempt to conquer. Imperialism is a dastardly enterprise. But to members of the polity—citizens of the empire—they are often institutionally more pluralistic and accommodating of heterogeneity and difference than nation-states. They tend to institutionalize pluralism better and suppress intergroup conflict, at least within the borders of the empire (they may amplify such conflict in the expansionary process and engender imperialism's evil twin, colonialism).

The foregoing helps explain why the destruction or crumbling of these empires—often under the auspices of "self-determination" and nationalistic ambitions—has too often stimulated ethno-nationalist aspirations and dreams of domination, and in a disturbingly high number of cases precipitated ethnic cleansing and genocide. As empires fall, solidaristic nationalist identities may give way to latent or subordinate group-based identities. There is no easy or simple way to unravel such associations. When diverse peoples have lived among each other for generations under imperial rule, it is far from clear or obvious how to divide themselves up: religion? Language? Culture? Ethnicity? And, for each one, who controls which territory?

This is why the dissolution of diverse, multi-ethnic empires, such as the Austro-Hungarian, Ottoman, or the Soviet Union and the Yugoslav Federation, each precipitated ethnic violence. When Yugoslavia fell apart at the end of the Cold War, that nationalistic identity was replaced by ethnic and religious identities between Serbs, Croats, and Bosnians—fertile soil for demagogues like Slobodan Milosevic and his dreams of Serbian nationalism.[150] The result was war in Europe. Nationalism, especially in larger regional contexts, is often linked with other identities based on tribe, race, ethnicity, or religion that can lead to or exacerbate othering.

Similarly, the destruction of the Ottoman Empire was one of the key events that led to the new Turkish state, whose leaders were bent on founding it around ethnic and religious identities, even if the state itself was intended to be secular. This helps explain the emergent nation-state's conflicts with Armenians and Greeks. The ailing Ottoman Empire and new Turkish state feared enemies abroad and within, and targeted Christian minorities with a variety of atrocities.

The dissolution of these larger political entities tends to unleash ethno-nationalistic ambitions. That's why the end of the Cold War precipitated a half dozen conflicts, some of which are called "frozen conflicts," including a war over a disputed region known as Nagorno-Karabakh, between Armenia and Azerbaijan, two former Soviet states. This dispute first arose, however, in 1918, after the fall of the Russian Empire. When Armenia and Azerbaijan joined the Soviet Union, this conflict was submerged under a new Soviet identity. It only reemerged after the dissolution of the Soviet Union. One resident embroiled in a brief war between the two countries in 2020 told the *New York Times* that he blamed politicians, not the people: "The people fight each other like dogs baited against each other."[151]

To be clear, our view is not that empires used their power to suppress these latent conflicts so much as the dissolution of the larger "we" embodied in the imperial (or Soviet) identity made these ethnic and nationalistic identities more salient, and thereby empowered demagogues who baited their people to war and conflict.*

---

* In some cases, such as the late-stage Ottoman Empire, it is probably true that imperial authorities took active steps to suppress intergroup conflict. But in other cases, the prevailing imperial or national identity acted as a natural flame suppressant by creating a larger "we" that rendered other identities less salient or secondary. The dissolution of these empires or weakening of certain nation-states, such as Iraq, made those subsidiary identities more salient, and thereby a source of potential conflict, easily exploited by demagogic identity entrepreneurs.

Not only does the dissolution of empires tend to revive latent ethnic or religious conflicts, but the defeat, destruction, or collapse of political entities itself can become a toxic stew of resentment and seething onto-logical anxiety—perfect conditions for demagoguery. Historians often cite the punitive terms imposed on Germany by the Treaty of Versailles in 1919 and subsequent humiliation experienced by the German people following World War I as a contributory factor in the rise of the Nazi Party.[152] As the US Holocaust Memorial Museum explains, the German people "faced poor economic conditions, skyrocketing unemployment, political instabil-ity, and profound social change. While downplaying more extreme goals, Adolf Hitler and the Nazi Party offered simple solutions to Germany's problems, exploiting people's fears, frustrations, and hopes to win broad support."[153]

With the benefit of more than a generation of hindsight, it now seems obvious that Vladimir Putin has similarly exploited the loss of status and the economic and political instability following the collapse of the Soviet Union to build and secure his political and economic power. *New York Times* columnist David Brooks asserts that Putin's most important achieve-ment has been "to help Russians to recover from a psychic trauma—the af-termath of the Soviet Union—and to give them a collective identity so they can feel that they matter, that their lives have dignity."[154] Putin regards the disintegration of the Soviet Union as a historical tragedy rather than the liberation of oppressed peoples. He propounds a narrative of victimhood, with the aggressor being the West, and America in particular.

Consistent with the emphasis on *change* as a backdrop to many of these othering dynamics, another set of conditions for othering includes cli-mate change or environmental changes. Research suggests that in societies primed with ethnic, religious, or tribal divisions, heat waves, droughts, and other exogenous shocks correlate with conflict outbreak. One study found that in a thirty-year period, nearly a quarter of all ethnic-fueled armed con-flict coincided with a climate-related calamity.[155] By contrast, in the set of all countries, war only correlated to climatic disaster about 9 percent of the time. Given the fact that the full ramifications of climate change are to be felt in the decades and centuries to come, it is likely that this dynamic will exacerbate and undergird more othering in the world.

In summary, demagoguery and fears of the "other" can arise in a range of varied circumstances, periods of economic insecurity, and large-scale social, political or environmental change. What these conditions have in common is that they heighten ontological insecurity. Change is scary and threatening, and if the sources of that change can be attributed to or blamed on a marginalized group, then the potential for demagoguery to fuel othering is limitless.

Future Threats

One of the most disturbing developments of recent years has been the growing support for and gradual ascendancy of ethno-nationalist or religious nationalist movements and political leaders all over the globe, from Marie Le Pen to Narendra Modi. The last time that nationalist movements were so potent, the result was history's most devastating world war.

As Francis Fukuyama observes, when diverse societies "try to base their national identities on race, ethnicity, religion, or some other, different substantive vision of the good life, they invite a return to potentially bloody conflict. A world full of such countries will invariably be more fractious, more tumultuous, and more violent."[156] The stirring up of ethno-nationalist sentiment may be initially motivated to build political power, but true believers will take their followers over the cliff's edge, as Hitler's German anticommunist supporters ultimately discovered.

More portentously, near the end of his book *Age of Anger*, Pankaj Mishra suggests that future historians may well regard current events as "commencing the third—and longest and strangest—and of all of the world wars: one that approximates, in its ubiquity, a global civil war."[157] Because of the similarities in the expressions of ethno-nationalism across the globe, Mishra sees these as part of a common pattern, just as the Thirty Years' War between Protestant and Catholics in Europe were a half millennia ago. What is clear is that "[h]ate-mongering against immigrants, minorities and various designated 'others' has gone mainstream."[158]

If he's right, not only will we see more episodic violence like the attack in Buffalo in 2022, but more mass and communal violence around the globe, pushed by demagogues spurring people to feel an acute sense of falling, loss of status, and fear of cultural displacement. One of the touchstones of white supremacist thought in the United States, and an apparent inspiration for the Buffalo shooter, is *The Turner Diaries*, a 1978 novel in which white supremacists overtake an US military installation and trigger a nuclear war. Yet the possibility of global holocaust is not simply the fantasia of right-wing literature like *The Turner Diaries*, with its idyll of a postapocalyptic world cleansed of nonwhite people and their allies. The end result of rising ethno-nationalism could be more wars driven by identity threats, ethnic conflict, and genocide. The forces of othering—violent ethno-nationalism, white supremacy, and the like—have a bloody record, including World War II.

These are not the histrionic warnings of historians, social scientists, or political partisans. Sober security analysts and intelligence agencies are sounding alarms that these trends pose significant security challenges for our near future and future generations. The FBI warns that white supremacist violence is the most prevalent form of domestic terrorism in the United States today.[159] The National Intelligence Council, which reports to the Office of the Director of National Intelligence, issued a report in 2021 with the ominous subtitle "A More Contested World."[160] The report warns that "societies are likely to fragment further based on identities and beliefs. People in every region are turning to familiar and like-minded groups for community and a sense of security, including cultural and other subnational identities as well as transnational groupings and interests."[161]

Not only does the report describe more divided societies and social disorder, but the report outlines five possible scenarios for the world around 2040. All but one are bleak. The report warns that we need to be proactive, and not reactive, to the challenges we face, among which, although unnamed, is the problem of othering.

The spark for a conflagration such as another world war or a nuclear disaster may not come from the West or even the global North. As the foreign policy journalist Murtaza Hussain recently observed in a chilling essay, "The looming threats of climate change, water shortages, and the presence of nuclear weaponry lead me to believe that the fraternal hatred and violence of the subcontinent has still not reached its apex. The combination of aggressive Hindutva in India and bellicose military-led Islamic nationalism in Pakistan may be enough to bring about something truly terrible in the coming century."[162] We can only hope such warnings can steer us off the danger path.

———

When facing the sharp end of the othering process, most victims or targets will quite understandably view it as deliberate, planned, and intentionally instituted through malicious design. Yet, in his history of humanity, *Sapiens*, Yuval Noah Harari essentially claims the opposite is true—that othering is essentially random. He claims that most group-based hierarchies originated as the result of a set of "accidental historical circumstances and [were] then perpetuated and refined over many generations as different groups developed vested interests in [them]."[163] We see the truth as somewhere between these two extremes—of seeing othering as essentially an accident that is then seized upon or as a deliberate and nefarious plan. We see elites manipulating identity categories or creating them generally for selfish purposes, with consequences that engender group-based inequality. It is the doubling down of self-interest that tends to deepen and extend the othering process and the forms of marginalization, but the initial arrangement is not usually one of engineered design. Instead, it is made easier or more difficult based upon initial and evolving conditions.

Perhaps this investigation into the sources and causes of othering can help us recognize the conditions in which demagogues and ethnonationalists flourish. If we are wise, we would use this knowledge to develop early warning systems and preventative strategies to thwart their rise and defuse them where they sprout. The history of demagogues shows that they either fade or are shamed into history's dustbin. Some of these strategies will be discussed in Part II. Now that we have a deeper understanding of the othering process—the specific dynamics that initiate or sustain othering, and the conditions that set these dynamics to work—it is time to turn to solutions.

Part II

Belonging

FIVE

Toward Belonging

As our investigation illustrates, the problem of othering is an ancient one, but any serious comprehensive effort aimed at addressing this problem requires novel approaches, creative thinking, institutional change, and a willingness to experiment with new modes and forms of organizing collective action, policy design, and implementation. Doing nothing or continuing forward along the current path is likely to lead to wider intergroup inequities and more societal polarization, fracturing, dehumanization, and worse.

Many previous efforts to reduce intergroup tensions and hostility have deepened or exacerbated the problem of othering. Segregation, for example, was thought to be a way to manage social divisions and tamp down intergroup violence, but it often worsened it, as the disasters of Partition in India and apartheid in South Africa demonstrated. Assimilation, similarly, was thought to be a way to reduce social divisions but resulted in devastating cultural erasure and trauma.

Prevailing frameworks like antidiscrimination laws, diversity programming, and equity and inclusion policies are in many ways far better, but ultimately fail to reach the aspiration desired. These policies, laws, and programs have helped reduced intergroup disparities along many objective dimensions, and improved representation in critical sectors and governing institutions, but have failed to heal the social fabric or inoculate against demagogic forces or tendencies that exacerbate social polarization and fragmentation.

Although these efforts have reduced objective deprivation and improved absolute conditions for many members of marginalized or historically disadvantaged groups, in some cases *relative* group disparities remain unchanged or have widened.[1] Universalistic policies like social or health insurance schemes intended to help the most disadvantaged may paradoxically maintain or even widen intergroup disparities.[2] Narrower policies that elevate relatively few members of marginalized groups to elite institutions or advantaged spaces may similarly do little to fundamentally change intergroup dynamics in the broader society. And many well-intended interventions, while laudable and producing tangible improvements in the lives of their beneficiaries, are simply too weak to overcome or fundamentally redirect broader societal patterns that constitute othering processes. At times, they may even reinforce them. The effort to include women and racial minorities into Ivy League institutions of higher education illustrates how.

In 1969, after centuries of gender exclusion, Yale University finally admitted women into its undergraduate class. While women were physically present and finally permitted into the classroom, it was clear that they did not *belong*. They remained marginalized within the institution and campus life in critical ways.[3]

Because so few had been initially admitted, women were readily tokenized in the classroom. They reported a high rate of sexual harassment. And they were not only barred from most extracurricular activities (this was before Title IX), but women were prohibited from certain social spaces, including having lunch at Mory's, a private dining club of social significance.[4] Decades later, the first women admitted described the feeling of attending Yale as "very unwelcome."

Although women were formally "included" in the undergraduate body, they were excluded from many settings (some university-based, others semi-private) that were critical for flourishing at Yale and beyond. By and large, the burden was placed on *them* to adjust to the customs and norms that had tacitly (and sometimes explicitly) defined Yale as a privileged white male institution for centuries.

Autobiographies of prominent alumni describe similar experiences at other Ivy League institutions in this period. In their respective memoirs, both Supreme Court justice Sonia Sotomayor and former first lady Michelle Obama reported a feeling of "not belonging" on Princeton University's campus of the 1970s.[5] Although arriving from vastly different social and economic milieus—the Bronx and the south side of Chicago, respectively—they experienced something strikingly similar on Princeton's campus as women of color.

One of the authors of this book observed this dynamic firsthand. Although arriving on Yale's campus in the fall of 1969 as a young Black man, his experience is remarkably similar and equally despairing. Here is an excerpt from a previously published account of that experience:

> On arriving at Yale, I found that I had underestimated the alienation and distance which existed between the law and me and my goals. Not only was Yale a strange and different place from Stanford, in many ways it was hostile. I often found both the faculty and subject matter at Yale to be incredibly callous and indifferent to my needs and to the needs of the people for whom I wished to work.
>
> The hostility at Yale, though, was not generated by personal animosity. Indeed, I would say that many of the people I met at Yale, like many who have been at the center of the legal power structure, were simply oblivious to those living in the margins of society. I found New Haven to be a socially conservative environment compared to the West Coast. . . .
>
> My fate at Yale was sealed by the [murder] trial of [Black Panther leader] Bobby Seale, which had just started in New Haven. It was not just the trial, it was my fellow students' reaction to it. Again there was a strange distance between the students and the discussions on campus and the reality of what I was experiencing. I decided that in order to make the future in which I wanted to live, I had to find a present environment in which I could live. I left and went back to my hometown of Detroit and worked for the remainder of the school year.[6]

What would it have looked like if Yale and other Ivy League universities had been guided by a paradigm of belonging instead of a narrower policy of inclusion?

From Inclusion to Belonging

To better appreciate the features of belonging, the light of contrast may prove most illuminating. We begin with the more familiar concept of inclusion as embodied in the opening vignette. Inclusion is a demand to admit members of groups who have been traditionally or categorically excluded. So, for example, if a particular group has been historically kept out of a particular arena or institution—such as the practice of law, universities and colleges, occupations, or social clubs, then allowing them in is formally known as inclusion. Yale University's decision, along with other Ivy League institutions, to admit women into their undergraduate body was a formal policy of inclusion.

Inclusive policies or initiatives come in many forms. They can come in the form of affirmative action, which are race- or gender-conscious policies that attempt to increase the representation of underrepresented groups.[7] Or they can occur by simply removing a barrier to inclusion, such as by categorically allowing women to apply, as Yale did in 1969. If there is a deliberate bar to inclusion, then removing that bar by disregarding that characteristic can result in a form of inclusion. Conversely, if the bar is not deliberate, but a product of social structures or outside forces, then a conscious awareness followed by remedial effort can achieve inclusion.

As important as inclusion is, inclusive policies can feel far from equitable or fair. Allowing a small number of women into a traditionally gender-exclusionary and male-dominated institution may seem like a major achievement, but if those entrants are tokenized, expected to serve as representatives of their group, or marginalized within the institution, then inclusion can feel anything but welcoming or inclusive to the intended beneficiaries. In fact, formal inclusion can reinforce their marginality by highlighting their lack of belonging within the institution.*

---

* Another expression of how othering may continue even in settings of formal inclusion is the phenomenon of "stereotype threat," the dynamic in which members of marginalized groups operate under asymmetric conditions with performance impacts and other negative outcomes. Claude Steele and Joshua Aronson, "Stereotype Threat and the Intellectual Test Performance of African Americans," *Journal*

To better appreciate this, consider the metaphor of being a guest. In-clusion can make members of the "included" group feel as if they were just guests. They are invited or admitted into the institution or setting, but as tokens or on a partial or conditional basis. Moreover, the norms and customs of the institution are likely both unfamiliar and perhaps even unwelcoming to the newly admitted, and the guests are expected to adapt and conform rather than change the institution to accommodate the guest.

Unfortunately, the limits of formal inclusion are not a remnant of the initial phase—a bumpy transitory period as inclusion leads to broader in-stitutional change. Such dynamics continue to define the experience of many members of marginalized groups in historically exclusionary institu-tions with inclusive policies or public spaces many decades later. To take a few examples: In 2018, a Black student at Yale fell asleep in her dormitory common area, and a white student called the police, leading to a tense en-counter and a seeming presumption of nonbelonging.[8] In 2014, Black stu-dents at Harvard launched a photo campaign titled "I, Too, Am Harvard."[9] The accompanying explanation asserted, "Our voices often go unheard on this campus, our experiences are devalued, our presence is questioned—this project is our way of speaking back, of claiming this campus, of stand-ing up to say: We are here. This place is ours. We, TOO, are Harvard." This is the language of belonging, and an assertion of it.

It is not just within elite private institutions that presumptions of non-belonging despite formal inclusion occur. The same month as the incident at Yale, a white woman called the police on two Black men who were hold-ing a cookout on the popular shores of Lake Merritt in Oakland, earning her the notorious epithet "BBQ Becky."[10] This incident occurred against a tense backdrop of ongoing gentrification, as Oakland transitioned from a predominantly Black to predominantly white city between 2010 and 2020. In response to this incident, community members in Oakland organized a series of events called "BBQ'n While Black," demanding equal access to the lakeside area.[11] Accompanying it was "#WeStillHere," a social media

of Personality and Social Psychology 69, no. 5 (1995): 797–811, https://doi.org/10.1037/0022-3514.69.5.797.

campaign with the explicit goal of creating a more equitable and inclusive Oakland.

This was hardly an isolated incident. A spate of encounters in public spaces where white people called the police on Black people for no apparent reason or for trivial reasons became social media memes and highly visible expressions of nonbelonging. Only a few weeks before the Yale incident, two Black men were arrested for trespassing at a Starbucks in Philadelphia, even though they were having a simple meeting, an ordinary event at a coffee shop.[12] A month later in San Francisco, a white woman called the police on an eight-year old Black girl for allegedly selling bottled water without a permit, earning her the epithet "Permit Patty."[13]

A more robust form of inclusion may go further than simply removing a barrier or formally extending admission, and proactively pursue meaningful representation, defined by a "critical mass." This critical mass is representation large enough that members of that group don't feel isolated or tokenized.[14] A complementary policy of equity may help ensure that resources and opportunities are fairly distributed within the institution, whether in the form of pay or benefits or access to prestigious scholarships, fellowships, or other privileges. Some equity policies may go further, and allocate *greater* resources to members of formally excluded groups or higher-needs populations, such as students with disabilities or English language learners, or other supports such as mentoring or counseling to ensure that members of socially marginalized groups are able to thrive and succeed within the institution.

Even still, equitable inclusion does not reach—or aspire—to the same bar as belonging. Inclusion is when space is made within an exclusionary institution for members of the excluded group. Equitable inclusion occurs when there is a conscious effort to ensure that inclusion is experienced on an equitable basis. But belonging occurs when the members of the group are made to feel as if they belong to the institution, and when members of those groups are empowered and have a say in the organization, design, construction or reconstruction of that institution.

Creating Belonging

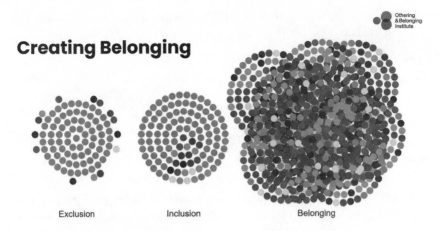

| Exclusion | Inclusion | Belonging |

FIGURE 2. Exclusion, Inclusion, Belonging.
Source: powell and Menendian.

Equity, especially, is primarily understood in material terms: access to or denial of resources, the tangible disparities that result, and the reduction of such disparities. Belonging incorporates but moves beyond the material. Belonging requires a more equitable distribution and access to societal resources, but it is more fundamentally about building a bigger "we." Belonging is constructed along more dimensions than equity.

We will return to the question of what is needed for belonging and the component elements of belonging. But we emphasize here that belonging is *partly* subjective—it is partly based upon how members of a group experience their setting and social environment, as well as the objective conditions that enable, facilitate, and advance belonging.

To return to our metaphor, inclusion is when members of an excluded group are permitted to join a long-standing social club. Equitable inclusion is when they are allowed to join on a fair basis, and able to fairly enjoy the benefits of the club. But in both cases, it's still someone else's party, and you are just a guest. Belonging confers full and unconditional membership. Belonging occurs when everyone feels as if they are not only welcome, but they are empowered and have a stake and a say. Under belonging, you are fully able to participate in the norms, setting, and, ideally, in co-creating the culture and life of the organization. This may include reconsidering the organization of the club, the purpose (vision/mission), charter and bylaws, and the event calendar. It may require other revisions or reformulations, from the trivial to the foundational.

In this sense, belonging is not simply about *presence*, nor is it about joining a thing "as is." After all, if belonging is merely a form of connection or affiliation, being a part of a thing—an institution, a community, or an organization—then does membership come with all the institution's baggage and flaws? Or, more pointedly, in the words one critic, "If we belong to this country, then this country belongs to us, every part of it, including its systemic anti-Black racism and its colonization of Indigenous peoples and land."[15] No, because this critique misunderstands what we mean by belonging.

The "bite" or the edge that belonging entails, which the other forms of inclusion, equity, and the like lack, is that it demands more both of the institution as well as of the individuals and groups involved. An inclusive institution does not necessarily have to change its norms, policies, or practices in any way beyond allowing a formerly excluded set of persons inside. A "belonging" institution has to do more work than that. Similarly, a person who is admitted but whose identity group has been traditionally excluded may feel, as a recently invited guest, inhibited from making demands or claims upon the institution or space. Belonging demands more. It demands active participation by all in shaping the institution, and if successful, will reciprocate with a greater sense of feeling, connection, and warmth about the institution. The "I, Too, Am Harvard" campaign is illustrative. We hope this brief sketch suffices to suggest what belonging looks and feels like in contrast to equity and inclusion. Let us dive deeper and specify the elements that define the practice of belonging.

Elements of Belonging

Like many important ideas, belonging is a complex, multifaceted, and multidimensional concept. It is also dynamic, meaning that it can exist in one context but disappear in another, or appear and reappear in the same context over time. For decades, scholars have sought to define belonging and decode the elements that appear to constitute it. One of the classic definitions is the "satisfaction of an individual's need to be personally involved with their environment and to feel part of a larger social entity—socially embedded."[16] More recent definitions, often emphasizing different elements, have been propounded.[17] In many ways, these efforts are similar to the efforts to measure and define "happiness," which is also a highly subjective experience and eludes a specific and singular definition.[18]

In lieu of agreement upon a specific definition for belonging, scholars have instead developed—and sought to validate—a series of scales capable of measuring belonging. One of the first, and probably the best-known of these instruments, is the "Sense of Belonging Instrument" (SOBI), published in 1995.[19] The SOBI is a long questionnaire (a 27-item survey with 49 questions) divided into two parts, "psychological states" and "antecedents." This instrument has been widely applied in a variety of contexts. But that has hardly slowed the creation of new measures. Intervening research and additional efforts have produced new scales and instruments, with their authors touting their advantages over the alternatives.[20]

Despite these impressive efforts, there remain many limitations to and criticisms of these instruments. Even if these instruments maintain predictive validity, that does not mean that they are capturing or illuminating the elements that constitute belonging. Paradoxically, they may be successful at *predicting* or *measuring* belonging, but fail as operational definitions or at generating such definitions.

Moreover, as the names of these instruments suggest, they are focused on a *sense* of belonging, and have limited ability to tell us why belonging is experienced or what sorts of conditions, traits, or interactions help generate that sense. By focusing on the respondent's personality, identity, or dispositional traits, many of these instruments fail to document or identify the contextual or situational factors that could provide further illumination on the material conditions that shape the experience of belonging.

Further research has sought to unpack different dimensions to belonging, with different researchers arguing for or against different components. For example, some emphasize the dimension of "connectedness," while others might emphasize "participation" or "recognition."[21] It is not our goal to resolve these debates here. Given the variety of circumstances in which belonging may be desired, it is possible that there is no comprehensive or complete set of elements sufficient to create or foster belonging in every possible context. Nonetheless, we can specify a few elements that may be necessary to belonging irrespective of context and a few related fundamental insights along the way.

———

In terms of general principles, first, we maintain that belonging is a compound concept, which incorporates multiple elements and/or dimensions. To the frustration of many, like other important compound or complex concepts, it is not reducible to a simple proxy or singular element, even "fit" or "feeling of home." Second, belonging is a relational concept, which means that it cannot be understood in a reductive, analytic mode of examining individuals or their psychological traits or attitudinal tendencies. We must examine the relationship itself, not simply the things that are in relationship. Third, and relatedly, belonging is both subjective and objective.*

As a concept measured by self-report, belonging may ultimately be subjective (existing or not according to subjective experience), but it nonetheless has a material substrate. This is a point we wish to emphasize: there exist socio-ecological preconditions that make the experience of belonging more or less likely. Thus, like othering, belonging is structured and patterned in society, not simply the experience of individuals. In general, the psychological instruments that measure belonging give insufficient attention to these conditions. To the extent that these preconditions are functionally "necessary conditions," whose absence makes belonging either impossible or extremely unlikely, we feel comfortable including them as definitional elements.[22]

———

* We recognize the inherent complexities and difficulties in the notions of "subjectivity" and "objectivity," but these concepts serve as close-enough heuristics or approximations to convey our intended meaning as it applies to belonging. Moreover, the focus throughout this book has been on the status and experience of groups rather than individuals, along with the broader societal conditions, meanings, and practices that generate othering. While not ignoring the subjective experience of belonging, we wish to emphasize that belonging is also materially grounded, patterned, and structured in society.

In terms of elements, we contend that, first, belonging encompasses and requires inclusion, and to some extent equity as well. This is part of the objective aspect to belonging. If extreme disparities persist or exclusion is maintained, then the conditions for belonging cannot arise or exist. Belonging may also require accommodation.* Norms, customs, or practices that are designed to be neutral, but have a persistent disparate impact, undermine belonging. If an institution, for example, provides food options that fail to recognize certain religious or dietary needs, then members of some groups may be or feel excluded. Similarly, if building design or other physical structures impede access for people with disabilities, then exclusion can occur even if formal inclusion is the policy. These and other examples are discussed in more detail later.

Second, belonging requires a sense of connection, with an emphasis on *sense*. Whether we wish it or not, most things exist in some sort of dynamic relationship, and belonging is no exception.[23] The experience of belonging is more likely when there is a tether or a tie, something that binds or affiliates a person to another person, community, group, or institution. That connection need not be intimate; nor must it be permanent. But the absence of a sense of connection is unlikely to generate a sense of belonging. This is part of the subjective aspect of belonging.

Furthermore, this connection generally comes with an emotional valance, often a sense of attachment, fondness, safety, or warmth.[24] This is what is meant by an "affective" component to belonging that is not generally acknowledged or emphasized in other equity and inclusion practices, even those that stress representation.[25] The affective element describes how individuals regard or feel about the object of belonging. This affective component cannot be known by simply scanning formal policies or objective conditions, but only by investigating the sense of connection itself.

----

*The incorporation of inclusion into a compound definition of belonging may be intuited from the fact that belonging is, in many ways, an evolution of the concept of inclusion and builds on it. It is difficult to peg exactly what minimal level of equity is required to create the material conditions for belonging, but it is likely a threshold that varies from context to context.

Third, belonging requires visibility or recognition.[26] The simple act of being seen can engender powerful feelings between people, even a sense of intimacy between erstwhile strangers. In the public sphere, people yearn to be heard and understood, especially if they feel neglected or overlooked. Recognition occurs when people feel that their social group is seen, respected, and valued. This is partly why representation is so important: if a person feels that their identity or their group is invisible in the community or institution, they are less likely to feel a sense of belonging. A feeling of belonging is fostered when a community or an institution affirmatively communicates that participants belong, and does so in a way that demonstrates that the community or institution sees and respects their identities.

Recognition may form the predicate for a sense of connection, which then becomes a reciprocal element: the subjective experience of belonging is more likely if the connection is in some way mutual, if the person holding the connection to the community, institution, or group simultaneously feels that they are visible, recognized, and valued. The sense of connection may be a by-product of feeling recognized and valued.

Mixed messages or subtle cues can undermine efforts to engender belonging. If the message feels more like a marketing slogan than an authentic expression of intent, it could weaken attachments rather than engender belonging. Such messaging should be grounded programmatically. It should resonate in the life of an institution.

Fourth, belonging requires agency. Agency is the sense or feeling of control people have over actions and their consequences.[27] Belonging requires a meaningful degree of actual agency in relation to the object of belonging. If barriers are removed, objective disparities are eliminated or reduced, recognition is accorded, and connection is forged, but agency is denied, then belonging is unlikely exist. Or if inclusion occurs, but some participants are given a voice and a say, but others are denied it, then belonging is thwarted for those who are treated less generously.

The requisite of agency brings *power* into the belonging formula. To have agency, one must individually and collectively have the power to act and the potential to influence. This goes beyond the classic formulation of "voice."[28] Having a voice means being heard, which is largely a corollary to being recognized or visible, our third definitional element. Agency goes beyond voice to "say," or influence. Having a say does not necessarily mean getting one's way, but it does entail more than the right to be heard; it means some degree of capacity to shape the proceedings or the deliberations. To foster belonging, we call for the empowerment of people, especially those from marginalized groups, to be able to fully participate in society. Belonging will arise when institutions and communities take steps to facilitate agency so that these participants ultimately feel that they have a say.

The potential for maximal agency—co-creation—is the most radical and potentially transformative aspect of a belonging paradigm. It is radical in the sense that it is not the default position for how most institutions or communities are organized, as our discussion of the contrast with inclusion demonstrated. But this form of radical agency is also intuitive due to its proximity to our conception of democracy, that people should have a say in creating and governing the society they are a part of, although for belonging, this principle would extend to virtually every aspect of our lives and not just to our formal political space. As James Baldwin wrote, "The place in which I'll fit will not exist until I make it."[29]

Although we encourage co-creation as a belonging principle, we wish to make a caveat: agency is definitional to belonging, with empowerment being the means to achieve it. But co-creation is merely an expression, perhaps the ultimate one, of full belonging. Not every member of a community or institution may wish to influence the proceedings or decision-making process of that community or institution, and their agency is not denied when they opt out of doing so, only when they are never given the choice or opportunity to begin with. Enforced passive participation lacks the agency necessary to full belonging. Conversely, active participation is an indicator, although not requirement, of belonging.

To a great extent, belonging exists only when members of a group feel as if they belong. This is the subjective component of belonging. If all the objective components of belonging exist, and agency is realized, but somehow participants feel as if they are unwelcome or less welcome than others, and this experience is shared across members of the group, then belonging is denied. What about the reverse? What if the conditions for belonging are absent and instead one is inhabiting deeply othering space? Can one

FIGURE 3. The Four Elements of Belonging.
Source: powell and Menendian.

belong or feel a sense of belonging? Although we find this extremely unlikely, we would nonetheless conclude that any self-report of belonging in
that context is illusory. In such a case, we would note a claim of belonging
but ultimately reject an assertion that belonging can exist without the requisite conditions.[30]

In summary, belonging exists when all social groups in society are included in critical institutions in society and in their communities; are recognized and accorded visibility within those institutions or communities;
have agency, including the ability to actively participate in shaping those
critical institutions and communities; and report a sense of connection or
feeling of belonging. Belonging is both perceptual and tangible; a feeling
and a practice; subjective and objective.

The Need to Belong

Before proceeding to a discussion of how to realize or foster belonging, we
need to sharpen the case for belonging, not just in terms of addressing the
problem of othering and social group inequities, but in more fundamental

terms. Belonging is more deeply rooted in the human condition and central to human societies than merely as a solution to the problem of othering. The need to belong is fundamental and universal to human survival and flourishing.

For rationalists and modernists, human well-being and desire are viewed in largely material or utilitarian terms. It is assumed that people seek to maximize their utility, and therefore strive for income, wealth, power, and security to achieve those ends. Such views of human nature have foundered against currents that flow through societies in which material desires and economic interests are trumped by other needs and motivations.

In his landmark 1943 paper titled "A Theory of Human Motivation," the American psychologist Abraham Maslow presented what he called "a hierarchy of human needs."[31] He asserted that human needs are ordered and stacked sequentially such that one only moves up in the hierarchy when lower needs are largely satisfied. In Maslow's model, the most basic needs are physiological, such as sleep, food, and water. But the second most basic need in his model is safety, followed by belonging in third.

While Maslow's approach is widely embraced, there have been a number of recent challenges to it, including the assertion that belonging may precede physiological needs and safety.[32] This assertion is based upon the observation that, in many cases, we cannot obtain our physical needs or achieve safety without belonging. Even in the context of complex modern societies, certain needs may only be satisfied if belonging or certain forms of membership exist. For example, health care or other vital services may be denied to people who are not citizens of certain nation-states. In ancient societies, political excommunication or expulsion meant certain death, not just a figurative social death.[33]

While there may be some disagreement as to the exact place or primacy of belonging in terms of a hierarchy of human needs, there is a consensus acknowledging its overall importance, including in terms of human survival and development.[34] It is easy to overlook the importance of belonging in a society that valorizes individualism and elevates the individual. But none of us would survive—or even be—without others. We are literally born attached to another human being, and remain dependent and helpless for an extended period of time. Although we sever the umbilical cord, we may never sever our need for attachment.

———

Healthy human development, not simply nutrition, shelter, and physical safety, requires bonds with other human beings. A variety of studies have probed the nature of this connection and the harmful consequences of isolation and neglect.[35] The main and consistent finding is that infants and children who receive the nutrients and physical care they require, but not the love and emotional bonds, become developmentally stunted in terms of brain development, IQ, impulse control, and emotional empathy, but also in terms of weight, height, and physical growth.

One classic study of infants in the 1930s and '40s found that children raised by incarcerated mothers were better off along a range of measures than children in orphanages.[36] Another study of Romanian orphanages found that a team of rotating nurses providing care and touch that simulated that of a natural mother resulted in the same developmental delays and disabilities, but that if the nursing was more intensive and focused, such that infants were able to develop a bond with particular nurses, many of these delays disappeared.[37] What matters was not just human touch or connection, but bonds, love, and attachment, and it matters as much as food, water, shelter, and physical safety to healthy human development.

Further research has uncovered a chemical basis for these observations. Certain hormones like oxytocin and vasopressin are associated with human bonding and connection.[38] Dopamine and endorphins are released in the brain in pleasurable, social settings where belonging is experienced. As a social animal, we require social connection to thrive. This helps explain consistent research findings on the harmful effects of isolation and loneliness in adults.[39] Researchers have found clear links between isolation and premature death as well as dementia and despair.[40] Social isolation has been found to increase risk of heart disease and stroke by 29 and 32 percent respectively,[41] and dementia by 50 percent.[42]

Similarly, recent research on solitary confinement has uncovered a causal connection not only to mental health, and psychosis in particular, but also to physical well-being.[43] Prisoners subjected to solitary confinement are more likely to attempt suicide, become addicted to opioids, and even commit murder after release.[44] Solitary confinement is punishment that denies a human need as basic as food and shelter. In other words, belonging may be more foundational than Maslow's hierarchy implies. These and other studies deepen our understanding of the importance of belonging, especially in more nuanced terms of modern medical science.

A lack of belonging takes a terrible toll on the human psyche. In his book *Tribe*, the journalist Sebastian Unger argues that suicide rates among veterans may be a consequence of the trauma of transitioning from a tight-knit combat unit into a hyperindividualistic society conspicuously lacking belonging and camaraderie.[45] Unger suggests that the best treatment for post-traumatic stress disorder (PTSD) may be greater belonging and social connection, and that failure to provide belonging can exacerbate it. Unfortunately, these problems are now evident on a wider basis.

Many modern societies are afflicted by a lack of belonging crisis, where both members of marginalized groups and members of formerly nonmarginalized groups report a lack of belonging, as we noted in the previous chapter. New measures and instruments have been developed in recent years to try to gauge the degree of belonging felt in workplaces, schools, and communities.[46] One of the most important new instruments was a survey created by Project Over Zero called the "Belonging Barometer."[47] Applied to nearly 5,000 respondents, they found that most Americans report significant feelings of nonbelonging. Specifically, "64 percent of Americans reported nonbelonging in the workplace, 68 percent in the nation, and 74 percent in their local community." Nearly a fifth of Americans "failed to report an active sense of belonging in any of the life settings."[48]

The various entangled crises of loneliness, isolation, and alienation—all expressions of lack of belonging and community—are finally drawing the attention of medical and political leaders. In May 2023, the nation's top doctor, the US surgeon general, issued a report titled "Our Epidemic of Loneliness and Isolation: The U.S. Surgeon General's Advisory on the Healing Effects of Social Connection and Community."[49] The report scrupulously summarized the medical and physiological harms of loneliness and isolation on physical and mental health, comparing loneliness to smoking a pack of cigarettes. But most importantly, it repeatedly emphasized the importance of belonging and recognized belonging as a fundamental human need, and then called for interventions to foster greater social connection and belonging. Around the same time, the United Kingdom issued a follow-up report to its 2018 initiative to tackle loneliness, sounding many of the same themes.[50]

As foundational as belonging may be to human needs in terms of physical and emotional health, there is yet another dimension to tease out. It is not just that human beings are social animals in the sense that we need human connection and the formation of human attachments, and that our physical and emotional well-being depends upon that belonging. Human beings seek recognition and respect, not just connection.

This is another area where materialistic accounts of human need and human nature fall short. They have a tendency to overlook what some commentators, drawing on Plato, denote to as "Thymotic" desires.[51] This is the need "to be seen, respected, appreciated" and is the hunger for recognition. Whereas Enlightenment philosophers tended to see human beings as principally motivated by reason and emotion or material or economic concerns, a perspective that emphasizes "thymos" sees status, relative standing, and dignity as a critical source of human concern. From this view, money and power and fame are not ends, but rather are means to achieve those thymotic needs, including belonging and dignity. Some observers argue that culture itself is driven by this need.[52]

As David Brooks points out, this need extends to social groups:

> Plato went on to point out that people are not only sensitive about their own self-worth, they are also sensitive about the dignity of their group, and the dignity of others. If a group is denied the dignity it deserves, we call that injustice. Thymotic people mobilize to assert their group's significance if they feel they are being rendered invisible by society. Thymotic people mobilize on behalf of those made voiceless by the powerful. As Plato indicated, thymos is the psychological origin of political action.[53]

In other words, group belonging is a thymotic need, and the lack of it is a wellspring of significant political dissatisfaction, organizing, and disorder.

A lack of belonging is a source of powerful populist resentments as well as resistance to the prevailing order. Recall the discussion of "sacred symbols" in Chapter 4 as an expression of thymotic needs over material needs. More broadly, it can be asserted that the demagogic characters described in that chapter are manipulating the need to belong by activating fears and panics over a perceived other to build, secure, and maintain power. They offer a home—a place to belong—within the exclusionary community they seek to construct. The need to belong is a source of their power.

This is no idle observation. In her landmark twentieth-century masterpiece, *The Origins of Totalitarianism*, Hannah Arendt identified loneliness and a lack of belonging as a critical ingredient in the conversion of supporters to totalitarian thought. As she explained, totalitarianism "bases itself on loneliness, on the experience of not belonging to the world at all, which is among the most radical and desperate experiences of man."[54] She also wrote, "The question is not, as it was for Hamlet, to be or not to be, but to belong or not to belong."[55]

———

In diverse, complex societies experiencing rapid change and rampant alienation, tight-knit groups provide belonging that is so often missing in the lives of too many people. Notorious cults such as the Branch Davidians, the People's Temple, or even Aum Shinrikyo are each examples of sects that offered such belonging, but whose charismatic leaders ushered their followers toward disaster.[56] Even extremist groups like ISIS operate on similar principles, offering a sense of purpose and community, along with a dash of "excitement and romance, a link to a grand history."[57] Outside observers wondered incredulously at how so many people, especially from affluent and well-educated families, could have been lured to their deaths, but miss the fundamental feature of belonging at the core of their appeal.[58]

Although many Western recruits to the Islamic State may have later regretted their affiliation, they were drawn to militant fundamentalist Islam by a sense of purpose and belonging that was absent in their communities.[59] Indeed, researchers found that ISIS recruits in Europe came primarily from communities that had the greatest difficulties integrating Muslim immigrants into their social fabrics, not from societies that were impoverished or had objectively less human development.[60] In fact, the opposite was often the case: the families of recruits and the nations of recruits may have been better off than those who did not join. Osama bin Laden himself came from an extremely wealthy family.

In this regard, the appeal of militant fundamentalist Islamic organization like Al Qaeda and ISIS have a similar foundation to white nationalist organizations. They even share similar recruiting tactics. Just as YouTube and social media were used to recruit ISIS soldiers, white identity groups are also using YouTube to radicalize young white boys and men.[61] White supremacist organizations are targeting disaffected and alienated young white boys as ripe targets based upon the social conditions in our society.[62]

A lack of belonging can be used to compel or manipulate disaffected or alienated peoples toward nationalistic, ethnic, or other chauvinistic visions of community or affiliation. Recall how much of Trump's support came from affluent voters, suffering existential, not economic, anxiety. The conservative commentator David French observes that Trump's most dedicated supporters are drawn to the deep sense of belonging offered by his "Make America Great Again" political campaign rallies: "They see a country that's changing around them and they are uncertain about their place in it. But they *know* they have a place at a Trump rally, surrounded by others—overwhelmingly white, many evangelical—who feel the same way they do."[63] The rallies instill a sense of community through a powerfully visceral experience, complete with a narrative arc, villains (media, Democrats, etc.), and sacred symbols.

Although a sense of belonging may explain the appeal of cults, most forms of nationalism or exclusionary belonging on offer today embody the same principle. This is the dark side of the need to belong: it may be exploited by the forces of othering. The power of othering is a by-product of the power of belonging.

―――――

The need to belong is not merely a source of power manipulated by reactionary demagogues; it is also a distorting influence on the political left. In his account of the failures of the Occupy Wall Street movement, insider Jonathan Smucker incisively notes the role that belonging played in building community among many disaffected radicals who felt alienated from a larger society that they felt was corrupt and evil.[64] Occupy offered belonging among like-minded individuals, replete with its own culture, symbols, and shared living space. In his account, the soothing balm of this community, and its "prefigurative" living arrangements, began to substitute for political strategy and ultimately inhibited the development and pursuit of a program for broader transformative social and policy change.[65] In short, the pleasure of activism and community became the ultimate end, and ultimately the end, of the movement.

The need to belong is a fundamental human one, as essential to human health, development, and survival as any material need. But this fact is also the wellspring of othering and the source of the existential fears that drive othering. If this need is as fundamental as science and social science suggest, then that in turn implies that we are, in some essential fashion, dependent, and not the free, autonomous creatures we imagine ourselves to be. Moreover, this dependence exacerbates the fears we harbor of other people: fears of violence, exploitation, or abuse. We harbor immense—perhaps even infinite—need and fear of each other. This is one of the paradoxes of human existence and belonging. If the need to belong is also the source of othering, our investigation must address an important question: Does belonging require an "other"? Or can we create belonging without othering?

Belonging without Othering

Before proceeding further, we should make clear the belonging we advocate for in this book. While the need to belong is, we believe, a foundational psychological and physical need and basic emotional reality, there are many ways of understanding or meeting this need. Some are more expansive and inclusive, and others are more exclusionary and limited, and some are both at the same time—the extension or expansion of membership by deepening exclusion for a particular marginalized group.

These possibilities raise a series of important questions: Does belonging depend upon or require some form of exclusion? Does belonging to one group mean not belonging to another one? For there to be an "us" or a "we," must there be a "they" or a "them"? More broadly, is it even possible to construct a society where no social group dominates? Or, more pointedly, does belonging require othering? We have seen how belonging is created through thick cultural units and strong ethnic, religious, and racial ties. Does this mean that belonging is based upon othering?

Although there are reasons to suppose so and adopt this view, we do not. We reject the claim that belonging requires an "other." It cannot be denied that many of the offerings of belonging around the world seem to be extended on an exclusionary basis under the leadership of a "strong charismatic figure." Indeed, this is the basis of the ethno-nationalistic projects surveyed in Part I. This kind of belonging has been described under the header of "blood and belonging" or could similarly be characterized in terms such as the Nazis' "Blood and Soil" slogan, with all of the attendant connotations.[66] While a vivid descriptor, we prefer to denote this kind of belonging as "bounded" or parochial. Thus, bounded belonging is a form of belonging constructed on a limited basis.

Quite often, the practice of belonging appears in the form of social solidarity generated by the exclusion of an other and the creation and maintenance of sharp boundaries between the "us" and "them." The problem is that this form of belonging—bounded belonging—adds to the difficulties in disestablishing othering and addressing the various forms of polarization and fragmentation associated with it.

As discussed in Chapter 4, othering is being weaponized by elites for power and material gains. What was not necessarily evident in that discussion, but should be obvious now, is that this danger is based in no small part on the need to belong. In fact, societies with more exclusionary boundaries and more punitive cruelties for those falling outside of those boundaries make belonging even more desirable and important. But this does not mean that othering is an inevitable by-product of the human condition or the process of creating belonging.

Much of the literature that argues for the evolutionary basis for othering as a necessary counterpoint to belonging tends to refer to our long existence spent in relatively small bands prior to the agricultural revolutions that started around ten to fifteen thousand years ago, where humans transitioned from nomadic life and settled land for farming.[67] A related but separate argument is based upon the scientific understanding, discussed in

Chapter 3, that the brain is wired to categorize, but that this fact naturally leads to human differentiation and ultimately othering. Let's briefly consider each of these assertions.

The latter assertion is logical and perceptual. In order to notice something and classify it as such, there must be a basis for differentiating it from what it is not. But noticing that things can be or are different tells us little about belonging and othering. Belonging and othering are not the same as simply differentiating or even categorizing. Difference alone does not require or compel differential treatment, let alone unfair differential treatment. As we have seen, some societies make one form of difference socially meaningful while others do not even regard the distinction as a social fact. Racial differences have as little meaning in some societies as Hindu caste designations do in others. The differences that ultimately matter are contingent and not predetermined. This means that othering is as well.

As to the evolutionary claim that belonging depends on othering, belonging for early humans was based on trust forged in daily interactions and interdependent needs.[68] From this view, all other people were categorical "others" and could not be trusted. Further, the argument here contends that even as we moved to larger human settlements, our prior wiring predisposed us to create a sense of belonging with our own group in opposition to all other others. Although viewed regrettably (much like human evolution adapted our bodies for a very different diet than our food system tends to produce), this predisposition is explained as a vestige of our evolutionary past, wired into our brain, and unavoidably activated. This is sometimes what is meant by *tribalism* when ascribing an inherited tendency to form in- and out-groups, and to prefer or favor members of in-groups.

Although there is some validity to the premises, the conclusions are overdrawn. In societies of tens or hundreds of millions of people, neither in-groups nor out-groups can be formed on the basis of daily interactions and mutual dependence. Most humans today will never meet the vast majority of people they share a social grouping with. Yet belonging abounds among people who have never met or between people who encounter each other for the first time. Attend a sporting event and it is readily experienced among fans of the same team, as strangers find themselves hugging

and slapping hands as their team succeeds. Neither belonging nor othering, as experienced today, can be clearly traced to our evolutionary past.[69]
Such claims are overly reductionist, as should be clear by this point. The
othering process is far more historically contingent.

———

Nineteenth-century nationalists emphasized biology and common ancestry as the ground for belonging. But the successful decoding of the human
genome upended folk taxonomies regarding blood.[70] Contemporary ethno-nationalists who favor particularistic (rather than universalistic or pluralistic) nationalism and antiliberals (fascists, theocrats, etc.) more broadly,
increasingly ground their appeals on a recognition of the power of the need
to belong. They justify their continuance of othering on that basis, except
in terms that are rooted, if not in blood and kinship or daily interaction,
then in terms of religion, shared heritage or territory, culture, symbols and
traditions, or language.

Thus another version of the argument that human beings are hardwired
to both belong and engage in othering replaces daily interaction or blood
with *culture* as the ground of othering and belonging. Yoram Hazony, for
instance, argues that nations constitute coherent cultural units that allow
their members to share thick culinary traditions, holidays, similar languages, and the like.[71] He and other defenders of ethno-states claim that
belonging can and should be established on a limited or non-universalistic
basis organized around culture (and that such cultural units can correspond to nation-state boundaries). The use of culture as a ground for circumscribed or bounded belonging addresses some problems with the prior
theories, but it leaves other questions unanswered.

It cannot be denied that culture is a powerful mechanism for fostering
belonging. A common culture can provide scripts, practices, and common
experiences that allow people who have otherwise never met to share
a sense of familiarity and belonging, in addition to ease of speaking the
same language. It also cannot be denied that cultural differences can be
profoundly alienating: lack of familiarity with cultural practices can make
people feel like outsiders while also making those who lack acculturation
seem different, strange, or rude.

These observations demonstrate, however, that the claim that human cultures necessitate belonging based on othering or make it inevitable is self-refuting. Culture is neither inherently othering nor supportive of broader belonging, but has propensities in both directions. Some cultural practices tend toward openness and inclusion, while others tend toward parochialism, insularity, and exclusion. What matters is the specific content of the culture, not the fact of human culture itself.

In any case, culture is far more malleable than belonging founded upon daily interactions in small bands or ancestry and blood ties. Ancestry cannot be changed (except by fraud), but many cultural practices, like language, behaviors, and practices, are inherently mutable and adoptable by newcomers. For example, over one million Russian Jews emigrated to Israel from Russia after the fall of the Soviet Union, leading to the fabrication of a unique and synthetic subculture of Russian speakers in Israel.[72] There is nothing inherent in culture itself that inscribes a line between one group of people or another, sorting people into out-groups and in-groups, except when a set of cultural practices or tradition are designed to do precisely that. Even places with thick cultures have traditions that evolve or can be nudged in one direction or another, emphasizing a more open and inclusive element over another, more exclusionary element.

Culture, then, could form the basis of othering *or* belonging, and help organize the relative degree of both in a society. Paradoxically, this is also implicit in the argument propounded many years ago by Samuel Huntington in his notorious tract *The Clash of Civilizations*.[73] Huntington claimed that religion and culture would become the chief bases of conflict in the post–Cold War world, a claim many insist has been borne out by subsequent events.[74] Huntington would then seem to be yet another voice in support of the general view that culture is the crucial ground for belonging based on othering in the contemporary world. But a key part of Huntington's argument was that the relevant cultural units extended beyond and across nation-states, and he therefore predicted that future wars would be fought between these supranational cultural units, not nation-states. Thus Huntington's argument was implicitly a critique of ethno-nationalistic arguments like Hazony's, which attempt to bind nation-state boundaries to cultural units as objects of belonging.

Huntington saw and described culture as a more unifying force than do contemporary ethno-nationalists.

————

A more sophisticated version of the cultural argument can be extrapolated from Gerhard Falk's theory of stigmatization noted in Chapter 2, which we introduced as a process of, and explanatory basis for, othering. In his theory, stigma plays a constitutive role, helping delineate insiders from outsiders while fostering cohesion among insiders.[75] Falk appears to be making a universal claim: that all societies use stigma to create or identify outsiders in order to bind together insiders. And every society he observes has stigmatized behaviors, conditions, or traits.

There are two problems with inferring the inevitability of othering based on the apparent universality of cultural stigma. First, even if stigma is universal, the basis for stigma is not. More specifically, stigma does not have to code to or attach to socially identifiable groups we describe as "the other." While some forms of stigma Falk identified were those attached to such groups (like Native Americans, the disabled, or the elderly), many of the forms of stigma are attached to professions (like tax or trash collectors), behaviors (like drug use), or illnesses (like leprosy, aka Hansen's disease), not social groups.[76] Thus it is possible to have societies with social stigmas that serve each of the purposes Falk describes but do not contribute to the othering process or create a categorical social "other," in the sense used throughout this book.*

The second problem with the argument that cultural stigmatization is universal, and that therefore belonging based on shared stigma must always entail othering, is that othering is nearly as universal as stigmatization. Yet the ubiquity of othering does not prove that othering is an *inevitable*

————

* Recall that our definition of the other is a social group category, not the experience of individuals being alienated or ostracized by or from society. Thus the societies we describe as having "belonging without othering" may nonetheless produce outsiders and outcasts, just not on the basis of categorical and immutable group identities. These forms of difference-making are more situational and conditional than categorical and durable.

by-product of human societies, just that it is a general tendency, much like violence or war, tendencies that must be restrained and prevented. If othering can be prevented or curtailed, then certainly the stigmatization processes that undergird it can be as well. In fact, that is part of the challenge: to combat othering with belonging means contesting dehumanization and challenging social stigmas associated with stigmatized groups.

———————

We must acknowledge, however, the gulf between practice and theory. Part of the recent emphasis on culture has to do with the fact that many other binding agents on offer seem to be lacking appeal or magnetic force or have been discredited. The events of the twentieth century went a long way to discrediting both nationalism and creeds like communism based on Marxism as models to affiliate or organize around.

In a brilliant essay, the cultural observer Amin Maalouf persuasively argues that the fall of communism through the collapse of the Soviet Union played a critical role in the revival of religion and religiously inspired movements in the decades since.[77] This is not just true of places like the former Yugoslavia or Russia itself, but across the world. Imagining the life of a young Arab man in the late 1990s, Maalouf illustrates the appeal of Islamist movements over the alternatives in that context:

> In the past he might have been attracted to an organization with Marxist tendencies that would have been sympathetic to his existential difficulties and initiated him, in its own way, into the debate about ideas. Or else he might have joined some nationalist group that would have flattered his need for identity and perhaps spoken to him of renaissance and modernization. But now Marxism has lost its attraction and Arab nationalism, annexed by regimes that are authoritarian, incompetent and corrupt, has lost much of its credibility. So it is not impossible that the young man we are thinking of will be fascinating by the West, by its way of life and its scientific and technological achievements. But that fascination would probably have little impact on his actions, since there is no political organization of any consequence that embodies that model he admires. Those who aspire to the "Western Paradise" often have no

alternative but emigration. [A]ll those who want to shake up the established order or are revolted by corruption, state despotism, inequality, unemployment and lack of opportunity, all who have difficulty finding a place in a fast-changing world—all these are tempted by Islamism. In it they find satisfaction for their need for identity, for affiliation to a group, for spirituality, for a simple interpretation of too-complex realities and for action and revolt.[78]

In the West, a similar reasoning process helps explain why contemporary antiliberals and ethno-nationalists argue that trust and belonging must be built on something more than ideals such as liberal universalism or pluralistic nationalism. This explains the presumption that religion and culture can serve as such a binding agent. In the words of Ezra Klein summarizing (but not espousing) this perspective: "Our truest identities are rooted in the land in which we're born and the kin among whom we're raised. Our lives are given order and meaning because they are embedded in the larger structure and struggle of our people."[79] The critique of universal liberalism is that it dissolves these bonds without adequately replacing them with something sufficiently deeply felt.

The eminent political scientist Francis Fukuyama has fretted along similar lines. He argues that "[liberalism] creates a spiritual vacuum, as individuals go their own ways and experience only a thin sense of community. Liberal political orders do require shared values, such as tolerance, compromise, and deliberation, but these do not foster the strong emotional bonds found in tightly knit religious and ethnonationalist communities."[80] Or, as Matthew Rose more pointedly summarizes the antiliberal and particularistic argument, liberalism "severs deep bonds of belonging, leaving isolated individuals exposed to, and dependent on, the power of the state."[81]

These arguments are not only extremely reductionist; they are tautological. There is nothing in social science or history to conclude that religious or ethnic bonds are *necessarily* "emotionally stronger" than those of national identity, professional identity, identities built around creeds, or any other identity. They only appear to be so because of the situational weakness of the alternatives on the menu. Indeed, the experience of the twentieth century showed how swiftly creeds like "communism" could swamp and suppress religious and ethnic identities and bonds, rendering them secondary or far less salient. To the extent that such cultural identities play a larger role in our lives, they may become so, but there is nothing inherent in their nature that renders them that way. Whether they will or not depends upon practices, activities, philosophies, narratives, and lived experiences of people or the threat presented to those identities.

————

As another example of how an ethical or philosophical commitment can rival other cultural forces, consider the commitment to egalitarianism across group boundaries now derisively described as "wokeness."[82] Wokeness is, in essence, sensitivity to systems, structures, cultural practices, and activities that tend to reinforce intergroup inequality—or othering. Wokeness is a sensing system for identifying and attempting to root out oppressive and marginalizing practices.

Yet this commitment can seem so powerful and overbearing at times that the linguist John McWhorter now compares it to a religion.[83] And the economist Tyler Cowen described wokeness as an American export that has gone global, in a surprising defense of it.[84] He, too, sees elements of a religion to it, which he calls "wokeism." He notes that "wokeism is a way of spreading ideas from a relatively feminized American culture to a world less supportive of women's rights." As he observes, "even the un-woke among us might think Francophone society and culture could stand to be a little more woke. The boss needs to know he doesn't have the right to sleep with his secretary."

It seems to us, therefore, that it is possible to have belonging without othering. There may be certain proclivities that undergird tendencies in the direction of either othering or belonging, but there appears to us nothing inherent in human biology or psychology that makes othering inevitable, let alone any particular expression. Any claim to the contrary is merely a new form of essentialism, or an attempt to naturalize historical contingencies.

Even if the claim is true, per social dominance theory, that social hierarchies appear to be intrinsic to human societies, those hierarchies do not have be based upon fixed or largely static social group identities.[85] They can rest on more fluid and dynamic categories than those upon which they currently tend to, such as professional identities, situational identities, service or leadership roles rather than gender, sexual orientation, religion, or racial or ethnic identification.* Nor does the existence of social hierarchies necessitate the domination by one group over others.

The possibility of belonging without othering does not mean that overcoming prevailing traditions or dominating hierarchies is simple or easy. In most cases, it will prove extraordinarily difficult. The question then becomes: How do we promote belonging and increase belongingness without othering?

Building Belongingness

What does belonging without othering look like? What are the conditions that support and advance this kind of belonging? At a societal scale, inculcating belonging on a broad basis requires certain cultural and normative commitments. Belonging is a fundamental need, but whether it can exist on a broad or a narrow basis is conditional on norms established by the dominant groups in society.[86] If culture, norms, and identity are established and promulgated on a broad and inclusive basis, then it is far more likely that belonging will exist more broadly than if those same things are promulgated on a narrow basis. Above all, belongingness entails an unwavering commitment to not simply tolerating and respecting difference (which is no small thing in a world of violent othering), but to ensuring that all people are welcome and feel that they belong in the society with agency and not as provisional guests.

Full belonging requires the possibility of an iterative and nuanced process of co-creation by all groups involved from a position of empowered

---

* To be clear, our position, although deeply egalitarian, is not anti-hierarchy per se. Not all social hierarchies are problematic from an othering and belonging perspective. A society that valorizes service, ethical leadership, or caring professions above some others is not one that we would necessarily object to. Rather, our concern is with social-group-based hierarchies that entrench intergroup inequality or subordination on a durable and categorical basis.

and active participation. We now turn to specific interventions that can promote both broad belonging in practice as well as help build support for a vision of belonging across society. It is not a form of cultural chauvinism or imperialism to observe that belonging depends upon a culture in which privileged social groups do not simply impose their will upon less advantaged groups. A society cannot hold itself free of critique by justifying its othering as a cultural practice.

———————

To pursue a paradigm of belongness requires a deliberate effort and strong commitment to that end. It must serve as an aspirational ideal, which, like many ideals, orients our actions and guides our efforts, even if that ideal is never perfectly achieved.* As Christine Wong Yap observes, "Like happiness, belonging isn't something that happens to you, which you have no power to increase. Belonging often happens because of intention, investment, support, generosity, and cooperation."[87] In short, every sector of our society, but especially our critical institutions, must be drafted into the effort.

In the short term, our goal should be to multiply sites of belonging and diminish societal practices of othering. This means deliberate "rehumanization" strategies, or efforts to "humanizing the other," challenging and rejecting negative representations and stereotypes of certain social groups. As noted before, belongingness interventions are more than equity interventions. In addition to structural and material conditions, they have a psychological and/or affective component. This means not only changing perceptions of othered groups in the broader society but also the perceptions of the othered group themselves. A prime example of how we might do this is by sending messages to out-groups that they belong and are welcome in our community and society.

In an effort to improve academic performance and graduation rates among its marginalized student populations, the University of Texas began

———————

* There mere pursuit of such a goal can have salutary effects, or what Jim Sidanius and Felicia Pratto call "hierarchy attenuating" effects, which can reduce or diminish othering and enhance the potential for belonging, even if it is never perfectly achieved. Sidanius and Pratto, *Social Dominance*, 104.

reaching out to at-risk students with welcoming messages.[88] Known as the "mindset intervention," researchers transmitted a series of messages to targets who they felt might have been at risk for dropping out. Those messages affirmed that they deserved to be on campus and were capable of academically succeeding. The message worked, and produced many positive observed effects.

The basis of this intervention was research that discovered that student performance was impacted by self-doubts of one's academic potential. This simple belonging-affirming messaging not only improved academic performance but also improved student health, with those who had received the message having significantly fewer doctor's visits in the study period.[89] Other so-called value-affirming messages have been established to have similarly salutary effects.[90]

As useful as they may be, there are also limits to the UT mindset intervention as an exemplar of belonging. In the intervention, messages were transmitted that affirmed recognition and visibility in a way designed to strengthen the sense of connection. But the intervention was largely unidirectional. It lacked the participatory component that ultimately generates a more fulsome sense of belonging. Thus the mindset intervention fails to meet our fourth element to our definition of belonging, but it could be combined with empowerment efforts to cultivate agency as well.

––––––––

The most obvious way in which this is expressed is through the constituting or reconstituting process, as when a community forms a government or constitution that bounds them together in a new form. But even when members join an existing community, belongingness can only exist when new members have the capacity to shape the future direction of the organization, institution, or community.

In that sense, belonging requires some stake—some alignment with the values, purpose, history, or mission of the group as it currently exists. For example, when one of the authors of this book joined the American Civil Liberties Union (ACLU) as the national legal director, that author embraced core tenets of the organization, even as he attempted to move the organization into new fields and new areas of work. The organization, in turn, made space for this.

It is this element—not just voice, but a meaningful ability to shape the institution or community to which they belong—that moves belonging, as a paradigm, fully away from and distinctive from a paradigm of inclusion. Recall that inclusion can arise in a form of "guest membership." As effective as the mindset interventions proved, they mainly turned anxious guests into welcome confident guests. In a private setting, guests are not full members, but admitted on a basis of conditionality or the prerogatives of full members. This conditionality is absent in a belonging paradigm. Belonging entails full membership, and with that the ability and capacity to engage as a full participant in shaping the vision, goals, values, and norms of that to which they belong.

But belonging does not necessarily mean that such agency gives rise to or requires the right to make demands upon that thing—that organization, institution, or community—and expect it to acquiesce. There are two reasons for this. First, having agency or a stake does not mean that one individual or group has the right to determine the direction for all. Rather, it is a right to contribute or shape the direction. The participatory element of belonging does not necessarily mean that the demands or asks of the marginalized group are adopted without amendment or compromise, but they are at least considered and weighed. This is an important but subtle distinction. Full belonging means having the same rights and privileges as any other members—no more and no less. It confers a right of full standing, rather than conditional or partial standing.

At a deeper level, the right to make demands connotes a separation inconsistent with a belongingness paradigm. In a space of belonging, the right to make demands is of oneself and community, rather than of the something external. For example, when students demanded changes at universities in the 1960s, they were asking for belonging because they felt that they did not have it. They wanted representation—a student senate—but they also wanted more than inclusion and representation—they wanted transformation. This is the genesis of ethnic studies departments.[91] Again, if they succeed, their success must yield a shared responsibility that they must then partially shoulder.

Belonging is a set of processes that engender the right to make contributions to and shape that which we seek to belong to. But belonging cannot remain a remote aspiration that simply guides or orients our actions and strategies. Belonging must and can be made real. If it is simply a utopian aspiration, in the sense of an unattainable ideal, then it is not a paradigm that can solve, let alone mitigate, the practical problems of othering in the world.

Institutional Belongingness

Belongingness must be more than expressive or aspirational; it must be institutional and institutionalized as well. Institutions play a critical role in advancing belonging. Most obviously, they provide for a well-ordered society by organizing conflict through politics rather than violence, and can advance egalitarian norms through policies enforced by the rule of law.[92]

At a more fundamental level, institutions generate and inspire social trust or erode that same trust.[93] Social trust is the glue that holds societies together. Those without it experience not simply a lack of faith in government, but also social alienation. Yuval Levin, a conservative scholar, asserts that "many of our struggles seem rooted in relational problems. Loneliness and isolation, mistrust and suspicion, alienation and polarization . . . fall into the blind spots of our individualist culture [as a] crisis of connectedness."[94] Harking back to Robert Putnam's landmark classic, *Bowling Alone*,[95] Levin laments the state of social disrepair in America, but does not call for an amorphous reweaving of American relations. Rather, his book *A Time to Build* calls for focused attention on institutions and institutional renewal.

Levin argues that we can't simply build social trust or even belonging out of a desire for it. Willpower is not enough. As he explains: "What we are missing is not simply connectedness but a structure of social life: a way to give, shape, place and purpose to the things we do together."[96] The failure, he says, is not a failure of connection, but a failure of institutions.[97] Therefore, our solution must lie there as well.

Levin's main argument, buttressed by data of falling rates of trust in key institutions such as Congress, government, police, military, corporations, and even religious institutions, is that our key institutions are no longer working well. Even if they perform their jobs within specified parameters (for example, make and sell goods, pass laws, protect public safety, etc.), they have lost their "formative" component. As he explains: "healthy institutions often function as molds for the people inside them."[98] The formative nature of institutions is that they create culture, trust, ethical frameworks, and even normative behaviors, obligations, and responsibilities. The problem is that most of our institutions no longer do this. Instead of acting as "molds," they have instead become "platforms"; not as "formative," but as "performative."

In this paradigm, the "institution-as-platform" means that people within institutions strive to use the institutions to advance personal celebrity, wealth, and stature rather than to create community and common purpose. For example, universities, corporations, government agencies, and hospitals are now vehicles for making "stars": celebrity doctors, academics, politicians, or CEOs. They advance individuals rather than the greater mass of people that inhabit them. This results in a lack of connection and belonging, since these institutions are not unjustifiably viewed as advancing narrow rather than collective interests. The challenge, then, of institutional revival is to rewire institutions to do the latter.

———

Adrienne Clarkson makes a similar point in her book on belonging.[99] As the former governor general of Canada, she counsels against trying to rely on intimate love as a basis for belonging. Instead she calls for reciprocal trust that can be practiced at a national level. The vehicle for this must be institutions and norms, which can support this for the larger society as opposed to the tendency for institutions and norms to promote distrust and competition.

Part of the impetus for the American common schools movement of the nineteenth century was the view that public schools would serve as molds for citizenship and civic life, not simply institutions for inculcating human capital and skills. This was a view held by a line of figures as diverse as Thomas Jefferson and Thomas Dewey, each recognizing the essential and vital role of public common schools to democratic life.[100] The centrality of public education as a formative mold was also recognized by the Supreme Court in its landmark *Brown* decision:

> Today, education is perhaps the most important function of state and local governments. Compulsory school attendance laws and the great expenditures for education both demonstrate our recognition of the importance of education to our democratic society. It is required in the performance of our most basic public responsibilities, even service in the armed forces. It is the very foundation of good citizenship. Today it is a principal instrument in awakening the child to cultural values, in preparing him for later professional training, and in helping him to adjust normally to his environment.[101]

Institutions are bonding agents in society—bringing people together in joint endeavors for the collective good. Segregated schools were formative institutions in the worst possible sense: socialization and institutionalizing separation and segregation. Unfortunately, too many of our contemporary institutions function like pre-*Brown* institutions: tending to pull us apart rather than bring us together, reinforcing class and geographic differences and advantages rather than binding us in a common endeavor. To take but one example, America today builds more prisons than universities. Little wonder so many of our institutions seem to be dysfunctional, decaying from within, or under significant pressure or attack.

Institutional pressure and dysfunction can be an impetus for renovation and reform. Americans in the late eighteenth century and early nineteenth century experienced a dizzying period of institutional innovation partly by opportunity but also by necessity. Not only was this the period of the development and adoption of the Articles of Confederation and the United States Constitution, but the colonies-cum-states were experimenting with constitutional and political forms. As one historian put it, that period was "the most creative period of constitutionalism in American history and one of the most creative in modern western history."[102]

Americans in the early twentieth century also experienced a period of great institutional renewal, known as the "association" movement, as novel associations, from those of neighborhoods and homeowners to those encompassing colleges and universities, came into being.[103] They formed organized to protect interests and advocate for policy and reform. Unfortunately, we are now in a period of institutional deceleration and decay. The forms and novelty of institutions are severely lacking. We need both energy and innovation to not only rebuild existing institutions but also create new ones capable of meeting the challenges of the moment, not least of which is the problem of othering and belonging.

———

The institutions we live with today foster inertia because they create the wrong kind of belonging. Australian anthropologist Ghassan Hage distinguishes between "homely belonging" and "governmental belonging."[104] This former is the ability to experience genuine membership and to feel "at home," enjoying security, community, familiarity, and opportunity. The other is "governmental belonging," which is a sense of ownership or entitlement to participate in consequential decisions, including the management of the space of the nation and who can belong there. This is a distinction between being granted national membership, on one hand, and being part of the collective that does the granting of membership, on the other. Hage wants to draw attention to the fact that these two are not coextensive, even in liberal multicultural societies. If we cultivate the former without the latter we will fail to at making belonging a deeper norm. Homely belonging lacks the empowerment and agency we call for.

Above all, we must redevelop the habit of institutional innovation and renovation. The fundamental, core problem is that the containers that bind our people—the institutions that serve—are weak or fraying. They are cracked, and crumbling. We live in a period of history where institutions are under attack and distrusted. We need a new set of containers—a new set of institutions, narratives, and stories about ourselves that are strong enough to weave our peoples together and create belonging. We must pay attention to the containers.

———

One container that has done a far better job of binding people together as an institution, and which may be one of the most resilient in American society, is the military. Although an often-troubling instrument of American desire for dominance and violence, the military, more than almost any other national institution, has managed cohesive diversity throughout the ranks. Although not without problems (sexual assault is a serious problem), the military is a unique institution that epitomizes the best parts of deliberate integration and bonding. Military bases and training facilities bring people from every sector of our society. As one Vietnam War veteran recounted:

> I was drafted into the U.S. Army at the height of the Vietnam War. Trained as an infantryman, I landed in a combat unit hard up against the DMZ. Though I didn't always share my comrades' worldviews, I learned how to rely on, work with and love the hillbillies, urban blacks, Native Americans, Chicanos, farm boys and misfits who had been thrown together in the platoon I came to think of as a family.[105]

More than that, the ties drawn within this institution are strong because the stakes—literally life and death—are so great. Unlike some institutions or the corporate sector, the military is integrated through every echelon of its ranks. This may be one of the most impressive accomplishments in our society: binding so many diverse people into a common purpose of honor. In short, the military not only directs people from different parts of society into the same place and same institution, but more than any other institution our society it naturally meets the conditions for positive intergroup contact.

Intergroup contact theory was first articulated in 1954 and later refined and developed by social psychologists to characterize the nature and conditions in which intergroup contact between peoples would reduce, rather than exacerbate, prejudice.[106] In the initial formulation, there were four such conditions: "equal status, intergroup cooperation, common goals, and support by social and institutional authorities." In what other institution can it be said that all four conditions exist to such a natural degree? Little wonder that the military—any nation's military—is a binding agent for social groups in that society.

The military not only draws from every sector of society, but it often draws from the least privileged sectors of society, which, in Western societies, comprise more people of color and immigrants. Thus it is a practical necessity that branches of the military tamp down ethnic and racial divisions and foster inclusion and belonging. This is true not just of the United States, but also of France.

In 1996, the French military ended compulsory recruitment and switched to a volunteer service, like the United States. In so doing, it began to recruit more heavily in working-class areas. The result is that children of Muslim immigrants from former French colonies became overrepresented, and now Muslims are believed to account for 15 to 20 percent of the force, roughly two to three times the Muslim share of the total French population.[107] A cohesive force could not be sustained without an institutional commitment to diversity and inclusion.

Even in "colorblind" and fractious France, where the immigrant diaspora of its former colonial projects live in starkly different neighborhoods and conditions than legacy Europeans, the military serves a similar role as it does in the United States in bringing people from different sectors of society together for a common role. But the French military goes a step further and is one of the few spaces where France's *laïcité*, or insistent public secularism, has given way to accommodation and toward belonging.

While much of French society has made it more difficult for Muslims to practice their religions—making it harder to build and open mosques, to practice religious customs in public institutions, and so forth—the French military has gone in the opposite direction.[108] Work schedules are adjusted to allow Muslims to pray on schedule. Religiously observant food is served. Muslim holidays are recognized. As an officer in the French Navy told the *New York Times*, "The tolerance that we find in the armed forces, we don't find it outside."[109]

———

The strong sense of purpose and joint initiative that comes from the military as an institution begins to point the way to how we can institutionalize belonging. Despite reservations and even deep concerns we may have about the use of American military power, sometimes in service of othering, there may still be things we can learn about building belonging from military institutions. How might we engage in institutional innovations drawing on the lessons of the military? Are there other public service platforms that might build belonging without othering?

An alternative is a different form of compulsory (or noncompulsory) public service. In his 2020 Democratic primary campaign for the presidency, military veteran Pete Buttigieg floated the expanding national service. Citing his time in the US Navy, Buttigieg explicitly endorsed the benefits to citizenship and communal bonds from service programs.[110] David Brooks argues that public service would not only serve these worthy ends, but also open up innovation and dynamism in our society.[111]

More recently, General Stanley McChrystal called on America to provide a national service program for a million American young adults, arguing that it would be "the most important strategy we can implement to ensure the strength and security of our nation," after witnessing the turmoil of the 2020 election.[112] Some pundits have suggested a "mega-AmeriCorps" that could give new high school graduates hope, purpose, and experience and pull them out of the rat race of college as foregrounding their future.[113] There are details to be worked out, but such an initiative could transform our society into one of much greater belonging.

Structural Belonging

Beyond providing the formative context in which belonging gestates, institutions play another role in shaping belonging: they facilitate the creation and maintenance of more inclusive structures. Institutions are not simply entities with power, resources, and authority, like government agencies. Institutions are also paradigms or legal regimes that shape culture, influence the distribution of resources and power, or facilitate collective decision-making.

For example, antidiscrimination norms embodied in civil rights laws play a significant role in promoting institutional inclusion, and ultimately, belonging. While it is true that such norms can provoke backlash, to the extent that they are successful at tamping down overt discrimination, they generate new norms and behaviors. The expressive component of such legislative achievements is not trivial. The effort needed to enact such regimes requires the mobilization of not simply legislative majorities, but significant public will. Thus the civil rights movement's legislative achievements of the 1960s reflected (and helped engender) changing attitudes and viewpoints.[114] The same is true for the wave of same-sex marriage legislation of the last two decades, culminating in a landmark Supreme Court decision constitutionalizing same-sex marriage in the United States.[115]

Yet antidiscrimination provisions, no matter how symbolic or substantive in terms of changing the societal fabric, rarely express true belonging. At most they serve as mechanisms for inclusion—for bringing members of formerly excluded groups into institutions. That does not necessarily put them at the center of societal regard.

Politically powerful interest groups rarely need to assert their influence or voice in order to persuade local, state, or even federal officials from representing their interests. Policies that would be anathema to those groups are rarely advanced, let alone seriously considered. The same is not true of marginalized groups. Specific norms or institutional rules could be considered to achieve a similar effect.

In this regard, a distinction should be drawn between antidiscrimination provisions, which protect discrete groups in particular contexts (such as women in employment), and more proactive or prophylactic measures. For example, the Americans with Disabilities Act, one of the most successful, landmark civil rights laws in American history, did more than prohibit discrimination; it required proactive accommodations to ensure that merely "equal" treatment did not produce or reinforce inequality.

The accommodations required by the ADA are ubiquitous: from access ramps to parking spots to the width of bathroom stalls and the design of new homes and buildings.[116] They have literally changed the built environment, but also the norms and expectations about it. Accessibility is now a design standard across American society.

And while certain accommodations may have been intended for persons with physical disabilities, they often make life easier for everyone. Closed captioning, elevators, and better lightning have made life easier for the able-bodied.[117] In an assessment of the elevators installed for a New York City subway station in 2013 over the course of an hour, a wheelchair user observed that "I have not seen a person with a disability yet ride that elevator. It's all been walking people."[118] A women with a baby and stroller used the elevator to reach the subway level, and it is assumed that people with vertigo or joint or knee problems, or even just the elderly, used the elevator.

The main point, however, is that the ADA institutionalized inclusion—and perhaps moved us toward greater belonging—by doing more than simply prohibiting certain forms of discrimination; it required proactive accommodations. There are other ways in which our law does this, and these are models for greater belonging.

———

The Affordable Care Act (also known as "Obamacare") amended the Fair Labor Standards Act (a New Deal–era law) to require employers to pro-vide nursing mothers a reasonable break time to express breast milk after the birth of a child as well a place for an employee to do that.[119] This 2010 law has resulted in lactation rooms and other accommodations for nursing mothers beyond a simple bromide not to "discriminate." In this case, the provision goes beyond formal equality, since there is no similar set of re-quirements (or needs) for men or non-nursing mothers.

Formal guarantees of equal protection or equal rights are often insuffi-cient to create inclusive structures. In those cases, what is required is either an accommodations regime or a process that gives *greater* attention or pro-tections to particular groups. Two notable, but quite different, examples are the Religious Freedom Restoration Act (RFRA) and Section 4 of the Voting Rights Act (before it was neutered).[120]

The RFRA was a law designed to protect religious practice and religious belief in several important ways. But the main provision requires that gov-ernment laws—at any level—do not substantially burden religious practice, and that if a generally applicable law is passed that has a "disparate impact" on a particular racial group in service of some important governmental in-terest, that interest must be served in the least restrictive or burdensome manner possible.[121] In other words, the law requires that well-intended leg-islation try to avoid interfering with religious activity, and that if it must, it should be done in the narrowest manner possible to avoid burdening that activity or practice. This is essentially analogous to the notion that laws that have a "disparate" racial impact be avoided unless proven to be necessary.

The difference is that even if they are shown to be necessary, the RFRA requires that they be implemented in the least burdensome manner available.

The RFRA is a beautiful example of a piece of structural legislation that requires government to consider the impact laws and policy have on social groups. Laws that are implemented carelessly, and with little thought for the impact or effect, should be more carefully scrutinized, especially with respect to religious activity. The RFRA requires proactive consideration of the impact a law or policy may have on a group's needs. The same concept could be extended on a broader basis, including to other marginalized social groups. Indeed, that is exactly the purpose of disparate-impact laws—they require government to avoid well-intended policies that harm marginalized groups.

Finally, the Voting Rights Act is another paradigm for structural belonging. Like the legislation just reviewed, the Voting Rights Act did more than simply prohibit discrimination on the basis of race in voting processes, procedures, and accommodations; it also provided an additional layer of institutional protection. Any proposed change to a procedure, no matter how seemingly innocuous, in a voting district that had a nefarious and proven history of discrimination, had to be screened and approved by either a federal court or the US Department of Justice.[122]

This procedure, known as "pre-clearance," was designed to ensure that no clever enactment would operate in a discriminatory or unfair manner against racial minorities, especially those that had been the subject of discrimination for so long. Section 4 of the VRA established a formula for pre-clearance. Unfortunately, the Supreme Court struck down the formula used to determine covered jurisdictions, and Congress has yet to replace it (although the late congressman John Lewis had proposed a bill that would do exactly that).[123]

The point is that the underlying principle, pre-clearance, much like the standard required by the RFRA or the accommodations regimes required by the Affordable Care Act through the Fair Labor Standards Act or the ADA, are notable instances in which federal legislation moves well beyond the simple norm of antidiscrimination, to require structural inclusion, and ultimately, greater belonging by extending regard to possible impacts on marginalized groups. It formalizes the regard and concern that must be part of any belonging paradigm.

The Practice of Bridging

However, creating structures for belonging or a belongingness policy agenda, while necessary, is also insufficient. As important as many of these structural interventions may be, in some respects they remain too shallow. Such structures are necessary ballast for societies that do not have belonging at their heart or are ambivalent about inclusion. Although legally potent remedies, many of these reforms are weak prophylactics for cultural change.

In addition to institutional or structural policy interventions designed to gestate social trust or extend societal concern and regard more widely, belonging requires deliberate practice. One of the critical steps toward reducing othering and promoting belonging is a practice known as "bridging." Bridging is a particular form of social capital which describes connections that link people across a cleavage that typically divides society (such as race, or class, or religion).[124]

Bridging is a practice where members of different social groups are not only brought into contact, but build social connections and rapport. Thus bridging activities can be as simple as an interfaith dinner or a multicultural concert or as complex and institutionally embedded as a leadership training program or an experiential course on cultural differences. The point is that members of different social groups are compelled, through bridging, to extend their attention and build connections across the boundaries of difference.

The heart of bridging is listening to and learning from and about the person perceived as different or even as "the other." Listening means hearing their story, not to confirm their facts or perspective, but to affirm their humanity. Listening is sometimes confused with agreement, although the former does not require the latter. The simple act of being heard has a powerful impact on both the speaker and the listener. Active and empathetic listening is perceived and felt as a form of caring and regard, and it builds trust.[125] Remarkably, it may have a greater tendency to induce change or shift opinion than listening for purpose of persuasion, to change a person's opinion.[126] Listening to persuade is not bridging, because it does not convey care or build trust.

The emphasis in bridging practice is centering stories and narratives rather than facts and data. The goal is not to arrive at "truth," but rather to better understand how another group sees itself and express what is important to it. Thus the groups do not necessarily have to agree on a set of facts, but they should strive to better understand each other's perspective. They should seek to recognize the identity of the group they are bridging with, even if they dispute the claims that accompany that identity narrative. We can acknowledge each other's humanity even in our disagreement.

One notable example of a bridging effort is the New Baptist Covenant, a movement launched in 2007 to bring Black and white Baptist churches into conversation and, ultimately, into covenant agreements.[127] But in the initial phase, the idea was that the congregations get to know each other, learn more about their shared histories, and engage in projects and trips together.[128]

The practice of bridging requires a curated space, a set of ground rules, and a strong moderator or facilitator. In its initial stages, bridging is not about resolving conflict. Over time, the practice of bridging will build the trust needed to negotiate such matters, and ultimately create the connections and trust that engender a wider sense of belonging. As groups get better at bridging, they will find it easier to bridge with more groups—even across longer bridges.

Bridging is one of the pillars to create a culture of belonging. Belonging calls for being heard and seen, as our four-element definition suggests. The deliberate practice of bridging strengthens our capacity to hold and maintain an empathetic space, something our societies desperately need, and people broadly want and desire. Too many of the spaces we inhabit— neighborhoods, schools, workplaces, politics—are defined by zero-sum competition and status-seeking rather than mutual recognition. We must inculcate bridging practices within all of our critical institutions. The more we do it, the better we will get, and the more the benefits will become manifest.

Critically, however, bridging does not mean that any individual or group must give up an identity that is meaningful to them. It is a practice for increasing empathy, compassion, and common ground that begins to erase lines drawn between groups on the basis of fear. It does not deny difference, but rather recontextualizes and softens it.

––––––––

The necessity of bridging does not mean that bridging is possible in every social context. Bridging would be impossible or unreasonable in a context in which one group is threatening another with immediate violence (although one of the more notable instances is the so-called 1992 "Watts truce" between Los Angeles gangs, which resulted in a dramatic reduction of gang violence).[129] Similarly, bridging does not mean one cannot take a political or moral position against a particular practice or ideology. While we embrace the practice and concept of bridging, we reject the ideology of group-based supremacy and dominance. This is a fundamental guardrail in any ideology or practice relating to group-based affiliation.

Bridging is an important form of social capital identified by social scientists, but it is not the only one. In addition to "linking" social capital, another common form of social capital is known as "bonding."[130] This is when members of a group turn inward, and focus mainly on each other and themselves. There is also a practice we call "breaking," which goes further than "bonding," and is actually the antithesis of social capital—it is where members of a group not only turn inward, but explicitly push members of other groups away. Bridging is the only way we will turn back the tide of a world of breaking, where social capital is degraded and destroyed, as we will describe next chapter.

We call for a world where everyone belongs; where we belong to each other, and ultimately, where that circle of widening concern extends even beyond the human realm, including to the earth itself.* The next two chap-

––––––––

* In our caring for each other, we must eventually come to recognize that caring for the planet is joint responsibility and point of connection that we all share. We recognize that our discussion of othering and belonging in this book has focused on these concepts principally in relation to humanity and the human realm and not to the environment or the so-called "natural world." Although beyond our current scope, these are themes we plan to take up in future work.

ters delve into how we rebuild inclusive identities and narratives to support those identities and advance a belongingness paradigm. In particular, the next chapter grapples with the most complex subject of the book: the deeply interrelated projects of building new narratives, identities, and, ultimately, selves with that of the structures, policies, and practices set out here.

SIX

From the Other to the Self(ves)

This book outlines the problem of othering and makes the case for the necessity of belonging. Both the ongoing problem of othering and the multiple crises of nonbelonging (despair, loneliness, fragmentation, and so forth) arise out of the same soil: the problems of identity and the relations among people.

The previous chapter teased out the elements of belonging and explored institutional and programmatic reforms, initiatives, and interpersonal and cultural practices that can lead to a world of greater belonging. But achieving that goal will require deeper change than widely embracing belonging as a global norm or the implementation a belonging policy agenda. This chapter digs into this deeper terrain.

Recall that the "other" is constituted by the othering process. Further, our group identities are relational, constituted in relation to each other. We also described the processes that constitute "boundary work," or the delineation of social group identity. Chapter 4 showed how this works in the real world, illustrating how othering is set into motion by elites wishing to build and hold power, initiating mechanisms that distribute resources, power, and meaning.

One implication, noted but not explored, is that the othering process does more than constitute the other; it also constitutes the non-other, dominant or higher-status groups. Every step of the othering process is relational. Both the "other" and the more favored "we" group (and indeed the nature and sense of the "we" itself) is constituted by the same processes and set of mechanisms. What this means is simple yet profound: the problem of othering cannot be solved by simply fixing the condition or situation of the marginalized or subordinated group. To believe this is a serious mistake.

Consider, for example, what was once called the "Jewish Question" or the "Jewish Problem."[1] This was the issue of how to manage the treatment of Jewish peoples in Europe, especially against a backdrop of pervasive antisemitic sentiment. Thus, the Nazis' "Final Solution" genocidal plan was chillingly framed as the answer to that question or problem. But as this example illustrates, the "problem" was not with the Jews of Europe, but rather with the Gentiles, and the Germans in particular. And so it is across the board with every case of othering. In that particular case, however, the attack on Jewish peoples was a way that German elites, particularly those in the National Socialist party, fostered belonging among non-Jews, creating a greater sense of coherence and belonging for the in-group.

In short, the problem of othering cannot be solved simply by improving the material conditions of the outgroup (although that can greatly ameliorate the effects of othering). While such efforts can reduce disparities and other indicia of inequality, they do not entail true belonging. When people feel invisible or unheard, their material conditions and economic well-being are not more important than their need for recognition, respect, and agency.* When social groups are situated differently in society in terms of power and status, any belonging intervention must begin with a recognition of the inherent relationship between groups. We must reject any denial of our relationality as a way of ignoring social cleavages or the need to bridge them. True belonging must touch and transform non-othered peoples as well as othered peoples; it must be universal rather than targeted.[2] How we do this is the focus of this chapter.

In the last chapter we explored the often-paradoxical interaction of belonging and othering. Belonging is such a powerful and fundamental human need that it is too easily weaponized to deepen or exacerbate othering. When

---

* Recall our discussion of thymotic needs in the last chapter.

this occurs, bonds of belonging are strengthened between members of one group while processes that engender group-based inequality and marginalization are strengthened for others. As we explained in the last chapter, the goal, then, is not simply greater belonging, but belonging without othering.

To create a world of belonging without othering will require a reweaving of our identities and a reconstitution of our sense of self. The very same processes of group-based identity formation and affiliation are what constitute the self as well. In other words, it is not only our group identities that are socially constructed, but also our sense of self. An exploration of the nature of the self is therefore the first topic of this chapter, a difficult and challenging matter that we have reserved until the last possible moment.*

A Brief History of the Modern Self

The "self," as most of us experience it, is surprisingly a relatively recent innovation in human history. Beginning around 1600, a revolution occurred in Western thought that forever changed the conception of the self, especially in the West.[3] Although there were many contributory sources, one of the leading lights of this revolution was a French mathematician, philosopher, and scientist named René Descartes.

Writing in the first half of the seventeenth century, Descartes is probably most famous for his phrase "cogito, ergo sum," or, translated from Latin, "I think, therefore I am."[4] Descartes was writing in the midst of a period we know as the Scientific Revolution, and helped usher in what is known as the Enlightenment (also known as the Age of Reason), which is the extension of scientific thinking and rationality to the many other realms and domains of life, from politics and law to the social sciences and the humanities.[5] These developments helped pull Europe out of the Middle Ages and triggered a furious period of invention and innovation that has hardly abated since.

---

*Many nuances and subtleties that were only previously hinted at should become clearer by the end of this chapter, as should the horizon of possibilities and the pathways for change toward a society of greater belonging.

Descartes's famous phrase emerged out of a deep inquiry into, and rumination on, the nature of existence. Descartes concluded that his capacity to think and reason proved the fact of his existence. In so doing, he—perhaps unwittingly—ushered in a new understanding of the self. His core self was primarily a mind, and a mind that reasoned and was itself accessible to reason and introspection. Philosophers sometimes refer to this as the Cartesian self or the Cartesian ego.[6] Perhaps a more accurate appellation would be the Western self.

Descartes's philosophical writings contributed to the formulation of several "dualisms" that are now embedded in Western thought and at the foundation of the Enlightenment, including mind over body and reason over emotion.[7] Building on Descartes's foundation, influential Enlightenment philosophers such as Immanuel Kant and Jean-Jacques Rousseau played critical roles in these developments.[8] Through the influence of the Enlightenment on the American and French revolutions, among other conduits, these assumptions migrated into our law, politics, and social sciences, where people are generally regarded as individuals, and as rational agents capable of restraining their "passions," or as actors seeking to maximize their utility. The social science of economics is in large part based upon these assumptions.[9] Ethics of justice and rules of law, including guilt, innocence, and culpability, are as well.[10]

Although Descartes helped distinguish between the idea of an inner self separate from society, other thinkers contributed to the valorization of the former over the latter. Martin Luther and the Protestant Reformation emphasized direct, individual communion with God over that mediated by religious authority, and therefore put the onus of religious faith—and salvation—on the individual.[11] The enlightenment philosopher Jean-Jacques Rousseau helped secularize this moral inversion, giving the "inner self . . . priority. . . over social convention."[12] Rousseau emphasized the conforming and constraining influences of society's codes and mores, and sought to free individuals from those restraints in order to achieve a greater good and reach a higher moral standard. Thus, both recognition of the individual self and moral autonomy were requisite to the development of the Western self, as embedded in law and ethics.

Another Enlightenment philosopher whose writings contributed to the modern self is John Locke, a British physician. Locke introduced the notion of a *tabula rasa*, or blank slate, as the primal state of the human mind prior to the imprint of society.[13] This revolutionary idea meant that human beings were largely shaped by their environments, and not by racial endowments or innate moral predispositions. This was both a much more generous view of humanity than was typical of the time as well as the root of the social construction of identity and the self.

But for Locke this also meant that people enjoy free will, and are responsible for their own actions and decisions—that we are a product of our own making as reasoning individuals. Thus, the separate, autonomous, reasoning individual is the essence of the self for these philosophers. What was left implicit, however, is that the Western self was also white, male, and able-bodied.[14] Locke emphasized property ownership as a condition of personhood status. This was based on his theory of the self-as-property, and his foundational assertion that "every Man has a Property in his own Person."[15] It follows from this that any person who does not own their self is not a full autonomous individual. This leaves women, children, and non-white peoples outside of this conception of personhood. This is why Imani Perry regards Locke as "the architect of patriarchy."[16]

Women fell on the "wrong" side of the Cartesian dualism, regarded as emotional creatures rather than rational individuals capable of governing themselves and society.[17] And non-white people, especially Africans and Native Americans, were widely regarded as backward peoples from barbaric and uncivilized societies, incapable of reasoning without emotions, by Enlightenment thinkers and their successors.[18] This served as the justification for slavery and subjugation, and limiting the right to vote and full citizenship only to those deemed worthy of it.

Although modern Western societies have jettisoned these associations formally, by extending full political rights to women and non-white people, they persist implicitly in many cases. It shows up when, for example, commentators assume that some societies are less suited for democratic self-governance.[19] And to the extent that societies or nations are based on an alternative set of principles, such as communitarianism rather than individualism, or harmony with nature rather than dominance and exploitation, then they are not infrequently viewed with suspicion or as backward or less advanced.

Moreover, even as the group-based associations have been formally discarded, the assumptions regarding the nature of the self (as rational, autonomous, accessible, etc.) persist. And although newer fields in social science, such as behavioral economics and implicit social cognition, are founded upon challenges to many assumptions regarding the rational, accessible, autonomous self, it remains the prevailing model of the self in the West.[20] While these critiques are noteworthy, they are largely peripheral to our discussion here.[21] Although we regard this theory of the self as deeply flawed, the important point here is that the construction of the Western "self" is inconsistent with our theory of identity development, and is a serious impediment to a belongingness paradigm.

———

In Chapter 3, we argued that social group identity development, meaning the formation of affiliative identities, was an intersubjective, social process, shaped by the push and pull of countless assertions, contestations, and interactions. These dynamics are a large part of the othering process. They fix the boundaries of group identity, shape the meanings that attach to those identities, and the relations between groups.* The idea of "group positionality" suggests the relational nature of social identities. It turns out that it is not simply group identities that are constituted in this way; our very sense of self is as well.

The American sociologist George Herbert Mead explained this idea 1934, where he wrote that "[t]he self, as that which can be an object to itself, is essentially a social structure, and it arises in social experience."[22] In his view, the self can only arise in a social context through social interactions with others. This insight has been elaborated upon by other philosophers and scholars.

Contrary to the idea of an authentic inner self, the political philosopher Francis Fukuyama observes that what most people "believe to be their true

———

* "Fix" may be an overstatement, but they create a stabilized matrix where these relations can exist in a way that allows for shared understandings, even as some individuals or groups strive to contest or challenge them.

inner self is actually constituted by their relationships with other people, and by the norms and expectations that those others provide."[23] The philosopher Charles Taylor explained in his opus *The Sources of the Self* that the process of "selfing" (of creating the self) is dialogical or intersubjective as opposed to monological.[24] The notion of a "dialogical self" is meant to suggest that we are constituted by and through our relationship to others rather than self-constructed in the Lockean sense. This dialogical sense of the self is captured by the idea that to have a self, we have to be seen by others as a self.[25] The reverse is also true; to see yourself, you also have to see other selves. The traditional African saying, Ubuntu, meaning "I am because you are," captures this idea, while also underscoring a sense of deep unity between people. Without connection, not only does one lose a sense of belonging, but also a sense of a self.

Part of being an adult is realizing that there are other selves in the world. This is the foundation of empathy, the golden rule, as well as Kant's categorical imperative.[26] But, to recognize and differentiate ourselves, we must first recognize others. So, the story of seeing oneself is already collective and social.[27] Our sense of self is far more relational than the disembodied Cartesian ego would admit. The key to knowing ourselves is not interiority or introspection, as Descartes believed, but rather the opposite: it is appreciating how our identities are shaped and reshaped by the social worlds we inhabit and are inextricably embedded within.

We suggested in Part I that many of our social identities are not just relational, but are defined in relation to each other. In both the United States and South Africa, whiteness was constituted by the social meanings of Blackness and/or African slavery. And in Europe, we saw how the identity of Christian, especially during the Crusades, was defined by contrast with Muslim and Jew. And how in India, upper castes are defined in contrast to lower ones. Recall further Gerhard Falk's theory of stigma, that stigma serves the social purpose of helping differentiate between insiders and outsiders, and thereby helps bind together disparate peoples into a new social group. The stigmatic exclusion of others creates the valorization of the favored group. In this sense, the identity of the insider group is bound up with the identity of the excluded group.

Although we experience our sense of self as individual and personal, it is not much of a leap in logic to recognize that if group identities are generated intersubjectively and socially, our individual sense of self is ultimately shaped in a similar way. After all, our sense of self is a compound, composite, or synthesis of many of these socially constructed identities.[28] And since these group identities that people affiliate with are also a product of the othering process, that means that our sense of self is also shaped by the othering process. In conclusion, selfing and othering are conjoined and related processes.[29]

Both the work of selfing and othering is largely a social project. Contrary to prevailing conception of the modern, Western self, the "self" is not only relational rather than autonomous and independent; it is also multiple or plural rather than unitary or single. Recognizing this is a key to belonging.

The Multiple Self

We have already emphasized the point that there is no such thing as a homogeneous community—that is, a community or society without social diversity or socially relevant distinctions. Even the most ethnically, racially, linguistically, and religiously cohesive communities contain diversity and difference along multiple dimensions, starting with gender identities, age groupings, and sexual orientation. Every society is plural. This principle also applies to the self.

We have just noted that our sense of self is partly a compound of our various identities. Even if we regard "the self" as a "thing," it is multiply faceted, like a gemstone with different colors and aspects depending upon the side, angle, and lighting. These selves come to the fore in different contexts and situations. In some contexts, certain facets of our "selves," certain identities we hold, become salient while others are quieted. This is what George Herbert Mead meant when he wrote, "There are all sorts of different selves answering to all sorts of different social reactions. It is the social process itself that is responsible for the appearance of the self; it is not there as a self apart from this type of experience."[30]

For example, when attending a parent-teacher conference, the identity of "parent" (or teacher) becomes salient, while it loses its social significance in a work meeting where children are absent. When traveling abroad, national identity (such as "American") for tourists becomes more salient than when sitting at home watching television or attending a local church service. Similarly, racial or religious identities will sometimes feel more salient when in diverse spaces or in contexts where that identity is implicated, such as a classroom discussion or a religious service.

Our different identities come to the fore when they are relevant or called forth. They may be relevant because they provide a basis for connection (such as familial or caring relationships or in communal spaces of worship), or because of an identity threat. We have seen how various identity threats, like patterns of discrimination or threats of violence, can impel people to make connections for solidarity, strength, and mutual protection. Thus, the Russian invasion of Ukraine helped reinforce Ukrainian national identity.

Contrary to the Cartesian ego, there is no such thing as a unitary or singular self. Each of us holds multiple identities *and* multiple selves.[31] We contain a myriad of identities and selves within us, which are activated in different contexts and relationships.[32]

Part of healthy human development and identity development is experimentally asserting different social identities, observing the reactions of others to these assertions, and ultimately striving to weave them together. The more integrated and consistent our identities are felt to be, the more they are regarded by psychologists as "coherent" and "continuous."[33]

When circumstances or contexts make this difficult or impossible, the dissonance can be disorienting and stressful.[34] When gay and lesbian people feel pressure to conceal or tamp down parts of their selves, like the Black comedian Jerrod Carmichael reported feeling when coming out of the closet, that can be experienced in extremely disconcerting ways, such as self-hatred.[35] In order to belong, some members of marginalized groups are forced to suppress or hide parts of their selves.

In contrast, identity coherence feels soothing and affirming. In his account of the Occupy Wall Street protest movement, Jonathan Smucker observes that part of the appeal of the communal living in the occupied spaces was the sense of identity coherence that the Occupy community provided.[36] It allowed people to bring to the fore their core values and self-expression to every aspect of their daily life in ways that are extremely elusive in a messier world outside of Occupy.

In his telling, however, the sense of belonging generated in this unique community movement became counterproductive, even intoxicating. The sense of "psychic completion" experienced when protesters could center their social justice values and receive communal affirmation meant that many participants began to place greater value on the community that had been created than on the goal of transforming the broader society.[37] Smucker regards this shift as a major strategic error and failing of the movement, but blames the insularity and parochialism of the movement, which he sees as a by-product of the seductive nature of the community that had been established.

This problem arises in many social justice movements. We noted before that mobilization is easier when the group's perceived well-being depends upon broad solidarity. The call to action is often a rallying based upon identity and a perceived injustice or relative deprivation.[38] It is easier to mobilize people in response to a perceived identity threat than a "shared, complicated, positive vision."[39] This helps explains the paradox of why some marginalized identities are held harder and faster than the corresponding identities held by members of dominant or higher-status groups. If one's gender, race, or religion is a source of danger, then members of that group are more likely to be conscious of that identity and alert to threats.[40]

In the last chapter, we noted how the need to belong and seductive appeal of belonging in thick cultural units explains part of the appeal of reactionary movements and cults alike. To that we can add radical movements as well as social justice movements. Many social movements resist identity multiplicity and openness and implicitly endorse essentialist accounts of identity. They wonder: "without coherent, stable identities, how can we move forward in a political movement that matters?"[41]

Such questions are to the detriment of our very being. Not only do they deny our multiplicity and fluidity; they reflect a discomfort with uncertainty and nuance. But the larger problem is that perfect identity coherence leads to social closure by members of the group. Members of a group develop such strong cohesion among themselves that outsiders become unwelcome or nettlesome.[42] It is in this way that the sense of, or desire for, increased identity coherence leads to insularity and what we call "breaking," deliberately turning inward, and shunning connections with members of other groups.[43]

———

The problem of social closure that arises either in the case of identity coherence or in hewing too tightly to a single primary identity, viewing the self in narrow or unitary terms, is eloquently captured by what the author Chimamanda Ngozi Adichie calls "the danger of the single story."[44] The "single story" is a dominant, essentialist narrative about the self or a social group that overwhelms all other aspects of identity. When a single story or narrative defines an identity or a person, there is no space for alternatives that can connect people across that identity boundary. Even worse, the reduction of identity to a single affiliation encourages the adoption of an attitude that is partial and sectarian, and sometimes intolerant, domineering, and violent.[45]

But a multiple self—a self that acknowledges its inherent multiplicity—creates space where people can come together across different identity bases. We might not share the same race, but perhaps we worship the same god. Or perhaps we have different gender identities, but we enjoy the same foods, music, and traditions. Or perhaps we are differently abled, but we cheer on the same sports team. Most of us share at least a few of the same social identities.[46] If we embrace rather than suppress our multiplicity, we can build bridges over the most daunting divides. No less a figure than Malcolm X can teach us how. As he explained in a letter to a friend in New York, "what I have seen and experienced on this pilgrimage has forced me to 'rearrange' much of my own thought-pattern, and to toss aside some of my previous conclusions."[47] Known reputationally in the America as a Black nationalist and separatist leader up to that point, Malcolm X elaborated upon an astonishing revelation made through a dramatic shift in context:

> During the past seven days of this holy pilgrimage, while undergoing the rituals of the hajj, I have eaten from the same plate, drank from the same glass, slept on the same bed or rug, while praying to the same God—not only with some of this earth's most powerful kings, cabinet members,

potentates and other forms of political and religious rulers—but also with fellow-Muslims whose skin was the whitest of white, whose eyes were the bluest of blue, and whose hair was the blondest of blond—yet it was the first time in my life that I didn't see them as "white" men. I could look into their faces and see that these didn't regard themselves as "white."

Malcolm X's religious identity allowed him to connect across a racial boundary that would have been largely inconceivable prior to this experience.

The more we hold open and multiple identities, the harder it is to have a categorical "other." Instead of falling on one side or the other, there are many sides to choose from, many allegiances to draw upon. In contrast, when the self is "hard" and "firm," when we hold too fast and tight to a certain set of narrow identities—when we are pressed to take sides or fall back behind identity lines—then the othering process becomes much more pernicious. A categorical self—a self that is categorically bounded and reinforced—is one that is extremely difficult to build bridges for.

Although it may feel less affirming—and even somewhat uncomfortable—the healthier balance is to maintain some identity dissonance. Only in that case can the multiplicity we actually embody be readily perceived and felt, and the illusion of unity and stability be disrupted. Moreover, only in that case can we build bridges and more deeply connect with people outside of our group, as currently experienced or defined.

This is imperative. Recognizing the multiplicity within and between us is one of the keys to belonging. Belonging requires a sense of a larger "we" that encompasses people that are not currently affiliated with or members of the same group along some meaningful social dimension. The larger "we" need not include every aspect of the self or every salient dimension of our identity, but it must exist for at least one such dimension.*

----

* We recognize that this is more difficult in contexts in which an identity threat is present or operative. As noted in in Chapter 4, identity threats make some aspects of our identity more salient. The greater the threat, the more that identity can swamp or overwhelm our other selves. But this must be resisted, even in moments of grave danger or peril. Otherwise, broader belonging is impossible.

As a cultural practice, bridging can help connect people across identity categories, and engender greater belonging, but it is mostly a waystation along the road to greater and deeper connection and belonging. Bridging is intentionally connecting across a social divide, with the goal of weakening the walls that separate us. It is a practice to build trust, rapport, and connection in fractured, divided, and fragmented societies. Ultimately, we need more than practices that build connection and social capital across existing identity boundaries. We need new and reimagined shared identities as well as narratives and cultural practices to support and ground those identities.

A healthy belonging society would do more than make space for others who are different. Too often it is assumed that any recognition of difference is harmful, a source of societal division. But difference is not harmful, only a basis or justification for harm. After all, any form of love, if it's not narcissistic, compels us to love others who are different, and accord them full humanity. Otherwise, only those who share our identities are worthy of love and regard. This is why the solution to othering is not "sameing"— trying to make others like us—but belonging, building community across and within group boundaries.

Because we are each multiply faceted, we are different from each other *and* more mysterious to ourselves than we generally perceive or understand. In a sense, we are also different from ourselves, not just each other. So, we both need to acknowledge that the self is not what we think it is (contrary to Descartes), but also recognize and create more open selves. The multiple self, the recognition of our multiplicity, creates a softer, more porous movement within and boundary between us and others.

Remaking the Self

If the reader is persuaded of our earlier point that group-based categories and the constellation of meanings associated with those categories is more fluid and less fixed than we generally perceive or realize, then it should follow that the self—individual identities in composite—is equally open and fluid. This is one of most poignant insights we wish to convey. If it is true, and the capacity to create belonging without othering depends upon a greater openness and recognition of the multiplicity in our sense of self, how then can we achieve that goal?

To some extent, this already occurs, but beyond conscious awareness or control. What happened to "Soviet" citizenship, identity, and even sense of self among members when the Soviet Union collapsed? Or, conversely, what happens to identity and sense of self as the European Union project becomes stronger and more deeply felt? As we go through large political and economic realignment, we often simultaneously go through remaking of selves. We are likely going through such realignment now. As our physical and social environment changes, so will our self, although not through our own conscious making or even to our conscious awareness.

Powerfully felt new identities can be fabricated within minutes. Interventions such as the Robbers Cave experiments and other so-called "minimal-group" studies reveal just how easily completely made-up identities can be adopted, embraced, and powerfully influence social dynamics.[48] One of the keys to belonging is to create or recreate identities that can bind more of us together, allowing us to create new connections, so that people who are "othered" or currently outside of our identity group are brought within our sphere of concern.

This idea has been experimentally established. Interventions that make the social identity of university students as such more salient than other identities had a dramatic effect on behavior, making students more generous.[49] Engendering belonging can be accomplished purposefully by forging new identities to bind people together, by surfacing submerged identities, or it can be done by participating in the revision of existing identities.

The self or selves are always being remade. Part of what we must do is become conscious and more aware of this process, and deliberate about how and purposeful in the "what," the content of our new identities. Just like words, identities and even our selves are constantly evolving—refusing to remain locked in a static state. We are participants in this process, whether we realize it or not.

———

Each of us belongs to many groups, has many concurrent identities, and in many of those cases, the dynamics between groups are constantly shifting.

We noted the existence of stacked identities in Chapter 2, but we did not emphasize the more dynamic nature of these identities and their interrelationship. This is both intuitive and extremely difficult to grasp.

As we suggested with our brief vignettes that opened Chapter 3, our experience and our cultures prime us to view our identities as more stable than they are, as if identities are frozen in time, either at the level of the group or the individual. Our moment-to-moment experience of identity feels quite consistent, even as it mutates or revolves rapidly.[50] It is difficult for human beings to recognize, even in ourselves, the fluidity of our identities across time and space.

Who we are as individuals, as racialized and gendered groups, as nations or peoples, is changing. Much like language, identity is not something that "is," it is something that is always *becoming*.[51] As linguist John McWhorter explains, "They tell you a word is a thing, when it's actually something going on."[52] Identity is the same way.

Identities are processes in flux rather than static categories. And they change for the same reason as words: their structure, being shaped by environment and practical utility, and relational nature, makes transformation and evolution inevitable. As we have seen, categorical social identities evolve to serve a set of needs, reflected in appellations that recede while others gain salience.[53] This insight extends to the self. As we have written elsewhere, "The self is not a rigidly defined construct, but is constantly in flux, shaped by environment and interactions, all of which are relationships."[54]

Usually, this change is too slow to notice. As we have seen, the human experience and life span is too narrow and short to appreciate the metaphorically tectonic changes that occur in social group identity. Change is happening at a pace that now falls within our cognizance, but with the further challenge that such rapid change generates significant discomfort and anxiety.* A changing world demands we change in turn. We believe, if it is to be a healthy change, it must be grounded in belonging without othering.

---

* Recall our discussion of LGBTQ identity and Latinx identity evolution in Part I as examples of both rapid change and discomfort with rapid change.

We cannot do this by abandoning the identities we hold dear, but by interweaving them with new identities. Thus, instead of creating the kind of stacked intersectional positions or stacked overlapping identities discussed in Chapter 2, which are largely exclusive, the goal is to create identities that interweave without undermining the integrity of each other.[55]

A New "We"

One general way to foster more inclusive identities is through what the anthropologist Marshall Sahlins calls "mutuality of being."[56] The idea is active "participation in one another's existence."[57] The intersubjectivity of identity and the self, then, must become deeper—it requires a connection that is based on interdependence or what Sahlins calls "a conjoint being." This is both the challenge and the risk because the fear of interdependence—of mutuality—is a powerful source of othering.

For many supremacists, fear of losing dominance or status advantage undergirds othering. When group identities or positionalities are based upon dangerous relationships or abusive interdependence, then those identities are inherently unstable and anxious. During British rule over India, colonial authorities made Bengal the official language in the province of Assam, marginalizing native Assamese speakers and denying them access to the best jobs. This historical fact probably contributed to the more recent effort to purge many Bengali speakers from the citizenship rolls in Assam.[58] In the U.S., antebellum southern planters were economically dependent upon the institution of slavery, but terrified that they or their families might be killed in a slave rebellion.[59] In such a context, only dominance and control, not mutuality, cooperation, and reciprocity, ensures safety for the dominant group.* This is the contemporary fear of the American foreign policy establishment: that if the American military is not dominant, it must be subordinate, and American interests and safety

---

* This helps explain why members of historically or traditionally dominant groups may tend to support authoritarian politicians in the face of a status threat, even within free and liberal societies.

are jeopardized. Dominance is both unstable and unhealthy. It generates the fear that impels toward greater domination and control.

The Mayan expression *Inlakesh*, meaning "You are my other self. We are one. I am another yourself," captures the recognition of interdependence and reality of mutuality. But it is based upon a different understanding of the self, one that directly rejects the Cartesian split and the modern Western concept of the self. As the actor Helen Mirren explained in a commencement address extolling this term, "if I'm you—I have a responsibility to you. If you're me—you have a responsibility to me. The Mayans just had a more beautiful way of saying 'we're all in this together.' We're all in this together—remember that, so that you can make some sense out of and fix this crazy, crazy world."[60] Recognition of our mutuality entails interdependence solidarity, and, ultimately, belonging.

———————

But there needs to be tangible supports, including cultural practices and social space, for such recognition of mutuality and connection. In this regard, we are particularly inspired by the suggestion, from Amin Maalouf, that everyone should learn three languages.[61] The act of learning a language is in service of communication, which itself is in service of connection and cooperation. To learn another's language is very close to, if not in fact, an act of bridging, and a cultural investment.

As Maalouf explains, "everyone needs three languages. The first is his language of identity; the third is English. Between the two we have to promote a third language, freely chosen. . . . This will be . . . the language of the heart, the adopted language, the language you have married, the language you love."[62] Maalouf endorses English as one of the three due to its widespread usage. We do not necessarily endorse the specific prescription here, but the general idea is a natural extension of the notion of multiplicity within and between our selves. What better way to recognize that multiplicity than through multilingualism? Moreover, this chapter has emphasized the need for more modes of connection and forms of affiliation, not fewer or less. Learning a language serves that overarching goal. In the next chapter, we will present an example of how this has been institutionalized in Singapore.

In addition to a cultural practice of multilingualism, another—perhaps more difficult—approach is to create a new language altogether to ground a broader identity. Francis Fukuyama claims that the founders of Indonesia and Tanzania "in effect created new national languages to unify their highly diverse societies" for that very purpose.[63]

If such measures prove insufficient or impossible, then another way to do this is to fabricate identities that bridge difference. Belonging requires agency, active participation, and, quite often, co-creation. This is a recognition of the relation between a person's inner and outer environments—the places we belong are also the places that help make us. Or, in other words, "We realize home is a place we make, and that makes us, again and again and again."[64] Our sense of self is remade as we build toward belonging.

One expression of this is through a concept Daniel Burns, a political scientist, calls "forged families."[65] This is the idea that family units can be created deliberately and intentionally through means other than blood relations, even in the contemporary West. It requires determination and commitment. But there are already models in our society of such alternative family arrangements. The anthropologist Kath Weston observes of her fieldwork studying the AIDS crisis, "The families I saw gay men and lesbians creating in the Bay Area tended to have extremely fluid boundaries, not unlike kinship organization among sectors of the African-American, American Indian, and white working class."[66]

Granted, the creation of new, bridging identities is easier said than done. But we can and must participate in this process, even if we cannot dictate the outcome. As we have seen, the process of identity development is iterative and complicated, but we can shape it with vision and imagination, and a degree of humility. In the short term, one thing we can do is recast one of our identities or open ourselves to new ones that we can incorporate into our (multiple) self.

Andrew Solomon suggests how this can happen: "The best way to get to these horizontalities is to find coherence, and in the wake of these stories, I recast my own narrative. I have a horizontal experience of being gay, and a vertical one of the family that produced me, and the fact that they are not fully integrated no longer seems to undermine either."[67] In other words,

without abandoning our vertical identities, we must try to build new horizontal identities that can bridge across existing forms of difference to knit
together a healthier society.

Andrew may have too much faith in the ability of individuals to shape
this process, but he is on the right track. We need to throw ourselves into
identities that can create new connections. Part of the fear on the far right
and left is that connections undermine the assumed purity and integrity
of prevailing identities, and their hostility is based on the view that intermixing as an existential threat. This undergirds some opposition to integration, and is the generally the central fear animating opposition to intergroup marriage.

The political scientist Robert Putnam calls for a similar recasting to
that imagined by Andrew Solomon, but at a societal scale rather than
something individuals can do. In his survey of American society during
the twentieth century, he claims that Americans swung from an "I" to a
"we" and back to an "I" society, one that is more individualistic, exclusionary, and less communitarian. Putnam finds that the "higher summit" and
most successful decades of American life occurred when the "promise of
'we'" was realized.[68] Many of the dysfunctions in our society are traceable
to the institutionalization of a smaller and more exclusive "we." In addition
to a political economy of greater community, inclusion, and solidarity as a
prescription to our current predicament, he recommends the creation of a
"new, more capacious sense of 'we,' a reconstruction of diversity that does
not bleach out ethnic specificities, but creates overarching identities that
ensure that those specificities do not trigger the allergic, 'hunker down'
reaction."[69]

─────────

Such a prescription may seem astonishingly ambitious, but it is essentially what nation-builders have done for centuries. Recall from Chapter 3 how the construction of identity was an integral part of building
new nation-states, such as Italy and Germany, out of countless smaller
units, in the 1860s and '70s. Some of these identities are built not over
decades, but centuries.[70] Modern state-builders have had to do this as
well, in places as diverse as India and South Africa. India's founders,

Gandhi and Nehru, erected the new national identity on top of existing elements but also helped forge the "idea of India."[71] The challenge
for us is to devise broader identities within existing nation states or
beyond them.

If the notion of creating new identities seems strange, it is also necessary. If we are going to end othering and build belonging, we need new
identities and new stories to ground and support those identities. James
Baldwin suggested this path when, in a high-profile Cambridge debate
against William F. Buckley Jr., he explained that "[w]e are trying to forge
a new identity for which we need each other."[72] Although he felt that this
was only possible after a reckoning, after white America acknowledged
what it had done, Baldwin recognized both the need for new identities and
that such a need was rooted in our mutual interdependence.

The Problem of Protective Breaking

In the last chapter, we briefly noted the problem of "breaking," the degra-
dation or destruction of social capital that occurs not when groups turn
inward, as in bonding, but when groups turn away from each other on a
fearful basis or deliberate manner. In a bonding experience, groups seek to
associate with each other to strengthen their connections or relations or to
foster group pride, as in the celebration during an ethnic pride parade or
festival.

Breaking defines the other not just as "different," but as threatening or
dangerous. As such, breaking tends not only to undermine belonging, but
to contribute to the othering process. There are different forms of breaking that themselves express, or may be responsive to, different forms of
othering. Strong breaking occurs when the subordination of the other is
constitutive of the identity of the dominant group and shapes policy and
practice. When this occurs, the exclusion of some group is fundamental to
the meaning or definition of the dominant group. Weak breaking occurs
in the form of neglect, whether benign or malignant, as to willful harm.

Excessive bonding—when members of the same group deepen their
relations, intimacy, and trust—can slip into weak breaking, the kind of
benign or willful neglect of other groups. This is because too much bonding

creates what Jonathan Smucker calls the "political identity paradox."[73] We have already alluded to this problem, but it describes the tendency of different social groups and movements to develop and foster a strong internal identity in pursuit of a political objective, but that this cohesion becomes an impediment to political struggle and success because that same cohesion leads to isolation and insularity.

One problem is that the intoxicating feeling of belonging generated from the experience of strong community (and extreme in-group cohesion) inhibits the outreach needed to achieve larger political goals while also alienating or repelling likely allies.[74] In the words of Jonathan Smucker, "we begin to swim in our own marginalization. We begin to act out the story of the righteous few."[75] This occurs when groups substitute tangible political goals (by accepting continual defeat) for the salve of identity coherence and community.

The antidote to this problem must be proactive efforts to build a bigger "we" and leadership that is outward looking rather than insular. Within any group, no matter its social location, there are powerful tendencies that tend toward insularity. As the journalist Bill Bishop noted in his early look at growing polarization, "like minded groups, over time, grow more extreme in the direction of majority view."[76] In any social context, people "find it socially advantageous to adopt a position slightly more extreme than the group average." Human beings are intensely status conscious, and the aggregate result of these tendencies is polarization.[77] This is tendency is difficult to disrupt, because naming it or challenging it can "call one's own belonging to the group" into question. Good leaders orient their groups outward toward the periphery rather than the core, and they do this by modeling that outlook and orientation.[78]

Excessive bonding is inimical to the fluidity and openness we are calling for. Moderate bonding is not necessarily dangerous, but it does not help build larger societal belonging (although it can create a greater sense of belonging within a group). For that, we must turn to bridging, as described in the last chapter. The practice of bridging can lead to a society of greater belonging by making the divides that separate us more porous, and can help us morph, recast and broaden our prevailing identities in a healthier direction.[79] Breaking, not bonding, is the antithesis of bridging. It is dangerous, and leads to fragmentation, deeper divides, and a smaller "we."

Breaking is most serious when a dominant group or the leading institutions and powers in society seek to exclude or harm another social group. When reactionary politicians seek to exclude people based upon their identity, by building a wall or issuing travel bans from Muslim nations, as President Trump attempted to do, that is a dangerous form of breaking that enlarges othering.[80]

But breaking can also occur in the other direction as well. Marginalized groups may practice breaking when they seek to curate spaces, form organizations and associations, or build community on an exclusive or exclusionary basis. Because there is so much othering occurring in certain societies, groups that have suffered the brunt of a particularly harmful othering process may tend to defensively or protectively break. When the dominant society is so hostile to a group and when the cumulative toll of daily life becomes unbearable, there is an understandable impulse to separate or seek safer spaces. The harmful effects may not be same, but breaking by marginalized groups is not harmless either.

A prominent example of "defensive breaking" is the demand among some LGBTQ people to preemptively ban cops at Pride.[81] In the wake of the murder of George Floyd, the Pride organizers in New York City, Seattle, and Denver sought to ban police, citing the history of police violence and brutality against LGBTQ people and other marginalized groups.[82] These efforts triggered a fierce debate, partly because many LGBTQ officers proudly participated in Pride.[83] The progressive mayor of New York City and liberal media voices condemned the ban as discriminatory.[84] Without resolving this debate, we simply note that this is a prominent example of defensive breaking, although it is between a broad social group and a professional rather than two social identities.

Sometimes breaking may be an understandable impulse for survival or protection, not simply a maladaptation to an oppressive society. Booker T. Washington's campaign for self-help under the oppression of Jim Crow segregation is an example of this.[85] If white-dominated southern society accorded no opportunities, then there was little alternative to a self-help regime. Breakaway or autonomous movements such as those initiated by the Kurds of northern Iraq are defensive breaking triggered by genocidal events, like when Saddam targeted them with chemical weapons.[86]

It is a disturbing trend, however, that the more sophisticated defenses of ethnic democracy—or ethno-nationalism—are justified on similar grounds. For example, a federal judge has defended Israel's symbolic and legal prioritization of Jewishness over its universalistic commitment to democracy and equal rights on the grounds that the state's ethnic identity was a response to the failures of liberal universalism to protect Jewish people from depredations of the Nazis and other antisemitic segments of Western societies.[87] This charge may well be true, but to respond to a violation of human rights by undermining a commitment to equality and democracy replicates the error and repeats the problem.[88]

If the solution to the failures of liberal universalism is more "particularism," the medicine is likely to engender more of the same disease. It will result in more ethno-states and ethno-nationalism, more conflict and fragmentation, and more war and genocide, not less. Societies or institutions that fragment into ever-smaller units multiply the reasons and possibilities for conflict. Even in its more benign form, this kind of breaking is inconsistent with an expansive belongingness paradigm.

Perhaps the most iconic example of "protective" or "defensive" breaking is the emergence of the "Black Power" movement. In 1966, Stokely Carmichael, who had by that point ascended to the chair of the Student Nonviolent Coordinating Committee (SNCC), gave an electrifying speech at UC Berkeley in which he propounded a philosophy of "Black Power."[89] Because of the intransigence of the white leaders and white communities to address the problems of racial inequality, poverty, and war, Carmichael called for "Black Power" as a way of building power outside of traditional power centers.

While well intended, the meaning, framing, and context exemplifies "breaking." Martin Luther King Jr., in particular, was perturbed by this philosophy. As one witness observed, "I will never forget Dr King's face when Black Power began to emerge—he looked like the most stricken man."[90] It undermined Dr. King's vision not only of a beloved community, but also of an integrated and multiracial civil rights movement. As he put it, "We must never forget that there are some white people in the United States just as determined to see us free as we are to free ourselves." As a colleague explained, "Dr King was not opposed to power. But to elevate so-called black power over white power would **break** that which he was seeking to build—a coalition among white and black people." As Dr. King elaborated in an interview involving Stokely Carmichael, "I feel that power is necessary, but it would be difficult for me to use the term 'black power' because of the connotative meaning that it has for many people and the feeling that this may represent a desire to rise from a position of disadvantage to one of advantage, thereby subverting justice."

Do not misunderstand us: The Black Power movement helped establish critical policy objectives among other productive ends, and articulated a powerful and compelling political vision that was lacking. But it is an example of defensive or protective breaking that ultimately does not bridge or build a larger "we." Should organizations whose mission is disestablishing anti-Black racism, for example, include white members? Or, more narrowly, non-Black members? Many social justice movements and organizations grapple with this dilemma—whether to found their efforts on a broader basis, or whether to narrow their focus, and exclude or marginalize participants based on identity.

Breaking, whether it is an expression of oppression or a reaction to it, is incapable of building greater belonging. It either leads to or reinforces a smaller "we." It tends to exacerbate polarization and furthers fragmentation. It can hobble or immobilize social justice movements and organizations through unproductive and ceaseless infighting.[91] And it has a tendency to lock the groups involved into a false categorical essentialism, rather than foster possibilities and social space for bridging and belonging.

Resist Essentialism

In broad strokes, this book describes the dominant or higher-status groups in society as the group that belongs and the marginalized, despised, envied, or pitied groups as the "other." Although we emphasized that different kinds of othering processes yield different kinds of "other," there is a tendency to reduce "them" to one or two salient dimensions of difference while regarding our own groups as more richly textured and multidimensional. In other words, we see ourselves and our own groups in nuanced terms, but tend to deny that complexity in other groups.

Remarkably, the tendency toward essentialist commentary, rhetoric, and analysis arises even—and perhaps most often—among those who profess to know better. Enter into any social justice convening space in the past ten years, and it is likely you will hear someone making an overly broad generalization about a group based upon their identity.

Beyond stereotyped or overly generalized claims about certain groups, a prevalent expression of essentialist thought is the emphasis on "authenticity," presupposing there is an "authentic" as opposed to prevailing or culturally scripted way to express or perform any particular social group identity, from gender to race. This is not to deny that some identities people hold are stigmatized or denigrated, and that this experience can be painful, as when segments of society deny a trans person's gender identity or a queer person's sexual orientation.[92] But we should be careful about essentializing any expression of these identities, or even identities themselves, as if their moral value or legitimacy depends upon it. Indeed, one of the arguments on behalf of gay rights was that gay persons are "hardwired" for same-sex sexual preferences, possibly even that there is a gene or epigenic trigger.[93] But their humanity and their right to belong cannot and should not depend upon whether an identity is biological or sociological.

It is critical to resist this tendency, and the larger sorts of essentialisms that tend to accompany discussions of social justice or group-based inequities. In any society, there are invariably members of a dominant or favored group that enjoy neither the advantages and privileges that are supposedly conferred by that membership nor hold tightly to that identity. For example, not all white people enjoy a dominant perch in American society in any meaningful way. Even in a society founded on the supremacy of white people over Black people, many whites were and are severely impoverished or otherwise disadvantaged.

And just as marginalization in one domain does not entail marginality in all, dominance or privilege in one context does not mean being favored in all. Without trivializing the reality of group positionality and durable social hierarchies, we are all likely to experience the sense of being "othered" in some spaces and conditions in our lives, even in our own families. Nonetheless, some social groups are systematically othered, and have very few places where they can comfortably belong. One of the goals of this book has been to shed light on this problem, but also to increase the number of places and times we can all belong.

———

Nor do all members of dominant groups endorse or support policies that reinforce their advantage. Imagine a policy proposal to lower taxes, but only in white communities. Not all white people would either benefit from or support such a policy. And even many white people who would benefit would oppose it on ethical or social justice grounds.

Such observations are not offered to suggest that white privileges or advantages do not exist, and conversely, that other group-based disadvantages do not exist, but rather to point out that all groups are heterogeneous for some purposes and in some contexts. Too often we conflate the ideology of whiteness or white supremacy with people who are phenotypically white.

Whiteness is as much a conceptual and ideological space as a physical descriptor. As such, there are multiple white identities. One strain is organized around domination and exclusion, but another is organized around equality and justice, as evidenced by the enormous surge in white participation in the Floyd protests. We must afford space to recognize the difference, and to connect with people racialized as white but who reject the ideology of white supremacy or dominance. Failing to do so will engender certain derangements, like the case of Rachel Dolezal on the one hand, or a situation where more white people bind themselves more tightly to a corrosive white identity under a perceived identity threat on the other hand.[94] This may be underpinning formations from the Tea Party to the "Stop the Steal" movement.[95]

Racial and ethnic categories are both necessary and fraught. They are necessary because we must have some taxonomy to track disparities and progress in reducing them, but they are fraught because they obscure many differences within groups. And, at a deeper level, they are necessary because, as James Baldwin wrote, "[i]dentity would seem to be the garment with which one covers the nakedness of the self."[96] At the same time, as we have seen, Native American, Black, white, Asian, and Latino are incredibly diverse groupings of human beings. In working with categories and telling large public stories, we should try to avoid reductive or simplistic characterizations.

One example of this is the idea of fragility, as contrasted with trauma. Robin DiAngelo has focused attention on what she calls *White Fragility*,[97] the notion that part of what is holding back racial progress is white sensitivity to being called racist. Or, more narrowly, such characterizations may be used to describe Trump supporters or white reactionaries as people defined by fear, waiting to be riled, easy targets for demagogues, set to a hair trigger, satisfied emotionally with the opportunity to vent their anger. And, further, that no careful expression of facts or complexity and nuance in disposition will blunt that.

Whether used to by conservatives to denigrate "liberal snowflakes" or by social justice advocates or reformers in characterizing white people or Trump supporters, the idea of "fragility" is profoundly anti-empathetic—it is something to be rejected or overcome, whereas trauma is regarded as something more serious, worthy of sympathy and regard. We challenge these assessments.

Such characterizations when applied to social groups are reductive and essentialist. They are too categorical for how people are actually oriented in the world. People are more complicated and often more fluid than this simple psychological framing. People are both resilient and fragile, altruistic and selfish, hopeful and fearful. Although some people acknowledge this, they gloss over it by ascribing general tendencies to groups. Even this misses the point by denying our multiplicity, but at the group level.

We saw in Chapter 4 how Trump activated part of his base with outgroup animus, specifically against Black people, Latinos, Muslims, and LGBTQ people. But what we missed is that many of his supporters (an estimated 6.7 million of them) had also voted for Obama, or were or had expressed racial egalitarian preferences at different points in their life.[98] One of the dangers of essentialism is that it insists that our differences are categorical, unchanging, and natural. This is an analytical error, but it is also a strategic error.

What ultimately matters is not whether a group falls into one category or the other (fearful and reactionary or hopeful and progressive), but how we can prime or appeal to the better angels in all groups. That is how Lyndon Baines Johnson won one of the largest landslide victories in American history *after* signing the 1964 Civil Rights Act, but was followed by the Nixon presidency on a wave of backlash. Or how some former Obama voters voted for Trump, and were among the mob literally storming the Capitol on January 6, 2021.

———————

In a famous passage, Walt Whitman wrote, "Very well, then I contradict myself, I am large, I contain multitudes."[99] Most people are complicated enough to contain contradictions. The same people who can be rallied to a moral cause can be riled up by the demagogue, not because they are ready and waiting to be set off, but because different parts of our selves are being called to the fore by different leaders and messages. What matters are the stories that shape our sense of self and the leaders who appeal to our hopes and aspirations or stoke our fears and activate our prejudices.

Although we must not reify categorical group meanings, we must also avoid believing that we can easily understand and address the problem of othering or build belonging simply at the individual level. We are all individuals and members of social groups at the same time, and both at the level of the group *and* the self, we are more fluid and multifaceted than is generally acknowledged, especially in Western thought. An authentic belonging paradigm must honor this dynamic. One way to do this is not to wear our identities too tightly, as James Baldwin's guidance, which serves as an epigram to this book, wisely counsels.

From Narrow to Broad Identities

If one of the keys to belonging is embracing our multiplicity, how can we practically accomplish this at a societal level? The answer is remarkably straightforward. Without abandoning any particular identity that is important to us and provides great meaning, we should simultaneously lean into the identities we hold that are broader and more inclusive, rather than those that are narrower and more exclusive. The tendency to do the latter produces what Francis Fukuyama calls "the crisis of identity" in modern societies, which is the rapidly growing number of identities combined with demands for public recognition.[100]

The Enlightenment and the conditions of modernity (especially urbanization, the movement of people out of small, traditional villages and towns and into larger, diverse urban areas) fostered an environment in which the crisis of belonging becomes most acute. When people are pulled out of thick cultural arrangements with strong local ties (like local villages) and thrust into large, impersonal institutions and settings like factories in bustling cities, the choices of identity become more salient and bewildering. The social closure of small towns may have less room for acceptance of difference, but the range of identities available to people is also more circumscribed. Urbanization has been observed to engender alienation, and greater acceptance of difference has not necessarily created more belonging. This dynamic was first characterized by nineteenth-century social theorists as the transition from *Gemeinshaft* to *Gesellschaft*, and has now happened on a global scale, from China to Brazil and everywhere in between.[101]

One effect of this dynamic is a yearning for nostalgia or pining for forms of human relations or connection that provide that sense of belonging that feels absent in modern life. Another is the tendency toward greater fragmentation in society and demand for recognition, along with the proliferation of identities.

Our response cannot be to reject these demands or smother individuality under a universalizing or totalizing identity. Nor can we turn back the clock, no matter what reactionary theorists suggest, and return to a premodern societal arrangement. This might increase a sense of belonging among non-othered peoples, but exacerbate the problem of othering. The solution lies in a balance between the two extremes of totalizing universalism and infinite fragmentation.

We all need identities, but what is more, all human societies need collective identities. The critical questions are: What kind of identities should we have, and what good they can serve? As we've seen, identities can be useful for many purposes—they create a sense of belonging or help organize around a common purpose. We have seen how many identities, but especially marginalized identities, are a by-product of the othering process. As such, they can become useful or liberatory for naming the oppressed group, resisting oppression, fostering solidarity, and helping organize and mobilize to reform underlying conditions.[102]

Chapter 3 described the processes that underlie the formation of group identities, and suggested that different social contexts and conditions not only make identities more significant or meaningful, but also help define and shape the boundaries of the group that the identity describes. "Black" identity, for example, was not a "natural" social grouping, but a by-product of racialized slavery and accompanying dehumanizing practices. But Black identity acquires significance and deep meaning beyond that, even as it continues to perform a function in resisting and countering racism.

To construct a society of greater belonging, we will need more encompassing shared identities, new *and* existing. Every identity we hold connects us with a large number of people. Among our existing identities, broader identities connect us with a greater number than narrow identities. Narrow identities are those that are more exclusive, and in which the boundaries between social groups are more rigid.[103] Broad identities are those in which membership is more porous, fluid, but also inclusive and encompassing. As Francis Fukuyama observes, "If the logic of identity politics is to divide societies into ever smaller, self-regarding groups, it is also possible to create identities that are broader and more integrative."[104]

Reactionary and nationalist movements as well as conservative or fundamentalist religious movements tacitly recognize the critical distinction here, by generally hewing tightly to particular or narrow identities and downplaying broader and more open identities. Ethno-states, in particular, are the ultimate expression of this. Ethno-states are nation-states that tie a particular set of identities, whether they are ethnic, racial, religious, cultural, linguistic, or based on some fuzzy idea of ancestry, to the identity of the nation-state, either in terms of citizenship or legacy citizenship. As noted in Chapter 3, ethno-states may codify these relationships in laws and constitutions or simply recognize them as a matter of tacit practice and symbolic expression, as on flags, currency, or in parades and commemorative marches.[105]

Although nation-states have the potential to transcend particularistic ethnic, religious, racial, and linguistic identities, by connecting through

208   Belonging without Othering

civic bonds people across these lines of difference, ethno-nationalism is an acid that corrodes this potential. It narrows and then tightens the range of possibilities within the political community. As George Orwell wrote in 1945, "The abiding purpose of every nationalist is to secure more power and more prestige, not for himself but for the nation or other unit in which he has chosen to sink his own individuality."[106] In other words, under nationalism, the self becomes narrowed and tightly bound to a particular object, such as the nation-state. Identity entrepreneurs (usually a chauvinistic demagogue) promoting particularistic (rather than universalistic or pluralistic) nationalism within nation-states are one of the most dangerous forces in the world today, and by emphasizing the binding of social group identity with the state, render the nation exclusionary, discriminatory, and narrow.

Conservatives and traditionalists may prefer more exclusive and narrower identities, but progressives exhibit an equally dysfunctional tendency to make identities either political or private without grappling with the more fundamental question of how to develop and generate inclusive collective identities. So, we either take identities as a political claim, like "Black and proud," or treat them as private, intimate matters, such as religious faith. Both impulses are mistakes. We need identities that can speak to and build collective belonging—purpose, meaning, groundedness—in something greater than ourselves, and which bind us to other people, especially members of different social groups.

The good news is that human experience is replete with examples of how this is accomplished. Some identity categories are by definition exclusive, intended to serve only a predefined community, and instilling or mandating rituals and customs that heighten differentiation rather than facilitate integration. But many identity categories were designed to be open and accessible to all. Indeed, Jewishness and Christianity are two contrasting examples. The former was defined by rituals, dietary restrictions, and even laws that were specifically and intentionally distinctive from the surrounding communities, apparently intended to heighten that distinctiveness.[107] The latter, by contrast, is universal in its ambitions, open to any and all who embrace its tenets and adopt its practices, irrespective of social class, status, race, ethnicity, gender, or any other identity characteristic.

Groups that are open to individuals of any background are denoted as "super-groups" by Amy Chua.[108] Chua classifies the United States as a "super-group" because its citizenship is open to anyone born on U.S. soil, regardless of ancestry or religion. Critically, she maintains that super-groups do not demand that their members shed or suppress their other identities. Thus new citizens to America can retain their ethnic, religious, linguistic, and cultural identities, fusing them with their new national identity. Super-groups layer, but do not displace, our other identities. In addition to new identities that supplement prevailing ones, we need to embrace broader identities that connect us to more people, perhaps in the way Chua describes.

Openness, Multiplicity, and Fluidity

Forging broader and more integrative identities is necessary but not sufficient. We not only need more encompassing social group identities; we need more pathways to join social groupings. We need broader identities, but we also need identities with more porous boundaries. We need identities categories that permit greater movement across the borders of identity. We have already noted the anthropological view that for most of humanity's prehistory, our species lived in relatively small bands of nomadic hunter-gatherers. While these facts are sometimes deployed to suggest that othering or belonging is evolutionarily built into this prehistory, one aspect that is generally overlooked is that such bands defined kinship more broadly and inclusively than we tend to recognize today.

Although kinship in most modern societies is defined in terms of biological relations, a fact that has only become more entrenched since the genomics revolution makes paternity an objectively verifiable fact, that is only a recent norm. Anthropologists studying so-called "traditional" societies found that kinship is created in a myriad of ways across different cultures. For New Guineans of the Nebilyer Valley, kinship is created by sharing certain culturally significant foods, such as mother's milk or tubers.[109] For the Chuukese people in Micronesia, surviving a dangerous journey at sea is sufficient to become kin.[110] Genomic analysis of burial sites suggests that many families or kin were not actually related by blood. As

David Brooks points out, "throughout most of human history, kinship was something you could create."[111]

But inclusive kinship is not an artifact of pre-agricultural societies. Within the Roman Empire, one of the heights of what is often regarded as "Western civilization," upper-class or patrician households routinely adopted males from lower-class households, endowing them with their titles, surnames, and estates.[112] Although such estates and titles would ordinarily pass to male offspring, high rates of mortality and the lack of male heirs meant that imperial nobles routinely adopted children in order to ensure succession of their names and estate. Senators, in particular, would bequeath their station to their heirs; adoption helped ensure that such titles would pass on, and other relations (sisters, wives, etc.) would be cared for. This is why fully grown adult men, even in their thirties and forties, were frequently adopted.

This imperative also helps explain why several notable Roman emperors were adopted heirs, including Augustus Caesar, the first, as well as the second emperor, Tiberius.[113] The practice of adopting adult men—a kind of family insurance policy—was so common even among patricians with male children that norms developed regarding how lower-class households should be compensated for losing their male heirs.[114] Roman law codified the possibility of more inclusive identities, and facilitated the means to incorporate outsiders into existing social formations.

As these examples demonstrate, and the concept of "super-groups" suggests, identity categories can be constructed on more exclusive and narrower terms, or on more inclusive and broader terms. But part of what makes identities exclusive or more inclusive is the permeability or accessibility of the identity. Whether an identity is drawn or constructed on a narrower or broader basis is a choice, not an inevitability associated with social identities.

The prevalence of birth-based criteria for many identities (caste, race, ethnicity, etc.) is partly explained by the fact that they provide clarity and certainty—they resolve ambiguities in taxonomies through definitions that are exclusive (that is, not overlapping between categories), can be independently verified, and are beyond the control of individuals. Although well-meaning in some cases, these efforts are antithetical to the reality of how identities develop and evolve. As just noted, some societies lean in to narrow identities because of a misguided belief that only thicker culture units with more cohesive identities provide a sense of belonging. In any case, societies can also devise or reconstruct classification systems in the opposite direction.

Fortunately, many societies are now beginning to recognize and codify fluidity and openness in identity categories. This is perhaps most advanced in the cases of gender and gender identity. In recognition of the extremely damaging and harmful consequences of not having one's gender identity align with one's perceived identity or physical characteristics, many governments, institutions, and communities (although certainly not all) have created ample space for individuals to select their own gender identity.[115] Facebook, for example, allows users to select among dozens of gender identity categories.[116] Organizations and institutions such as hospitals and universities are similarly expanding the range and options for gender identification. This process of inclusion in the opening of identity categories for gender is not without challenges or difficulties, but it one that much of the medical establishment now endorses, especially for adults.[117]

A recent phenomenon perhaps associated with this greater openness is the significant increase in the percentage of the population that identifies as LGBTQ or nonbinary.* In 2023, Gallup found that about 7 percent of adult Americans identified as such, roughly double the percentage found in the 2012 survey.[118] Even more dramatic, however, were the generational differences. More than 20 percent of people born between 1997 and 2003 identified as such, compared to just 10.5 percent of millennials (born between 1981 and 1996), and far more than the 2.6 percent of baby boomers.

The obvious explanation for both developments is the weakening stigma of nonheterosexuality and greater societal and institutional acceptance for nonheterosexual persons, noted in the last chapter. (One analogy here is that the number of people who identify as left-handed increased after American schools and families stopped trying to train

---

* As noted in Part I, we take care to avoid conflating sexual orientation identity and gender identity, but individuals who express nontraditional gender identities are probably more likely to express a nonheterosexual orientation.

kids out of it).[119] Rather than celebrate this development, however, some commentators, pundits, and politicians, especially those on the more conservative end of the ideological spectrum, have reacted with alarm and concern.[120]

Some of the worry is based upon traditional values, concerns over family formation, and falling rates of fertility, but others are rooted in fears of progressive or fashionable "social contagion" and teenage mental health.[121] Although it may be some time before researchers pinpoint the exact cause of this change, and the relative weight of influences, it strikes us as predictable that a variety of sexual orientation identities would proliferate following the weakening of the norm of heterosexuality, or heteronormativity. That norm ushered people, uncomfortably and forcibly in some cases, into an identity and set of prescribed scripts that they neither wanted nor embraced.*

While midcentury psychologists found that men were more likely to have same-sex encounters or preferences, one of the more interesting findings from the recent Gallup survey was that women were far more likely to report LBGTQ identification. And although most of the LGBTQ-identifying respondents identified more specifically as bisexual (57 percent), women were far more likely to identify as such. The number of young women identifying as bisexual appears to be a major driver of both upward trends. One conservative scholar, surveying multiple survey data sets, concludes that a "more sexually liberal and modernist culture, one which values difference, best accounts for the new trend. This culture has its greatest impact on the most sexually fluid and perhaps easily influenced groups: the young, the very liberal, and women."[122]

Given all the confusion and consternation around these developments, some readers might wonder if the solution is to discard all categories, and simply "let people be individuals." While an appealing argument, and one

---

* One of the problems with normativity itself is that it tends, by definition, to mask itself and make itself invisible by seeming "normal" and "natural." Thus the norm of heterosexuality, like the norm of gender binaries, has a tendency to simultaneously suppress alternative identities and make those alternatives seem deviant. As norms weaken, we should expect those alternatives to emerge with greater force.

that is grounded in philosophical liberalism (perhaps taken to its logical endpoint), it is merely an attractive mirage. The reasons should be evident by this point.

First of all, this suggestion assumes that we can throw off shared identities and retreat into utterly idiosyncratic ones of our own design or making. As explained in Chapter 3, human beings naturally form categories. In fact, we could not function without categories. The content of those categories is not predetermined, and the categories themselves as well as the set of social meanings associated with them can and will change. We may not always have certain categories, but if institutions or governments stopped using classification systems for identities, that would not cause them to go away or disappear.* They would retain their social salience; they just would not be endorsed or managed by the state. We cannot wish them away in favor of the Western, individual self. Therefore, the best path forward is to push prevailing identity categories toward a broader and less exclusive basis, not to subscribe to the illusion that they can be waved away. We cannot dispense with social identities, but we can reconfigure them for better ends.

In American political discourse, a variant of the anti-classification view shows up in arguments over "identity politics." This is the strategic counsel that talking about certain identities or the needs of certain groups in public discourse is alienating to other groups. Critics of so-called "identity politics," including, most prominently, Mark Lilla, in the aftermath of the 2016 presidential election, argued that identity politics alienates the white voters that Democrats need to win elections and thereby enact policy reform.[123]

From this perspective, identity politics is viewed as a "breaking" strategy, that, by centering the needs and grievances of marginalized peoples, fractures the community. Thus the phrase "All Lives Matter" is deployed as

---

* Some conservative commentators, not recognizing this distinction, have advanced this recommendation. See, for example, *Classified: The Untold Story of Racial Classification in America*. While we do not agree with the recommendation that states should stop classifying people based upon popular identity categories, we suggest instead that states should find ways to accommodate identity fluidity rather than reify narrow or exclusionary identity categories.

an alternative to the more pointed phrase "Black Lives Matter." The obvious problem with this alternative is that it papers over, masks, or denies the disproportionate reality of excessive police violence experienced by Black people. This denial reinforces othering by undermining policy reform aimed at solving this injustice.

If, as Francis Fukuyama observes, "identity politics is everywhere a struggle for the recognition of dignity,"[124] then the solution cannot be to smother, repress, or ignore those demands. Rather, we must find ways of accommodating them without succumbing to the Scylla of infinite fragmentation on the one side or the Charybdis of rigid essentialism on the other.[125] We can only do this by leaning into broader identities where possible and embracing our multiplicity so that all of us hold—and recognize—at least some identities that bind us together.

True belonging requires that we bind ourselves together, although without the dangerous illusion that there is an "authentic" rather than a grounded way to do so. The solution, therefore, is not rejecting identity, but rather refashioning it to serve our needs. The multiplicity of identities we already hold—a condition of modernity—means that we have more identities to draw from in making those connections with others. The malleability and mutability of those identities makes it possible to extend them ever more widely rather than fall into the trap of continuing fragmentation.

The problem, however, is that identity formation along these lines are enterprises we cannot accomplish by ourselves. They are nuanced and complex collective processes. Still, we can and do participate in the process, not only identity making, but also meaning and world making. The critical word is participate.

Transracialism

If we are right about the nature of the self and the other, then it radically reconfigures many of the traditional debates we seem currently stuck over. Our societies have, to a significant extent, acknowledged the fluidity of identity when it comes to gender, accepting, respecting, and dignifying individual determinations with respect to gender (as distinguished from biological sex). But there are far more cases of identity where this fluidity is denied.

Despite the nuanced and precise variations of Blackness developed in the Jim Crow South (octorooon, quadroon, etc.), prevailing ways of classifying people by race remain largely exclusionary, meaning that people are generally sorted into one category or another (white, Black, Asian, etc.). For example, Barack Obama, a person of mixed-race ancestry whose mother and maternal grandparents (who helped raise him) were white, was by and large referred to as the nation's first "Black" president, a categorization that was no small controversy prior to his election.[126]

A more recent controversy was the case of Rachel Dolezal. Ms. Dolezal was the president of the NAACP chapter in Spokane, Washington, but was forced to resign after a news reporter accused her of misrepresenting her racial identity.[127] Although her parents alleged she was white, Ms. Dolezal not only publicly identified as Black, but subtly changed her appearance at times to make it seem so, all the while raising Black children of her own.[128] She appears to have befriended several Black men she regarded as father figures (which, in at least some cases, they reciprocated)* as well as claimed Black siblings adopted by her biological parents.[129]

After being accused of lying about her race, and presenting in "Blackface," she not only resigned her position, but was ostracized from the communities and organizations whose mission she served and appeared to fervently believe in. After an intense backlash covered by national media and an unwillingness of community-based racial justice organizations to hire her, she resorted to relying on food stamps to survive. She explained that she never meant to offend anyone, but added, "If somebody asked me how I identify, I identify as black. Nothing about whiteness describes who I am."[130] If sincere on that point, does her sincerity make a difference to either her identity or how we might regard her?

Due to her apparent prior deception (and an apparent pattern of deception generally), critics were quick to see Ms. Dolezal's statements as self-serving, and her claim of Blackness as a basis for social and material

---

* Considering the preceding discussion, we should avoid dismissing claims of kinship just because they are not based on biological or blood relations.

advancement. But her case raises the intriguing question, why can a person have gender fluidity and transcend their sexual physiology but not enjoy a parallel acceptance of a similar claim for race?

The answer to this paradox is to remember that identity remains a complex social process. Even in cases where individuals are granted the freedom to determine their identity, that is because the broader society—or at least critical segments or institutions—have granted or extended that ability to individuals. The mistake that Ms. Dolezal made was assuming she could do this all by herself, and her (deceptive or misleading) attempts to claim Blackness in a context in which that category was not made socially or institutionally available to her.[131] The predictable backlash was fierce, making Ms. Dolezal a pariah and social outcast. Attempts to defend Ms. Dolezal themselves spawned new controversies, which we lack space to fully recount here.[132]

We do not describe this case to rehabilitate Ms. Dolezal, who might have anticipated and proactively addressed the predicament she faced by acknowledging the difference between her individual assertion of identity and the facts upon which others might classify her (which she, belatedly, did). Especially given her career work, she should have known her assertion would be transgressive, and even offensive to some.

However, we should consider another meaning when she says she rejects whiteness. Instead of denying her ancestry, a more generous interpretation might see her rejection of whiteness as a way of challenging the meanings and ideological function of whiteness. No less a figure than James Baldwin invited white people to do this, when he wrote, "Because they think they are white, they do not dare confront the ravage and the lie of their history. Because they think they are white, they cannot allow themselves to be tormented by the suspicion that all men are brothers."[133]

Perhaps her rejection of whiteness as an identity was a way of acknowledging, rather than denying, her connection with others—a gesture toward bridging. The manner in which she pursued this may have been less than adroit and, in many ways, insensitive, but she was following the logic of Baldwin's admonition, and part of the backlash risks—dangerously—re-essentializing race.

There have been multiple cases of university professors claiming Native American or other non-white identities, ostensibly to advance their

careers.[134] One of the stranger cases is that of Jessica Krug, a history professor at George Washington University. In 2020, Professor Krug published
a Medium post claiming that she had systematically deceived students and
colleagues by claiming to be an "Afro-Latina" when in fact she was a Jewish
woman from the suburbs.[135] Her "confession" was uncomfortably self-
disparaging and had a religious tone that critics felt was disingenuous.[136]

Although some of the cases appear self-serving and career motivated,
we are willing to consider the possibility that some of these people are
trying to distance themselves from whiteness and white identity because
they genuinely believe that adopting such an identity is harmful or inconsistent with their deepest values and commitments.[137] We are not endors-
ing the way they did it but we do believe this is an issue that should be more
thoughtfully engaged.

———

Not only is race a social construction, but certain facets of racial identity
can be viewed as ideological. We have already noted that some part of
whiteness is ideological: it is exclusionary and manifested to maintain
certain privileges and prerogatives. Denying those who reject that label
and sanctioning, punishing, and then ostracizing them threatens to re-
essentialize race once again, and bring us full circle.

Similarly, what if some portion of Generation Z who identify as LGBTQ
or nonbinary, especially those who identify as bisexual, are doing so not out
of an authentic sexual interest in people of different genders, but out of a
deeper desire to connect across difference or based on the social currency of
holding a more marginal identity and therefore bridge a social divide? That
is, what if, since sexuality is one of the few places where identity fluidity is
not only permitted by more widely accepted, it is a means to connect with
people across lines of difference, by self-describing, not only as bisexual but as
nonbinary, or pansexual? Similarly, what if some people identify as "queer"
not based upon sexual experience, but out of a desire to rebel against certain
gender and sexual orientation norms and traditional hierarchies?[138] If one
function of identities is to engender belonging and connection, then we fail
to see the harm in allowing this to happen without the kind of downward
scrutiny and sanctimonious disdain that some commentators maintain.

We should permit, if not encourage, people who seek to bridge, to grasp for a new or different identity, especially across deep social cleavages, and to do so with less trepidation. This does not mean we should automatically acquiesce to those making such claims. But we should welcome the negotiation and contestation that such claims commence, rather than fear it. The mistake that Ms. Dolezal made was not that people can change identities; it's that doing so is not an individual process (something she could do by herself), but a collective and social one. Although there may be limits, there must be the possibility of change because evolution is inevitable.

In fact, in a healthy, belonging society, the role of formative structures, institutions, and even narratives and culture would be to make these identity boundaries more porous and facilitate greater identity fluidity and multiplicity, by responding to our group needs and solving our collective problems. As those problems are resolved, some of these social identities would recede or lose social significance. In such a society, not only will our identities be more situational, and thereby fluid across multiple dimensions and axes, but we should also *experience* that fluidity and multiplicity more than we tend to do today. In practical terms, that means that none of us, in an ideal sense, should spend our entire life consigned within a single salient identity category; and, if we do, such an experience suggests that something is wrong—that the othering process is operating to make those identities more rigid, categorical, and entrenched than a healthy situation would warrant.

———

Both our identities and our very sense of self are constructed in relation to other identities and other selves through the othering process. Given the relational nature of both the self and the component identities, the solution to othering cannot occur by focusing exclusively or even primarily on the condition of marginalized groups.

The "Jewish problem" was not a problem of Jews, but rather a problem found in the larger antisemitic societies in which this question was framed and discussed. Thus, the problem of othering cannot be addressed simply by correcting or changing the characteristics or even the conditions of the subordinated group alone. If a group is tagged as being lazy or dishonest or violent, then the apparent solution is to make members more industrious and honest and peaceful. This is a seductive error: the temptation to believe that othering can be solved simply by improving or rectifying material conditions (often the policies of the political left), or changing habits or behaviors or even characteristics of marginalized groups (often the policies of the political right).

If the othering process constitutes both the other and the non-other, then the solution must be found in both places and at the source. The heart of the othering process is something that occurs when a powerful or dominant group organizes and then behaves in service of their own advantage and interests to the exclusion or disadvantage of another social group, an "othered" group. This is partly why an investment strategy is never sufficient to solve othering: improving the conditions of marginalized groups without reconstituting the dominant group and unwinding the processes that engender the dominance and marginality of both groups will fail to achieve its intended goals.

This chapter began to show how we might do that, by broadening our prevailing identities to reconstitute them along different lines, and by creating new possibilities for connection toward belonging—to build a bigger "we." This requires a recognition of our internal multiplicity and a willingness to cast ourselves into new identities that reconnect us and put us into a different set of relationships.

We have done this before, and can do this again, but we need more than a willing desire and a clear objective. We need a better understanding of the methods by which deliberate and conscious participation can move us in this direction. How do we ground and support new, more inclusive and encompassing identities to build the bigger "we"? The answer is the subject of our concluding chapter.

SEVEN

Hope for an Uncertain Future

This chapter brings us to the final question of this book: *How* can we build a more inclusive future collectively, a world where everyone belongs? We already reviewed many of the policy-based reforms and structural changes that can ease us into a world of greater belonging. But more is needed than policy and remedy. We need to reorient our ways of being and foster habits of connection, with more bridging and less breaking.

The greater challenge is to go be beyond bridging across boundaries and difference, and toward deeper forms of connection based on a recognition of our mutual interdependence and a larger "we." In the short term, we need to multiply and amplify spaces for bridging and curtail breaking, but in the longer term we need to develop and sustain containers that emphasize our shared humanity and enlarge our sense of a collective that is not defined by difference without denying difference. We must expand our "selves," broadening our prevailing identities (while creating new ones) as well as the stories and narratives we create and deploy to give meaning to those identities. This is our ultimate challenge and calling.

This is a critical moment in history, not simply because of the collective crises (ecological, epidemiological, economic, technological, and political) that confront humanity, but because it is a moment of institutional flux and change. Faith in existing institutions has declined while the multiple crises we face are beyond the capacity of individual nation-states to solve.[1]

In many critical particulars, the postwar order is faltering.* Western democracies are jettisoning establishment political parties. Surging support for outsider candidates in Europe and the United States reflects a desire for more fundamental change. But where this desire for change will go is unclear.[2] What is clear is that it can either tend toward deepening polarization, fragmentation, and othering or it can run in the opposite direction, fostering belonging with less othering, a culture of bridging, and building a bigger "we."

The main problem is that the repulsive forces that pull us apart are often stronger than those that bring us together. Demagoguery offers simple solutions to complex problems, preying on our prejudices and the pervasive anxieties that accompany large-scale and rapid change. This explains the ubiquity of ethno-nationalist movements, xenophobia, and reactionary political narratives regarding the traditional family, the role of women, or dangers of social mixing.[3]

Even where diversity is celebrated and valued, one of the fundamental tensions in multiculturalism is whether we are building merely pluralistic societies—where all groups are accorded equal respect and dignity—or societies in which our interdependence is acknowledged and realized, and everyone is afforded the agency to participate in its ongoing co-creation. One can read policy platforms rooted in equity and social justice and come away with the impression that "separate but equal" balkanization is an acceptable, even desirable, societal outcome.

We cannot create true belonging in a world in which everyone is clinging to or cornered into their most narrow, fearful selves, as currently constructed. This does not mean we can ask people to abandon their current identities, and plunge themselves into ontological death. The hint of such a demand from a place of equity and justice is partly what created the strange cases of Rachel Dolezal and Jessica Krug. We must supply the alternative.

After all, ontological anxiety and the deep need to belong has brought us to this juncture. But we must imagine something beyond our current selves. This is not as far-fetched as it may seem. There are ample cases

* More deeply, one could argue that the order since Westphalia or the Enlightenment is faltering.

already described in this book of how this has happened in the past. But what has not yet been foregrounded, and must now be discussed, is the role of narrative. To appreciate the possibilities contained within this insight, we need to begin by reexamining the role of stories.

The Power of Narrative

The previous two chapters noted the role of culture in fostering belonging and othering, and the need to recognize the multiplicity of the self to open new possibilities for identity development. But realizing them requires stories and narratives that can bring these identities to life and practices and habits that ground them.

In *Sapiens*, a wildly popular "big history" of humanity, the historian Yuval Harari makes several interesting claims that shed light upon the problem of othering and the path toward belonging. Among them, he asserts that our species lived in scattered small bands for most of our existence, and that our species was neither physically stronger nor necessarily more intelligent than other groups of *sapiens*, such as Neanderthals or Denisovans (in fact, Neanderthals were probably stronger). What allowed our species to win out—and more controversially, ultimately wipe out—other groups of *sapiens* was a "cognitive revolution" that occurred between 70,000 and 30,000 years ago.[4] The archeological evidence developed thus far shows that wherever *Homo sapiens* settled, competing *Homo* species disappeared, along other mega-fauna, and anything else in our way.[5]

At the heart of this revolution was the use of language, not simply to communicate or convey information, but to tell stories that centrally featured the people involved. More specifically, Harari points to the emergence of what he calls "collective common myths"—stories and narratives that created a larger "we" and enabled *Homo sapiens* to coordinate collectively in a manner and at a level that far surpassed our ancient competitors.[6] Even though smaller in number and weaker in stature, this coordination and cooperation allowed *Homo sapiens* to overcome stronger, faster, and fiercer competition. Instead of merely operating in bands of a dozen, our species could coordinate activity or action at almost any scale, from hundreds to thousands to millions and even theoretically billions of people.

The narratives that enabled collective widescale cooperation also provided spiritual meaning and shared social identities. They told us who we were and specified our role and place in the universe. Although Harari refers to these narratives and the concepts embedded in them as "myths," he does not intend to trivialize them. Quite the contrary, as he explains, these "collective common myths" or "imagined orders" become embedded in the material world (in "stone and mortar"), and ultimately shape our wants and desires, programming us in ways that are potent and far-reaching.

As Joseph Campbell's seminal works remind us, these "myths" can be more powerful, influential, and meaningful to us than any verifiable fact.[7] They give our lives meaning, provide scripts for behavior, connect us to places and people, and much more. As Joan Didion famously wrote, "we tell ourselves stories in order to live," even as she grappled with the consequences of the unravelling of shared narratives in the fragmentation of the late 1960s.[8] Didion's insight, however, is that our shared collective narratives structure our lives in profound ways. Or, as Angus Fletcher, the award-winning author and research lead of Project Narrative at Ohio State, explains, "the secret or super-power" that humans have and allowed us to dominate the planet is not our capacity for reason, as was thought by Enlightenment philosophers, but instead is "narrative—the ability to link causes together, to establish sequences, to tell stories."[9]

In this regard, narrative appears to play a central role in both processes of othering and belonging. The story we tell and live by plays an oversized role in the construction of belonging and creation of the social other. We have already described how the elites circulate different stories about those who belong ("us") as well as those who don't belong ("them"), and the role of dominant groups in establishing norms and cultural practices that either promote broad belonging or belonging based on othering.

There does not appear to be anything fixed or rigidly determined about the story we tell and live in. Humans have an uncanny ability to expand narratives indefinitely, graft new elements into old stories, mix and recombine elements, and build an organizing narrative about society of ever-increasing complexity. If this is right, it becomes imperative that we pay much greater attention to our stories, or organizing collective narratives (it may be misleading or trivializing to call them stories). Every society is framed by organizing narratives. Every community has shared myths, legends, commitments, and beliefs. Every set of core moral values and ethical principles is embodied in stories and narratives. What matters is the content of those stories, and the meaning attached to them.

———

Why do some stories take hold while others do not? As Harari notes, telling effective stories is not easy: "The difficulty lies not in telling the story, but in convincing everyone to believe in it."[10] Convincing people to subscribe to a particular religious faith or national origin story were among the most difficult projects in human societies, but also the most powerful.

As one example of such an imagined order facilitating collective activity, Harari cites America's founding myths and documents. The organizing narrative is the story of the American Revolution, the rebellion against tyranny, a republic established on universal, liberal principles, and the novel concept of political equality for all people. Harari acerbically notes that although little in the most famous language in the Declaration of Independence is technically accurate, it has oriented millions of people to believe that if they live according its principles, they can "cooperate effectively, living safely and peacefully in a just and prosperous society."[11] As this example shows, our organizing narratives help to give meaning to events in our past and future, and who we are.

The construction of identity is a complicated process, and one important element of the process that we haven't addressed yet is the role of history and historical narratives in the construction of group-based identities. "Who we are" is based upon narratives of what our people have accomplished, suffered through, or collectively experienced.

Narratives of shared endeavors and sacrifices are usually central to the building of nation-states and as well as solidifying religious orders, as both the Crusades and the resistance to them illustrated for European Christians and Muslims of the Middle East alike. Conversely, narratives of trauma and dispossession may also shape identity development. Both Jewish and Armenian peoples, in surveys, have said that their respective genocides are "central" to their identity.[12] Similarly, dispossession has fundamentally shaped Native American identity.[13]

The organizing narratives that shape the construction of collective identities are far more than a dispassionate and factual recounting of events. They are not purely historical accounts. Moreover, what is called "history" is actually an organizing narrative disseminated and directed for the purpose of providing collective meaning, purpose, and identity. According to a Sioux proverb, "A people without history is like wind on the buffalo grass."[14] History tells us who we are. This explains why history is such a fierce zone of contestation. Competing accounts of history are far more than technical or esoteric disputes over facts, dates, or events. Different historical narratives provide different accounts of collective identity and meaning.[15]

The Golden Age Fallacy

Perhaps one of the stranger phenomena of our era is the persistence of bizarre and factually unfounded claims about the past, what Francis Fukuyama calls "nostalgic fantasy for a time that never existed."[16] Hindu nationalists in modern India have propagated a mythology that is positively bizarre in some respects. They claim, for example, that ancient Indians invented aircraft thousands of years ago and could travel to other planets.[17] Along similar lines, a noted Serbian pseudo-historian claims that ancient Serbs erected pyramids during the last Ice Age, and that these structures were used to communicate with interstellar civilizations.[18]

These strange claims have each arisen in the soil of ascendant ethnonationalism, and are supplied as "proof" of a "great civilization."* One observer describes this (modern) view of ancient India in stark terms:

It is seen as a time of pure Hinduism, created by Sanskrit-speaking people who had always lived on the Indian subcontinent, with a unified,

---

*While these claims may appear especially bizarre in the contemporary context, supernatural elements are common to religious narratives, and there are legends and mythologies that lay at the root of many of the world's civilizations. For example, both the Chinese and Japanese emperors were said to be descended from divine beings.

homogeneous religion and culture free of the foreign presence to come in later centuries, especially with the entry into India of Islam and then the West. In this paradisiacal ancient India, the Hindu right finds evidence of a wide array of modern devices and technologies.[19]

This explains why such claims have found receptive audiences. Mythologies of past greatness serve several critical functions. First, they assure their communities that, whatever travails may be upon them today, they are a "great" people, with remarkable accomplishments and capabilities. In some cases, they are used to even denote divinity or divine aegis to the group.

Second, they are used to shape or anchor the identity of the group. They are designed to instill pride and strengthen affiliative bonds. Thus, nostalgia for some past moment is part of the process of identity creation and definition. More than that, "collective nostalgia" anchors not simply individual identity, but helps create or reshape group-based identities in a broad and public way. The role of these narratives is to help define and affirm contemporary collective identities, and we have seen how there can be an exclusionary aspect to this.

Contemporary archeological research suggests that the Exodus story contained in the second book of the Torah and the Old Testament of the Bible may have been conceived in the sixth century BC—more than six hundred years after the events supposedly occurred—as "a political manifesto to unite Israelites against the rival Egyptian empire as both states sought to expand their territory."[20] In other words, it was a shared collective narrative designed "to give an origin and history to a people and distinguish them from others by claiming a divine destiny."[21]

These narratives, by specifying a particular moment or period and the people involved, indicate who belongs and who does not. In his delineation of the elements of fascism, the American philosopher Jason Stanley claims that harkening to a "mythic past," where the "'we' descend from a glorious, patriarchal past," and "'they' threaten that legacy," is one of the ten pillars or fascism—and is so central that he lists it first.[22]

This helps explain why ethno-nationalist movements appear to be such fertile soil for the creation of these myths, no matter how bizarre. After all, what is "Make America Great Again" if not an effort to claim some past moment of greatness while binding together MAGA as a group identity with its own totems, symbols, and vernacular? One need not deny greatness to aspects of the American political experiment to acknowledge that the MAGA slogan is reaching for a mythical past, not some concrete period of defined greatness.

Third, these narratives anchoring "our identity in the past helps give us a sense of stability and predictability."[23] Reaching for the past is a reaching for a time of homogeneity and stability in terms of "knowing one's place." Recall our discussion about how rapid change triggers anxiety in human beings. By anchoring people to the past, these narratives offer stability in a period of turmoil and anxiety. In short, these mythologies are propagated as ways to contend with, and resolve, anxieties about the complexity of modern life, a feature that goes all the way back to Hesiod, who saw corruption, wars, and moral decline, even in eighth-century BCE Greece.[24]

Hesiod wrote wistfully of the "legend of the golden age," which he and his people regarded as a much earlier and (even for the poet) ancient time of forebears who lived in peace, harmony, and prosperity.[25] In this conception, some distant earlier period was the pinnacle of human history, with each generation a regress from those happier heights, on the downward slope.

———

Indeed, something quite similar can be found at the root of the Abrahamic tradition in the tale of the Garden of Eden, and the expulsion of man from paradise. There is some evidence that the notion of the "golden age" and pining for the "good old days" goes back even further to ancient Mesopotamia. Sumerian cuneiform contains examples of this both in prose and poems.[26] This notion seems to be so common that some commentators have labeled it the "Golden Age Fallacy."[27]

The psychological needs that nostalgic mythmaking serve are universal, especially in periods of change and instability. The reason the golden age fallacy is a fallacy is that the past being valorized was not usually better in any objective sense, but rather the human societies harkening back to the past characterize that period as such for easily understandable psychological reasons, usually to grapple with humiliations or anxieties about the present. Our identities are rooted in ways of being, expressions of culture, and particular places and periods of time. When some part of our story is lost or challenged, perhaps by changes that we did not invite or at the hands of enemies or other groups, this causes pain and grief. We need new stories to help us cope, but this is difficult to do in periods of rapid change.

The southern "Lost Cause" narrative was a powerful salve for the wounds of the Civil War among the white planter class and white southerners generally, even though it performed incredible injustice to freedmen and their descendants. This narrative was a mythical rendering of the antebellum South, out of which sprang the nation's most popular film (and, when adjusted for inflation, still highest-grossing of all time), *Gone with the Wind*.

Much as China's apparent ambitions over Hong Kong and Taiwan (and Tibet before them) harken back to some earlier period before being humiliated by European imperial powers, Vladimir Putin's invasion of Ukraine appears rooted in overcoming the humiliation of the fall of the Soviet Union while harkening back perhaps to the Russian Empire under Catherine the Great.[28] His grand state solution is to unite some ancient Slavic diaspora and the Russian-speaking world, or "Russky Mir."[29]

The Balkan corollary to Russky Mir is "Greater Serbia," what ethnonationalists in the former Yugoslavia hoped to build with ethnic cleansing in Bosnia and Kosovo, before being driven back by NATO. In both cases, as one observer notes, "no matter what their past crimes, [these nations] see themselves as sufferers, not aggressors, and whose politics and psyche revolve around cults of victimhood nurtured by resentment and grievance against the West."[30] These narratives and their psychological underpinnings help explain how such strange claims regarding Neolithic-era advanced-technology Serbian pyramids in Bosnia could find a receptive audience.

These golden age narratives are fallacious, in part, because they are highly selective claims that focus on a particular point in time or period of time to the exclusion of others. It is a case of history being "molded to the imperatives of the present."[31] And to that, we might add, the fight over the future. Whether it is Russia and parts of Ukraine, Azerbaijan and Nagorno-Karabakh, China and Tibet, or Israel and Jerusalem, each territorial claim is based upon control over the land area and people in question at some defining historical moment or period.[32]

Yet each one of these claims ignores points in time in which they historically lacked control over that territory or the deeply contested and fluctuating nature of that control. A century-over-century territorial map of ethnic Armenia over the past two millennia would be a kaleidoscope of shifting boundaries and borders to a comic degree. While an extreme case, much the same could be said of most ethnic and cultural communities on the globe on a long enough time frame. This is why the idea of a "proper territory" being defined by a historical account is a hopeless and deeply flawed endeavor.[33]

In truth, all of history is a partial account subject to being revised, reframed, or amended in some way. What is emphasized or celebrated and what is forgotten or unspoken shapes historical memory and gives meaning to the present. The American Revolution, for example, has been framed as more than another colonial rebellion, but in world-historical terms, as the creation of an epochal republic, and a model for the entire world, the city shining on a hill.[34] In short, all history is framed or given a gloss in some way that indicates what is important and what is not, and aspects of history that are embarrassing may be obscured or repressed.

This also helps explain contemporary fights over history books, including discussions of slavery and race in American textbooks and classrooms. These are the same dynamic at a different scale as various "memory laws," laws that prohibit the expression of historical claims that diverge from or challenge the official interpretation of the past (see our supplemental chapter for more on this). The Soviet Union prohibited speech on the mass famines of the early 1930s in Ukraine and Kazakhstan, laws that have carried over into post-Soviet Russia, just as Chinese authorities have criminalized—and will censor—any effort to memorialize the student rebellion in Tiananmen Square in 1989.[35] History is always selectively deployed to serve the ambitions and needs of the moment.

But the myth of the golden age is fallacious for another reason. We have noted how ethno-nationalists and ethno-states attempt to justify the binding of national identity with a particularistic (rather than pluralistic) set of racial, ethnic, cultural, or ancestral claims. Crucially, these fantasies about the past—these nostalgic yearnings—suggest a time or a period where people were bonded around some core identity categories or broad cultural idea, whether it is racial or ethnic homogeneity, religion, or a deep national tradition. That is also part of the fantasy, because there never was such a time free of difference or division.

Contestations over history are only superficially about the past. They are primarily about the present and the future, as the psychological underpinnings of the "golden age fallacy" reveal. This is why public debates over the past are not principally the province of esoteric academic debate or erudite scholarly journals, but large public narrative. Contestation over the past, and the impetus for the various forms of historical mythmaking and "nostalgic fantasy," are more about quieting anxieties experienced in the present, overcoming humiliations, and striving to reclaiming a particular future from the "past."[36]

Human societies propagate organizing narratives that instill pride and suppress those that are embarrassing or humiliating. Critically, we should not view this tendency merely as the cynical tactic of a cunning leader. Such collective organizing narratives would not take root if people rejected them. They must offer something appealing for them to take hold in the minds and imaginations of their recipients. The alternative is not just confusion and chaos, but a different story, propounded by someone else, that is ultimately embraced. The cunning and effective leader propagates organizing narratives that appeal to their people, even if that means a highly selectively or largely fabricated reading of history.

If this theory is correct, then nostalgic yearnings and nostalgic fantasies should intensify in periods of rapid change and uncertainty, as human anxieties surge, and political entrepreneurs tap into these anxieties by promulgating such fantasies. Even a cursory glance around the world today suggests that we inhabit such a time. Because of globalization, every community and culture feels as if it cannot safeguard its heritage.[37] The prevalence of these fantasies across cultures and societies reflects the common root to these fantasies.

If narratives of the past are collectively constructed for more immediate exigencies, helping affirm or amend and then anchor contemporary identities, then narratives of the future can be similarly constructed for the same ends. And if narratives of the past can be designed to exclude, narratives for the future can advance a more inclusive belonging vision for society.

From the Imagined Past to the Imagined Future

Although stories are not enough, we cannot call a world into being that we cannot begin to imagine. There is a reason that demagogues and ethno-nationalists pine for a past that never was instead of embracing a future that is rushing onward. If we can imagine a past that never was, then can we imagine a more hopeful future? Can we imagine a world where no group dominates? Although the past remains with us, neither it nor the future is set in stone. We can and must together dream of, and call for, a future where we all belong.

One of the paradoxes of the fight for social justice is that identities of marginalized people are constituted out of the process of marginalization, or, in the nomenclature of this book, the "othering process." Thus we have seen how Native American identity has been forged in reaction to dispossession and genocide, to take but one example.

The reason this is paradoxical is because justice might seem to require a rejection of those identities along with the equalization of material conditions and opportunities. Thus, as Black South Africans strive to achieve political and economic equality by overcoming the legacies of colonialism and apartheid, wouldn't it also follow logically to reject the racial paradigm that defines them as Black in favor of some pre-colonial identity or alternative construct? "Race" was a European invention of the seventeenth century. After all, Black South Africans are indigenous, with millennia of traditions and culture that have endured, unlike their counterparts farther north who were brought in chains to the Americas and were stripped of so much.

But the paradox here is the similar to the paradox of colorblindness. As an aspiration, colorblindness has a certain logic—but as a practical matter, it makes little sense. Although Black South Africans have many other overlapping identities (religious, ethnic, etc.), racial identity continues to help organize collective efforts toward the aspiration of a free and equal society. A "Zulu" identity, one of the largest ethnic groups among indigenous South Africans, tends, in contrast, to divide and fracture that political interest and undermine solidarity between formerly colonialized peoples.

A similar problem exists for the identities of members of nonmarginalized groups (for example, "white," "Christian," "Hindu," "Han," etc.).

Even as many of these identities have problematic features or tendencies, we cannot ask people who hold them to simply abandon them. Doing so either results in a direct ontological threat, which will deepen the hold of that identity, with often violent results, or produces a different kind of de-rangement like the case of Rachel Dolezal.

We can't ask people to suffer ontological death by abandoning a core identity.* It is not even clear people could do that if they wanted to with-out a great deal of social and collective help. People need identities and selves. We can't ask people to slip off meaningful identities—even cor-rosive ones—without offering an alternative or dissolving all material or contextual bases on which those identities form (like the disintegration of the Soviet Union or breakup of Yugoslavia). As meaning-making animals, the loss of meaning has a profound impact upon us. But for members of dominant or higher-status groups, ontological threats are even more likely to lead to radicalization, support for authoritarianism, and out-group violence.

Although we shouldn't ask people to reject or abandon identities that have given their life meaning, we should take seriously the call to devise alternative identities, not on a narrow basis, but on a broad and inclusive one. If certain forms of affiliation are toxic or corrosive, our only resort is to provide alternatives that are just as compelling and meaningful. It cannot suffice to condemn certain bonds of belonging without offering or afford-ing a healthier alternative. We must offer an imaginative belonging alterna-tive. That alternative must include community, an estimable identity, and purpose. Just as nation-builders have had to create new identities since time immemorial, so must we strive to create new identities today.

The chief difference between creating new identities and grappling with the harmful tendencies of existing ones is the influence and inertia that our prevailing identities hold, and the imaginative vision needed to persuade people to embrace a new organizing story. A belonging vision will require us to collectively recast our identities into healthier forms.

---

* Demanding that people repress, shed, or hide parts of their identities is not only an ontological identity threat, but it is also an expression of othering. Consider the self-abnegation required to stay in the "closet" as a condition of belonging.

This can't be accomplished by ourselves. It becomes possible if we open ourselves to new relationships (rather than hold tightly to our narrowest selves), but we still need public narratives, cultural practices, and social supports to ground them and weave them into our social lives. This is the essence of co-creation—imagining together. Although all of us play a role, our public leaders play an outsized one.

We noted in the first chapter that one of the reasons "tribalism" fails as a descriptor of othering is that not all human societies properly characterized as "tribal" are exclusionary, insular, or parochial. Whether they are depends upon the norms and outlook of the group. These attitudes and tendencies in turn depend in no small part on leadership modeled within such groups. Leaders can tell an organzing story and embody an outlook that is hopeful and inclusive or one that is fearful and parochial.

Rapid change produces anxiety in humans and other mammals. We live in a time of enormous and accelerating change. Demagogic leaders by and large have taken that anxiety and curdled it into fear, resentment, and anger, especially among members of traditionally dominant groups. They have nurtured a story of loss and being replaced. This not just a story about climate change or jobs disappearing; they are telling a story about losing the collective self. In other words, this not just a story about losing stuff, but also about losing being. And, in their telling, the source of this loss is not just technology, natural disasters, or epidemics and the environment, but the dreaded "other."

Although inevitable, change is anathema to those afraid of it. You can't allay fear of change by asserting the world is going to change anyway. You must present a positive and compelling vision of the future. The key fact is not the reality of change, but the meaning attached to that change. The meaning-making process happens in large part through public narrative, stories promulgated by public leaders and media.

Public leaders can inspire societies with visions of a more hopeful belonging future, in the same way that demagogues can frighten them into division. Dr. Martin Luther King Jr. was one such leader, but there are many others, whose words and thoughts can inspire and galvanize, from

Lincoln to Mandela. This does not mean that such public leaders are free of opprobrium or opposition. The key is not their public standing, but the message they convey and the reach that message ultimately has.

A good story must respond to our anxieties and fears while directing our hopes and aspirations. An instructive example occurred at the outset of the space race, in response to shock and fear that shuddered through American society with the launch of the Soviets' Sputnik. President Kennedy's moonshot speech sought to allay those fears while calling on the nation to send a man to the moon within the decade.[38] It is not enough to admonish people not to be afraid; a good story must help people channel that anxiety or fear into collective energy and serve as an inspiration or plan of action, as when another president told Americans in the depths of the Great Depression that "the only thing we have to fear is fear itself" as a pledge to action.

A notable leader who both expressed and embodied a hopeful, belonging message was Ireland's Mary Robinson, elected as the nation's first female president in 1990 and who served until 1997 before becoming the UN's high commissioner on human rights.[39] In her inauguration, she told a story of Ireland's past, present, and future, painting a portrait of a "new Ireland" that would be more "open, tolerant, and inclusive."[40] She enlarged Ireland's national identity to include its extended diaspora and to connect it to Europe's postcommunist future. By the end of her tenure she was one of Europe's most popular and admired leaders.

As one commentator observed: "history has a way of turning into myth, but the reverse can also be true: Myths have a way of making history. Fortune also tends to favor fervent believers."[41] This appears to be one of the critical secrets to belonging: the way to defuse the demagogue is not through condemnation and cauterization, but by telling a better story, one so compelling that it draws followers and attracts adherents. As this book has sought to reveal, stories and narratives play a critical and powerful role in shaping who we are, how we make meaning, and what may possible. If Harari is right, that stories are central to the story of human survival and success, and if history is partly myth, then we have the power to collectively imagine a better future. In the words of Hannah Gadsby, "[s]tories hold our cure."[42]

Telling Better Stories

Narrative is one of the principal ways we construct a sense of belonging today, just as it has been for millennia. Since at least *The Iliad* and *The Odyssey*, stories shape our collective imagination and tell us who we are and our place in the world. Some stories are exclusionary and preclude a large, belonging "we." Stories of cultural or religious or racial dominance are also about a set of relations, and how and why those relations should be arranged and maintained. They are about who is "worthy," chosen or deserving, and who is not.

Demagogues tell stories to frighten and divide. Although we wish it were otherwise, the best evidence suggests that demagogues cannot be defeated or defused by railing against them, castigating them and their followers. Instead, the best path to defeating them is by telling a better story. Whatever its content, an effective belonging story must provide dignity and a future for all people. This is the key.

Many of our prevailing narratives seem to have a strong in-group and a strong out-group. If we are going to build belonging without othering, we have to confront a simple question: Is it possible to create a powerful story without a villain or an out-group? Some scholars claim that all movements depend upon a villain—whether it is immigrants, a racial other, Muslims, government bureaucrats, or perhaps, in the case campaigns like those organized by Bernie Sanders, billionaires and large multinational corporations. In his study of mass movements, the American philosopher Eric Hoffer maintains that "[m]ass movements can rise and spread without belief in a god, but never without belief in a devil."[43] One foreign affairs observer claims, as an application of this principle, that the Iranian political regime depends upon a view of the United States as the "great Satan."[44]

Yet, experts on narrative and stories are not completely convinced on this point, at least in terms of the compelling reach and staying power of an organizing narrative. They find that the best stories—the most interesting and enduring stories—are not so categorical either in their moral structure or their moral delineation among characters. Although superficially following the traditional "hero's journey" and the archetypal and Manichean fight of good against evil, the central character of *Star Wars* is a fallen figure who redeems himself in the final moments of the original trilogy. Presented as the ultimate villain, Darth Vader is in fact a tragic and conflicted figure. The most compelling stories feature complex characters.

Strangely, many of the most enduring stories are neither those that conform to nor complicate the moral order, but those that invert it, introducing chaos, randomness, and chance, where ambiguity is embraced. Experts call this the "fairy-tale twist" because it is so common among the stories in oral traditions that survived over generations.[45]

———

Even if it is possible in a broad social and political context to create and promulgate a compelling story without a villain or out-group, how would such a story be disseminated or absorbed? We may need both a powerful set of stories and even better storytellers. Fortunately, this is something humanity is already quite skilled at from time immemorial.

One strong reservoir of this is fiction, both literary and mass entertainment. One of the reasons that the science fiction television show and film series *Star Trek* proved so compelling is that it projects a future of greater hope and belonging. It was one of the first network American television shows to depict a truly diverse cast, and even included a Russian and Black bridge officer at the height the Cold War and the civil rights movement. Countless engineers and scientists have drawn career inspiration from that vision. Even Jeff Bezos, the entrepreneur who founded the space exploration company Blue Origin, told one of the *Star Trek* actors as much.[46]

More deliberate efforts in this regard can be found in strains of speculative fiction, such as Afro-Futurism. Some of these stories imagine societies of belonging by reconceiving identity in a variety of ways, as by recasting the possibilities for Black life and community. Octavia Butler's numerous award-winning novels deal with diversity and difference in ways that challenge and inspire.[47] The film *Black Panther* shattered box-office records by conveying a similarly moving tale drawing upon Afro-Futuristic narrative elements, proving that they have broad appeal.

Black Panther also models a story without a categorical hero or villain. Despite its provenance as a "superhero" genre film with characters cast in those roles, as the backstories are revealed, their roles prove surprisingly fluid and dynamic. By the end of the film, the antagonist is in many ways a sympathetic, tragic figure, and the "hero" has ultimately discovered flaws and errors of his own.[48]

We must be able to tell stories that hold the complexity of people and life. But a story that builds a bigger "we" must have a place for all groups, including members of a formerly or traditionally dominant groups. It must remind us, in the words of the comedienne Hannah Gadsby, that "your story is my story, and my story is your story."[49] It must be rooted and based on reality and representations of reality as well as a project of imagination. This means it must acknowledge our flaws, but not as permanently flawed or fallen.

———

In an interview with Ta-Nehisi Coates and Nikole Hannah-Jones, Ezra Klein probed the acclaimed journalists on the power and potential of narrative and story: "stories matter because you build upon them, and then what? Are we just changing who the good and bad guys are of the story, or what is being built on this?"[50] Coates answered that in a complex "human" story, "[t]here is no place where you reside and you get to feel like you are the good guy in the story."

That may be true in a narrow sense, but in a cultural sense, that kind of story is not going to bind us together, fostering connection and affinity. A belonging, "bridging" story must be one that contains nuance for all groups, without painting any social group into the role of permanent villain or fallen condition.[51] It must offer positive, aspirational scripts for each group, even if those scripts provide different templates or roles for different groups within the larger narrative. Our larger belonging narrative must be a story about the world and all of the people in it that is unifying rather than dividing. It must have the possibility of redemption and renewal for all people and groups. No group can be consigned to the role of villain or antagonist.

There are many challenges. Consider the so-called problem of "toxic masculinity," the idea that behaviors and scripts traditionally offered to men are dysfunctional or even harmful, both to men themselves and to others, in modern societies.[52] It is clear that certain behaviors that were once brushed off as "boys being boys" are no longer acceptable (if they ever were), including behaviors in the workplace that are now described as vestiges of the "*Mad Men* era."[53] Scholars and pundits alike have come up with widely divergent solutions to the so-called problem of "masculinity" and manhood in contemporary society,[54] but the real problem may be the lack of available scripts to guide what a reconstituted and healthy masculine gender role can and should be in modern societies. We need larger belonging narratives that delineate the role of men in society—without denying different gender identities—while providing positive scripts for those identities, including young men.

A similar set of questions arise regarding race. Specifically, can we tell a story about racial injustice and Black suffering while effecting space for the guilt or shame that whites might experience while also creating a space for their stories and aspirations as well? Not a story where white people must dominate or white needs are centered, but neither a story where white people must be (or are presumptively and irredeemably) racist, fragile, or a challenge to be overcome?

Some might wonder: Why should we tell a story that includes whites or any other traditionally privileged group? How can we embrace white people given the history of white supremacy in this country and in the world? This question deserves a careful and deliberate answer.

In lifting up a few possible reasons why we must, we should first emphasize that there is no available alternative. Our more hopeful public story about the future must include these groups as part of the story or else it will falter and fail. We cannot pull people out of harmful organizing narratives that shape their sense of identity and community without offering a positive and functional alternative. As David French noted on the allure of Donald Trump's MAGA rallies and the community it affords despite the derangements that MAGA-devotion seems to entail, "You can't replace something with nothing. And until we fully understand what that 'something' is—and that it includes not only passionate anger but also very real joy and a deep sense of belonging—then our efforts to persuade are doomed to fail."[55]

Moreover, people who do not see themselves in a story of the future (or only as villains) will inevitably reject it, often violently. This explains the fight over history and national identity we have seen in statehouses around the United States and other countries.[56] The fight over the past is often more intense because it is a fight over our very essence and the possibility of a redemptive future. Commenting on the visceral and charged reaction to the 1619 Project by Hannah-Jones,[57] which posited a different founding for the United States, Ezra Klein asks, incisively: "Why is there so much more electricity over how we understand our past than how we describe our present? What are the stakes? What changes when the story a country tells about itself changes? What changes when who has the power to tell that story changes?"[58]

To the extent that groups believe they are fighting for their very being, there will be no space to see the other side or make common ground. In the words of Amin Maalouf, "any human community that feels humiliated or fears for its existence will tend to produce killers."[59] Again, plunging white people into ontological death means derangements like Dolezal on the one hand or Timothy McVeigh and Dylann Roof on the other, head-rushing to claim a non-white racial identity or holding to it too tightly on the path to radicalization and mass violence.

Another reason we can and should include non-othered peoples in our belonging story is that we can and should distinguish between people and ideology. We can decouple people racialized as white from white supremacy as an ideological project. As we argued earlier, the hard focus should be on supremacy—or dominance—of any sort. In order to forge belonging without othering, we must replace dominance with nondominance, not one form of dominance with another form of dominance. We are against group supremacy in all its possible manifestations.

Emphasizing nondominance can help mitigate the status threat engendered by inclusion and equity and help inoculate against various replacement theories. It must be stressed that the goal is not to replace one group's social position in society with another group, but to forge a society in which no group is dominant or supreme. Our focus is against supremacy, dominance, and othering, not white people, Han, Hindus, or any other people.*

---

* The struggle against dominance and supremacy should not be confused with a fight against numerical predominance. The proportion of white or non-white

Our focus must be on caring, cooperation, mutuality, and belonging, not zero-sum competition, revenge, or reverse supremacy and dominance.

We acknowledge how difficult this can be. Just as much of the "the bipartisan, Washington-based, foreign policy elite that believes maintaining the United States' global dominance is essential to ensuring American safety and international peace,"[60] many dominant groups fear that a loss of their group position will lead to chaos, disorder, and great harm. We must find ways to convince them that a healthy world is achievable through healthy competition, cooperation, diversity, and balance of power, rather than dominance.

The challenge is even greater when the scripts afforded these identities were oriented around dominance or attempts to dominate, as is the case for traditional male gender roles. Creating new scripts for men and masculinity oriented around nondominance is no easy task. One possible alternative is to emphasis protection, service, and caring within a larger belonging narrative that regards the male role in a positive light, rather than as a problem to be mitigated, contained, or erased. Only if men who embrace a masculine gender identity are offered a positive role will they participate in the belonging narrative. If they are denied a positive role, they will reject the narrative and too often fall prey to the siren call of the demagogue.

Positive intergroup contact is achieved by working together toward common goals in a context of relatively equality. The narratives that can serve our goal of belonging should be similarly structured: everyone is needed in service of a larger, shared vision. This narrative should posit the possibility of peaceful coexistence and cooperation as beneficial to all.[61]

Another element of the effective story is that it can evoke feeling and even sympathy while simultaneously humanizing the groups involved in the story, which some scholars call the "sentimental story."[62] While the

---

people does not ultimately tell us much about the values or tendencies and norms of the community, institution, or group. A plurality or bare-majority white institution can be far more pernicious in its exclusionary tendencies or norms than a heavily white institution, especially if the white people in that institution feel an identity threat. In fact, emphasizing numeracy over values, norms, and the like will tend to engender fears of identity threat.

sentimental story is also a tool of the demagogue, it is also effective as a bridging practice and organizing belonging narrative.

Another way to overcome the fear of status threat is by leaning into broader identities, as discussed in the last chapter, or emphasizing overarching identities that bridge a salient social cleavage, within the story. We saw how certain identities can be forged or made salient to reduce the salience of others. Effective belonging stories should seek to do this.

To the extent that people are members of a dominant group, such "dominance," as it is actually experienced, may be quite limited or provisional. White dominance or any other kind may only be dominant as an ideology in relation to competing worldviews, and not an inevitable artifact of the identity it is tethered to. For example, white supremacy does not mean that most white people are material beneficiaries of such an ideology. Members of the group raced "white" may get symbolic status from that ideology. But status and material condition are not always in sync. Often it is not, as the ironic term "wages of whiteness," coined by Du Bois, suggests.

But even if there are material benefits from dominance or enjoying higher-status group membership, that does not mean that members of the formerly dominant group will be materially worse off if their identity loses its relative social position of predominance. Not being part of a dominant group does not mean that they may only then exist in a subordinate state or will cease to exist. This is another way to understand the fear of the American foreign policy establishment: that if the American military is not dominant, it must be subordinate. Yet, thoughtful reflection should reveal the shallowness of such fears. A world where American taxpayers and soldiers are not shouldering the burden of military dominance could make a stronger nation, not a weaker one, and a safer world, not a more dangerous one.[63] The key is imagining and positing a future where all may be better off under conditions of non-hegemony.

As we push for social justice and advance a belonging organizing narrative, it must demonstrate that every group has a place and belongs. Our imagined future requires a very large "we" and absent any group domination. We must advance a vision in which everyone can see themselves and plays an active and participatory role, and is extended dignity and respect.

Telling this story will be difficult, and living it will be harder still. We must breathe life into our vision. Within our new belonging narratives, we need new scripts that guide behavior and model positive action. But above all, we must foster practices and devise institutions that embody that story. Bridging is such a practice, but we need to do more than bridge. We need to promulgate institutional forms, collective rituals, and behavioral norms that reinforce that vision. This includes cultural practices that inculcate these stories and ground such identities as well as laws and policies that circulate these stories into public educational curriculum.

But we cannot avoid the responsibility or do so from a distance or from a high remove. We are the story, and we play many different parts with mutual fears and aspirations. We must articulate, present, and convey a story of belonging and love to compete and win over the story of fear and domination. The better story will prevail.

Telling a compelling, inspiring, and effective organizing story in this way is difficult for liberal democracies. Although liberal democracies have inspiring origin stories and ethics of egalitarianism, it is difficult in a free and open society to maintain large social projects that can bring people together. Liberal societies tend to provide maximal autonomy to individuals to create meaning and purpose for themselves, which means that it is much harder to galvanize a public around a joint endeavor, the primary and notorious exception being a war.

Liberal democracies tend to devolve into technocratic issues, matters that are enormously important, such as health care, employment, etc. but which can also seem trivial and relatively unimportant from a larger point of view, lacking a sense of history or grand purpose. Some inspiring movements are organized around electoral campaigns, but the energy dissipates when the campaign is over—like the "hope and change" campaign that Barack Obama led in 2008 illustrated.

The most effective stories are those that create a common cause, bring together the greater part of society in pursuit of that cause, and inspire people to a higher and often nonmaterial goal or purpose. The very best stories are those that make people feel as if they are involved in a historical endeavor. But we cannot rest on our laurels. This is the challenge for every generation. Our story will never be complete because we will never be complete. As Stuart Hall reminds us, our identities "have histories," but "like everything which is historical, they undergo constant transformation. Far from being eternally fixed in some essentialized past, they are subject to the continuous 'play' of history, culture and power."[64] Our histories and our identities are subjects of continuous revision. Likewise, our belonging story must be pages in the process of being written.

If telling effective new organizing narratives with identities and meanings that foster belonging and a larger "we," and convincing people to buy into them seems daunting, we should remember that this leap of imagination is no greater than the mythologies we have worked so hard to create and sustain in so many other realms. The question before us is simple: How can we create an imagined future instead of an imaginary past? After all, the act of imagination for a future is necessarily more open and replete with possibility than the effort to rewrite a past, which must contend with an actual historical record. The future is ours to write.

The Demographic Opportunity

Across the world, demographic changes are making the question of the imagined future quite important. In the United States, higher birth rates among non-whites is making the question of national identity more salient, just as higher birth rates among immigrants and Muslims are in Europe, or birth rates among Arabs in Israel. Demographic change has a way of making this debate urgent. We are in a period of rapid demographic, political, technological, environmental, and economic change, which entails rapidly changing identities, including pressures around diversity. We need to offer alternative stories for making meaning of these developments that do not center fears of replacement and dispossession. The right wing is trying to pause this change, or, more extreme, reverse it and return to a mythological past. But the future will come whether we are ready or not. Trying to hide in an imagined past is a risky ploy.

The demographic transition refers not simply to the shift from white to non-white racial composition through migration, but more critically for our belonging future, through intermarriage and intermixing of racial (and other) group identities. Interracial marriage is on a very large upswing in the United States, and as a society, we have neither prepared for the consequences nor adequately considered the possible implications. It may not be true that demography is destiny, but it certainly will have an impact.

Prohibitions against interracial marriage were only declared unconstitutional as recently as 1967, and opinions regarding it were slower to catch up. The General Social Survey tracked public opinion on this issue for decades. In 1990, roughly six in ten non-Black Americans (63 percent) said they would be opposed to a close relative marrying a Black person. This share fell by about in half by 2000 (at 30 percent), and halved again to about 14 percent today.[65]

Perhaps as a result of these attitudes, interracial marriage remained somewhat uncommon for decades. In 1967, only about 3 percent of all new marriages were interracial, and by 1980 only about 3 percent of *all* marriages were interracial. Now, about 15 percent of all marriages are interracial.[66] These figures also do not include cross-cultural or inter-ethnic marriages, like Chinese Americans marrying Indian Americans. As the proportion of the population that is non-white in the United States grows, interracial marriages will become more common, approaching a tipping point, where it may quickly accelerate as taboos fall away.[67]

Unsurprisingly, these marriages are yielding multiracial and multi-ethnic children. According to the Pew Research Center, 6.9 percent of American adults are now mixed-race, a figure that is certain to climb much higher in coming years.[68] In particular, the 2020 census revealed a huge increase in multiracial Americans, the largest percent increase of any group.[69]

We only have glimmers of what this will mean in the long run. We know it will challenge existing racial categories, and the criteria on which people will be sorted into those categories. As there are more multiracial people, it will be harder to maintain taxonomic categories that are exclusionary rather than fluid.[70] But the implications and potential extend far beyond that. By some accounts, multiracial and multi-ethnic families will be the plurality by the end of the century. All these projections are somewhat contingent on the existing categories holding, and that is not given. Yet, our language, institution and systems often struggle to describe or characterize these peoples.

The case of Kamala Harris is instructive, as she was elected to the vice presidency in 2021, more than a decade after Barack Obama was elected president. But she was more often referred to as the first Black-Indian vice president than Obama's mixed-race heritage was foregrounded.[71] A careful analysis shows that Harris has not actually changed how she presents, but rather South Asians more visibly embraced her candidacy as an identity milestone, shifting how the broader public viewed her in the process.[72]

But as this example illustrates, most Americans have difficult classifying people who seem to elude neat or clear racial categories. One commentator asserts that "[u]ltimately, it is a mixed person's prerogative to be fluid in their identity, for them to sometimes hold one, or both, and for that to change over time."[73] While we do not necessarily disagree with this, we note that a single individual—even the vice president—has limited power to assert identities that are not accepted by the wider public. And that is where we should work: creating a greater comfort level with racial multiplicity and fluidity, and by extension, identity multiplicity and fluidity.

Perhaps no place in the United States epitomizes this—or the potential upside of this—more than the state of Hawaii. While hardly a racial paradise, mixed-race people are so common and frequently encountered that people living in Hawaii appear to have helped create a very different context in which racial meanings operate. With so many mixed-race people (a quarter of the state population, according to Pew), mainland assumptions and stereotypes about people of an identifiable race are no longer as stable or readily made.[74]

A study by a Tufts professor on 4–11-year-old children in Hawaii and Boston demonstrates the difference. Children in Boston were quick to make and hold racial stereotypes on the basis of race ("that blacks were aggressive or, on the flip side, good at basketball; that Asians were submissive and good at math").[75] In contrast, although children in Hawaii were familiar with such stereotypes, they were more weakly held and less consistently applied, especially to racially ambiguous persons. The study's author did not conclude that Hawaiian children were race-blind, but rather that they did not impute character traits on the basis of race as consistently. In fact, one study suggested that they were more nuanced at reading and relating across race.

One theory advanced to explain this is that multiracial identity, paradoxically, makes race less salient as a taxonomy for making fast and dirty assumptions about people, and therefore people are evaluated on alternative bases.[76] It does not take much imagination to see how this hybridity and fluidity could upend forces that maintain othering—or group-based marginalization—and help us move closer to a world of belonging. Perhaps most remarkable is the fact that simply visiting places like Hawaii can "rub off" and help rewire ways of perceiving and thinking about group identity, even at an unconscious level.

While Hawaii might point us toward a hopeful future on these issue, Brazil might give us pause. The fluidity and racial taxonomies established in Brazil are far greater than those of the U.S. By some accounts there are over two hundred different color categories.[77] And while it is hard to make meaningful direct comparisons, there are reasons to question the model of Brazil as an aspirational future for addressing these issues.[78] Colorism and pigment-based hierarchies appear firmly entrenched in Brazil, despite the multiplicity of racial categories.

Nonetheless, the demographic trend toward multiracial identity will create possibilities for different stories and understandings that a more categorical world impedes. We need new and more open identities and powerful stories to convince and persuade people of a vision of a larger "we." These demographic changes make the status quo inherently unstable, without telling us exactly what the future should hold.

Globalization

Demographic change is not the only force that can help us recast identities and build new narratives to support them. Globalization presents threats and opportunities for belonging identities. On the one hand, it's clear that globalization provides a greater scope for exploitation and global marginality—othering processes now have a larger canvas on which to operate. On the other hand, globalization also weakens traditional categorical boundaries and connects individuals to a myriad of new, horizontal identities and communities, such as those Andrew Solomon surveyed.

Global networks of trade and exchange have unquestionably weakened national boundaries in many respects. The chief resources and assets of a nation are no longer natural resources for extractive industries, but tend to be the human capital and technologies they contain. This is how tiny Taiwan has an outsized economic influence due to its cutting-edge factories and techniques for computer microchip development.[79]

The swift flows of capital, currency, and even people and technology across national borders have significantly altered the underpinnings of the Westphalian model of the nation-state. Many nation-states are today exceeded in power and resources by the largest multinational corporations.[80] The globe now has many weak nations, and weak nations produce weaker national identities and feeble loyalties.

Although typically viewed as processes relating to trade and economic exchange that connect and bind nations together, globalization extends beyond the economic sphere. Forces of globalization have led to movements of capital as well people, migration, and identity itself. There are musicians, athletes, and corporate chieftains all across the world who have homes in three or more countries. Russian oligarchs are notorious for buying properties in London and New York. The American football quarterback Tom Brady, for example, was married to a Brazilian supermodel, vacationed in a compound in Costa Rica, and has homes in multiple states.[81]

Although derisively described as "cosmopolitanism," it is the case that many people on our planet are effectively global in outlook and living patterns, rarely anchored to a certain place or even country. The world's largest metropolises are thriving hubs of diversity, with residents from across the globe. Little wonder that the viewpoint described as "cosmopolitan" is one that embraces diversity, change, density, and inclusion, and is less wedded to the traditional nation-state.

As discussed in more detail later in this chapter, some versions of the weakening bonds of the nation-state model are being institutionalized through new and alternative political models, such as the European Union. In this model, there are free flows of workers and capital, and as a corollary, a layering of national identities with a more inclusive and broader belonging through European citizenship.

Neo-nationalists and ethno-nationalists are keenly aware of the fact that a broader, more inclusive outlook is inconsistent with a stronger attachment to the local and the parochial. This is why resurgent nationalists so strongly oppose both a cosmopolitan outlook and supranational institutions as well as globalization. They seek belonging, but belonging as a bonding agent to the local and the insular by creating harder edges and more exclusive and smaller "we."[82] Even commentators from the conservative-libertarian Cato Institute can spot the danger with this position: "Alas, this [vision] is limited by the boundaries of what the nation is: a bigger tribe, which is very often ruthless toward those who do not belong to it."[83]

In this sense, the trend of globalization is both an opportunity and a threat to belonging.[84] It is a mechanism by which greater belonging can be realized. But the weakening of national borders, especially to capital, has spurred forces that drive more migrants out of weak states. This, along with certain imperious tendencies inevitable in supranational experiments like the European Union, is fomenting a powerful backlash. The reactionary right hates the European Union at the same time that surging migration has strengthened currents of reactionary and perhaps ascendant ethno-nationalism.

In Europe, people who hold this view seek to keep out immigrants and refugees, especially from the Middle East and Global South. In the United States, this view is represented by an opposition to immigration, principally from Latin America, but especially demographic change. Is there a space between cosmopolitan globalism and reactionary ethno-nationalism?

Fundamentally, the impetus for globalization is neither economic nor technological, strictly speaking. The organization of human communities into distinct nation-states undermines human capacity and potential for, if not the necessity of, cooperation and coordination.[85] Looming threats like climate change or more immediate threats like the Covid-19 pandemic do not remain confined to national borders or obey international law. As the Unger quote that serves as an epigraph to this book emphasizes, and as Harari's theory suggests, our cooperative capabilities will determine the ultimately potential of our species.

The forces of globalization are more than the economic flows of capital and labor or the narrow province of trade agreements and intellectual property enforcement. They are powerful currents that buffer our world. We need institutions and capacities that reflect humanity's shared circumstances and respond to our collective needs. To some extent, NGOs already do this, helping coordinate responses to pandemics, the spread of disease, or nuclear threats. But we need more than technocratic multilateral institutions or coordinating mechanisms. We need institutions that can help us recast identities on a larger backdrop and weave new connections among disparate peoples. The internet has powered new communities across global boundaries. We need more deliberate ways to pursue similar goals. On a concrete level this should affect how we think about travel, education, and sharing resources and responsibility.

We can anticipate that new identities are emerging as a result of globalization, and this is an opportunity as well as a challenge. A globalized world is a more interdependent world, and therefore a world in which we are more tied together and vulnerable with each other. But it is also a world where othering processes can magnify in scale and intensity.

Rainbow Nations

Given the patterns of demographic change and mass migrations flowing out of globalization, many if not most of the nations of the world are grappling with a fundamental tension discussed throughout this book: whether nation-states that promise equal protection of laws and democratic governance can be sustained if they give privileges, prerogatives, and priorities to particular religious or ethnic groups.

The problem of ethno-states has been a recurring subject of discussion throughout this book, from the role of identity in the formation of states (and vice versa), to the efforts of ethno-nationalists to bind national identities to certain cultural units, whether they are ethnic, religious, linguistic or otherwise, to the role of ethno-nationalism in narrowing the set of salient social identities. The existence of ethno-states is perhaps one of the central contradictions in the world today, especially in liberal democracies, as well as a wellspring of othering.

Almost nowhere is the vision of broad inclusion and institutional belonging manifest (even setting aside the problem of citizenship and immigration). But there are places that are further along this trajectory than others, however imperfectly realized. With so many problems in the world, and othering at the heart of them, we want to point the way to places that have succeeded, however imperfectly, like Canada, which celebrates inclusion in a different way. We can point to other places and nations that have explicitly adopted multicultural, inclusive national identities, and devised institutional supports to structurally ground those identities. These institutional developments can inspire us to forge similar arrangements in other places. Notably among them are South Africa and India's post-apartheid and post-independence constitutions, Singapore's institutional management of diversity, and the Dayton Accords and Good Friday Agreement.

During the CODESA period that negotiated the end of apartheid, there were many competing visions for the future of South Africa. White nationalists and Zulu nationalists had competing exclusionary visions.[86] It would have been understandable, after decades of oppression, to embrace an exclusionary alternative, especially one that exacted a degree of revenge.[87] But Nelson Mandela, despite his long incarceration, pushed his country toward an explicitly inclusive vision. Borrowing a term coined by Archbishop Desmond Tutu, Mandela invoked the idea of a "Rainbow Nation" as a theme of his inaugural presidential address to connote an inclusive, multicultural country, reborn from the ashes of apartheid.[88] Mandela built upon the idea during his first month in office, describing his vision for South Africa where "[e]ach of us is as intimately attached to the soil of this beautiful country as are the famous jacaranda trees of Pretoria and the mimosa trees of the bushveld—a rainbow nation at peace with itself and the world."[89] Although this vision is far from achieved, it has made substantial accomplishments, most notably shaping a respected and proud South African national identity.

Similarly, Mohandas Karamchand Gandhi (aka Mahatma Gandhi) helped lead a movement that resulted in the independence of India from British imperial rule. As with South Africa at the end of apartheid, there were competing visions for the future of the new country. Like Mandela,

Gandhi hoped for a multi-ethnic, multireligious nation and rejected the Hindu nationalist vision that left out Muslims, Sikhs, and others and would have entrenched caste "untouchability."[90] Accordingly, Gandhi also opposed the partition of India into two separate countries, forcibly segregating people by religion across new national borders.[91] In fact, Gandhi had proposed, as a counterbalancing mechanism, that the new Indian nation's first prime minister and cabinet be filled exclusively with Muslim ministers, to solidify a multireligious and multi-ethnic new nation, and to prevent partition.[92]

Although he lost the debate over partition, he won the debate over India's national identity, for several generations at least. In the wake of partition, spasms of violence spread across the new nation, with cycles of reprisals against both Muslims and Hindus alike. In his final significant fast, begun on January 12, 1948, Gandhi pushed himself to the brink of starvation to persuade Hindus and Muslims to end the cycle of violence and work toward peace.[93] Although he succeeded in this, it was a temporary measure that had yet to be fully institutionalized. India was ultimately constitutionally founded as an inclusive, multicultural and multiracial secular liberal democracy, although Gandhi did not live to see it, as he was assassinated by a Hindu nationalist less than two weeks after breaking his fast.[94] As with South Africa, this was a contested vision from the start and one that more and more Indians have expressed doubts about, but unlike South Africa (so far), India has moved increasingly away from it.[95]

These examples show how formative institutional developments can provide a foundation for an expanded sense of "we" or "us." One of the clearest and lesser-known examples was how Lee Kuan Yew built Singapore's new city-state by insisting on a "multiracial, multireligious, multicultural model to provide a cohesive identity for the new nation."[96] Because he was forming a new nation, there was no national identity. Yet the peoples that would form the new state were diverse—Chinese, Malaysian, Indian, and "other." About 15 percent of the citizens of Singapore identified as Malay, and about 7.5 percent identified as Indian, and a majority were Chinese. This diversity was managed in a number of clever and farsighted ways.

First, everyone in the city-state was expected to be bilingual—and not just as an educational offering, but a state decree. Recognizing the importance of language to identity formation, Singapore instructed all citizens in English, as well as the language that corresponded with their ethnic identity. In that way, there was a shared language for the new state.

Second, they adopted English, the colonial language of the state before independence, as the official language of the government, rather than one of the ethnic groups' language, and Malay as the national language, recognizing Malays as the indigenous people of the region.[97] The national anthem was, accordingly, in Malay. This was specifically done to avoid ethnic conflict.

Third, Singapore deliberately integrated the diverse peoples by residence and geography. Public housing was required to be integrated—the exact opposite of what the United States did in the same time period. Singapore's leaders understood that cohabitation was a social glue, and that separation and segregation deepened social division.

A related feature was the way that the state venerated—rather than suppressed—religious diversity. Although only about 1 in 3 are Buddhist, 1 in 5 are Christian, 1 in 7 were residents were Muslim, 1 in 10 are Taoist, and about 1 in 20 were Hindu. Mosques and temples were rebuilt or refurbished, and churches can be found everywhere. In fact, two Jewish synagogues were designated national monuments.[98] Every religious group was respected and recognized in society.

Finally, and though it may seem extreme or untenable in a liberal democratic society, Singapore explicitly prohibited hate speech. Singapore enacted a "Sedition Act" that prohibited actions or speech "promot[ing] feelings of ill-will and hostility between different races or classes of the population of Singapore."[99] While this may be hard to imagine in Western democracies, many in Singapore feel that they "engaged together in a meaningful national project."[100] As a friend of the philosopher Kwame Anthony Appiah observed, people in Singapore do feel watched, but also seen.

In democracies, managing pluralism and an array of diverse religious and ethnic identities can be more difficult, especially if political leaders present themselves as representing a particular group. But there are still examples of where political settlements have sought to tamp down such divisions and build more inclusive institutional structures that provide a context in which more cohesive national identities can develop.

Perhaps the best example comes from the region whose name is a metaphor for fragmentation, the Balkans. Following the Bosnian War, the Dayton Accords was a landmark negotiated treaty that has brought peace to a deeply divided region.[101] As a by-product of the settlement, the new Bosnian and Herzegovinian Constitution created a tripartite presidency. Croats (Catholics), Serbs (Christians), and Bosnian (Muslims) are each represented in the presidency at all times. There have been at least seven elections where this model has worked, despite its complexity.[102]

Another example is Northern Ireland following the Troubles. The 1998 Good Friday Agreement set up a power-sharing arrangement that essentially gave both unionist (Protestants) and nationalists (Catholics) power sharing in the government at all times.[103] It doesn't mean that these settlements have been perfect. Even as the Bosnian and Herzegovinian political settlement proceeded, the country permitted ethnic and culturally segregated and distinct primary and secondary education curriculum. This is an example of the educational system undermining the goals of the political settlement, and also the longer-term chances for a new narrative and national identity reconstruction. As imperfect as these examples are, they have succeeded in preventing communal violence for more than two decades. They are helpful places to think about where the most extreme conflict has turned into at least relative calm and stability, with functional institutions and democratic governance.

Although the stability and relative peace that these institutional arrangements have created is worth the price alone, these innovations have done more than that. They have created a space for the emergence or evolution of new and existing identities. More than two decades after the Good Friday Agreement, census takers have found a surge of residents in Northern Ireland identifying as both British and Northern Irish, both Irish and Northern Irish, or all three. One scholar attributed this to "a growing situation in Northern Ireland of this willingness to have hybrid identities reflecting this post-agreement generation."[104]

What is notable about many of the examples just canvassed is that they are a product of highly intensive, fraught, and often deeply negotiated and contested political settlements in a period of rapid change. The CODESA agreements, the Dayton Accords, and the Good Friday Agreement were all negotiated in the 1990s, after the end of the Cold War, an era of unprecedented global peace and prosperity. And yet this was a period of tumult, as societies struggled with unleashed nationalism emitted by the unraveling of the Soviet Union and the end of the Cold War.

What each of these examples reflects is institutional innovation. In each case, leaders were trying to find a way to preserve communal rights and human dignity in deeply divided and fracturing societies. In that respect, we would argue that each of these settlements, imperfect as they are, can point us to a path forward. Remarkably, despite the pressures that these settlements and accords have experienced, they have endured for more than two decades now. This suggests that it can be accomplished, but only with deliberate effort.

Although these settlements resolved problems in places with the most extreme violence and divisions, virtually every place in the world has tremors of the same to a lesser degree. This reaffirms the argument for institutional innovation and renewal made in Chapter 5. What we need are versions of these settlements drawn across every society. However, we need institutional arrangements that recognize difference without reifying it.

In contrast to the durable (so far) arrangements in these cases, Lebanon stands out as a cautionary tale. Following a devastating sectarian civil conflict, the country adopted a quota system in a manner that is so intricate and detailed as to put any of the previous examples to shame. Although it has largely succeeded in tamping down intergroup violence, it has produced immense governmental dysfunction,[105] and has deepened identity-based attachments to certain offices and government benefits.[106]

Neither unrestrained majoritarianism nor the opposite system of intricate quotas and sectarian checks-and-balances is the ultimate solution. Nonetheless, we need formal ways of recognizing each other, of ensuring fair representation, of power sharing, if we are to have a globe where we can live together. These arrangements each embody, in various ways, this goal.

————

But it has yet to be determined whether, over the long term, it is in fact possible for different human social groups to peacefully coexist. Although we believe the overwhelming evidence supports the affirmative answer, along with the fact that there may be no alternative option, the ongoing wars and violence in the negative column cast continual doubt. Violence can be repressed through force, as in Nagorno-Karabakh, but that is not the same thing as a truly legitimate and sustainable peace through institutional renewal. Once the enforcement mechanism is withdrawn, the violence will recur.

Somehow, we have to find a way to persuade the people of this planet that there are only two options: one is to continue to try to build communities and coerced settlements drawn by domination and control. In this option, the end result is perpetual warfare and possibly the end of the planet as we know it. The other option is to try to find a way to coexist, not just between ethnic states, whether democracies or autocracies, but as integrated, diverse places of belonging. This is obviously our preferred path, but it is one that will require great effort, negotiation, and institutional innovation to secure it.

Nation-states are a double-edged sword as a weapon to combat othering. On the one hand, they are a powerful tool for exclusion, and the principal vehicle for contemporary demagogues, ethno-nationalists, and warlords to weaponize identity, binding it on a narrow basis, cultural, ancestral, ethnic, linguistic, or religious. On the other hand, nation-states (much like ancient empires of the past) play a critical role in eroding the supremacy or dominance of racial, ethnic or religious loyalties, counterbalancing them with a new set of communal bonds and compelling principled legal commitments. In this way, nation-states citizenship can bind and connect people across each of these differences in a powerful way. Thus citizenship within the United States (today) is formally extended to members of all racial, ethnic, and religious groups. In this regard, that nation-state is potentially a tool for belonging, not simply an instrument of othering.

This fact, the role that liberal pluralistic nation-states play in tamping down ethnic or religious divisions in favor of more salient national identities, is one of the reasons that some ethno-nationalists regard them (and not just supranational institutions) with knee-jerk disdain and suspicion. The American conservative thinker Patrick Deneen asserts that liberal universalism constitutes a form of "anticulture" that has "dissolved all forms of preliberal culture," and ultimately uses the power of the state to insert itself into and control every aspect of private life.[107] This is strikingly similar to Matthew Rose's observation from Chapter 5, that liberalism leaves societies more dependent upon the state. One problem is that the conclusion does not follow from the premise. Just because pre-liberal cultural bonds are diminished or rendered less salient in modern societies does not create any more dependency upon the state than was the case in ancient eras or under the great pre-liberal empires that preceded the nation-state. Rather, the critiques reveal the authors' preferences for bonds of belonging that tend to engender othering. This must be resisted.

At a level beyond that of tinkering with institutional mechanics, the deeper challenge for nation-states is to establish a national identity that is not tied to a particular social group, racial, ethnic, religious or otherwise, and not just formally, but in practice as well. This path actually points to a third path between the two options described immediately above. There are very few nations in the contemporary world that do this explicitly (state-based religions were far more common in the past) and codify it in law or constitutions (although, we have mentioned a few), but there are many more places where "legacy" identities are viewed as de facto national identities. When nation-states found or refound themselves on terms that are not based or rooted in a particular set of ethnic or religious identities, but recognize and celebrate diversity within the nation, like Canada or South Africa, they are a powerful vehicle for belonging. The concept of a rainbow nation is a powerful expression of this, but there are others we have similarly noted.

The fundamental challenge of belonging at the national level is to reduce the salience of any particular social or ancestral identity in relation to national identity, and to leverage critical institutions, such as constitutions, courts, and legislatures, in service of that ideal. Although the nation-state is a powerful instrument for achieving this goal, in some cases this can only happen beyond the national level.

Supranational Belonging

As we saw in earlier chapters, premodern forms of supranational belonging were often successful at keeping ethnic or religious domination at bay, or at least managing that diversity and pluralism more successfully than successor nation-states were, often led by the belief in Wilsonian "self-determination."[108] While sounding good in theory (especially in a world—at that time—dominated by large European empires), in practice self-determination often means the right to dominate ethnic or religious minorities within the form of new nation-states.

In a highly polarized and fragmented world, some forms of belonging must cross national boundaries and overcome the barricade of nation-state form. In Europe, the struggle to disentangle religion (and specifically the Catholic Church) from the state was a multicentury project, and a source of centuries of warfare. On the other hand, we saw how empires were surprisingly facile, relative to nation-states, at incorporating and accommodating difference. For ancient Rome, loyalty to empire trumped religion, ethnicity, color, and tribe. Even more recent empires, like the fractious Ottoman Empire, managed to create space for the myriad of jostling groups within its borders. Although there were purges and pogroms, they were often not as oppressive or endemic as the violence that marginalized peoples experienced within the form of successor nation-states.

The institutional form plays a critical role in fostering or dampening belonging. Recall the discussion in Chapter 5 on the role of national institutions as "molds" for connection and belonging. Supranational entities and associations can also serve as such molds. A prime example of how a political settlement and institution building can set the stage for a larger, more inclusive "we" is the European Union project.

To understand the impetus for the European Union, we must first remember that in the first half of the twentieth century, Europe was the epicenter of two world wars, which resulted in the deaths of more than a hundred million people. The European Union was an effort to create institutions which would move toward greater European integration, and hopefully hold at bay the violent and aggressive nationalism that had become an existential threat. The founders of the European Union, Robert Schuman and Jean Monnet, recognized that the only way to do this was to tamp down the exclusive and chauvinistic expressions of national identity that underpinned this violence and aggression.[109]

In addition to trading community, and then later political institutions, the most tangibly felt aspect of the European Union was a shared currency and Schengen Zone, which ensured freedom of movement across borders within the EU.[110] Like the Dayton Accords or Good Friday Agreement, this settlement created a space for identity development.[111] There is some evidence to suggest that a European identity—and attachment to that identity—have grown over several generations, especially among younger people.[112] The emergence of this new "European" identity was grounded principally by the creation of EU institutions. The latter preceded the former, and gave this new identity something to bind itself onto, something to ground it. The symbols of the EU—the flag, anthem, currency—provide further cultural grounding.

This also shows why nationalists despise the European Union as a project, and pine for its failure. By reconfiguring identity in a more inclusive way, and as a model for doing so, it is an existential threat to the Westphalian model of organizing societies, especially those that are tacitly or explicitly ethno-nationalist in their form. In this regard, the African Union is an interesting contrast with the European Union.

The European Union began as the European Economic Community, a charter based on a 1957 treaty that sought greater regional economic integration.[113] In 1993, it was incorporated into the EU, and ceased to exist by 2009. From the outset, the Organisation of African Unity (OAU), founded in 1963, envisioned greater political *and* economic integration, and recognized the need for solidarity to challenge and eventually overcome colonization.[114] The African Union superseded the OAU and formally came into existence at the turn of this century. Among its explicit objectives are "To achieve greater unity, cohesion and solidarity between the African countries and African nations," and "To accelerate the political and social-economic integration of the continent." This vision, a by-product of

Pan-Africanism noted at the beginning of this book, has not advanced as politically or institutionally as far as European integration, but the potential is there.

While there may be a legitimate debate about the future of the nation-state, and its utility in a deeply interconnected world, one need not call for its abolition or seek its demise to recognize the simultaneous possibility for supranational belonging in a globe organized primarily around nation-states. Human beings can have dual, without divided, loyalties, affiliations, and commitments. In fact, this was part of the fundamental settlement at Westphalia: that religious loyalties did not have to bind national loyalties.

Religious communities have long transcended national boundaries. Millions of Muslims from all over the world make the hajj pilgrimage every year to Mecca, in Saudi Arabia, from Denmark to Indonesia. Recall how such a pilgrimage was a key part of Malcolm X's political and spiritual evolution, and allowed him to connect across a racial divide that he previously felt incapable of traversing. Nor are such forms of belonging across identity boundaries unique to Muslim pilgrimages. There are many religious communities—and indeed many other communities—that transcend national boundaries. Although some chauvinist groups may assert the incompatibility of multiple loyalties (as when nineteenth-century Know-Nothings decried "papists" in America, for fear that loyalty to the Catholic Church would trump loyalty to country), pretty much every major nation-state on the globe has found ways to accommodate at least some diversity of religious adherence or loyalty. Similarly, no major religion demands citizenship or allegiance to a single or particular nation-state, even though some world religions are closely bound to certain nations, like the Catholic Church and the Vatican, Sunni Islam and Saudi Arabia, or Hinduism and India.

The point is that many supranational identity-based communities have been accommodated into the modern nation-state, in ways that most people simply take for granted today.[115] Supranational belonging is no more incompatible with national identity and loyalties than being a mother is incompatible with being a doctor or a teacher. Multiple identities—with different commitments and responsibilities—can coexist without undermining the other. We all sustain multiple allegiances, to family, work, and community. This is so ordinary that it can seem remarkable only when re-marked upon or when pressed to take a side. In this way, supranational belonging can and does exist in a world organized around nation-states.

In fact, in some ways, such layered identities may be complementary or even reinforcing, not simply "compatible." Rather than undermining na-tional citizenship, the full expression of what it means to be "French" or "German" may have deeper resonance—as well as greater meaning—from also being a citizen of the European Union. In reflecting on the tragedy his countrymen set upon in deciding to leave the European Union, the British comedian Russell Brand lamented that "[u]ltimately, it is the island of self that we must either leave or remain trapped within."[116]

Our Belonging Future

In this book, we made our strongest possible the case for the concept of "othering" as a framework that can help us make sense of seemingly dis-parate yet similar dynamics across the globe, and for "belonging" as an equally capacious and important response to these problems. But it is not just that these frameworks are more accurate in some abstract and concep-tual sense. These frameworks readily lend themselves to connecting dispa-rate movements and linking efforts, so that every social justice movement is both a challenge to specific expressions of othering and othering itself.

The alternative is, in a larger sense, loss and defeat. Even if we are suc-cessful at overcoming some expressions of othering, a world in which we only care about the well-being and justice of some groups, and not others, is not the world we want to call into being. As Martin Luther King Jr. said, "Injustice anywhere is a threat to justice everywhere."

If we are successful in much of the above, in building upon the demo-graphic opportunity, of telling a more effective and compelling story of be-longing, of building a bigger "we," of fostering belonging across traditional boundary lines, then we will have accomplished a great achievement and averted many tragedies.

We currently inhabit a world that is nominally dictated by othering. If the twentieth century is a guide regarding the ethno-nationalist presenti-ments bubbling up around the world, our current trajectory is one of more conflict and ethnic violence. This is the future that intelligence threat analysts are bracing for. But we also see a world where people aspire to bridge and where belonging is widely desired. The challenge is to translate these aspirations into durable practices and formative institutions.

As meaning-making symbolic and cooperative animals, we have great potential for othering or belonging. Belonging and othering are not necessarily a binary but exist along a dynamic spectrum. We are calling for belonging without othering. We are calling for as much agency and co-creation as possible. We are calling for checking or curtailing power "over" and supporting power "with." We need new institutions, laws, and stories to realize these demands.

Despite any shortcomings, we hope that this book has not only persuaded you of the importance of belonging without othering as a general principle, but has also inspired you to participate in the co-creation of this idea in your own life and community. Your participation and experimentation is vital. We invite and welcome you into this joint venture.

Climate change, pandemics, the migration of people, demographic change, technology, and much more will not allow us to retreat into the past or to hunker down in the present. Change is coming. As we've seen, change can be challenging and even difficult, especially as the speed of change accelerates, but it can also be enlivening and rewarding. To an unhealthy degree, our societies remain stuck in a mythical past while ignoring a future that is rushing forward. The future is not set, but it will arrive nonetheless.

A vision where all belong must be the aspirational ideal to stir us into this future. We can contribute to its creation and move forward into a more open and inclusive world or slide back into a world that is more exclusionary and fragmented.

There is no formal blueprint and many unknowns and some unknowables. There must be bold and serious experimentation at every level of society and within our interpersonal lives. We need institutional reform and renewal, so that our critical institutions facilitate connection rather than deepen division. We need leaders that inspire and build community instead of those that prey on fear and prejudice. We need media and social media that prevent radicalization rather than draw people down spirals of hatred and bigotry. We need collective projects that open minds and

enlarge our hearts. We need bridge-builders, weavers, and social connec-
tors in every community.[117]

We see some of that experimentation already, and applaud it. But we
must do much more.

We can continue to other or we can embrace belonging without othering. We cannot predict which direction humanity will choose, but the
choice is enormously consequential. Not only could we destroy the planet
and each other on our present course, but we are hobbled from achieving
the full expression of our humanity and ourselves.

The Mechanics of Othering

In Part I, this book explained the complex manner in which group identities emerge, are contested or inscribed, and become socially meaningful, signaling a location in the social order, and the general manner in which political and economic elites create, fan, or stoke fears of the "other" and inflame social cleavages, rendering these identities politically or socially salient. Yet what remains unexplained, or only hinted at, is how these identities and processes are institutionalized or otherwise structurally embedded into societies such that they produce and reproduce group-based inequality, or what Charles Tilly called "categorical inequality."[1] In other words, how does "othering" produce systematic group inequality? This supplemental chapter will attempt to answer that difficult question by identifying the specific mechanisms at work.

———

Any effort to answer this question must begin with several caveats. First, while it is not in vogue among social scientists, we describe the forces that generate group-based inequality in terms of "mechanisms." By "mechanisms" we refer to generally applicable or universal forces and processes as well as to specific instantiations of those in law, social behavior, customs, norms, or policy. This is not to suggest that there is anything automatic or "mechanical" about these forces. In many of these cases, these forces were fiercely contested and strongly opposed. Rather, the use of the term *mechanism* suggests a set of common instruments and techniques that recur across space and time in different cases, and can be found to help explain and contribute to group-based inequality.

Second, these mechanisms are not exhaustive of the forces that generate group-based inequality. In addition to these mechanisms, there are often unique or idiosyncratic processes or forces that help generate or inscribe group-based inequality. The forces surveyed here, however, are common enough—in the sense in which they are present or found in enough instances of "othering"—to warrant being described as "mechanisms of othering." In most cases of group-inequality found across the world or over time, these forces described here are present or play a central or significant role.

Third, the "mechanisms" identified are pitched at a level of generality that is specific enough to describe a particular force, but general enough to describe a broad class of behavior, conduct, and processes. That does not mean that they do not interact or overlap, as they often do. The mechanisms described herein not only interact, and reinforce each other, but they generally co-occur. Our theory of othering would predict this—that through boundary work and emulation, othering in one sphere will spill over into another domain of life.

It should be noted, however, that drawing and policing or sustaining categorical boundaries that generate inequality is difficult. Each of these mechanisms involves extensive organization, coordination, resources, or energy among participants and institutions. Although not technically a mechanism itself, these mechanisms also rely on the prior establishment of a "partial frontier and defined social relations across that frontier" to make social closure possible.[2] Durable, categorical inequality is only possible when the powerful, inadvertently or by design, use their power to maintain those distinctions in various ways.

Violence

Violence is the most obvious and fundamental instrument of social control routinely deployed to enforce group boundaries, privileges, and prerogatives. Violence is used to assert as well as maintain dominance and power.

Violence is direct, powerful, and—in the proper context—unambiguous in its purpose and intent. Group-based violence is so ubiquitous that one could substitute ethnic conflict for a study of othering. For this reason, it is impossible to provide an exhaustive account of this mechanism, so a brief survey must suffice.

Of course, not all mass violence is based upon group identity or directed at a social group or members of a social group: much historical collective violence is based on ideology, natural or material resources, or territory. And individual psychological factors or interpersonal dynamics (grievances, perceived hostility, etc.) may contribute to violence, and metastasize into communal episodes.[3] But beliefs, resources, and territory are often intricately connected with identity or social groupings. This is amply demonstrated by the wars over land and territory inflicted on indigenous people worldwide by colonial aggressors. In the nineteenth century alone, the United States government fought more wars against Indian tribes than foreign powers, decimating American Indian communities.[4]

Religiously motivated violence may be one of the largest sources of violence, especially in the context of European history. Although wars of religion racked Europe during the sixteenth, seventeenth, and eighteenth centuries, often between various Protestant sects and Catholic states, or between civilian and religious authorities, perhaps the most notorious example of religious wars were the Crusades, a series of European-sponsored invasions of the Middle East between 1096 and 1291.[5] These endeavors resulted in enormous bloodshed, with the main victims being Muslim and Jewish peoples in the besieging and sacking of Nicaea, Antioch, Jerusalem, and Constantinople.[6] The Crusaders were reported, at the siege of Jerusalem, for example, to have slain Muslim soldiers who surrendered, and to have killed women and children as well.[7]

One of the chief architects of the first crusade, Pope Urban II, urged Christians of Western Europe in a series of speeches to undertake a military expedition to "liberate" the Holy Land from Muslim rule.[8] Although a territorial war in the narrow sense, this was not a war for control over economically productive land. The pope promised that God would spiritually reward anyone who fought to "free" the Holy Land. At least one hundred thousand European knights, vassals, and serfs traveled under the cross to

engage a Muslim enemy, creating in the mind of the Crusaders a sharp religious "other" as a religious foe that had largely not existed in either the
Middle East or Europe before then.[9]

Critically, however, one of the by-products of this endeavor was increased violence against Jews and Muslims in European lands, not simply
faraway enemies. Not only did the Crusaders terrorize Jewish communities
en route to the Holy Land, but local nobles initiated a series of pogroms
destroying Jewish communities, most notably in Mainz, Cologne, and
Worms, in a series of events known as the "Rhineland massacres" of 1096.[10]

———

Violence directed against a discrete and insular group is highly suggestive
of group-based marginality, especially if there is a widespread or episodic
pattern of violence, as the Rhineland massacres reflect. But to take a few
examples out of headlines in recent years, consider the Pulse LGBTQ
nightclub shooting that killed forty-nine in Orlando Florida[11]; the Tree
of Life synagogue shooting that killed eleven in Pittsburgh, Pennsylvania[12]; the mosque shooting that killed fifty-one in Christchurch, New
Zealand[13]; or the shooting that killed nine Black Christian parishioners
in Charleston, South Carolina.[14] Each of these examples of extreme out-
group violence occurred across a salient social cleavage (even if the motives
are contested).

Small religious sects or isolated social groups are particularly vulnerable
targets for this kind of violence, as the plight of the Yazidis discussed in
Chapter 2 or the case of the Roma in Europe suggest.[15] But another example in the American context is the attacks on Mormons in 1830s and '40s.
Joseph Smith, the author of the Book of Mormon, had been systematically
hounded out of New York State and Ohio. When he and his followers settled in Missouri, they were regarded as enemies of the state. In October
1838, the Missouri governor issued an "extermination order" demanding
that all Mormons be driven out or killed.[16] A militia attacked the Mormon
settlement and raped, mutilated, and murdered seventeen Mormons, loot-
ing and burning their property in the process. These acts were justified by
narratives that denigrated Mormons as a "degenerate, non-white race" and
"foreign reptiles" even though the religion originated in the United States,

was perhaps uniquely tethered to the American Revolution, and emerged out of the "Great Awakening" of the 1820s.

————

Although violence can be episodic or continuous against marginalized groups, the longer and broader the pattern, the greater the degree of marginality that may be inferred, either as a cause or effect. For instance, between 1877 and 1950, the height of the Jim Crow era, there were more than four thousand lynchings, and nearly three-quarters of victims were Black.[17] Lynching was so widespread that the NAACP's first major campaign after its formation 1909 was to make lynching more visible and to try to stop it. Violence of this order is often ritualistic and therefore cultural. People would attend lynchings with their children and families. Postcards and keepsakes were made and distributed. This ritualistic violence was formative for the entire society on status of Black people, not just a message or warning to Black freedom advocates.

Even small-scale or interpersonal violence may be influenced by relative power dynamics and group positionality. One of the most notorious in the American context was the brutal murder of Matthew Shepard in 1998.[18] A student at the University of Wyoming, Shepard was pistol-whipped with a gun by two assailants who then tied him to a fence in freezing conditions and set fire to him before leaving him to die, which he subsequently did.[19] Shepard's death led to hate-crimes legislation against LGBTQ people.

The spate of violence against transgender people, especially Black transgender people, in the United States is a pattern that a human rights organization described as an "epidemic."[20] In 2018, there were at least twenty-six transgender women who were murdered. In one particularly gruesome instance, the body of Bee Love Slater, a Black transgender woman from Florida, was found burned beyond recognition in a car.[21] Even the American Medical Association called for new policies to stop this epidemic.[22]

————

Similarly, gender violence—including rape—remains a widespread problem in many parts of the world, especially in places such as India or parts of

Latin America, and in those contexts is connected to patriarchal societal structures.[23] A 2018 survey found that India was the most dangerous place in the world for women.[24] A woman in New Delhi was gang-raped on a bus in 2012, an incident that drew attention to the enormous number of rapes reported in that city.[25] Just a few months earlier, a sixteen-year-old girl was raped by eight men, an incident that was attributed in part to a sense of patriarchal impunity and cultural silence and dishonor from reporting such crimes.[26]

In 2019, another incident shocked the Indian public, when a sixteen-year old was found beheaded on the side of a highway, with evidence that her face may have been burned by acid as well.[27] Aside from the brutality of the incident, the most shocking part of the story was that the father appeared to have orchestrated her murder as an "honor killing." Apparently, she went to visit her boyfriend on his birthday, transgressing norms restricting girls' freedom and ability to date.

Religiously or culturally inflected gender violence is hardly foreign to the Global North. Compared to the several dozen women executed by the colonies as 'witches' in New England, an estimated sixty thousand (mostly) women were tried and executed in Europe in the sixteenth and seventeenth centuries.[28] The greatest concentration of violence in that period appears to have occurred in Scotland and Germany, which experts attribute to unique religious, cultural, and legal features of those places.[29] The Catalonia government has recently issued pardons in those cases,[30] and the Scottish government is considering a similar step, in recognition of the harm caused by the hysteria, and has already issued an apology.[31]

———

It should be emphasized that violence is not simply reflective of group-based marginality or vulnerability; it is also a cause and contributory element to the position of marginality. Violence is used both to enforce group position as well as to create it. Systemic violence against a discrete and insular group can be a mechanism of social control. In the Jim Crow context, the victims of lynching were often those who challenged prevailing social norms, especially those around race and sexuality.

Legal commentators and feminist scholars immediately noted that Supreme Court justice Samuel Alito's leaked draft opinion overturning the constitutionally recognized right to abortion announced in *Roe v. Wade* contained a number of curious citations to an obscure seventeenth-century jurist.[32] The jurist, Matthew Hale, not only presided over several witchcraft trials and sentenced women as such,[33] but his treatises on rape—which took the position that women could not be raped in marriage—influenced the direction of American law broadly but also resulting in miscarriages of justice in actual criminal trials.[34] The extensive citation to the views of such a jurist in an opinion that withdrew a vital right to reproductive freedom and access to health care for women in the United States was bitterly fitting, given the view that such reproductive restrictions are ultimately forms of social control.[35]

On the other hand, extreme violence—especially genocide—is more than social control; it is a form of social exclusion and closure. For example, the expulsion of Armenians from western Anatolia during World War I by the Turkish state or the Holocaust itself,[36] the expulsion of Jewish peoples from Nazi Germany and Nazi occupied or Allied territory, and mass murder, was more than social control. Even in the Rwandan genocide of 1994, the Hutu majority decided to try to systematically eliminate all of its minority Tutsi population, resulting in around 800,000 deaths.[37]

The line between violent expulsions and genocide is not always easy to draw. In 1492, Queen Isabella and King Ferdinand ruthlessly implemented a policy of "pure blood" or *limpienza de sangre*, resulting in the forced expulsion or murder of hundreds of thousands of Jews and Muslim Moors, despite the large population of Moors in Spanish lands at the time. Indeed, much of what we call the Spanish Inquisition, under Torquemada, was the violent expulsion of Jews and Muslims.[38]

As noted in a landmark examination of racial residential segregation in the United States, "violence [was] foremost among the tools whites used to construct the ghetto" and thereby build racial segregation into urban areas.[39] Black racial pioneers seeking to move into white neighborhoods routinely encountered violent resistance, property violence, and vandalism, or the threat thereof. Black movers would have burning crosses on their lawns, windows broken, rocks thrown at them, other vandalism, and even bombs or Molotov cocktails thrown into their homes.

————

It is important to emphasize that group-based violence need not be motivated by group animus to function as a mechanism or cause of othering. Whether white people attacked Black racial pioneers "because of" racial antipathy or concerns around the effects on property values, racial comfort or community is frankly irrelevant because the result was the same.

A more recent example that inspired a considerable degree of reporting and reflection was a murderous rampage in Atlanta-area massage parlors. In March 2021, a twenty-one-year-old Georgia man entered three massage parlors in the region and shot and killed eight people, six of whom were Asian women.[40] Reports suggested that the attacker was a deeply troubled evangelical Christian who attacked sex workers to dampen his libido. The event occurred at a time when several other violent incidents involving Asian American victims were widely reported.[41]

Commentators and journalists situated the Atlanta attacks in this context. Conservative analysts were quick to dispute this narrative, pointing out that there was no obvious or clear evidence of anti-Asian animus in this attack and further accusing the media of advancing a "narrative" of white supremacy and misogyny.[42] This response misses the point: the unique vulnerability and position of Asian women in this part of the sex industry, as servicers for massage parlors. Intent is not irrelevant to the effect of violence as a mechanism of othering, but these are cases where the victims' identities are relevant to their structural positional vulnerability.

Communal violence as "othering" may have an ambiguous or complex relationship to the state, as the example of the attack on the Rohingya or the Jim Crow lynchings in the American South suggest. So-called "riots" or mobs may be instigated, supported, or perhaps just given a blind eye by state actors, or even coordinated. For example, in the Jim Crow South, many local sheriffs or law officers were also night riders or protected night riders. Public officials often looked away or refused to investigate or protect victims of such violence. In Myanmar, public servants were often involved in training and arming the Buddhist attackers. Complicity is the norm, and involvement not uncommon. Incidental or mob violence is sometimes escalated in state hands, in which case it acquires a new, more pernicious role.

Between 1917 and the early 1920s, the United States experienced a spate of what the white press reported as "race riots."[43] In fact, however, these were episodes of communal violence directed at Black communities. For example, in 1919, a white mob mobilized to attack Blacks in Washington, D.C., and the fighting, which included returning World War I veterans, lasted five days. One riot that took place in Chicago in July 1919 lasted thirteen days and left thirty-eight people dead, 537 injured, and a thousand Black families without homes.[44] This incident was so traumatic it inspired one of the nation's first major commissions to examine the events, the Chicago Commission on Race Relations, which published a massive report in 1922 that prefigured the Kerner report and the Ferguson report.

Perhaps the most egregious instance of communal anti-Black violence was the Tulsa Massacre in 1921, which destroyed "Black Wall Street," a thriving Black financial hub, and resulted in hundreds of injuries, thousands of arrests, and as many as three hundred dead (although the official death toll was just below forty), as dramatized in the HBO show *Watchman*.[45] The more infamous, though, may have been the St. Louis massacre of 1917, where more than three thousand whites marched into Black neighborhoods to kill and maim, resulting in more than a hundred deaths and thousands left homeless.

As our survey of othering would predict, there are similar cases found elsewhere. Gujarat province in India has had a persistent pattern of caste-related violence, often turning into so-called "riots."[46] Such episodes occurred in 1969, 1975, 1981, 1985, and more recently. The 1975 episode was triggered by "reservations," the system of reserving employment and other opportunities to lower-caste Dalits.[47] The 1981 episode was more violent, however, and involved fifty deaths, mostly from marginalized groups. In 1985, the violence extended beyond Dalits to Muslims as well, and approximately one hundred were killed, and thousands of homes destroyed.

Human rights organizations claim that violence against Dalits increased since the 1990s in response to movements for Dalit rights. According to one estimate, between 1995 and 1997, a total of 90,925 cases were registered with the police nationwide as crimes and "atrocities" against lower castes.[48] More recently, a government agency claimed that caste-based violence increased by 46 percent between 2015 and 2017, including many murders.[49] It should be noted that one of the sixteen-year old Indian girls murdered in an incident described above was Dalit.

In the context of a civil war, the state/nonstate distinction can break down. In Sri Lanka, a twenty-five-year civil war provoked sporadic intergroup violence. Most Sri Lankans are Buddhist, about seven out of ten, and they generally speak Sinhalese, just as the minority Hindus in Sri Lanka speak Tamil. Conflict between the Tamils and Sinhalese intensified during the twentieth century, with episodes like a 1958 riot in which 150–200 people were killed.[50] A separatist movement among the Tamils, triggered by perceived threats around cultural survival, contributed to the long civil war. Muslims—about 10 percent of the Sri Lankan population—were caught in the middle, and the victims of atrocities by both sides in the war. After the Tigers were defeated in 2009, Sri Lanka's newly emboldened Buddhist nationalists targeted Muslims. Right-wing groups attacked Muslim-owned shops, painted pigs on the walls of mosques, and tore down a shrine to an Islamic saint.[51] In 2014 and 2018, riots erupted in different parts of the country, during which Muslims and their properties were targeted.[52]

Discrimination

Violence may be the most obvious mechanism and expression of othering, but discrimination is probably the most easily morally intuited as such.*

---

* Violence is—with well-defined exceptions—almost universally regarded as a cardinal violation of the civil order, but acts of violence often arise in contexts or circumstances that make it harder to know the degree to which a victim's identity played a central, primary, or motivating role. See infra, the discussion of the killing of Matthew Shepard and the Pulse nightclub shooting, which targeted marginalized

Discrimination occurs when a person is treated differently—generally worse—because of their group membership or identity. When a person is denied an opportunity—a job, a promotion, the right to vote, the chance at an education, or the privilege of joining a club—because of their identity (such as their gender, religion, race, or LGBTQ status), it has a deleterious effect on that person's well-being and life chances. When members of a particular group are consistently or routinely discriminated against in society, it negatively influences the well-being of that group as a whole. In short, discrimination is a major cause of intergroup inequality, or othering.

Upon closer inspection, however, discrimination is a surprisingly slippery concept. As a legal principle, the term itself is something of a misnomer, or underspecified. To discriminate is simply to distinguish between things or people.[53] Most forms of discrimination are legal, if not enshrined in law, such as age-based restrictions on voting or purchasing alcohol or certain privileges or benefits to veterans or the elderly. We permit employers, sports teams, and schools to select among people based upon different skills, abilities, and relevant characteristics without worrying too much about this. For example, selecting a sports player based upon speed or strength is considered acceptable, while doing so based on race or religion might be deemed unacceptable.

In a technical sense, discrimination occurs when selecting someone because they were a member of a previously excluded group. For example, if a court finds that women were excluded by a trucking company because of gender, the law may permit, or even in some cases require, an equally qualified one to get the nod over a man. As recompense for past harm, this kind of discrimination is widely understood as ethical.

To help distinguish between distinctions drawn for laudable reasons and those motivated by animus, the law distinguishes between "invidious" and benign distinctions. Moreover, most legal codes will establish norms protecting certain classes of individuals from discrimination, clarifying

---

people but had complex and murky motives. Even in cases of genocide—the most obvious cases—violence is sometimes based on concerns of national security or integrity, targeting groups as an "enemy within."

which distinctions should be regarded as presumptively invidious and which should be broadly permitted or at least unregulated. In terms of othering, the types of discrimination that are most concerning are those that contribute to intergroup inequality, treating all members of one group differently, or allowing actions and policies to differently affect them.

More subtly, it is not discrimination that the law seeks to regulate, or that contributes to intergroup inequality; it is *actions*, decisions, or policies based on discriminatory distinctions. It isn't necessarily a problem that an employer recognizes that an employee is Black. The legal harm of discrimination occurs when they refuse to hire or promote or decide to fire or otherwise deny a benefit on the basis of their race.

Another ambiguity related to discrimination is the problem of intent. Discrimination is generally treating someone different because of their identity or social group. The words "because of" have proven legally significant. Some people—and courts—interpret that kind of language to require that consideration of race was "motivational," meaning that the identity of the actors involved formed at least part of the motivation for the differential treatment. Although discrimination can be blatant and obvious, as when an employer or a university explicitly refuses admission on the basis of a racial, ethnic, gender, or religious identity, it can also be subtle and covert, as when an employer provides a pretextual reason for refusing to hire or promote an individual, unrelated to their identity or social group. Discovering the difference can be quite challenging, especially if such decision making is unconscious or based on unconscious associations.

There is another subtlety here as well. What if an employer refuses to hire someone, not because of hatred or animus against a particular group, but because of stereotypes about that group? For example, what if an employer holds no ill will or hatred toward people of a particular group, but assumes that they are lazier or less hardworking? Or, what if they refuse to hire someone because they assume that people in their workforce might have a hard time working with them or experience discomfort? For example, military commanders may have no personal animus against women or LGBTQ persons, but many have raised concerns that having them in regiments could undermine military cohesion. Or, what if a factory foreman refuses to hire a women (or an Irishman) for a factory position because of the assumption that it would be disruptive to regular efficiency? Should the prejudices or tendency of a workforce be a ground for discrimination, even in the absence of animus or invidiousness? Antidiscrimination law generally regards negative stereotypes as impermissible.

Discrimination does not usually occur because of an identity category per se. Rather, it occurs because of stigmatic associations with that category. Thus the operative language "because of" race, religion, age or gender is, in effect, extending to such assumptions and associations, not just the identity category. As suggested above, it would be more accurate to say a person was not hired because of the bias of the person making the hiring decision or the considerations and associations the hiring manager used, not because of the applicant's race.

―――――

A related and difficult nuance to the problem of discrimination is when a law does not target or single out a group or members of a group for differential treatment, but in fact does the opposite: purports to treat everyone the same, even though few can deny that the underlying purpose is to stigmatize or oppress. This problem arises in several forms. Perhaps the most infamous example is that of *Plessy v. Ferguson*'s infamous legal principle: "separate, but equal." This doctrine required separate (segregated) public accommodations for Black and white persons, ostensibly treating them exactly the same (and thus complying with the formal requirements of the Fourteenth Amendment's rule that the state provide equal treatment of laws). But in practice, these facilities were anything but equal.

In this way, discriminatory laws are not always those that explicitly differentiate between groups. Very often it is the systematic and unequal *application* of a law to a particular group that signals its discriminatory purpose. For example, loitering laws in the United States have been broadly used to target Black Americans doing otherwise perfectly lawful things, like standing outdoors.[54] Certain traffic violations are known to be selectively used as a pretext for surveilling or harassing motorists of color.[55] These discriminatory laws can be recognized through their disparate impacts or disproportionate effects.

Superficially neutral laws can produce unequal effects not only through unequal application or selective enforcement, but also by design.* In France, headscarves were banned in schools in 2004, and in 2011 certain face coverings and veils were also banned, with the possibility of a fine.[56] Although ostensibly neutral on religion, these laws targeted practicing Muslims in France. In 2022, Marine Le Pen went so far as to propose a ban on headscarves in public places, even though such a rule would superficially apply on a universal basis.[57]

The foregoing issues are among the reasons why some courts and legislatures interpret the words "because of" or similar language to encompass actions that produced disproportionate effects on a protected group, even in the absence of discriminatory intent or motivation. The Voting Rights Act and the Civil Rights Acts of 1964 and 1968 encompass this kind of "effects language."[58] For example, if a decision was based upon stereotypes or unconscious bias, it could have resulted in such effects even in the absence of a purposeful intent to discriminate. In the stilted language of law, this is sometimes called "discriminatory effects" or "disparate impact." Policies can have disparate effects, and thereby discriminate, even in the absence of intent.[59]

But not all discriminatory laws produce disparate impacts. Compared to "separate, but equal," a less blatantly hypocritical discriminatory law purporting to treat people the same are versions of the antimiscegenation laws discussed in Chapter 3. These laws, originating in the colonial period, prohibited marriage between races, until they were struck down in the aptly named case of *Loving v. Virginia* in 1967.[60] Although such laws were promulgated on grounds of preserving racial purity, the obvious and undeniable purpose was not to protect Black Americans from white blood, but the reverse. Such laws are obviously discriminatory even though they are facially neutral and can have no obvious disproportionate impact by race. Only by examining them in context can we recognize their true purpose.

----

* It is a mistake to presume that the goal of law is to be neutral. This mistake is based on the conflation of the concepts of neutrality with fairness. Consider the accommodations required in ADA. It is anything but neutral.

Marriage laws that prohibit marriage between different social groups may be among the most revealing examples of discrimination that are most difficult to detect as discriminatory because they are apparently neutral in both design and effect. Because of the centrality of marriage to human intimacy and reproduction, laws that ban certain forms of intergroup marriage may be among the most pernicious and harmful in terms of amplifying othering. Unfortunately, such laws are not a relic of the past.

Under the leadership of Modi's Bharatiya Janata Party, India has promulgated laws that restrict interfaith marriage.[61] Although the Indian Constitution protects religious freedom and diversity, such laws are broadly supported in Indian society. A Pew survey found that most Indians oppose interfaith marriage, especially when the woman is Hindu or Sikh.[62] As of 2021, police in India are literally interrupting marriage ceremonies and arresting couples violating the law.[63]

By encompassing intentional acts and behavior, those that are either unconscious or simply disproportionate in its effects, or simply laws and policies that are designed to oppress, discrimination plays a powerful role in the othering process. It structures access to jobs, education, and other critical life-shaping and enhancing opportunities and institutions.

––––––

Discrimination is paradoxically both more and less important to the production of intergroup inequality—to the othering—than is probably understood. On the one hand, any single instance or form of discrimination may be of limited significance by itself. In Burundi, for example, women are prohibited by law and custom from playing the "sacred" drums.[64] While such a prohibition does not significantly curtail the ability of women to find work, it is symbolic of a gender hierarchy and patriarchal culture.

Similarly, if a member of a group is denied admission to a university because of their race, or employment with an employer because of their sexual orientation, or a home because of their disability, it is unlikely that that denial forms a complete bar to university education, employment, or a home. Even if a particular landlord or realtor discriminates against an individual on the basis of their identity, there may still be a chance that another does not. There may be alternative universities to consider, jobs that hire, or homes to purchase. Only when discrimination is broad and widespread does it become an absolute bar.

On the other hand, even a single instance of discrimination can have a compounding and cumulative effect when examined over time or across domains.[65] Thus a single denial—depending on the relative importance of that opportunity—can have a much larger cumulative effect over time. For example, Lilly Ledbetter took a job as a shift manager at Goodyear Tire & Rubber in 1979. Company policy prohibited her from discussing her pay with colleagues. Nearly twenty years later she discovered that, despite her superior performance, she was paid substantially less than her male colleagues. Starting out at a lower rate of pay can compound to much larger amounts over time, if promotions and raises are based on the initial salary. Indeed, some employment experts argue that the inequality in pay rates for the same job may be partly explained by different levels of negotiation between men and women for starting salaries, and that this initial difference grows wider over time.[66] The courts threw out her suit on a technicality, and the Congress passed a law in her name to overturn the basis for decision in 2009.[67]

Another area in which discrimination can have long-term effects is in denying access to education. Discrimination in university admissions, unfortunately, is an American tradition. Women, minorities, and people of color, among others, have been regularly excluded from critical institutions of higher education. People of Jewish ethnicity were broadly discriminated against by Ivy League universities in the first half of the twentieth century, just as women were entirely barred from many of these universities until 1960s.[68] Many Ivy League administrators and their alumni viewed these institutions as serving not only the educational aims of the institutions, but the social role of training the nation's Protestant upper class. For this reason, although informal quotas had been suspected of trying to keep Jewish applicants out, in 1922, Harvard president Abbot Lawrence Lowell presented a plan to limit Jewish applicants to no more than 15 percent of the student body.[69] Although this proposal was ultimately rejected, this explicit admission was one example of a wider effort to suppress Jewish attendance in the Ivy League at the time.

Yale's policy was perhaps even more explicit in its discriminatory intentions. In a report submitted to President James Rowland Angell in 1922, the chairman of the University Admissions Board wrote that "[t]here seems to be no question that the University as a whole has about all of this race that it can well handle."[70] The annual report of the Board of Admissions of Yale University for 1944–45 reiterated this concern: "The Jewish problem . . . continues to call for the utmost care and tact. . . . The proportion of Jews among the candidates who are both scholastically qualified for admission and young enough to matriculate has somewhat increased and remains too large for comfort."[71]

Discrimination need not affect a profound area of life, such as university admissions or job opportunities, to harm well-being. Another example of identity-based discrimination is Saudi Arabia's ban on women driving. Reportedly instituted in 1957, this gender-based driving ban significantly curtailed freedom of movement for women.[72] This restriction made it difficult for women to pursue or secure jobs, get an education, mix socially, or do anything that free people enjoy. Only affluent or rich women could afford chauffeurs or private drivers that would allow them that freedom.

Periodic protests against this driving ban occurred in 1990, 2007, and 2011–12, resulting in many arrests, punishments (such as confiscating passports), and other consequences and criticism by international human rights groups.[73] The most recent campaign against this ban, however, proved successful. In 2017, Saudi leadership announced that they would review this ban, and in 2018, they ultimately overturned it.[74] Despite this, one of the leaders of the campaign was initially sentenced to nearly six years of imprisonment.[75]

Resistance to discriminatory laws or regulations in the form of protests can trigger reprisals of state violence. In this way, violence is used to enforce discrimination, working hand in glove. One of the most recent examples of this is the case of Mahsa Amini, a twenty-two-year old Iranian woman who was arrested by the religious morality police on September 16, 2022, for violating the country's hijab law, which requires her to cover her hair.[76] Her suspicious death in custody triggered more than six weeks of massive protests across the country as well as a violent state crackdown.[77]

One human rights group estimates there were over two hundred deaths as a result of the state response.[78]

The Saudi gender-based driving ban, like many systems of discrimination, was part of a much larger and more encompassing system of gender discrimination in the Kingdom, a so-called "Guardianship" system.[79] In addition to the driving ban, it included restrictions on women's freedom to attend concerts or movie theaters, male relatives' permission to travel abroad, and legal discrimination in the workplace, as well as additional requirements to secure government documents and forms.[80] These kinds of interlocking discrimination are clearly more oppressive than discrimination in just one area or one facet of life. It should also be noted that the Kingdom has executed dozens of women for witchcraft in recent years.[81]

––––––––

In terms of the othering process, certain forms of discrimination are more harmful than others. When a state discriminates as a matter of policy—as occurs when excluding a group from military service or denying access to a critical resource—the harm is likely greater than when it is done simply in private by a single individual or entity. There are two reasons for this. First, when the state discriminates against a group, there is a symbolic and expressive component that may not exist in a situation of widespread but diffuse private discrimination. This imprimatur of government conveys a message and connotes a public stigma.

But the larger problem with state-based discrimination is that institutional or state-based discrimination tends to be more systematic and broad-based. Fundamentally, law is a formal mechanism of social control, and reflects the considered judgment of the political and legal community.[82] When an individual discriminates against a member of a group because of their group status, that act is limited to a particular site. When the state discriminates, the sites of discrimination are multiplied, and the instances may become systematic. The result tends to be more extensive and damaging. Law plays a critical role in the othering process.

Ancient legal codes are replete with legal distinctions based on identity and reflect both the othering processes of the societies in which they emerge as well as contribute to ongoing othering. One of the earliest known written legal codes, the Roman Republic's "Twelve Tables," required new-borns with visible disabilities to be put to immediate death.[83] The Code of Hammurabi, perhaps the earliest known legal code, divides society into two genders and three classes, superiors, commoners, and slaves or ser-vants, and ascribes different punishments depending upon the identity of a perpetrator of a crime or the victim.[84] A section of that code defining penalties for assault and battery is illustrative. It states that if a superior person strikes another superior person, they have to pay nearly a pound of silver. If a common person strikes another commoner, they have to pay ten shekels of silver. But if a slave strikes the body of a superior person, his ear "shall be cut off."[85] As one historian observes, the code essentially suggests that "the life of a female commoner is worth thirty silver shekels and that of a slave-woman twenty silver shekels."[86]

Although more common in ancient law codes, differential treatment based upon negative stereotypes or beliefs is hardly restricted to them. More recently, the doctrine of "Don't Ask, Don't Tell" was a discrimina-tory military service rule that, while allowing gay and lesbian persons to serve in the military, required that they keep their sexuality a secret.[87] If their sexual orientation was discovered, they could be summarily expelled from service, as thousands were.[88] Similarly, until 2015, the U.S. military excluded women from combat role.[89] These policies were more systematic than if a particular officer discriminated against women or LGBTQ per-sons. The symbolic component of 'Don't Ask, Don't Tell' signified a social stigma on same-sex relationships in the military that cannot be discerned in the case of individual-level cases of prejudice, even if quietly allowed.

Perhaps the most notorious form of discrimination in American mil-itary service was a 1792 federal law that prohibited African Americans from serving until the Civil War (although Black troops did fight in prior wars).[90] Even when allowed to serve, however, Black troops were organized into segregated units, given unequal pay, and served entirely under white senior officers, the most famous of which is probably the 54th Regiment of Massachusetts Volunteers.[91]

Antidiscrimination laws can have a powerfully salutary effect in miti-gating the harm of discrimination, even as they may be unable to entirely eliminate it.[92] For example, the integration of the American armed forces by President Harry S. Truman in 1948 was a major step toward the fight for civil rights in other areas of life, and gave wind to the civil rights movement.[93] Thus the presence—or nonexistence—of antidiscrimination legislation can be a very important indicator of othering in a society—or belongingness, as was discussed in Chapter 5.

Segregation, Secession, and Expulsion

Segregation is the separation of people across space or within or across institutions. Segregation can occur on virtually any basis or in any life arena. The most well-known forms of segregation are residential, occupational, educational, or in public accommodations (like buses and restaurants). The most common bases for segregation are racial, gender, caste, religion, profession, and (dis)ability. But like othering itself, it can occur on any basis or in any realm of life.

Violence and discrimination are more obvious mechanisms for propagating intergroup inequality and elements of the othering process, but segregation is in many ways more insidious and pernicious. The reason for this is that violence and invidious discrimination are difficult to justify or disguise within prevailing ethical frameworks or commonsense universal notions of justice. Segregation, however, can appear neutral, fair, and even be characterized as benevolent paternalism or justified on the basis of peace and harmony. Moreover, some forms of segregation may be desired by some members of marginalized groups, as a protective cordon or community enhancing.

The problem, however, is that segregation almost always results in disparate and unequal life outcomes between the groups being segregated. Wherever segregation exists between social groups, disparities are usually observed in terms of wages, income, wealth, educational attainment, health and wellness (life expectancy, morbidity, etc.), and social and economic mobility.[94] In religiously segregated Northern Ireland, for example, Irish Catholic life expectancy is 74.1 years compared to 81.7 for Protestant men.[95] Protestant women live 4.7 years longer than Catholic women. This is strikingly similar to the disparities that exist in the United States on the basis of race. In the San Francisco Bay Area, for example, life expectancy is about five years greater in segregated white neighborhoods (84 years) than highly segregated Black/Latino neighborhoods (79 years).[96] Although the bases are different (race compared to religion), both forms of segregation are associated with a five-year disparity in life expectancy.

There is a voluminous literature across the social sciences documenting the harmful effects of segregation.[97] Less well understood is why these effects arise.[98] The answer has to do with the overlay of social groups with critical life-enhancing resources and social networks. Whether by design or accident, resources are almost always inequitably distributed in society. Some communities are rich in natural resources (fertile soil, timber, arable land, etc.) while others are deserts. The same is true of economic and social resources. Tax-base capacity, economic growth rates, and public provision tend to be unequal between communities, despite many compensatory mechanisms. Even within uniformly great schools, some teachers are better than others.

Because resources are always unevenly distributed across space and within institutions, segregation tends to extend more or better resources to one group (often through proximity or channeling) and restrict or limit those resources or opportunities to other groups. This is the function and purpose of segregation, and why it has a powerful tendency to generate intergroup inequality. To illustrate: If, within a school, every member of one group was assigned to a classroom with the best teacher, and every member of another group was assigned to a classroom with the worst teacher, the outcomes would be predictable: persistent educational disparities between the classrooms and also between the groups. But if both groups were well mixed across both classrooms, group-based disparities could not arise due to segregation, even if one classroom performed better than the other.

If there were no difference between segregated spaces, there would be less reason to segregate. Segregation is doing more than keeping groups apart. It was not that the Negro Baseball Leagues, for example, were lacking in talent or management. Rather, they chiefly lacked equal resources to field and organize the game.[99] Similarly, the chief complaint of Black parents during Jim Crow was not the fact of different school assignments per se, but the vastly unequal and inadequate resources supplied to Black schools: the lack of adequate materials, facilities, and other resources.

Nonetheless, the NAACP attorneys who developed the strategy that culminated in *Brown* recognized that a legal strategy aimed at equalizing resources would never suffice to achieve equal educational opportunity.

The reason for this is that critical life-enhancing resources are not always
tangible, such as taxes, revenues, or services. In many cases, these resources
are intangible, taking the form of social capital and social networks, political connections, or reputational prestige. Even if every concerted effort is
made to equalize material resources between the groups being segregated,
it is essentially impossible to equalize every intangible resource across a segregated boundary.

This is why the Supreme Court in *Brown v. Board of Education* ruled
that segregation was unconstitutional: it afforded inherently unequal educational opportunities. However, in an oft-overlooked nuance, the court
emphasized that the harms of segregation could not be rectified by simply
equalizing tangible resources, as the parties had stipulated that southern
states were doing.[100] This is also why the Supreme Court struck down the
state of Virginia's female-only alternative to it is prestigious military institute in the case of *U.S. v. Virginia*.[101] As the court noted in that case,
the Virginia Military Institute's reputation, unique history, and alumni
network could not be duplicated at a sister institution, no matter how
well resourced. And in *Brown*, the court observed that segregation itself—
irrespective of the distribution of resources—connotated the inferiority of
Black citizens. Segregated education is separate and unequal, and can never
be made so.[102]

The inequitable distribution of resources across space and large, complex institutions is inevitable. But what is not inevitable is that such inequities must become drivers of intergroup inequality. That only occurs
in the condition of segregation, when groups themselves are unevenly distributed or isolated across space and relative to each other, when there are
separate neighborhoods, jobs, classrooms, or schools for Black and white
children, girls and boys, Catholics and Protestants, upper-caste Brahmins
and lower-caste Dalits. As long as all social groups are relatively integrated
and evenly dispersed relative to each other across these critical spaces, the
uneven geographic distribution of resources cannot translate into unequal
group-level outcomes.

Segregation can also result when a social group is persecuted and driven into a protective space. Across the United States, many LGBTQ people fled into tight urban corridors where they could find refuge from an opprobrious and disapproving society.[103] So-called "gay villages" or "gayborhoods" were residentially and culturally segregated spaces with a high concentration of LGBTQ persons. Greater societal acceptance, along with the innovation of dating apps and economic forces, have contributed to the dispersion and increased integration of LGBTQ Americans.

It is sometimes maintained that segregation is a form or by-product of discrimination (or violence).[104] We view it as a mistake to regard segregation as a species of discrimination rather than a separate and independent driver of othering and mechanism of intergroup inequality. It cannot be denied that many forms of segregation are institutionalized by rules, laws, or regulations, and that such rules and regulations have been promulgated for obvious purposes of social control, social closure, and opportunity hoarding.[105] But segregation can arise even without relying on the state, law, formal rules, or even broad forms of institutionalized or market-based discrimination.

Segregation can occur because of background conditions, initial conditions, or differences between groups wholly unrelated (at least in any obvious way) to discrimination or the threat of it. There are communities that maintain separation to preserve certain cultural practices that are extremely unusual in the mainstream society. Amish and Mennonite communities in the American Midwest epitomize this.[106] As these communities do not regularly use many of the conveniences or practical necessities of modern life, integration between their members and the mainstream society may be extremely difficult to manage or balance. Thus, to preserve those ways of life, segregation may be preferred, and not a product of discrimination or violence.[107] Such segregation probably contributes to "inequality" as measured conventionally along dimensions such as educational attainment, income, and wealth.

Another example of how segregation can arise is differences in income between ethnic, religious, or racial groups in a society due to tenure (some groups may be recent immigrants or refugees who left behind businesses or family wealth), where legacy members of that society have access to the best neighborhoods or schools, and more recent members do not, generating spatial disproportionality and patterns of residential segregation. These differences in income and wealth (assuming all are new arrivals), as well as simple differences in local knowledge as part of the housing search process or (resettlement) procedures, can result in residential segregation absent violence or discrimination.[108]

Although segregation is a powerful mechanism of othering, that does not mean the harm is always greater than the benefit. Paradoxically, recent immigrants to a new country may find the most opportunity in ethnic enclaves. This "port of entry" effect reflects the fact that job opportunities, connections, cultural comfort, and social capital may be richest and thickest in such locations.[109] Many recent immigrants have limited proficiency with the predominant language, and thus such enclaves allow a more fluid discourse, learning of job opportunities, familiarity, and comfort. While such segregation may be harmful for second- or third-generation immigrant children, these enclaves may be the first step on the ladder of opportunity for first-generation immigrants.[110]

Similarly, members of deaf communities may be best served by moving into segregated deaf communities. The reason for this has to do with simple communication and culture. As the vast majority of hearing people are not fluent in sign language, they cannot easily communicate with or understand people who communicate primarily through sign language. This form of segregation may not necessarily produce harm—or, at least, may counterbalance the costs and the benefits more squarely than is the case when people are forced into segregated communities by compulsion or lack of choice.

Although the most notorious instances of segregation are probably Jim Crow segregation in the American South and South Africa's apartheid regime, segregation is ubiquitous in human history and across human societies. In its earliest known expression, segregation was initially devised to maintain differences among emergent professional classes (such as clerics and craftsmen),[111] but it has evolved in almost every corner of the globe in almost every complex society to separate certain groups or classes of people from privileges, resources, networks, and opportunities. India's ancient caste system, for example, deems the lowest caste, Dalits, as "untouchables."[112] This is not simply a colorful label, but a literal article of faith among many Hindus. In many villages, Dalits are forbidden to drink from upper-caste wells or to worship at their temples.[113] In 2020, a seventeen-year old Dalit was shot and killed for entering a temple "belonging" to an upper caste.[114]

Similarly, as noted earlier in the case of the Saudi "Guardianship" system, men and women are systematically segregated in public spaces. Within this system, women and men are assigned separate seating areas and entrances in theaters, restaurants, and concert venues.[115] These forms of so-called "public accommodations" segregation, based on gender or caste, bear more than a striking resemblance to Jim Crow segregation. The resemblance is less surprising, however, once the function of segregation is more deeply appreciated and understood.

In addition to the periodic communal violence and pogroms against Jewish communities, segregation was also a critical part of the process of "othering" Jews in the late Middle Ages and early Renaissance Europe. In 1516 Venetian authorities ordered Jewish residents to move into a carefully demarcated zone within the city.[116] Similarly, under the "Cortes of Toledo" agreement, Isabel and Ferdinand segregated Jews in Spain, requiring them to live in different neighborhoods than Christians, and to remain indoors during the day, certain professions excepted.[117] Walls were even built around the Jewish quarters, resulting in so-called "ghettos." Segregation was used to control Jewish lives and livelihoods.

Segregation is one of the oldest and most effective mechanisms of othering. It is both a driver and by-product of othering. But spatial segregation is not always feasible or possible. Many people with horizontal identities are difficult to segregate, and gender or sex segregation is especially difficult to facilitate residentially, as men and women tend to cohabitate. This is why segregation occurs on other bases or arenas, often institutionally, not simply by residence or neighborhood.

Occupational segregation occurs when members of a certain group are restricted to certain departments or roles within an institution, such as when women are permitted to be secretaries or nurses, but not doctors, or when Black men in the South could become porters, barbers, waiters, or custodians, but not managers or foremen.[118] In this way, occupational segregation powerfully restricts the wages and incomes of members of certain groups, circumscribing them to a certain part of society (neighborhoods, roles, etc.).

Occupational segregation can also occur when employers believe that mixing certain groups undermines efficiency. This is the reason that women were locked out of combat operations in the military, and also why many employers, historical or contemporary, might refuse to hire women (or men). So a machine shop steward or a mining foreman might refuse to hire women on the misguided theory that a gender-integrated work environment could undermine workforce cohesion.

Occupational segregation and educational segregation may be related, however. If women were refused admittance to the bar, then schools might have a reason to refuse to admit women to law schools (or vice versa). Educational segregation is when women and men, for example, attend single-sex schools. Because women were not admitted into many private colleges and universities, institutions arose to serve them. So instead of the Ivy League, women matriculated to the "Seven Sisters" schools. Many girls' schools or women's colleges were formed to provide education for women who were not served by mainstream institutions. Similarly, because African Americans were kept out of even public colleges and universities, historically Black colleges and universities (HBCUs) arose to serve them.

Public accommodations (segregated restaurants, railways, buses, theaters, etc.) and occupational segregation were accomplished with such aggressive sweep in the Jim Crow South that virtually every facet of life was segregated. This was also the case in South Africa under apartheid (1948–94). In both cases, segregation was built piece by piece, law by law, brick by brick, encompassing nearly every facet of life. But cross-cultural observers could see the parallels between societies. As the prolific mid-twentieth-century journalist John Gunther observed, "Atlanta is supposed to rank fairly high among Southern cities in its attitude toward Negroes, but it out-ghettoes anything I saw in a European ghetto, even in Warsaw. What I looked at was caste and untouchability—half the time I blinked remembering that this was not India."[119]

As the preceding examples illustrate, that segregation is not simply a static condition of human societies. It is a mechanism for increasing or decreasing the overall degree of othering experienced. For example, the residential segregation of Catholics and Protestants in Belfast, Northern Ireland, increased rapidly during the twentieth century and accelerated during the period of the so-called Troubles, which were at their height between 1971 and 1991.[120] One scholar found that 60 percent of the city was segregated in 1901, but that rose to 77 percent by the end of the century.[121] The advent of the Troubles in 1969 triggered a "sharp increase in residential segregation with forced housing moves as a consequence of rioting, violence, and intimidation."[122] A similar process occurred between 1920 and 1923, a period of rioting, in which Catholics left areas in which they had lived near Protestants.

And, as should be clear by now, the segregation of people results in increasing disparities in life outcomes. During the Troubles, the Protestant "unionists" gerrymandered Northern Ireland to cement their political power, while also routinely discriminating against Catholics in employment and housing. As one resident noted, "everyday chauvinism said Catholics were poor because they were backward and dirty, and brought it on themselves. 'That's a Protestant-looking house,' mothers would chirp after tidying up."[123]

Strikingly similar patterns have been discovered for racial residential segregation in the United States. Black neighborhoods were stigmatized as disordered and declining. Measured levels of segregation grew rapidly in the first half of the twentieth century and then peaked around 1970, easing off largely due to the adoption of the federal Fair Housing Act.[124] And, as was true of the Troubles, the urban rebellions in American cities in the mid and late 1960s accelerated white flight from the urban cores and into the suburbs, which also accelerated and intensified racial residential segregation.[125] Indeed, race or religious riots usually accelerate segregation, while also becoming a cause of such rebellions, creating a vicious circle of segregation, inequality, and discontent.

France learned this the hard way in 2005, as the suburban "banlieues" outside of Paris erupted in anger.[126] For years, Arabs from Algeria—a former French colony—had migrated to France for work. Many of these immigrants settled and raised families. Too many of these families were restricted to living in shantytowns resembling the townships in South Africa. Eventually, however, these structures were cleared for safe and sturdy housing built by the state. These communities, although possessing many of the outward forms of stable residential life, were socially divided from the mainstream of Parisian life. Companies were disinclined to hire applicants from these areas, and Arab surnames were also discriminated against in employment. As one resident of a French banlieue told the *New Yorker*, "You do everything for France, to be accepted, but you feel you're not welcome."[127] Thus segregation reproduces social isolation and economic division, even in the heart of Europe.

As alluded to earlier, despite the manifold harms of segregation, segregation is often promoted or defended on ostensibly benign or beneficent grounds. In particular, one ground frequently advanced is religious or spiritual practice. For example, "Purdah" is a practice of physical and social separation of women in some Hindu or Muslim societies, and is based on seemingly benign notions of chastity and well-being.[128] However, research suggests that it has harmful psychological and health outcomes, and reduced women's political participation in those societies.[129] Similarly, the 1480 segregation of Jews in Spain was based upon a concern among the monarchs that some Jews were falsely converting to Christianity, and that segregation was needed to ensure obedience to civil and holy law.[130] Recall that Hindu caste segregation is also based on religious grounds of purity and holiness.

White supremacist advocates of Jim Crow, for example, argued that segregation was necessary to maintain racial harmony, and that compulsory or forced association would lead to more racial antipathy. Indeed, the United States Supreme Court majority in *Plessy* explicitly adopted this argument. It wrote:

> If the two races are to meet upon terms of social equality, it must be the result of natural affinities, a mutual appreciation of each other's merits and a voluntary consent of individuals. As was said by the Court of Appeals of New York in *People v. Gallagher*, 93 N.Y. 438, 448, "this end can neither be accomplished nor promoted by laws which conflict with

the general sentiment." . . . Legislation is powerless to eradicate racial
instincts or to abolish distinctions based upon physical differences, and
the attempt to do so can only result in accentuating the difficulties of
the present situation.[131]

Often, paradoxically, segregation is proposed or advanced on the basis of
solving, or tamping down, intergroup conflict, rather than a desire to hoard
resources and expand the prerogatives of a dominant group. Thus there was
a widespread assumption in nineteenth-century America that the routine
or daily interaction of races would lead to conflict and violence, and so
segregation was advanced (although disingenuously) on the grounds that
it was necessary for the well-being of both races. The ultimate partition
of India in 1947 was intended to prevent or forestall further religious and
ethnic conflict, although it resulted in much worse.[132] The Japanese Internment was justified on a similar ground, of corralling an internal "threat."

During World War II, President Franklin Delano Roosevelt issued
Presidential Proclamation No. 2537, an executive order requiring aliens
from World War II–enemy countries—Italy, Germany, and Japan—to
register with the United States Department of Justice, as a follow-up to
the Alien Registration Act of 1940.[133] A month later, Roosevelt signed Executive Order 9066, which began the internment of ultimately more than
one hundred thousand Japanese Americans. They were forced out of their
homes and into camps along the West Coast through the war. In the infamous *Korematsu* decision, the Supreme Court upheld this notorious order
over an equal protection claim largely on grounds of national security.[134]

In 1983, the Commission on Wartime Relocation and Internment of
Civilians investigated the episode and found that the underlying basis for
internment was fear and racism, including harmful stereotypes.[135] The
commission's recommendations resulted in a reparations payment to internment victims or their immediate family members and a formal government apology. The internment of Japanese Americans was justified by
wartime security but is now viewed as an embarrassing mistake.

But an interest in peace, order, harmony, and security has been invoked
in recent years as well. For example, when sectarian tensions began to esca-
late in Baghdad during the early years of the American occupation of Iraq,

L. Paul Bremer, the U.S. administrator, segregated the city into sectarian enclaves in the name of peace. As a result, Iraq in 2009 was much more segregated than in 2003, unwittingly replicating a colonial trope.[136] Indeed, there is evidence that pan-Iraqi national identity was much stronger before the Bremer regime asked citizens to identify sectarian affiliation.

The segregation of Baghdad Green Zone was the basis for a possible larger cleaving. In 2006, then-senator Joe Biden even proposed dividing up Iraq into three different countries—a proposal that many viewed with similar skepticism to the oft-maligned Sykes-Picot Agreement, which shaped the national boundaries in the Middle East after World War I and the fall of the Ottoman Empire.[137] A similar proposal for carving up India was suggested by the British in the negotiations leading up to independence.[138]

The idea of segregation to resolve long-standing communal tension is recurring in the international context. The Dayton Accords, which ended the Bosnian War, "effectively engraved ethnic and religious divisions by carving out turf for the Serbs, Croats and Bosnian Muslims."[139] One of the ways in which it did this was by sanctioning segregated schooling. There are around fifty schools around Bosnia where ethnic Croats, who are mostly Roman Catholic, and Bosnian Muslims are separated in the same building or into different buildings. The separation extends to a different curriculum as well, with approved ethnically and culturally prescribed textbooks. The Organization for Security and Co-operation in Europe has raised concerns that the "'ethnically oriented curricula' impede reconciliation, perpetuate divisions, 'limit economic development and jeopardize the long-term stability and security.'" In other words, rather than tamp down tensions, segregation may be perpetuating divisions and animosities that filter from and toward the broader society.

What may begin as a well-meaning effort to stem communal violence may have longer-term, othering effects. The segregation of space as a short-term solution to a larger problem reinforces the problems that gave rise to the notion in the first place. Indeed, the United States was confronted with this in very real terms in 2005, when it was asked to review the constitutionality of the California Department of Corrections' policy of segregating prisons on their basis of race to prevent "violence caused by racial gangs."[140] The California Department of Corrections may well have been correct that segregating prisons reasonably prevented some intergroup violence. But what role did that separation have in reinforcing identities and the social fabric within the prisons that made such violence more likely? The policy merely underscores the harm: when the state segregates, it is acquiescing to private prejudices or reinforcing them. The deeply divided court ruled that the U.S. Constitution prohibits racial segregation of prisoners, and struck down the policy.

When the federal government segregated public housing to acquiesce to southern sensibilities and concerns about violence and harmony,[141] it doubled down on a process that extended segregation nationally and more extensively than it was before. Even if the government initially plays no role in promoting or engendering private prejudices, it has a duty and a responsibility to avoid deepening it. Or, as the Supreme Court justice Sandra Day O'Connor framed the matter in another context, local governments mustn't become a "passive participant" in a system of racial exclusion.[142]

Although there may be valid cultural reasons for segregation, we should be skeptical of arguments that defend segregation on equity or anti-othering grounds. One version of this argument maintains that separation is a necessary short-term step toward building an independent power base, so that integration may occur on a basis of equality and mutual choice. Indeed, the concept of "Black Power" was to some extent based on the notion that only by providing autonomous and separate Black-owned and operated businesses, schools, etc. could equality be constructed.[143] This assumption was based on the not-unreasonable premise that white-controlled institutions such as school districts or legislatures would never otherwise accord Black communities those resources.[144] Although hardly a Black nationalist or separatist, the *New York Times* opinion columnist Charles Blow has advanced a version of this in his manifesto calling for descendants of the Great Migration to return to the South to build and secure a countervailing, antiracist political power base.[145]

To some extent, this position betrays its insecurity or disbelief in the possibility of a society where Black and white people are regarded as equal and co-creating society, and therefore equality can only occur at a safe remove rather than in a joint endeavor. This is a kind of pessimism in the possibility of progress embodied by the later writings of Derrick Bell and others.[146]

Another version of this argument defends segregation on the basis of self-protection, not just solidarity. Sometimes members of marginalized groups are given subtle cues—even in the absence of overt discrimination or threats of violence—that they do not belong, and may self-segregate to avoid microaggressions and discomfort. The idea here is that segregation may create a protective space free from the abuse or discrimination in mainstream society.*

A third variant is not necessarily pro-segregation, but it is deeply ambivalent about the project of integration. These pro-equity voices assert that the answer to intergroup inequality is not integration, but rather equalization of resources.[147] So, for example, instead of trying to integrate schools, these advocates simply call for equal resources or additional, compensatory investments to attempt to equalize educational opportunity.

The problem is that these calls are tantamount to enforcing *Plessy's* "separate, but equal" tenet, not as a fraudulent cover, but in reality. And, as the Supreme Court accurately recognized in *Brown v. Board of Education*, separate is inherently unequal. The mistake that separatists make is to assume that this can be overcome by equitably allocating resources in the face of segregation. But, as the court in *Brown* further recognized, segregation is not simply about the segregation of material, tangible resources. It is also about the intangible. As the court explained, "[s]egregation of white and colored children in public schools has a detrimental effect upon the colored children. The impact is *greater* when it has the sanction of the law, for the policy of separating the races is usually interpreted as denoting the inferiority of the negro group."[148] Indeed, the VMI case is a more recent reminder of this, that even if you could equalize all of the resources between the two institutions, they would never be equal in terms of prestige, social networks, or alumni.

There are, however, arguments occasionally advanced that segregation can be used to provide additional or specialized supports, not simply

---

* This is a form of "defensive breaking," described in Chapter 6.

equalize resources. Thus, for example, special classrooms can be curated for children with certain disabilities. Or, gender-segregated swimming or educational classes may be appropriate, it is argued, on certain grounds, such as comfort or religion, at certain times. Increasingly, however, the expert consensus is moving away from consigning children with disabilities into a stigmatized classroom, based upon evidence that these children perform better with able students.[149] Cities and states are also rethinking gifted and talented education for the same reason.[150]

While we can never rule out the possibility of improved outcomes due to group segregation, we must express a strong dose of skepticism, not just on the basis of evidence, but also of history. For example, we can look at historically Black or women's colleges and conclude that they provide a great education. But we should remember that these institutions were by-products of exclusion.

If instances of segregation can actually be shown to produce more equitable outcomes, then they should not be automatically dismissed as "segregationist," but there are reasons to be skeptical even if material aims are established. Although the principal function of segregation is resource hoarding (over both material and intangible resources), segregation also promotes othering by fraying the social fabric, deepening division and further fragmentation. Groups that are separated or distanced are easier to demonize, caricature, or "other."[151] Only an integrated society can become a true "nation" and create a fulsome sense of belonging, a matter that the Kerner Commission recognized, and a topic we addressed in the last chapter of this book.

At a functional level, however, there is a fundamental contradiction within the segregationist impulse. It assumes that the new political or communal unit will be culturally cohesive or largely homogeneous. This is a delusion. No community—even one that shares the same language, culture, customs, race, ethnicity, and religion—is entirely homogeneous. Even among the most homogeneous places on the planet, like the Korean peninsula or countries like Poland, there are deep divisions in society relating to sexual minorities, reproductive freedom, and equality of women, among other divides, including geographic (for example, north/south, urban/rural).

No form of segregation can fully cleave people apart or solve the inter-group tensions that gave rise to the impulse in the first place. Rather than promote peace and harmony, segregation tends to beget more segregation, hostility, and violence. Perhaps is this nowhere more obvious than the cases of Northern Ireland, Berlin during the Cold War, or the bloody partition of India.

Ireland's secession from the United Kingdom in 1922 may have been motivated by a desire for freedom from the British Empire and self-determination, but the Protestant majority counties of northeast Ireland were determined to stay.[152] This resulted in the partition of Northern Ireland from Ireland, and the resulting tension was a source of violence for decades and the critical institutional background conditions that allowed the Troubles to arise. The Protestant "unionist" majority in those counties kept Northern Ireland in the United Kingdom but left the new Catholic minority embittered and wishing to reunify with Ireland. The violence and mayhem that spilled out of this is the conflict known as the "The Troubles," which resulted in thousands of deaths and led to an armed insurgency and ultimately the greater segregation of neighborhoods in Northern Ireland by religion.[153]

The Good Friday Accords of 1998 is the political settlement of that conflict. It laid out a complex power-sharing arrangement that ultimately kept violence at bay for more than two decades but never fully resolved the underlying grievances. In fact, the Brexit decision of the United Kingdom to leave the European Union has heightened tensions. As a separate nation, Ireland remains part of the European Union, raising the specter of a new hard border between Ireland and Northern Ireland, a provision against which was a key component of the Good Friday Accords. Unsurprisingly, violent rioting has flared up again in the wake of the conclusion of Brexit.[154] In June 2021, local leaders warned that unless the "protocol" that is currently functioning as a hard border is dismantled, there will likely be more serious violence in the near future.[155] Simultaneously, Northern Ireland has undergone demographic transitions, with the Catholic minority on its way to the majority,[156] and with that shift, perhaps a greater desire to reunite with Ireland itself, further undermining the Good Friday Accords.

When the Iron Curtain fell across Europe, Germany divided into West and East, with the former being a liberal democratic state and the latter being a communist state under the influence of the Soviet Union. Berlin, however, was cleaved in two, East and West, although it was entirely encircled within East Germany. Berlin was a partition within a partition. Its strange circumstance made it the focus of much political hay during the Cold War, and its infamous wall became a symbol of oppression.

The partition of India presented similar problems. Following independence, India's partition sought to cleave out predominantly Muslim communities into a new nation-state but resulted in spasms of violence, and endless internal conflict for both countries as a result, as well as the equally interminable dispute over Kashmir. More than one million people died in the resulting violence, and more than 15 million were displaced.[157] Rather than calm passions or increase security as its authors hoped, the partition enflamed them. Indeed, the partition of India into India and Pakistan triggered yet another partition—as the eastern part of Pakistan seceded and became the independent state of Bangladesh in 1971, after a brutal war.[158] These examples show the boundless logic of secessionism: once Pandora's box is opened, there is no logical stopping point, as happened in both the case of Germany and India, producing great misery and death.

Secession and secessionism is a form of segregation, albeit at a different scale. Whereas most segregation occurs within national boundaries, secession is actually segregation between new borders. Although not imposed like most forms of segregation, secessionism suffers from most of segregation's flaws. Not only does it generally fail to resolve intergroup violence, it does not resolve the problem of the "other." In fact, it deepens it by binding group-based differences on to national identities.

Under the auspices of Wilsonian "self-determination," secessionist movements seek to cement shared cultural, ethnic, religious, or cultural identities into a national one. Thus secessionist breakaway movements are usually led by nationalist entrepreneurs, touting a common heritage and denying communal bonds with other people with whom they currently share territory. This is why Bangladesh seceded from Pakistan, and what such movement leaders claim on behalf of Quebec in Canada, Catalonia in Spain, and Scotland within the United Kingdom.[159]

In Canada, Quebec nationalists wanted to amend the Canadian constitution under the auspices of the Meech Lake Accord to recognize the province as a "distinct society."[160] Their reasoning was that they needed that recognition as such to maintain their language and education in a predominantly English-speaking continent. The measure failed, but separatism continues.

Political parties arise dedicated to these projects, like the New Flemish Alliance in Belgium.[161] This party's primary project is to split Belgium—peacefully—into two new countries. But Belgium itself was created in 1830 as a breakaway territory from the Netherlands, with the support of France. Not coincidentally, French became the dominant language in the new country, with Dutch being the minority. More than that, Dutch speakers were looked down upon, and their culture viewed as backward.

South Sudan, whose existence was intended to resolve racial and ethnic oppression by breaking away from Sudan, simply reversed them in the boundaries of the new state, creating a new majority. Shortly after coming into existence, South Sudan was riven by civil war.[162] And although a fragile peace was negotiated in 2015, the conflict is spilling over the new nation's border.[163] Segregation creates a new minority. Secession begets secession. As one veteran of the Yugoslav wars questioned: "Why should I be in a minority in your country when you can be a minority in mine?"[164] This is a formula for endless territorial disembowelment. There is no stable logical endpoint.

But beyond the logical flaws in such endeavors, there is the deeper problem of heterogeneity itself. The assumption behind such efforts is the possibility of a largely monolithic society. But, as Kwame Anthony Appiah reminds us, "As a rule, people do not live in monocultural, monoreligious, monolingual nation-states, and they never have."[165]

The case of the Kurds, one of the world's largest ethnic groups without a nation-state, epitomizes the problem. They have long dreamed of an autonomous Kurdistan out of parts of Syria, Turkey, and Iraq, but instead they got what one *New York Times* headline called "endless war."[166] Their dream—also promising gender equality beyond the norm for the region—has turned into a nightmare. The problem is partly math, and not simply power. In the autonomous regions of the Middle East controlled by Kurds, only 55 percent of the population—by their own estimate—are actually Kurdish.[167] There are also large numbers of Arabs and Assyrian Christians, along with smaller populations of Turkmen, Armenian, Circassian, and Yazidi minorities. How can their dream be realized without marginalizing the groups that would become new minorities in a Kurdish ethno-state? Only by further secession, segregation, and expulsion.

This is why the flip side of secession is expulsion: the forced removal of a group of people. Whereas secession may occur on the basis of "self-determination," expulsion is the forced removal of a people from a territory, state, or area.[168] Like secession, expulsion creates segregation across boundaries, but it is often more violent and harmful than either occupational, educational, or residential segregation or secession. Expulsion can look like, and come quite close to, ethnic cleansing, even if the goal is not violence but separation.

In addition to the municipal segregation of Jews in medieval Europe or even pogroms aimed at them, there were instances of compulsory expulsion. In fact, one led to the other. Under the Alhambra Decree (an expulsion edict), Queen Isabella of Castile and King Ferdinand of Aragon expelled many Jews and more than three hundred thousand Muslim Moors from Granada, Toledo, Andalucía, and other Spanish cities in 1492 and 1493.[169] In Zurich, expulsion orders were issued in 1425, 1435, and 1436 for Jews, but historical evidence suggests that the orders were not strictly enforced. On the other hand, they were finally expelled in 1634.[170]

Probably the most infamous expulsion, at least in Western history, is the mass expulsion of Native Americans from their homelands and tribal areas into reservations across the desert Southwest.[171] Known as the "Trail of Tears," a campaign was undertaken in 1838 and 1839 that produced mass illness, death, and dislocation. Older authorities estimated more than 4,000 of 15,000 Cherokees died during or as a result of removal, but some recent recalculations suggest a higher death toll of approximately 8,000 out of 21,500.[172] The Cherokee were removed from ancestral lands and held for months in concentration camps where clean water, food, and adequate shelter were lacking. Several thousand died from dysentery, whooping cough, measles, and "fevers," which were likely malaria. Those who survived were then marched west, and another 1,500 died because they were already weak and sick from trauma, exposure, and malnutrition. Even more died once the weakened Cherokee arrived in Oklahoma, with the entire affair resulting in the death of approximately 25 percent of the 16,000 who were forced from their homes.[173]

By the time of the Trail of Tears, forced removal and relocations had occurred many times before. And there were many more "removals" after the Indian Removal Act, each deadly. The allied Sauks and Mesquakies lost 85 percent of their population after being moved four times between 1832 and 1869.[174] Similarly, the Navajo (or Dines, as they prefer) were evicted from their land and marched in what is known as the "Long Walk," resulting in more than 2,500 deaths of disease and starvation.[175] Scholars maintain that many contemporary problems, including "severe poverty, addiction, suicide and crime on reservations all have their roots in the Long Walk."[176]

Rather than resolve conflict, expulsions tend to foster new grievances and provide fertile soil for fantasies of revenge. This can result in cycles of expulsions. After the end of the Cold War and the dissolution of the Soviet Union, Armenia and Azerbaijan went to war over Nagorno-Karabakh, a region situated between both countries, which both countries claim as national territory. The Nagorno-Karabakh War resulted in control over the region by Armenia and ethnic Armenians for more than two decades, even though the region was internationally recognized as part of Azerbaijan's national territory. The *New York Times* reported that half a million Azerbaijanis were expelled from the territory after that war, and that 10 percent of Azerbaijan's population are people who lost their homes as a result.[177]

As one ethnic Armenian resident stated, "To live together is, put simply, impossible."[178] Armenia's failures to facilitate coexistence sowed the seeds of its people's expulsion several decades later. In September 2020, Azerbaijan launched an offensive into the disputed territory.[179] Using drones, Azerbaijan pounded Armenian lines and gradually gained control of key strategic routes and ground. Thousands of soldiers died, and dozens of civilians. But the end result at the conclusion of the conflict was that Azerbaijan had gained control of significant parts of the territory. Tens of thousands of ethnic Armenians fled the territory, in what could be regarded as a forced expulsion, based upon fear of retaliation for what had occurred decades before.[180] As this case illustrates, the failure of both states was the failure to find ways to live together in the disputed territory once each state had gained control. They succumbed to a segregationist logic and paradigm. This is true despite the fact that both Azerbaijanis and ethnic Armenians had lived in peace and relative harmony for generations during the Soviet Union.

Citizenship

Violence, discrimination, and segregation are the most common mechanisms of intergroup inequality and elements in processes of othering, but they are not the only common elements. Citizenship, as the primary form of *membership*—or belonging—in contemporary human societies,[181] plays a surprising but critical role in perpetuating the othering of marginalized social groups.[182] While citizenship alone does not guarantee belonging, it is difficult to imagine belonging in the modern nation-state without citizenship.[183] However, the centrality or importance of citizenship is not a recent one, a post-Westphalia innovation. Indeed, citizenship was a prize status in the Roman Empire, ensuring that a person could not be sold into slavery and guaranteeing certain legal immunities.[184] It was granted on a restricted basis, through inheritance, rather than birth (until AD 212), and often extended as an award by generals or consuls for exemplary service to the empire.[185] In contemporary nation-states, citizenship appears to play an even larger role in extending protections and rights and in generating or maintaining intergroup inequality.

In most societies, citizenship entails privileges and rights that are extended to citizens and denied to noncitizens. These rights may include the right to vote, run for office, and otherwise participate in the political process, but also include social and economic supports such as the right to a free, public education, the right to travel freely within the jurisdiction of the state, and the right to social security or unemployment insurance, disability, and other welfare benefits. In short, citizenship matters.

It should not be surprising, then, that contestation over citizenship frequently is a debate over who should belong and who does not. For that reason, historically, citizenship often takes on a racial, ethnic, or religious dimension. In the words of one scholar, "[c]itizenship is the key institutional mechanism for establishing boundaries of inclusion or exclusion in the nation-state."[186] The citizenship debates in India, Myanmar, South Africa, and the United States, among many other places, illustrate this vividly.

Members as citizens are extended benefits and privileges denied to noncitizens. This is why Frederick Douglass urged Black recruits to join the Union Army, not just to fight slave owners. He accurately surmised that Black military service would provide a stronger foundation for eventual citizenship.[187] Indeed, since ancient times, military service has been a vehicle to gain not only freedom, but also equality, citizenship, and dignity. The Civil War helped prove Douglas's point, with the service of Black soldiers bolstering the case for citizenship, but it wouldn't be until World War II that it was more firmly validated. Through World War I and World War II, Black troops fought for respect and to avoid being relegated to menial roles, as well as greater demands in the postwar societies.[188] As with Douglas, W. E. B. Du Bois was an enthusiastic backer of America's involvement World War I because he saw the potential for advancing the cause of Black equality.[189] What these Black soldiers and their supporters were pressing was not just the right to serve with respect but a full expression of belonging in society that military service and valor entails.

It was World War II, in particular, that had a dramatic effect on postwar American life. Black soldiers not only fought overseas for American freedoms, but were treated decently and democratically by whites for their first times in their lives. As the journalist John Gunther recounted in his massive exploration of the United States, *Inside U.S.A.,* "the consequent fermentations have been explosive. . . . One famous remark is that of the Negro soldier returning across the Pacific from Okinawa. 'Our fight for freedom,' he said, 'begins when we get to San Francisco.'"[190]

———

The importance of citizenship to belonging runs in the other direction as well. The denial, or worse, the stripping of citizenship, is a critical and not uncommon mechanism of othering in the world today.

In August 2018, the northeastern state of Assam, India, published a "national register of citizens" list that omitted no less than 4 million residents who claimed citizenship.[191] Those left off the list have had their life upended.[192] Without citizenship, residents cannot get an ID card, which affords many privileges and benefits.[193] Although Assam authorities are allowing residents left off the register to appeal by providing documentation, they must prove that they or their parents or family were residents of India before 1971. For many rural, illiterate people in the region, this has proven an insurmountable obstacle.[194]

It is not a coincidence that Assam is one-third Muslim.[195] Authorities claim that millions of Bangladeshi moved into the state illegally during or after 1971, when Bangladesh won its independence from Pakistan. Political leaders, especially those from the governing Hindu nationalist Bharatiya Janata Party (BJP), regard these residents as "foreigners," even though they may have lived in the state their entire lives. One woman, born in 1968, was left off the list, even though she was born there, although her parents fled from Bangladesh. Amit Shah, a leader of the BJP, called them "infiltrators."[196] The BJP has spread a fear that Muslim migrants into the region will be working for foreign powers.

Officially, the government claims to be enforcing a 1985 law that made all undocumented migrants to the state after 1971 illegal, but the timing and circumstances both suggest that it is part of a larger process of resurgent Hindu nationalism. Not only are the migrants and their children disproportionately Muslim, but Assam has been a site of repeated ethnic and religious violence. In 1983, over two thousand migrants were massacred in Nellie, a village in central Assam.[197]

In many critical respects, this crisis resembles the Rohingya crises on the other side of the Bay of Bengal in western Myanmar. In both cases, ethnic and religious cleavages, historical enmity, and a citizenship law are at issue. Although the Muslim minority in Assam have not been subject to the mass slaughter in recent years that the Rohingya experienced in Myanmar, such an incident is not difficult to imagine. The same rhetoric and government role in the 1983 massacre has been documented.

Another relatively recent expression of this issue is the treatment of Haitians in the Dominican Republic. The Caribbean island of Hispaniola is home to two nation-states: the Spanish-speaking Dominican Republic in the east and the French/Haitian Creole-speaking country of Haiti in the west. Unsurprisingly, people of Haitian descent make up the largest ethnic minority in the Dominican Republic (DR).

Like many ethnic minorities, Haitians in the DR have long been subject to discrimination and violence. According to one report, *haitianos*, as they are regarded in the DR, "make up an underclass that is the backbone of the country's labor force, tending its farms, cleaning its floors, building its houses and skyscrapers, staffing its all-inclusive resorts."[198] Haiti is one of the poorest countries in the Western Hemisphere, and like many other countries, the DR is dependent upon a steady and reliable stream of inexpensive labor.[199] But this is not a problem of massive undocumented immigration. It is a problem of "otherness" within a country itself.

In 2013, the Dominican Republic's constitutional court announced a decision that retroactively stripped an estimated 210,000 ethnic Haitians of their Dominican citizenship.[200] The government subsequently created a program to try to validate the citizenship of anyone who could provide proof with a birth certificate. When the deadline passed in June 2015, an estimated 200,000 people were left stateless.[201] This is one of the largest groups of stateless people in the world.[202] Thousands who had never even been to Haiti streamed over the border into it. Others were threatened with expulsion.

This matter occurred against a backdrop, as in Myanmar and India, of historical discrimination and violence and deep divides on the basis of identity. Along the lines sketched in Chapter 3 on identity formation, Dominican identity, or *dominicanidad*, was fabricated by the DR's 1930s leaders, including General Rafael Trujillo, who became president.[203] This concept was used to create national unity, but like whiteness in the United States, it was defined more by what it was not, with Haitians as the foil. In this case, Dominicanness was defined by being the opposite of "all things Haitian." Markers of Haitian identity in the DR include a "francophone" name and dark skin. Haitians were regarded as "untrustworthy" and "lazy." And although spurious, Dominicanness assumes that its people have more European ancestry than their Haitian counterparts.

Periodically, anti-Haitian sentiment has been used by demagogic DR leaders to build popular resentment, justify the exploitation of ethnic

Haitians, and secure political and economic power. This sentiment, called "antihaitiano nationalism," remains a politically powerful force. And, unsurprisingly, it has precipitated spasms of violence. In 1937, DR soldiers reportedly massacred ethnic Haitians or anyone who appeared to be an ethnic Haitian near the border, known as the "perejil massacre."[204]

And, as in the other two cases, the issue of citizenship in the DR did not arise out of nowhere: it had been building in fits and starts. In 2004, the Dominican Congress passed a law denying citizenship to anyone who was "in transit," even if born in the DR. After being sharply criticized by international human rights groups, the government took further steps in the same direction. In 2010, the government convened a national assembly to draft a new constitution, which formally excluded even the children of people residing "illegally in the Dominican territory" from citizenship altogether.[205] Some right-wing DR politicians have even proposed, without a lick of originality, building a border wall.[206]

The foregoing are instances where citizenship laws have revoked standing in society, creating chaos and engendering greater group-based marginality. But there are many other efforts afoot that would do the same elsewhere. In Israel, for example, there have been many proposals—and surveys show strong support—for laws that would strip Israeli citizenship from Arabs.[207] In particular, support for this is strongest among Israeli youth, suggesting that this could well be a serious governance issue in coming decades.

In the United States, citizenship was no less than anywhere else a mechanism for othering—for determining who belongs, and who doesn't, and facilitating the marginality of those deemed not to belong.[208] Today citizenship rights are denied to an estimated ten million undocumented immigrants living in the United States, including the so-called "dreamers." Historically, citizenship was denied on an even larger (relative) scale.

The precise nation of national citizenship was undefined prior to the Civil War. State citizenship was determined by the individual states. The federal Naturalization Act of 1790, enacted by Congress and signed by President George Washington, provided the rules by which immigrants could be naturalized and become national citizens, or citizens of the United States.[209] The law specified that only "free white persons" could be naturalized, and thereby excluded Blacks and Native Americans, among many others.

But it was not clear whether free Black people born in free states, who regarded them as citizens of those states, were also citizens of the United States. For example, were freeborn, Black citizens of Massachusetts also citizens of the United States? Remarkably, this question was unresolved by the Constitution or by the Congress.[210] It was not until the infamous *Dred Scott* decision that the Supreme Court decided it.

Dred Scott v. Sandford (1857) was a complex case involving many interrelated issues, but the facts are relatively simple. Dred Scott and his wife and two daughters were slaves, but their owner took them both to federal free territory and a free state, before returning with them to a southern slave state. Scott sued for his freedom in federal court under the "diversity of citizenship" clause, which allows plaintiffs to bring suits so long as they are citizens of a different state than the other party. Although circular, Scott's suit for freedom assumed and raised the issue he sought to establish: that he was a citizen of Missouri.

The Supreme Court could have resolved the case many different ways while ruling against Dred Scott and his family. They could have held that Scott was not a citizen because upon his return to a slave state, he returned to slavery (or slavery "reattached"). They could have held that he was not a citizen because he was born into slavery, and left his current status unresolved. Or they could have even ruled that although he had been emancipated either by virtue of residing in a free state or free territory where slavery was prohibited, he did not become a citizen of the state of Missouri or of the United States.[211]

Chief Justice Roger B. Taney, cementing his place in infamy, wrote a notorious and now-reviled opinion that went further than deciding against Scott's citizenship. Taney held that Dred Scott was not a citizen, but not because of any reason relating to his residence in free territory or even his slave birth. Writing on behalf of the court, Taney held that Scott was not a citizen because persons of African descent were not contemplated by the framers of the Constitution to be United States citizens, and, further, could *never become* United States citizens. In legal terms, he believed that persons of African descent, freeborn or enslaved, did not form part of the political community that created the United States.

Although the chief justice drew a racial line into the heart of American citizenship, he thought he was resolving a political crisis between the slave states and free states through the judicial power. Instead, he enflamed that crisis, and helped usher in the Civil War.

It took the Fourteenth Amendment to the Constitution, enacted in the aftermath of the Civil War, to overturn the *Dred Scott* decision by declaring in Section 1 that "all persons born or naturalized in the United States and subject to the jurisdiction thereof, are citizens of the United States and of the state in wherein they reside." This language, while definitively extending national—and state—citizenship to freed slaves and their descendants, has nonetheless been a source of controversy. By extending so called "birthright" citizenship, it ensured that citizenship rights could not be stripped from freedman, but it also allows undocumented immigrants to give birth to citizens.

The citizenship clause was a radical solution to the problem of national nonbelonging. Even today, very few nations permit birthright citizenship, and some that had have eliminated it, including Ireland in 2004.[212] There is a move in Ireland to restore it, just as there remains powerful voices wishing to reverse it in the United States. As president, Donald Trump reportedly considered issuing an executive order that would end birthright citizenship.[213]

Not only did the Trump administration seek to restrict legal citizenship and drastically curtail even refugee resettlement, but they undertook a series of revocation proceedings targeting naturalized citizens who it believed may have lied on their naturalization forms.[214] Although not on the scale of the other measures stripping citizenship, it is of a similar type.

Restrictions on immigration are a related mechanism of othering. If expulsions or citizenship stripping is not politically available, then immigration restrictions can perform a similar function, regulating who can belong and who does not. This is especially true when such restrictions target a particular social group, either by design or in effect. In the 1880s, Congress passed discriminatory laws that restricted Chinese immigration, and in the 1920s, it further restricted immigration from Eastern Europe. It was not until the Immigration and Naturalization Act of 1965 that larger numbers of non-white immigrants could migrate to the United States legally, resulting in a demographic revolution. Nonetheless, the Trump administration issued a series of executive orders created travel restrictions into the United States from predominantly Muslim countries.[215]

In Europe, although citizenship status has been extended to many immigrants from colonial territories, some European politicians have called for a superior status for "legacy" Europeans. For example, Marine Le Pen's National Rally Party (formerly the National Front) has advanced plans for "dual" national citizenship, which would prioritize "native-born" French citizens for jobs in the private sector and civil service, as well as in access to social housing, health care, and social benefits.[216] This would create a two-tiered citizenship, discriminatory in intent and effect.

As the foregoing examples show, citizenship is a critical mechanism of exclusion, defining and distributing rights and privileges based upon the resources and power of the state. But citizenship is not just about inequality. The extension or denial of citizenship is, in modern societies, the principal expression of membership, and therefore belonging.

Dehumanization, Denialism, and Othering Narratives[217]

Not every mechanism of othering and driver of intergroup inequality is legal or administrative. As we have seen, violence against a marginalized group or segregation of the same may be organized by the state, or it could be organized from the ground up, gradually fermenting in the culture or society. In fact, one of the predominant mechanisms of othering is nothing more abstract and intangible than prevailing narratives. The stories advanced by our leaders and in the media play a surprisingly large role in shaping public meaning and who is accorded dignity and respect and who is to be denied it.

Chapter 7 emphasized the role of narrative and telling effective stories as part of the larger project of building belonging, but we must also understand its antithesis: how imagery, narrative, tropes, and anecdotes regarding a social group contribute to othering. We have seen repeated cases in which the othering process is undergirded by dehumanizing rhetoric and stories that stigmatize or impugn the honor, loyalty, or value of a group to the larger community. Dehumanization through stories and rhetoric is a common element in the othering process. Yet there are aspects of it that remain unspecified. In particular, denialism is one of the most common mechanisms of othering.

In November 2017, the mayor of Osaka, Japan, severed "sister city" ties with San Francisco over the erection of a monument dedicated to tens of thousands of Chinese, Korean, and Philippine "comfort women" who were detained and raped by Japanese soldiers before and during World War II.[218] Tens or perhaps hundreds of thousands of people were killed by Japanese soldiers in 1937–38 when Japanese soldiers attacked Nanking, the capital of the Republic of China.[219] In addition to the murders, tens of thousands of women were raped and many were pushed into prostitution.[220] To this day, Japan refuses to acknowledge the extent of the war crimes. Unsurprisingly then, the mayor of Osaka pleaded with the leadership of San Francisco to take down the memorial, promising they would renew their relationship as soon as that happened.

In October 2018, London Breed, the mayor of San Francisco, reiterated that the city would not remove the memorial, calling it a "symbol of the struggle faced by all women who have been, and are currently, forced to endure the horrors of enslavement and sex trafficking."[221] She added, "These victims deserve our respect and this memorial reminds us all of events and lessons we must never forget." Yet that is exactly what denial narratives ask. Denialism is a narrative that refuses to acknowledge—and therefore reconcile—actions made by one group to another.

Denialism narratives come in many forms. In its most blatant form, denialism is an outright rejection or contestation of known and verifiable facts. Perhaps the most familiar expression is Holocaust denialism, narratives that deny either the fact of the Holocaust or its extent.[222] Another form of denialism was the "Lost Cause" mythology that rewrote the Civil War, framing the South as a benevolent and genteel society, and slavery as a positive good.[223]

Denialism is sometimes expressed in softer forms. Denialist narratives may accept the underlying truth, but reject the extent, claiming that the

Holocaust, for example, was much smaller in scale than reported. Other denialist narratives attempt to complicate the narrative. Turkey's denials or the Armenian Genocide assert that the death of between 500,000 and 1.5 million ethnic Armenians during and before World War I were the result of mutual hostilities rather than a systemic, largely one-sided slaughter.[224] The significance of certain horrors can be lost if smothered in false equivalencies, as when Supreme Court justices rejected arguments in favor of affirmative action for Black college applicants after asserting that America was a "nation of minorities," as if immigrants from all over the globe with their own travails and encounters with prejudice arrived in the same manner and overcame the same obstacles as the descendants of enslaved Africans.[225]

Denialism also exists when authorities downplay the official role of participants. The Ottoman Empire tried to cover up official complicity (but not the underlying atrocities) in the Hamidian massacres of ethnic Armenians in what is now Turkey in the final years of the nineteenth century.[226] Similarly, denialist narratives of the Srebrenica massacre in 1995 have gathered strength in recent years.[227] It is not that local officials deny the underlying fact that many Bosniaks were killed but that they contest the degree of official complicity or systematic effort behind them.

Sometimes denial occurs through a "conspiracy of silence" and willful forgetting, as one historian described the aftermath of the 1921 massacre of Tulsa's "Black Wall Street."[228] Even these "softer" forms of denial can be highly effective, especially if given the imprimatur of the state as official dogma. In Israel, the *nakba*, the expulsion of more than 75 percent of the Palestinians from Israel in 1948 to make way for Jewish settlers, is routinely denied or dismissed.[229] Schoolbooks omit it entirely, and state funding cannot be appropriated to organizations that teach it.

A more pernicious version of this tendency is when denial is made policy, and contesting the official (denialist) narrative is a violation of law. In India, censorship laws have been used to curb or prevent the distribution of media or narratives that would contradict mainstream denialism. For example, the filmmaker Anand Patwardhan has struggled against a powerful bureaucracy intent on silencing his work.[230] Just as Israeli narratives often downplay the violence that accompanied the expulsions at the founding of the state, India frowns upon historical narratives that grapple with what he calls the "psychosis of partition." His more recent documentaries, including *Reason*, a film that investigates the murders of four Indian activists who were targeted for their resistance to orthodoxy, has been directly challenged by the state's censor boards, and resulted in threats to the filmmakers' life.

Censorship laws that enforce denial and their counterparts—those that criminalize truth—are called "memory laws," and they attempt to enshrine an official interpretation of historical events.[231] The denialist versions of such laws have sprung up with alarming frequency in recent years. In 2018, Poland passed a law that ostensibly sought to tamp down slander against the state, but also had the effect of chilling—if not criminalizing—recognition of the state's complicity in the Holocaust.[232] Specific provisions to this effect were repealed after Israel objected, but the general law is still on the books. The Soviet Union passed memory laws relating to the mass famines of the early 1930s in Ukraine and Kazakhstan, laws that have carried over into post-Soviet Russia.[233] Recently, state legislatures began pushing similar laws in the United States in 2021, attempting to hold at bay criticisms in classrooms of America's racial past or discussion of gender identity. At least a dozen states have considered such laws and half a dozen have adopted them.[234]

Punishments and sanctions for violating denialist narratives are not restricted to citizens or residents. When Pope Francis acknowledged the Armenian Genocide in 2015, Turkey retaliated by withdrawing its ambassador from the Vatican.[235] Until Biden formally acknowledged the same, American presidents had for years avoided doing so for fear of retaliation by Turkey.[236] The American military and NATO relies heavily on Turkish airspace and bases as a staging ground for wars in the Middle East.[237]

Another form of denialism is when it renders a subject taboo. Although not an outright contestation or denial, avoidance of a difficult subject can have a similar effect. Avoidance through taboo makes it difficult, if not impossible, for a society to heal from a violent episode, for a marginalized group to achieve greater inclusion, and for a society to remain free and open. The Turkish scholar Taner Akçam has long maintained that Turkey's national taboo on discussing the Armenian Genocide has contributed to its antidemocratic tendencies.[238]

A similar dynamic occurred in post-Franco Spain. In 2022, the Spanish government passed a law intended to bring justice and "reparation," including an expediting process to exhume victims of the Spanish Civil War and General Francisco Franco's dictatorship.[239] Conservatives, however, opposed this law, and argued that exhumations of the mass graves would reopen old wounds, even as the exhumations were designed to bring closure to the victims' families.[240] If they should regain control of the government, it is likely they would end the exhumations and repatriation of remains.

A more extreme and sometimes more tangible form of denialism is outright erasure. Erasure occurs not when a subject is taboo or a set of facts are insistently contested, but rather when culturally significant landmarks, memorials, or histories are quietly demolished, removed, or deliberately omitted and forgotten.[241]

Erasure can occur on multiple scales. It happens when, to take a few example, mosques, shrines, and religious sites in western China have been removed or demolished in recent years.[242] Similarly, in India, Hindu extremists destroyed a mosque in 1992, and more recently, the government scrapped plans for a museum meant to showcase the arms, art, and fashion of the Mughals, the Muslim rulers who reigned over the Indian subcontinent from the sixteenth to the eighteenth centuries, and replaced those plans with a museum that would showcase "India's Hindu majority, leaders and history."[243]

It is important to distinguish between erasure as the practice of demolishing culturally important artifacts and the removal of monuments to historical figures whose reputations have been reappraised according to contemporary standards.[244] The destruction of the Buddha statues at Bamiyan in Afghanistan or Islamic shrines in China's Xinjiang region is not the same thing as the removal of Confederate monuments or statues of Confederate generals. Structures erected to demarcate appreciation or acclaim for an individual or institution may merit reassessment as new information about that person or institution comes to light. Christopher Columbus's brutality has contributed to such a reappraisal, no matter how significant his historical role. A monument erected for the purpose of glorifying or honoring can be removed without erasing that historical role, and perhaps put into a better context, such as a museum, where the expressive symbolic component can be better calibrated.

Similarly, when colonial names of places are changed, such as Bombay to Mumbai or Malacca to Malaysia, that is not an erasure of the kind described here, but rather an attempt to reclaim indigenous heritage that *had* been erased by the colonial legacy.[245] Indeed, removing statutes erected to tyrants, as when Saddam Hussein's was toppled, or emblems of colonial masters, as when Union Jack flags and statutes of Queen Victoria were torn down in the wake of India's independence, is hardly accompanied by an attempt to suppress history, but rather a redistribution of public valor.

The reason that denialism (as well as its variants, such as erasure) constitutes a mechanism of othering is that denialism is a process by which othering is perpetuated and undergirding mythologies are propounded or propagated. This is why Ibram X. Kendi calls denial the "heartbeat of racism."[246] Denialism sustains narratives that render certain groups as the "other," even in the face of incontrovertible fact. Denialism creates an alternative historical reality, one that fails to acknowledge not only the fact or extent of some horrible event or series of events, but culpability and accountability. Most fundamentally, denialism is the tendency or desire to avoid grappling with injustice, and thereby with moral guilt and evil.[247] It impedes the process of reparation, by which the breach of othering is healed, and inclusion and belonging can flower.

This is why truth-and-reconciliation commissions have been established.[248] In contexts in which full accountability seems impossible, public acknowledgment can at least initiate the healing process. Without the minimum of acknowledgment, not only will the wound remain, but it may fester. As a special advisor to the war crimes tribunal in Sierra Leonne noted, countries that suffer national trauma and try to move forward without consequences or contrition are unable to heal:

> Countries that skip the accountability phase end up repeating 100 percent of the time—but the next time the crisis is worse. . . . People who think that the way forward is to brush this under the rug seem to have missed the fact that there is a ticking time bomb under the rug.[249]

In the American context, perhaps the most widely known form of denialism related to slavery and Reconstruction. The so-called Dunning school of historiography at Columbia University in the first half of the twentieth century claimed both that slavery was a benevolent institution in a civil society and that the Reconstruction period, in which the rights of freedmen were pursued, was retrograde and evil.[250] It was in this context, in which myths of the antebellum and Reconstruction periods flourished, that new monuments to the Confederacy were erected. The "Lost Cause" mythology was southern denialism at its apogee.[251]

It is useful to contrast that with Germany's more forthright acknowledgment of its crimes against humanity. In the immediate postwar period, Germany had difficulty acknowledging the extent of the state's role in the Holocaust. The Holocaust itself was a state secret, and the Nazi leadership made great efforts, like the Ottomans before them, to restrict knowledge of it and avoid documentation.[252] In the wake of the death and devastation, Germans had little interest in grappling with the full extent of the crimes of their leadership or their complicity. As in the aftermath of the American Civil War, rebuilding was prioritized, not justice.

But as the generation of postwar children reached maturity, they pressed their parents and grandparents into a reckoning and Germany accepted greater responsibility.[253] In the postwar period, Germany has paid more than $90 billion in reparations, mostly to Jewish survivors and Israel.[254] As late as 1988, Germany agreed to another $125 million payment to enable remaining Holocaust survivors to receive monthly payments of $290 for the rest of their lives.[255] In addition, Germany erected monuments and memorials to the Jewish dead, including turning former concentration camps into memorial sites where visitors can learn much more about the horrors of the Holocaust. For example, in 2005, Germany opened the "Memorial to the Murdered Jews of Europe," also known as the Holocaust Memorial, in Berlin. Germany has even criminalized Holocaust denial.[256]

This is not to say that these efforts have been perfect.[257] In fact, even as Germany has made tremendous strides in combating Holocaust denial and paying reparations, it denied for decades that its colonial practices in Namibia amounted to genocide. From 1904 to 1908, the German colonial government killed about eighty thousand Herero and Nama people. Germany finally and belatedly acknowledged this fact in May 2021, and apologized.[258] And, to its credit, Germany has offered a reparations payment of

$1.3 billion, which Namibia accepted.[259] Critics, though, contend that it is a woefully insufficient offer.[260]

Overall, Germany's efforts have been markedly better at grappling with the reality and responsibility for the Holocaust in key respects than the United States' has been for racial slavery. The U.S. has never offered reparations, has allowed denialist narratives to thrive for nearly a century, and has struggled, even in recent years, to bring down monuments to Confederate leadership.[261]

Assimilationism and Cultural Imperialism

Erasure is more than a variant of denialism and denialist narratives; it can also appear as a form of "assimilationism." Assimilation refers to the process by which members of one group are socialized into the culture, mores, and norms of another group or society.[262] Assimilation was a mode of resolving ethnic differences in American society when immigrant groups arrived into the metaphorical "melting pot."[263] This is how Germans, Irish, Polish, and many other European ethnic groups became "white" and adopted English as the primary language spoken in the United States.

In its most ideal form, as the melting-pot metaphor suggests, assimilation is a reconstitution of group identity, allowing groups to blend and merge into a larger, new group. This would seem to be following our suggestion for larger, more encompassing identities. In practice, however, assimilation is largely hierarchical and asymmetrical: it demands that the marginalized group adopt the identity of the dominant group, leaving the latter's identity intact while erasing or repressing the former's. Thus the European white "ethnics" traded in their language, traditions, and behaviors for a mainstream "white" culture, and were instructed to leave behind those other group identities.[264]

In this way, assimilationism, as a mechanism of othering, is very similar to Iris Marion Young's notion of cultural imperialism, noted in Chapter 2. It is a way of asserting that the cultural practices of the dominant group are the only acceptable norms. Conversely, the culture of the new groups should be marginalized or rendered as the "other." Habits, traditions, and behaviors that are regarded as foreign, non-normative, or alien to the society are then rendered as "other." It is cultural othering.

As a mechanism of othering, "assimilation" characterizes the efforts of many governments, most notoriously the American, Australian, and Canadian, to "civilize" Native and aboriginal populations. In the American context, this was epitomized by Captain Richard H. Pratt's infamous 1887 tract, "Kill the Indian, Save the Man."[265] The main idea was that Native peoples needed to be "Americanized." The simple title denotes the violent nature of this process as well as connotes the asymmetry of it.

For more than a century, and well into the middle decades of the twentieth century, hundreds of thousands of Native children in Canada and the United States were sent to thousands of boarding schools.[266] In these schools, Native children were stripped of their culture, language, and religious practices in an effort to assimilate them into the dominant culture. They were also taken from their families to do this. One estimate figures that nearly 83 percent of Native American school-age children were attending such schools by the 1920s.[267]

With respect to the asymmetrical and hierarchical nature of assimilation, the marginalized group is the only group whose identity is suppressed (as in "Kill the Indian") and cultural practices are curtailed. This means that assimilation is actually a practice of cultural and identity erasure. Although unlike the erasure discussed in the previous section pertaining to statutes, monuments, or "memory laws," assimilation was a more direct form of erasure: the erasure of identity and cultural knowledge.

It should be noted, however, that like all forms of othering, Western and predominantly white nations lack a monopoly on assimilationist tendencies. Indigenous peoples in nearly every part of the globe have suffered cultural destruction and erasure, mostly from proximate rather than far-off powers. The Ainu, for example, the indigenous peoples of Japan's northernmost island, suffered for centuries as "Japanese assimilation policies have stripped the Ainu of their land, forced them to give up hunting and fishing for farming or other menial jobs, and pushed them into Japanese-language schools where it was impossible to preserve their own language."[268]

Like segregation, assimilation was often propounded by seemingly progressive reformers. It was honestly believed in many cases that assimilation was a "solution" to the difficult problem of othering and interactable differences between groups in societies. Indeed, many Americans of the late nineteenth century believed that assimilation was the only alternative to exterminating Native Americans, and therefore that assimilation was benign, or even a social good.

The fallacy of that view is now as obvious as the fallacy of "separate, but equal," but the point is that we cannot simply resolve the issue of whether these practices were benign or not through intentions and motives. What matters, ultimately, is the effect on those groups and on society as a whole. It is nonetheless a reminder that many of the causes of group-based inequality were actually and originally thought or believed to be "solutions" to these problems of group difference.

Rather than reduce intergroup inequality or marginality, assimilation sought to erase the differences that the dominant group found unacceptable, and which help justify othering. In this way, any differences or disparities would disappear with the erasure of the marginalized group. While this may be true in some technical sense of a government ledger (and underscores the danger of assuming that the reduction or elimination of disparities is the ultimate test of social justice), such efforts produced and maintained othering.

A more contemporary example is eerily reminiscent of these earlier colonial examples. In western China's Xinxiang province, disturbing and extreme systems of surveillance and control appear to have been established by the Chinese government. Media reports estimate that as many as a million Uighurs and Kazaks in Xinxiang were rounded up and placed into mass detention and "reeducation" camps.[269] Leaked documents revealed that Chinese authorities were concerned about "separatism" and potential Islamic terrorism, describing the region as a "powder keg."[270] While justifying the system on grounds of stability and peace, the result in many ways resembles previous systems of marginalization: children taken from families and other family separations, boarding schools for acculturation and assimilation, and installing ethnic Han control over key parts of the provincial government, even though the region is supposed to be an autonomous one.[271] There are even reports of forced sterilization, presumably with an eye toward gradually changing the demographics of the region,[272] prompting human rights organization and the United States to declare it a "genocide," as defined under international law.[273]

———

This chapter reviewed the most common mechanisms of othering—the forces that shape group-based marginality and generate and sustain intergroup inequality in the world. We did not purport to exhaust the potential ways of operationalizing othering, but we did describe the prevailing drivers. That these are the more common ways of enforcing othering does not render them the only such mechanisms possible. New tools and enforcement measures would likely crop up if these were seriously curtailed.

This review shows the complexity of the challenge in disestablishing othering—the sources of othering are varied, multiple, and disparate. There is no silver bullet, but there are answers. The remedies must be as encompassing as the causes.

Acknowledgments

There are many colleagues, friends, and peers who have shaped my thinking and influenced our collaborative project. Although too many to name individually, I will note Manuel Pastor, Gary Cunningham, Kim Samuel, Claude Steel, Paul Hudson, and Rachel Godsil as a few among the many. Special thanks to Karen Bouris and Cecilie Surasky for their respective roles in helping marshal this project forward. Their acumen and publishing insights proved invaluable.

As the director of the Othering and Belonging Institute (formerly the Haas Institute for a Fair and Inclusive Society) at UC Berkeley, I would be remiss if I did not express gratitude for the many funders and philanthropic donors who have ultimately made this work possible by supporting our projects and staff, starting with our first and foundational supporter, the Evelyn and Walter Haas Jr. Fund.

The Othering and Belonging Institute has been a central hub for developing these ideas and testing and applying them in a variety of contexts, and will continue to be going forward. Among our myriad of projects, we are pushing to make belonging without othering a global norm. I hope you will follow our work and participate, where possible, by joining our newsletter and following our work at https://belonging.berkeley.edu/.

I know that it is not usual to acknowledge one's coauthor, but my relationship with Stephen is not usual. We share a profound journey that implicates the world and each other. It is a wonderful and challenging journey to be on with a similarly curious and heartfelt fellow traveler.

john a. powell

In a project of this sprawling scope and long gestation, there are many people who deserve acknowledgment for their contributions, direct and indirect, to our effort. To begin, I would like to thank people who lent me encouragement and emotional support on this project, especially during the more intense periods of research, drafting, and revision. This includes family and close friends.

I would also like to express our gratitude for the hard work and research support given by the many students, past and present, who contributed in a variety of ways to the development of this manuscript. They include major research contributions, insights, and general editing assistance from Tatum Hurley, EJ Toppin, Darren Arquero, Catherine Robeson, Rhea Vermani, Martine Johannessen, Ruqayah Ghaus, and Darlene Reyes, and additional research help from Skyler Pemberton, Maria Rojas, Noelle Forougi, Josephine Okudoh, Elsadig Elsheikh, Hannah DuVivier, and Sherry Pablo.

We would also like to thank our colleagues at the Othering and Belonging Institute generally, but especially those who provided written feedback or participated in the staff discussion of the manuscript in August 2022, including Cecilie Surasky, Shadrick Small, Ashley Gallegos, Ashlin Malouf, Wendy Ake, Charlotte Taylor, Emnet Almedom, Christian Ivey, Puanani Forbes, Hossein Ayazi, Jake Tompkins, Karen Bouris, Aoyuan(Eve) Liao, Miriam Juan-Torres Gonzalez, Olivia E. Araiza, Samir Gambhir, Denise Herd, Mora Tulián Gamondè, and Rachelle Galloway-Popotas. I would also like to thank Professor Michael Omi, who has always held his door open for a conversation, encouraging me, and sharing our vision of what this manuscript could be, while spurring us forward.

Please forgive me if you expected to see yourself mentioned here, and your name is omitted. You have my gratitude as well.

Finally, I would like to thank john powell, and express my deep appreciation for our two-decade continuing collaboration. We started upon this particular path of our journey searching for a framework that could simultaneously connect accounts of difference, differentiation, and marginality and organize the day-to-day work at the Institute, and this is the culminating destination of that endeavor.

Stephen Menendian

Notes

EPIGRAPHS

1. James Baldwin, *The Devil Finds Work* (1976; repr., New York: Vintage Books, 2011), 64.

2. Roberto Mangabeira Unger, *The Religion of the Future* (Cambridge, MA: Harvard University Press, 2014), 98.

3. W. H. Auden, "September 1, 1939," *New Republic*, October 18, 1939, https://newrepublic.com/article/113208/wh-auden-september-1-1939.

CHAPTER 1

1. W. E. B Du Bois, "To the Nations of the World," July 25, 1900, First Pan African Congress, London, transcript and audio, https://www.blackpast.org/african-american-history/1900-w-e-b-du-bois-nations-world/. The line was famously repeated in one of his most admired published works. See W. E. B. Du Bois, *The Souls of Black Folk*, Lit2Go ed. (Chicago: A. C. McClurg, 1903), accessed February 28, 2023, https://etc.usf.edu/lit2go/203/the-souls-of-black-folk/, in which he wrote "the problem of the twentieth century is the problem of the color line—the relation of the darker to the lighter races of men in Asia and Africa, in America and the islands of sea."

2. This "scramble" or "conquest" is generally described as occurring between 1884 and World War I, with the Conference of Berlin, in which these powers attempted to regulate colonization, marking the official onset of this period. Thomas Pakenham, *The Scramble for Africa: White Man's Conquest of the Dark Continent*

from 1876 to 1912 (New York: Avon Books, 1992); Scott J. Keltie, *The Partition of Africa* (London: Edward Stanford, 1893).

3. W. E. B Du Bois, *Black Reconstruction in America: Toward a History of the Part Which Black Folk Played in the Attempt to Reconstruct Democracy in America, 1860–1880* (San Diego: Harcourt, Brace, 1935).

4. 163 U.S. 537 (1896). See also john a. powell, "The Law and Significance of *Plessy*," *Russell Sage Foundation Journal of the Social Sciences* 7, no. 1 (2021): 20–31, https://www.rsfjournal.org/content/7/1/20.

5. Comer Vann Woodward and William S. McFeely, *The Strange Career of Jim Crow* (1955; repr., Oxford: Oxford University Press, 2002).

6. For example, in a *New York Times* op-ed discussing the election of Sadiq Khan as the mayor of London, one commentator wrote that unemployment rates, health outcomes, and educational attainment may have more to do with "racism" than lack of integration. See Mehdi Hasan, "Sadiq Khan and the Future of Europe," *New York Times*, May 13, 2016, http://www.nytimes.com/2016/05/14/opinion/sadiq -khan-and-the-future-of-europe.html. See also Sahar F. Aziz, *The Racial Muslim: When Racism Quashes Religious Freedom* (Oakland: University of California Press, 2021); Key Sun, "Examining Racial Profiling from a Cognitive Perspective," *International Journal of Humanities and Social Science*, no. 13 (2011): 65–69, https:// www.researchgate.net/publication/264927052_Examining_Racial_Profiling _from_a_Cognitive_Perspective.

7. Jeffrey Goldberg, "The Obama Doctrine," *Atlantic*, March 17, 2016, accessed April 1, 2016, http://www.theatlantic.com/magazine/archive/2016/04/the-obama -doctrine/471525.

8. Jeffrey Goldberg, "French Prime Minister: 'I Refuse to Use This Term 'Is-lamophobia,'" *Atlantic*, January 16, 2015, accessed February 15, 2015, http://www .theatlantic.com/international/archive/2015/01/french-prime-minister-manuel -valls-on-islamophobia/384592.

9. There has always been ambivalence, for example, among African Americans for integration. Stephen Menendian, Samir Gambhir, and Arthur Gailes, "The Roots of Structural Racism Project," Othering & Belonging Institute, University of California, Berkeley, June 21, 2021, last modified June 30, 2021, https://belonging .berkeley.edu/roots-structural-racism.

10. john a. powell, "Will Humanity Survive? The Philosophy of john a. powell," video, Othering & Belonging Institute, University of California, Berke-ley, August 5, 2021, https://belonging.berkeley.edu/video-will-humanity-survive -philosophy-john-powell. ("[T]he reason Europe moved to the EU [European Union] is they said, with a bunch of little countries fighting over resources, within less than fifty years we've had two world wars. Two. And so part of the integration

of the EU was say can we do something to create a larger we? Can we create a European identity so we can stop killing each other? Because each war becomes more deadly. And the capacity that existed in World War Two is nothing compared to the capacity that we have now.")

CHAPTER 2

1. Matthew Smith, "'They Gave Them Long Swords': Preparations for Genocide and Crimes Against Humanity Against Rohingya Muslims in Rakhine State, Myanmar," *Fortify Rights* (2018): 12–13, http://www.fortifyrights.org/downloads/Fortify_Rights_Long_Swords_July_2018.pdf.

2. Jeffrey Gettleman, "Rohingya Recount Atrocities: 'They Threw My Baby into a Fire,'" *New York Times*, October 11, 2017, https://www.nytimes.com/2017/10/11/world/asia/rohingya-myanmar-atrocities.html.

3. Tomás Munita et al., "How the Rohingya Escaped," *New York Times*, December 21, 2017, https://www.nytimes.com/interactive/2017/12/21/world/asia/how-the-rohingya-escaped.html.

4. Smith, "'They Gave Them Long Swords,'" 20.

5. Robbie Gramer, "Tillerson Finally Brands Myanmar Crisis 'Ethnic Cleansing,'" *Foreign Policy*, November 22, 2017, https://foreignpolicy.com/2017/11/22/tillerson-finally-brands-myanmar-crisis-ethnic-cleansing-rohingya-muslims-war-crimes-genocide-state-department-asia-refugees/. The United States has since declared the event a genocide. Lara Jakes, "U.S. to Declare That Myanmar's Military Committed Genocide," *New York Times*, March 20, 2022, https://www.nytimes.com/2022/03/20/us/politics/us-rohingya-genocide.html.

6. Smith, "'They Gave Them Long Swords,'" 21.

7. Nick Cumming-Bruce, "Myanmar Generals Should Face Genocide Charges Over Rohingya, U.N. Says," *New York Times*, August 27, 2018, https://www.nytimes.com/2018/08/27/world/asia/myanmar-rohingya-genocide.html.

8. Krishnadev Calamur, "The Misunderstood Roots of Burma's Rohingya Crisis," *Atlantic*, September 25, 2017, https://www.theatlantic.com/international/archive/2017/09/rohingyas-burma/540513/.

9. Smith, "'They Gave Them Long Swords,'" 36.

10. A. K. M. Ahsan Ullah, Diotima Chattoraj, *The Unheard Stories of the Rohingyas: Ethnicity, Diversity and Media* (Bristol, England: Bristol University Press, 2023), 43, https://doi.org/10.2307/jj.5186775.

11. "UNHCR Global Trends 2013: Stateless Persons," United Nations High Commissioner for Refugees (UNHCR), 2013, http://www.unhcr.org/protection/statelessness/546e01319/statistics-stateless-persons.html, quoted in Smith, "'They Gave Them Long Swords,'" 37.

12. Julia Edwards, "Obama Says Myanmar Needs to End Discrimination of Rohingya to Succeed," Reuters, June 1, 2015, https://www.reuters.com/article/us-usa-myanmar-obama-idUSKBN0OH37C20150601.

13. *"They Tried to Kill us All": Atrocity Crimes against Rohingya Muslims in Rakhine State, Myanmar* (Washington, DC: United States Holocaust Memorial Museum & Fortify Rights, 2017), 5, https://www.ushmm.org/m/pdfs/201711-atrocity-crimes-rohingya-muslims.pdf.

14. Sir Geoffrey Nice and Francis Wade, "A Genocide in the Making," *Foreign Policy*, November 30, 2016, https://foreignpolicy.com/2016/11/30/a-genocide-in-the-making-burma-myanmar-rohingya/.

15. Nice and Wade, "A Genocide in the Making."

16. Nice and Wade, "A Genocide in the Making."

17. Calamur, "The Misunderstood Roots of Burma's Rohingya Crisis."

18. Rhonda Itaoui and Elsadig Elsheikh, "Islamophobia in the United States: A Reading Resource Pack," Othering & Belonging Institute, University of California, Berkeley, September 2018, https://belonging.berkeley.edu/global-justice/islamophobia/resource-pack.

19. Francis Wade, "The West Bank of the East: Burma's Social Engineering Project," *Los Angeles Review of Books*, November 7, 2015, https://lareviewofbooks.org/article/west-bank-of-the-east-burmas-social-engineering-project/.

20. Richard C. Paddock, "Aung San Suu Kyi Asks U.S. Not to Refer to 'Rohingya,'" *New York Times*, May 6, 2016, https://www.nytimes.com/2016/05/07/world/asia/myanmar-rohingya-aung-san-suu-kyi.html.

21. Erin Blakemore, "Who Are the Rohingya People?," *National Geographic*, February 8, 2019, https://www.nationalgeographic.com/culture/people/reference/rohingya-people/; Lindsey Kingston, "Protecting the World's Most Persecuted: The Responsibility to Protect and Burma's Rohingya Minority," *International Journal of Human Rights* 19, no. 8 (2015): 1. Also, the United Nations, at the time, called them the "most persecuted minority in the world" (as per both cites listed).

22. There is even evidence that such differentiation and warring was experienced even prior to the establishment of civilization as we know it. Archeological evidence suggests that *Homo sapiens* wiped out other *Homo* genus species as recently as 33,000 years ago, when the Neanderthals disappeared. Shirshendu Kundu, Shakilur Rahman, and Srikanta Thakur, "Ancient DNA and Neanderthals Mystery," *International Journal of Scientific & Engineering Research* 5, no. 4 (2014): 1189, https://www.researchgate.net/publication/306057454_Ancient_DNA_and_Neanderthals_Mystery; Nicholas R. Longrich, "Did Neanderthals Go to War with Our Ancestors?" BBC Future, November 2, 2020, https://www.bbc.com/future/article/20201102-did-neanderthals-go-to-war-with-our-ancestors; William

E. Banks et al. "Neanderthal Extinction by Competitive Exclusion," *PLOS ONE* 3, no. 12 (2008): 4, https://doi.org/10.1371/journal.pone.0003972.

23. See, e.g., Jed Rubenfeld and Amy Chua, "The Threat of Tribalism," *Atlantic*, September 13, 2018, https://www.theatlantic.com/magazine/archive/2018/10/the-threat-of-tribalism/568342/.

24. Yuval Noah Harari, *Sapiens: A Brief History of Humankind* (New York: Harper, 2015).

25. Jared Diamond, *The World Until Yesterday: What Can We Learn from Traditional Societies?* (New York: Viking Press, 2012), 148.

26. Except that, perhaps, the use of the terms reflects racist cultural baggage or assumptions about the society invoking. See Christine Mungai, "Pundits Who Decry 'Tribalism' Know Nothing about Real Tribes," *Washington Post*, January 30, 2019, https://www.washingtonpost.com/outlook/pundits-who-decry-tribalism-know-nothing-about-real-tribes/2019/01/29/8d14eb44-232f-11e9-90cd-dedb0c92dc17_story.html.

27. See also David Graeber and David Wengrow, *The Dawn of Everything: A New History of Humanity* (New York: Farrar, Straus & Giroux, 2021), for a unique account of premodern life.

28. Dominic Parker and Jay Van Bavel, "The Myth of Tribalism," *Atlantic*, January 3, 2022, https://www.theatlantic.com/ideas/archive/2022/01/tribalism-myth-group-solidarity-prejudice-conflict/621008/.

29. See, e.g., Shakil Choudhury, *Deep Diversity: Overcoming Us vs. Them* (Toronto: Between the Lines, 2015); David Berreby, *Us and Them: The Science of Identity* (Chicago: University of Chicago Press, 2005); Ian Bremmer, *Us vs. Them: The Failure of Globalism* (New York: Portfolio, 2018).

30. Ibram X. Kendi, *Stamped from the Beginning: The Definitive History of Racist Ideas in America* (New York: Nation Books, 2016).

31. Lonnae O'Neal, "Ibram Kendi, One of the Nation's Leading Scholars of Racism, Says Education and Love Are Not the Answer," Andscape, September 20, 2017, https://andscape.com/features/ibram-kendi-leading-scholar-of-racism-says-education-and-love-are-not-the-answer/. ("Self-interest drives racist policies that benefit that self-interest. When the policies are challenged because they produce inequalities, racist ideas spring up to justify those policies. Hate flows freely from there. *The self-interest*: The Portuguese had to justify their pioneering slave trade of African people before the pope. *The racist idea*: Africans are barbarians. If we remove them from Africa and enslave them, they could be civilized.") See also Matthew Clair, "Stigma," in *Core Concepts in Sociology*, ed. J. Michael Ryan (Hoboken, NJ: Wiley, 2018), 318–21.

32. Clair, "Stigma," 318–21.

33. Genesis 43:32 (King James Version), https://www.biblegateway.com/passage/?search=Genesis%2043&version=KJV.

34. Leo Rennie, "Gay-Related Stigma and HIV Transmission," American Psychological Association, April 2012, https://www.apa.org/pi/aids/resources/exchange/2012/04/public-policy; "HIV Stigma and Discrimination," Centers for Disease Control and Prevention, July 12, 2022, https://www.cdc.gov/hiv/basics/hiv-stigma/index.html.

35. "Kosher Food: The Kosher Primer," Kosher Certification Service, accessed December 28, 2022, https://oukosher.org/the-kosher-primer/.

36. David Livingstone Smith, *Less Than Human: Why We Demean, Enslave, and Exterminate Others* (New York: St. Martin's Press, 2011), 26. This volume is an excellent study and theoretical examination of dehumanization.

37. Isabel Wilkerson, *Caste: The Origins of Our Discontents* (New York: Random House, 2020).

38. "'Break Their Lineage, Break Their Roots': China's Crimes against Humanity Targeting Uyghurs and Other Turkic Muslims," Human Rights Watch, April 19, 2021, https://www.hrw.org/report/2021/04/19/break-their-lineage-break-their-roots/chinas-crimes-against-humanity-targeting.

39. Mujib Mashal and Suhasini Raj, "Could Ethnic Conflict in India Become an Issue Modi Cannot Ignore?" *New York Times*, July 30, 2023, https://www.nytimes.com/2023/07/30/world/asia/india-manipur-modi.html; Suhasini Raj and Alex Travelli, "A Rising India Is Also, in One Remote Pocket, a Blood-Soaked War Zone," *New York Times*, June 9, 2023, https://www.nytimes.com/2023/06/09/world/asia/india-manipur-conflict.html.

40. Kimberlé Crenshaw, "Mapping the Margins: Intersectionality, Identity Politics, and Violence against Women of Color," *Stanford Law Review* 43, no. 6 (1991): 1241–99, https://doi.org/10.2307/1229039. "[The term] was coined in 1989 by professor Kimberlé Crenshaw to describe how race, class, gender, and other individual characteristics 'intersect' with one another and overlap." . . . "The lived experiences—and experiences of discrimination—of a black woman will be different from those of a white woman, or a black man, for example." Jane Coaston, "The Intersectionality Wars," Vox, Last modified May 28, 2019, https://www.vox.com/the-highlight/2019/5/20/18542843/intersectionality-conservatism-law-race-gender-discrimination.

41. Kimberlé Crenshaw, "Demarginalizing the Intersection of Race and Sex: A Black Feminist Critique of Antidiscrimination Doctrine, Feminist Theory and Antiracist Politics" *University of Chicago Legal Forum*, no. 1, article 8 (1989): 139–42, https://chicagounbound.uchicago.edu/uclf/vol1989/iss1/8. See also Patricia Hill Collins and Sirma Bilge, *Intersectionality*, 2nd ed. (Cambridge: Polity Press, 2020), 2.

42. This insight was preceded by earlier critiques of prior feminist scholarship given insufficient attention to how gender was constructed in different ways across cultural, religious, ethnic, and racial groups. See bell hooks, *Ain't I a Woman?* (Boston: South End Press, 1981), 2–3, 12.

43. Kimberlé W. Crenshaw, *On Intersectionality: Essential Writings* (New York: New Press, 2017)

44. Rebecca Beatrice Brooks, "The Salem Witch Trials Victims: Who Were They?" History of Massachusetts, August 19, 2015, http://historyofmassachusetts .org/salem-witch-trials-victims/.

45. Shazia Nigar, "Violence Against India's Dalit Women on the Increase," *Asia Times*, July 23, 2018, https://asiatimes.com/2018/07/violence-against-indias-dalit -women-rises-as-perpetrators-go-scot-free/.

46. "Infographic—Religiousness of Polish Inhabitants," Statistics Poland, December 22, 2016, https://stat.gov.pl/en/infographics-and-widgets/infographics/ infographic-religiousness-of-polish-inhabitants,4,1.html.

47. Alex Travelli and Hari Kumar, "Under Hindu Nationalist Leaders, Sectarian Violence Flares in India," *New York Times*, August 1, 2023, https://www .nytimes.com/2023/08/01/world/asia/india-hindu-muslim-violence.html.

48. See generally Benny Morris and Dror Ze'evi, *The Thirty-Year Genocide: Turkey's Destruction of Its Christian Minorities, 1894–1924* (Cambridge, MA: Harvard University Press, 2019); Benny Morris and Dror Ze'evi, "When Turkey Destroyed Its Christians," *Wall Street Journal,* May 17, 2019, https://www.wsj.com/articles/ when-turkey-destroyed-its-christians-11558109896; Jim Yardley and Sebnem Arsu, "Pope Calls Killings of Armenians 'Genocide,' Provoking Turkish Anger," *New York Times*, April 12, 2015, https://www.nytimes.com/2015/04/13/world/europe/ pope-calls-killings-of-armenians-genocide-provoking-turkish-anger.html.

49. Nadia Murad, "Outraged by the Attacks on Yazidis? It Is Time to Help," *New York Times*, February 10, 2018, https://www.nytimes.com/2018/02/10/ opinion/sunday/yazidis-islamic-state-rape-genocide.html; Nick Cumming-Bruce, "ISIS Committed Genocide Against Yazidis in Syria and Iraq, U.N. Panel Says," *New York Times*, June 16, 2016, https://www.nytimes.com/2016/06/17/world/ middleeast/isis-genocide-yazidi-un.html.

50. Ezra Klein, *Why We're Polarized* (New York: Avid Reader Press, 2020): 49–53; Matti Bunzl, "Between Anti-Semitism and Islamophobia: Some Thoughts on the New Europe," *American Ethnologist* 32, no. 4 (2005): 499–508, https://doi .org/10.1525/ae.2005.32.4.499; Nasar Meer and Tehseen Noorani, "A Sociological Comparison of Anti-Semitism and Anti-Muslim Sentiment in Britain," *Sociological Review* 56, no. 2 (2008): 195–219, https://doi.org/10.1111/j.1467-954X.2008 .00784.x; Lindsey Green, "Islamophobia: The New Anti-Semitism?" Humanity

in Action Nederland, October 2010, https://humanityinaction.org/knowledge _detail/islamophobia-the-new-anti-semitism/.

51. William I. Brustein and Ryan D. King, "Anti-Semitism in Europe before the Holocaust," *International Political Science Review* 25, no. 1 (2004): 38, https://doi .org/10.1177%2F0192512104038166.

52. Brustein and King, "Anti-Semitism in Europe Before the Holocaust," 38.

53. Eleanor Beardsley, "France's Burqa Ban Adds to Anti-Muslim Climate," NPR, April 11, 2011, https://www.npr.org/2011/04/11/135305409/frances-burqa -ban-adds-to-anti-muslim-climate.

54. Robin Privman, Starr R. Hiltz, and Yiran Wang, "In-Group (Us) vs. Out-Group (Them) Dynamics and Effectiveness in Partially Distributed Teams," *IEEE Transactions on Professional Communication* 56, no. 1 (March 2013): 33–48, https:// doi.org/10.1109/TPC.2012.2237253.

55. For an excellent account of difference, see Scott E. Page, *The Difference: How the Power of Diversity Creates Better Groups, Firms, Schools, and Societies* (Princeton, NJ: Princeton University Press, 2008).

56. Robert M. Sapolsky, "Peace Among Primates," *Greater Good Magazine*, September 1, 2007, https://greatergood.berkeley.edu/article/item/peace_among _primates.

57. Sapolsky, "Peace Among Primates."

58. Gavin I. Langmuir, *Toward a Definition of Antisemitism* (Berkeley: University of California Press, 1990), 301–2, quoted in François Soyer, *Medieval Antisemitism?* (Leeds, England: Arc Humanities Press, 2019), 9–10 ("[A]ntisemitism can indeed be traced as far back as the medieval period in Christendom and he went even further, claiming that it actually has its origins in medieval Europe: 'If by "antisemitism" we mean not only its racist manifestations but all instances in which people, because they are labeled Jews, are feared as symbols of subhumanity and hated for threatening characteristics they do not in fact possess, then antisemitism in all but name was widespread in northern Europe by 1350, when many believed that Jews were beings incapable of fully rational thought who conspired to overthrow Christendom, who committed ritual crucifixions, ritual cannibalism, and host desecration, and who caused the Black Death by poisoning wells—even though no one had observed Jews committing any of those crimes.'")

59. Léon Poliakov, *The History of Anti-Semitism*, vol. 1, *From the Time of Christ to the Court Jews,* trans. Richard Howard (Philadelphia: University of Pennsylvania Press, 1955).

60. "Pogroms," United States Holocaust Memorial Museum, https:// encyclopedia.ushmm.org/content/en/article/pogroms.

61. Elizabeth Beck et al., "Undoing Islamophobia: Awareness of Orientalism in Social Work," *Journal of Progressive Human Services* 28, no. 2 (2017): 59, https://doi .org/10.1080/10428232.2017.1310542.

62. Claire Cain Miller, "Americans Value Equality at Work More Than Equality at Home," *New York Times*, December 3, 2018, https://www.nytimes.com/2018/12/ 03/upshot/americans-value-equality-at-work-more-than-equality-at-home.html.

63. For a critique of the deployment of "alienation" as a description of othering, see Elizabeth Hinton, *America on Fire: The Untold History of Police Violence and Black Rebellion Since the 1960s* (New York: Liveright, 2021), 176–77.

64. Paul Chatterton and Andre Pusey, "Beyond Capitalist Enclosure, Commodification and Alienation: Postcapitalist Praxis as Commons, Social Production and Useful Doing," *Progress in Human Geography* 44, no. 1 (2020): 27–48, https:// doi.org/10.1177/0309132518821173; John Horton and Manuel Moreno, "Alienation and the Class Struggle in Advanced Industrial Societies," *Synthesis* 2, no. 3 (1978): 1–30, http://www.jstor.org/stable/43783348.

65. Susan Fiske, Amy J. C. Cuddy, Peter Glick, and Jun Xu. "A Model of (Often Mixed) Stereotype Content: Competence and Warmth Respectively Follow from Perceived Status and Competition," *Journal of Personality and Social Psychology* 82, no. 6 (2002): 878–902, https://doi.org/10.1037/0022-3514.82.6.878.

66. "According to recent theory and research in social cognition, the warmth dimension captures traits that are related to perceived intent, including friendliness, helpfulness, sincerity, trustworthiness and morality. . . ." Susan T. Fiske, Amy J. C. Cuddy, and Peter Glick, "Universal Dimensions of Social Cognition: Warmth and Competence," *Trends in Cognitive Sciences* 11, no. 2 (2007): 77, https://doi.org/10 .1016/j.tics.2006.11.005.

67. Fiske, Cuddy, and Glick, "Universal Dimensions of Social Cognition," 77. See also Guido Peeters. "Relational and Informational Pattern in Social Cognition," in *Current Issues in European Social Psychology*, ed. Willem Doise and Serge Moscovici (Cambridge: Cambridge University Press, 1983), 201–37. ("Motivationally, warmth represents an accommodating orientation that profits others more than the self, whereas competence represents self-profitable traits related to the ability to bring about desired events (Peeters, 1983). In short, actors distinguish individuals and groups according to their likely impact on the self or ingroup as determined by perceived intentions and capabilities.")

68. Pascal Molenberghs and Winnifred R. Louis, "Insights from fMRI Studies into Ingroup Bias," *Frontiers in Psychology* 9, no. 1868 (2018), https://doi/10.3389/ fpsyg.2018.01868.

69. Max H. Bazerman, *Better, Not Perfect: A Realist's Guide to Maximum Sustainable Goodness* (New York: HarperCollins, 2020), Figure 2.1; Susan T. Fiske,

Amy J. C. Cuddy, and Peter Glick, "Emotions Up and Down: Intergroup Emotions Result from Perceived Status and Competition," in *From Prejudice to Intergroup Emotions: Differentiated Reactions to Social Groups,* ed. Diane M. Mackie and Eliot R. Smith (Philadelphia: Psychology Press, 2002), 247.

70. The cold-competent cluster (Asians, educated people, Jewish people, men, professionals, and rich people) elicited envy and admiration, but little contempt or pity. For this cluster, envy correlated with admiration and contempt, suggesting an ambivalent emotional response to these groups." Fiske, Cuddy, and Glick, "Emotions Up and Down," 256.

71. Amy J. C. Cuddy, Susan T. Fiske, and Peter Glick, "Warmth and Competence as Universal Dimensions of Social Perception: The Stereotype Content Model and the BIAS Map," *Advances in Experimental Social Psychology* 40 (2008): 69, fig. 2.1, https://doi.org/10.1016/S0065-2601(07)00002-0.

72. Peter Glick and Susan Fiske, "An Ambivalent Alliance: Hostile and Benevolent Sexism as Complementary Justifications for Gender Inequality," *American Psychologist* 56, no. 2 (2001): 109–18, https://doi.org/10.1037/0003-066X.56.2.109.

73. Cuddy, Fiske, and Glick, "Warmth and Competence," 85, fig. 2.4.

74. Amy Cuddy, Susan Fiske, Virginia Kwan, et al., "Stereotype Content Model Across Cultures: Towards Universal Similarities and Some Differences," *British Journal of Social Psychology* 48, no. 1 (2009): 1–33, https://doi.org/10.1348/014466608X314935.

75. Cuddy, Fiske, and Glick, "Warmth and Competence," 67–68. ("Emotions can be viewed as the engines that drive behavior and 'changes in action readiness.' Affect often mediates the effects of cognition on behavior, which is a central tenet of appraisal theories of emotion, including IET, which propose a cognitive appraisal of emotion behavior sequence. Because of this more direct link to behavior, past research suggests that effect often predicts discriminatory behavior better than stereotypes.")

76. Cuddy, Fiske, and Glick, "Warmth and Competence," 71.

77. Iris Marion Young, "The Faces of Oppression," in *Justice and the Politics of Difference* (Princeton, NJ: Princeton University Press, 2011), 48–62.

78. See also Iris Marion Young, *Throwing Like a Girl and Other Essays in Feminist Philosophy and Social Theory* (Bloomington: Indiana University Press, 1990); Iris Marion Young, *Intersecting Voices: Dilemmas of Gender, Political Philosophy, and Policy* (Princeton, NJ: Princeton University Press, 1997); Iris Marion Young, *Inclusion and Democracy* (New York: Oxford University Press, 2000).

79. Young, *Justice and the Politics of Difference,* 53.

80. Young, *Justice and the Politics of Difference,* 50.

81. Young, *Justice and the Politics of Difference,* 51.

82. Young, *Justice and the Politics of Difference*, 53.

83. Something we see recurrent in cases of othering. See Chapter 4 section on this. Young, *Justice and the Politics of Difference*, 54.

84. Young, *Justice and the Politics of Difference*, 55.

85. Young, *Justice and the Politics of Difference*, 56.

86. Young, *Justice and the Politics of Difference*, 58–59.

87. However, some claim that sex-selective abortion in places like India is a form of gender violence. Madhurima Verma, "Sex-Selective Abortions: A Heinous Form of Gendercide," Punjab University, 2019, https://www.progressiveconnexions.net/wp-content/uploads/2019/06/MadhurimaVerma-violence-dpaper.pdf;   Navtej Purewal, "Sex Selective Abortion, Neoliberal Patriarchy and Structural Violence in India," *Feminist Review* 119, no. 1 (2018): 20–38, https://doi.org/10.1057/s41305-018-0122-y.

88. "The savage is a distant, alien, uncivilized being, unaware of either the benefits or burdens of modernity. Lacking in sophisticated institutions of government and religion, ignorant of property and laws, without complex social bonds or familial ties, living in a state of untamed nature." Robert A. Williams Jr., *Savage Anxieties: The Invention of Western Civilization* (New York: St. Martin's Press, 2012), 1.

89. Sherry B. Ortner, "Is Female to Male as Nature Is to Culture?" in *Women, Culture, and Society*, ed. Michelle Z. Rosaldo and Louise Lamphere (Stanford, CA: Stanford University Press, 1974), 67–87.

90. "Yet the trifecta view of homosexuality as a crime, an illness, and a sin remains potent" (16; goes into more detail until 18). Andrew Solomon, *Far from the Tree: Parents, Children, and the Search for Identity* (New York: Scribner's, 2012), 16–18.

91. Solomon, *Far from the Tree*, 2.

92. Solomon, *Far from the Tree*, 2.

93. Brené Brown makes the point that othering is worse when it happens inside the family. Brené Brown, "Dehumanizing Always Starts with Language," Brené Brown, May 17, 2018, https://brenebrown.com/articles/2018/05/17/dehumanizing-always-starts-with-language/.

94. Solomon, *Far from the Tree*, 16.

95. Lindsay Sheehan, Katherine Nieweglowski, and Patrick W. Corrigan, "Structures and Types of Stigma," in *The Stigma of Mental Illness: End of the Story?*, ed. Wolfgang Gaebel, Wulf Rössler, and Norman Sartorius (Cham, Switzerland: Springer, 2017), 43–66.

96. Gerhard Falk, *Stigma: How We Treat Outsiders* (New York: Prometheus Books, 2001). This study expands upon Erving Goffman, *Stigma: Notes on the Management of Spoiled Identity* (Hoboken, NJ: Prentice-Hall, 1963). Based upon the

foregoing discussion, it should be clear that there is a much greater overlap between existential stigmas and othering than between othering and achieved stigmas.

97. Dena F. Dincauze, "Open Season on Sacred Cows," *Archaeology of Eastern North America* 6 (1978): 82–87, http://www.jstor.org/stable/40914171.

98. Herbert Burhenn, "Understanding Aztec Cannibalism," *Archive for the Psychology of Religion* 26, no. 1 (2004): 1–14, https://doi.org/10.1163/0084672053598003; Bernard R. Ortiz de Montellano, "Aztec Cannibalism: An Ecological Necessity?" *Science* 200, no. 4342 (1978): 611–17, https://doi.org/10.1126/science.200.4342.611; Boyce Rensberger, "Experts on Aztecs Deny Withholding Cannibalism 'Facts,'" *New York Times*, March 3, 1977. https://www.nytimes.com/1977/03/03/archives/experts-on-aztecs-deny-withholding-cannibalism-facts.html; Jan Jelínek, "Human Sacrifice and Rituals in Bronze and Iron Ages: The State of Art," *Anthropologie (1962–)* 50, no. 2 (2012): 199–208, http://www.jstor.org/stable/26272402.

99. Sandra Boehringer, Stefano Caciagli, and Anne Stevens, "The Age of Love: Gender and Erotic Reciprocity in Archaic Greece," *Clio: Women, Gender, History*, no. 42 (2015): 24–51, https://www.jstor.org/stable/26273656. "The study of ancient Mediterranean societies clearly exposes the defects in any such essentialist conceptualization of sexuality. Because, as we have seen in the case of classical Athens, erotic desires and sexual object-choices in antiquity were generally not determined by a typology of anatomical sexes (male versus female), but rather by the social articulation of power (superordinate versus subordinate), the currently fashionable distinction between homosexuality and heterosexuality (and, similarly, between "homosexuals" and "heterosexuals" as individual types) had no meaning for the classical Athenians: there were not, so far as they knew, two different kinds of "sexuality," two differently structured psychosexual states or modes of affective orientation, but a single form of sexual experience which all free adult males shared—making due allowance for variations in individual tastes, as one might make for individual palates." From David M. Halperin, "Is There a History of Sexuality?" *History and Theory* 28, no. 3 (1989): 257–74, https://doi.org/10.2307/2505179. See also Jennifer Jigour, "LGBT through the Ages," *USA Today Magazine* 142, no. 2828, (2014): 50–52, https://law-journals-books.vlex.com/vid/lgbt-through-the-ages-636155221.

100. A more precise description might be the idea of "incommensurability." See Thomas Kuhn, *The Structure of Scientific Revolutions* (Chicago: University of Chicago Press, 1962). If certain taxonomies have no basis in other contexts, then the idea is not even translatable from one context to another. We imagine this is how ancient Greeks or Egyptians would encounter the idea of racism.

101. Nicholas J. G. Winter, "Masculine Republicans and Feminine Democrats: Gender and Americans' Explicit and Implicit Images of the Political Parties," *Political Behavior* 32, no. 4 (2010): 587–86, https://doi.org/10.1007/s11109-010-9131

-z; Peter K. Hatemi, Rose McDermott, J.Michael Bailey, and Nicholas G. Martin, "The Different Effects of Gender and Sex on Vote Choice," *Political Research Quarterly* 65, no. 1 (2012): 76–92, https://doi.org/10.1177/1065912910391475.

102. See, e.g., Manisha Krishnan, "Dear White People, Please Stop Pretending Reverse Racism Is Real," Vice, October 2, 2016, https://www.vice.com/en/article/kwzjvz/dear-white-people-please-stop-pretending-reverse-racism-is-real. For a forceful rejection of this position, see Ibram X. Kendi, *How to Be an Antiracist* (New York: Random House, 2019). One of Kendi's most important insights is that individuals can be simultaneously racist and antiracist, or oscillate between those two modes over time or their life course. Note that this section of our work does not attempt to refute this idea that marginalized groups cannot be racist against superordinate groups, but rather focuses on the idea that marginalized groups can contribute to the marginalization of other marginalized groups, including their own. However, we think one problem with the former claim is that it contains an overly simplistic notion of power. Even the most marginalized social groups are not entirely powerless, yet the claim noted here often views power in binary terms rather than as a continuum.

103. Barbara Krauthamer, *Black Slaves, Indian Masters: Slavery, Emancipation, and Citizenship in the Native American South* (Chapel Hill: University of North Carolina Press, 2013); Ryan P. Smith, "How Native American Slaveholders Complicate the Trail of Tears Narrative," *Smithsonian*, March 6, 2018, https://www.smithsonianmag.com/smithsonian-institution/how-native-american-slaveholders-complicate-trail-tears-narrative-180968339/; Jack Healy, "Black, Native American and Fighting for Recognition in Indian Country," *New York Times*, September 8, 2020, https://www.nytimes.com/2020/09/08/us/enslaved-people-native-americans-oklahoma.html.

104. William Glaberson, "Who Is a Seminole, and Who Gets to Decide?" *New York Times*, January 29, 2001, https://www.nytimes.com/2001/01/29/us/who-is-a-seminole-and-who-gets-to-decide.html.

105. Mark Walker and Chris Cameron, "After Denying Care to Black Natives, Indian Health Service Reverses Policy," *New York Times*, October 8, 2021, https://www.nytimes.com/2021/10/08/us/politics/indian-health-service-freedmen.html.

106. Arrell Morgan Gibson, "Native Americans and the Civil War," *American Indian Quarterly* 9, no. 4 (1985): 385–410, https://doi.org/10.2307/1183560.

107. See, e.g., Tamoghna Halder, "Coming to Terms with Gandhi's Complicated Legacy," Aljazeera, April 7, 2021, https://www.aljazeera.com/opinions/2021/4/7/coming-to-terms-with-gandhis-complicated-legacy, which describes Mahatma Gandhi's anti-Black racism, including an excerpt from a letter in which Gandhi wrote, "a general belief seems to prevail in the Colony that the Indians are little

better, if at all, than savages or the Natives of Africa. Even the children are taught to believe in that manner, with the result that the Indian is being dragged down to the position of a raw Kaffir."

108. David Marchese, "Jerrod Carmichael Was Scared of Coming Out. He Still Is," *New York Times*, July 11, 2022, https://www.nytimes.com/interactive/2022/07/11/magazine/jerrod-carmichael-interview.html.

109. Marchese, "Jerrod Carmichael."

110. Mark Lopez, Jens Krogstad, Eileen Patten, and Ana Gonzalez-Barrera, "Latinos' Views on Selected 2014 Ballot Measure Issues," chap. 2 in *Latino Voters and the 2014 Midterm Elections*, Pew Research Center, 2014, https://www.pewresearch.org/hispanic/2014/10/16/chapter-2-latinos-views-on-selected-2014-ballot-measure-issues/. See also Nicole Narea, "Yes, Most Latinos Are Christian. No, That Doesn't Make Them Anti-Abortion," Vox, September 20, 2022, https://www.vox.com/the-highlight/23322487/abortion-latino-voters-roe-midterms-election.

111. Emma Bubola, "Nigeria Arrests Dozens Over Same-Sex Wedding," *New York Times*, August 30, 2023, https://www.nytimes.com/2023/08/30/world/africa/nigeria-same-sex-wedding-arrests.html; Mariel Ferragamo, "Where African Countries Stand in Their Struggle toward More Inclusive LGBTQ+ Laws," PBS, Jun 18, 2023, https://www.pbs.org/newshour/world/where-african-countries-stand-in-their-struggle-toward-more-inclusive-lgbtq-laws.

112. Wajahat Ali, "We Muslims Used to Be the Culture War Scapegoats. Why Are Some of Us Joining the L.G.B.T.Q. Pile-On?" *New York Times*, June 23, 2023, https://www.nytimes.com/2023/06/23/opinion/lgbtq-muslims.html.

113. Tom Perkins, "'A Sense of Betrayal': Liberal Dismay as Muslim-Led US City Bans Pride Flags," *Guardian*, June 17, 2023, https://www.theguardian.com/us-news/2023/jun/17/hamtramck-michigan-muslim-council-lgbtq-pride-flags-banned.

114. David Weigel, "The GOP's New Muslim Outreach," Yahoo, June 13, 2023, https://www.yahoo.com/lifestyle/gop-muslim-outreach-220648472.html.

115. Jon Blistein, "Kyrie Irving Boosts Antisemitic Movie Peddling 'Jewish Slave Ships,'" *Rolling Stone*, October 29, 2022, https://www.rollingstone.com/culture/culture-news/kyrie-irving-boosts-antisemitic-movie-peddling-jewish-slave-ships-theory-1234620125/; Stuart Thompson, "Kanye West's Posts Land Him in Trouble on Social Media," *New York Times*, October 9, 2022, https://www.nytimes.com/2022/10/09/business/media/kanye-west-antisemitic-racist-twitter-instagram.html.

116. Margot Roosevelt, "In California's Largest Race Bias Cases, Latino Workers Are Accused of Abusing Black Colleagues," *Los Angeles Times*, August 22, 2022, https://www.latimes.com/business/story/2022-08-22/california-racial-discrimination-cases.

117. Ed Park, "Confronting Anti-Asian Discrimination During the Coronavirus Crisis," *New Yorker*, March 17, 2020, https://www.newyorker.com/culture/culture -desk/confronting-anti-asian-discrimination-during-the-coronavirus-crisis.

118. William Leonard, "Black and Irish Relations in Nineteenth Century Boston: The Interesting Case of Lawyer Robert Morris," *Historical Journal of Massachusetts* 37, no. 1 (2009): 65–85, https://www.westfield.ma.edu/historical-journal/ wp-content/uploads/2018/06/William-Leonard-combined-spring-2009.pdf.

119. David Zahniser, Julia Wick, Dakota Smith, and Benjamin Oreskes, "Nury Martinez Resigns from L.A. City Council in Wake of Audio Leak Scandal," *Los Angeles Times*, October 12, 2022, https://www.latimes.com/california/story/2022 -10-12/la-me-nury-martinez-resigns.

120. David Brooks, "This Is What Happens When Race Is Everything," *New York Times*, October 13, 2022, https://www.nytimes.com/2022/10/13/opinion/la -city-council-racism.html.

121. Historians maintain that some American slaves, such as house servants or maids, came to identify with the interests of their masters or owners over the outdoor laborers. C. W. Harper, "House Servants and Field Hands: Fragmentation in the Antebellum Slave Community," *North Carolina Historical Review* 55, no. 1 (1978): 42–59, https://www.jstor.org/stable/23535381.

122. Brandy Zandrozy, "YouTube Tested, Trump Approved: How Candace Owens Suddenly Became the Loudest Voice on the Far Right," NBC News, June 23, 2018, https://www.nbcnews.com/news/us-news/youtube-tested-trump-approved -how-candace-owens-suddenly-became-loudest-n885166.

123. Channing Hargrove, "'White Lives Matter' Kanye Is a Provocateur Who Dismisses Black Pain," Andscape, October 14, 2022, https://andscape.com/ features/white-lives-matter-kanye-is-a-provocateur-who-dismisses-black-pain/.

124. Angela Dewan, "India the Most Dangerous Country to Be a Woman, US Ranks 10th in Survey," CNN, June 26, 2018, https://edition.cnn.com/2018/06/25/ health/india-dangerous-country-women-survey-intl/index.html.

125. Esha Miltra, "Some People in a Cheering Crowd Called for Her to Be Raped. Many Were Women," CNN, February 5, 2022, https://www.cnn.com/ 2022/02/04/india/india-delhi-rape-victim-shamed-intl-dst-hnk/index.html.

126. Glick and Fiske, "An Ambivalent Alliance," 110.

127. Glick and Fiske, "An Ambivalent Alliance," 110.

128. Glick and Fiske, "An Ambivalent Alliance," 115, fig. 2.

CHAPTER 3

1. Social psychologists use a similar technique called the "twenty statement task," which is designed to help people tap into different aspects of themselves and

make connections. Jay Van Bavel and Dominic Packer, *The Power of Us: Harnessing Our Shared Identities to Improve Performance, Increase Cooperation, and Promote Social Harmony* (New York: Little, Brown Spark, 2021), 22.

2. For an overview of how words evolve, see John H. McWhorter, *Words on the Move: Why English Won't—and Can't—Sit Still (like, Literally)* (New York: Henry Holt, 2016).

3. United States v. Cartozian, 6 F.2d 919 (D. Or. 1925), Justia Law, https://law .justia.com/cases/federal/district-courts/F2/6/919/1551454.

4. In Re Halladjian, 174 F. 834 (1909), Caselaw Access Project: Harvard Law School, https://cite.case.law/f/174/834/.

5. United States v. Cartozian, 6 F.2d 919 (D. Or. 1925); Earlene Craver, "On the Boundary of White: The Cartozian Naturalization Case and the Armenians, 1923–1925," *Journal of American Ethnic History* 28, no. 2 (2009): 30–56, http://www.jstor .org/stable/40543386.

6. Kendi, *Stamped from the Beginning*, 394. As a contrast, *white* was used in reference to good, life, purity, etc., as in "That, when they shall be opened, black Macbeth / Will seem as pure as snow." William Shakespeare, *Macbeth* (Oxford: Oxford University Press, 1992.), 4.3.60.

7. Stokely Carmichael and Charles V. Hamilton, *Black Power: The Politics of Liberation in America* (New York: Random House, 1967); Joane Nagel, "Constructing Ethnicity: Creating and Recreating Ethnic Identity and Culture," *Social Problems* 41, no. 1 (1994): 152–57, https://doi.org/10.2307/3096847; Ben L. Martin, "From Negro to Black to African American: The Power of Names and Naming," *Political Science Quarterly* 106, no. 1 (1991): 83–107, https://doi.org/10.2307/2152175.

8. Meghna Chakrabarti and Zoe Mitchell, "'Say it Loud': 50 Years Ago, James Brown Redefined Black Pride," Radio Boston, July 24, 2018, https://www.wbur .org/radioboston/2018/07/24/james-brown-black-pride.

9. Precious Adesina, "The Birth of the Black Is Beautiful Movement," BBC, August 3, 2020, https://www.bbc.com/culture/article/20200730-the-birth-of -the-black-is-beautiful-movement. See also Meeta Rani Jha, "Black Is Beautiful: Anti-Racist Beauty Aesthetics and Cultural Resistance," in *The Global Beauty Industry: Colorism, Racism, and the National Body* (London: Routledge, 2016), 31–51.

10. Martin Luther King Jr., "I Have a Dream." transcript of speech delivered at the Lincoln Memorial, Washington, DC, August 28, 1963, https://avalon.law.yale .edu/20th_century/mlk01.asp.

11. Robert Penn Warren, *Who Speaks for the Negro?* (New York: Random House, 1965).

12. Otto Kerner et al., *Report of the National Advisory Commission on Civil Disorders* (New York: Bantam Books, 1968), https://belonging.berkeley.edu/sites/

default/files/kerner_commission_full_report.pdf?file=1&force=1. See also, "1968 Kerner Commission Report," Othering & Belonging Institute, https://belonging .berkeley.edu/1968-kerner-commission-report.

13. Stephen L. Carter, "What Thurgood Marshall Taught Me," *New York Times Magazine*, July 17, 2021, https://www.nytimes.com/2021/07/14/magazine/ thurgood-marshall-stories.html.

14. Carter, "What Thurgood Marshall Taught Me."

15. K. K. Rebecca Lai and Jennifer Medina, "An American Puzzle: Fitting Race in a Box," *New York Times*, October 16, 2023, https://www.nytimes.com/interactive/ 2023/10/16/us/census-race-ethnicity.html.

16. Godwin Constantine, "The Biological Basis of Performativity of Identity-Linking Scientific Evidence to Social Theory," *Journal of Ethnic and Cultural Studies* 4, no. 2 (2017): 88–95, https://doi.org/10.29333/ejecs/82; Anne Fausto-Sterling, "Biology and identity," In *The SAGE Handbook of Identities*, ed. Margaret Wetherell and Chandra Talpade Mohanty (Newbury Park, CA: Sage, 2010): 165–85, https://dx.doi.org/10.4135/9781446200889.n10; Andrew Brown, "Identities in and around Organizations: Towards an Identity Work Perspective," *Human Relations* 75, no. 7 (2022): 1205–37, https://doi.org/10.1177/0018726721993910; Margaret Somers, "The Narrative Constitution of Identity: A Relational and Network Approach," *Theory and Society* 23, no. 5 (1994): 605–49, https://doi.org/10.1007/ BF00992905.

17. Judith Howard, "Social Psychology of Identities," *Annual Review of Sociology* 26, (2000): 367–93, http://www.jstor.org/stable/223449; William B. Swann Jr., Jolanda Jetten, Ángel Gómez, Harvey Whitehouse, and Brock Bastian, "When Group Membership Gets Personal: A Theory of Identity Fusion," *Psychological Review* 119, no. 3 (2012): 441–56, https://doi.org/10.1037/a0028589.

18. In fact, some theories of polygenesis thought that different racial groups had different human origins. See George M. Fredrickson, *The Black Image in the White Mind: The Debate on Afro-American Character and Destiny, 1817–1914* (Middletown, CT: Wesleyan University Press, 1971), 71–96.

19. Floyd James Davis, *Who Is Black? One Nation's Definition* (University Park: Pennsylvania State University Press, 1991).

20. Rice v. Cayetano, 528 U.S. 495 (2000) (treating ancestry classifications like racial classifications). See also Trina Jones and Jessica L. Roberts, "Genetic Race? DNA Ancestry Tests, Racial Identity, and the Law," *Columbia Law Review* 120, no. 7 (2020), accessed December 22, 2020, https://columbialawreview.org/wp -content/uploads/2020/11/Jones-Roberts-Genetic_Race-DNA_Ancestry_Tests _Racial_Identity_and_the_Law.pdf. "Modern accounts recognize that race is inherently and inseparably tied to social context. The problem with genetic race

is that it conflates genetic ancestry with socially constructed racial categories and attendant experiences. Yet, contemporary understandings of race reflect more than some distant, centuries-old connection to a geographical place. Indeed, as we discuss above, race has a particular history in the United States. Courts and other law-makers have strategically deployed race to justify, among other things, the capture and enslavement of African people and the system of Jim Crow segregation that continued well into the twentieth century. This history informs contemporary understandings of race in the United States. Genetic race leaps right over this layered, contextualized history and attempts to replace it with another simplistic, biological conception of race, this time based not on skull circumference but on the results of DNA ancestry tests. We discuss the social implications of genetic race below." Jones and Roberts, "Genetic Race?" 1970.

21. UNESCO, *Statements of Race and Race Prejudice* (Paris: UNESCO, 1950, 1951, 1964, 1967); Ashley Montagu, *Man's Most Dangerous Myth: The Fallacy of Race* (New York: Oxford University Press, 1974), 125, quoted in Anthony W. Marx, *Making Race and Nation: A Comparison of South Africa, the United States, and Brazil* (Cambridge: Cambridge University Press, 1998), 3.

22. Kendi, *Stamped from the Beginning*, 312–32.

23. "Census, Race and Science," *Nature Genetics* 24 (2000): 97–98, https://doi.org/10.1038/72884.

24. Max Roser, Cameron Appel, and Hannah Ritchie, "Human Height," Our World in Data, published 2013; last modified May 2019, https://ourworldindata.org/human-height.

25. Daphna Joel and Cordelia Fine, "Can We Finally Stop Talking About 'Male' and 'Female' Brains?" *New York Times*, December 3, 2018, https://www.nytimes.com/2018/12/03/opinion/male-female-brains-mosaic.html; Daphna Joel et al., "Sex Beyond the Genitalia: The Human Brain Mosaic," *Proceedings of the National Academy of Sciences of the United States of America* 112, no. 50 (2015): 15468–73, https://doi.org/10.1073/pnas.1509654112.

26. Although it is widely assumed that "gender" is socially constructed and "sex" is biological, Judith Butler has made a powerful case for the social construction of both. Judith Butler, *Gender Trouble: Feminism and the Subversion of Identity* (1990; repr., New York: Routledge, 2010).

27. Scott Plous, ed., *Understanding Prejudice and Discrimination* (New York: McGraw-Hill, 2013), 219–4, https://psycnet.apa.org/record/2003-06587-000.

28. Simone de Beauvoir, *The Second Sex* (Oxford, Oxford University Press, 1949). For a summary, see Susan Moller Okin, *Justice, Gender, and the Family* (New York: Basic Books, 1989), 6.

29. Okin, *Justice, Gender, and the Family*, 6.

30. See, e.g., Tressie McMillian Cottom, "In the Name of Beauty," in *Thick: And Other Essays* (New York: New Press, 2019), 37–72; hooks, "The Imperialism of Patriarchy," in *Ain't I a Woman?*; Madeline E. Heilman and Suzette Caleo, "Gender Discrimination in the Workplace," in *The Oxford Handbook of Workplace Discrimination*, ed. Adrienne J. Colella and Eden B. King (Oxford: Oxford University Press, 2018).

31. Butler, *Gender Trouble*.

32. Joseph J. Ellis, *The Cause: The American Revolution and Its Discontents, 1773–1783* (New York: Liveright, 2021). In this respect, identity is a bit like a gestalt or a Kuhnian paradigm: even if one did not see the world that way, it is hard to unsee it unless replaced by a different paradigm. Once an American citizen or a "white" or "Black" person, it is hard to imagine oneself before those identities. This is why such identities seem "natural" and "stable," even when they are fluid and highly dynamic, as discussed in Chapter 6.

33. Richard J. Evans, "The Coming of the Third Reich," *New York Times*, March 14, 2004, https://www.nytimes.com/2004/03/14/books/chapters/the-coming -of-the-third-reich.html; Heinrich von Sybel et al., *The Founding of the German Empire by William I: Based Chiefly Upon Prussian State Documents* (New York: Thomas Y. Crowell, 1890–98), 15–16, 131.

34. Brooke Allen, "Italy's Fragile Union," *New York Times*, December 2, 2011, https://www.nytimes.com/2011/12/04/books/review/the-pursuit-of-italy-a-history -of-a-land-its-regions-and-their-peoples-by-david-gilmour-book-review.html; Matthew Wills, "Libya's Italian Connection," JSTOR Daily, February 26, 2016, https:// daily.jstor.org/libya-italian-connection/.

35. Roger Cohen, "The Unlikely Triumph of Italian Nationhood," *New York Times*, August 14, 2020, https://www.nytimes.com/2020/08/14/opinion/italy -coronavirus.html.

36. David Rothkopf, *Power, Inc.: The Epic Rivalry Between Big Business and Government—and the Reckoning That Lies Ahead* (New York: Farrar, Straus & Giroux, 2012), 47–48.

37. Audrey Smedley and Brian D. Smedley, *Race in North America: Origin and Evolution of a Worldview*, 4th ed. (Boulder, CO: Westview Press, 2012); Robert P. Baird, "The Invention of Whiteness: The Long History of a Dangerous Idea," *Guardian*, April 20, 2021, https://www.theguardian.com/news/2021/apr/20/the -invention-of-whiteness-long-history-dangerous-idea; National Museum of African American History and Culture, "Historical Foundations of Race," accessed August 10, 2022, https://nmaahc.si.edu/learn/talking-about-race/topics/historical -foundations-race.

38. Audrey Smedley and Brian D. Smedley, "Race as Biology Is Fiction, Racism as a Social Problem Is Real: Anthropological and Historical Perspectives on the Social

Construction of Race," *American Psychologist* 60, no. 1 (2005): 16–26, https://doi
.org/10.1037/0003-066X.60.1.16; Audrey Smedley, "'Race' and the Construction of
Human Identity," *American Anthropologist* 100, no. 3 (1998): 690–702, http://www
.jstor.org/stable/682047; Audrey Smedley, "The History of the Idea of Race . . . and
Why it Matters," paper presented at the Race, Human Variation and Disease: Consensus and Frontiers Conference, Warrenton, VA, March 14–17, 2007, http://www
.understandingrace.org/resources/pdf/disease/smedley.pdf.

39. This fact is the source of considerable confusion, especially when treating
historical subjects or subject matter from a modern lens or paradigm. See, e.g., the
debate over casting a Black actress as Cleopatra in a historical drama. Vivian Yee,
"Whose Queen? Netflix and Egypt Spar Over an African Cleopatra," *New York
Times*, May 10, 2023, https://www.nytimes.com/2023/05/10/world/middleeast/
cleopatra-netflix-race-egypt.html; Gwen Nally and Mary Hamil Gilbert, "Fear of a
Black Cleopatra," *New York Times*, May 10, 2023, https://www.nytimes.com/2023/
05/10/opinion/black-cleopatra-netflix.html.

40. Winthrop D. Jordan, *The White Man's Burden: Historical Origins of Racism
in the United States* (New York: Oxford University Press, 1974), quoted in George
M. Fredrickson, "Why Blacks Were Left Out," *New York Review of Books*, February
7, 1974, https://www.nybooks.com/articles/1974/02/07/why-blacks-were-left-out/.

41. See Albert Szymanski, "Race, Sex, and the American Working Class," *Social
Problems*: (1974): 706–25. "The perpetration of racism by dividing . . . blacks from
whites within the working class prevents the development of a class consciousness,
and all segments of the working class are worse off as a result. . . . [T]he oppression
of . . . blacks by white males serves as a safety valve for the frustration of white
males. Instead of taking out their hostilities on the system, white males demand
servile behavior from . . . blacks as compensation for their own misery." See also
Pascal Robert, "The Obsession with the Black/White Wealth Gap Protects the
Elites," *Newsweek*, December 21, 2021, https://www.newsweek.com/obsession
-black-white-wealth-gap-protects-elites-opinion-1661910. "The racial wealth gap is
a reality that should not be ignored. And yet, its remedy is rooted in a class-based
economic agenda that will benefit all working class and poor people, while considering the specific conditions of the Black working class and poor. . . . The political
advances of Black America have always been made as part of multi-racial coali-
tions. It's time that the poor and working-class majority of Black America forged
their own political destiny based on their material interests, rather than a charade
of racial unity that ends up only benefiting an unscrupulous, rapacious, and utterly
cynical elite."

42. Marx, *Making Race and Nation*, 2.

43. Marx, *Making Race and Nation*, 2.

44. Eric Foner, *A Short History of Reconstruction, 1863–1877* (New York: HarperCollins, 1990).

45. Michael Omi and Howard Winant, *Racial Formation in the United States* (New York: Taylor & Francis, 2014).

46. David R. Roediger, *The Wages of Whiteness: Race and the Making of the American Working Class* (London: Verso, 1999), 133–56; Liam Kennedy, "How White Americans Became Irish: Race, Ethnicity and the Politics of Whiteness," *Journal of American Studies* 56, no. 3 (2022): 424–46, https://doi.org/10.1017/S0021875821001249.

47. Marx, *Making Race and Nation*, 131.

48. Eileen Dugan, "Jerusalem in the Crusades: 'Crescent and Cross,' Kingdom of Heaven, and the Fall of the City in 1099 and 1187," in *The Contexts of Religion and Violence*, ed. Ronald A. Simkins, *Journal of Religion & Society*, Supplement 2 (2007): 4–13, http://moses.creighton.edu/JRS/2007/2007-1.pdf.

49. Eric Hoffer, *The True Believer: Thoughts on the Nature of Mass Movements* (New York: Harper & Brothers, 1951), 89.

50. Gerhard Falk, *Stigma: How We Treat Outsiders* (New York: Prometheus Books, 2001), 13.

51. As a consequence, they are likely to challenge both the exclusion and the set of meanings associated with identity.

52. Nario-Redmond, Michelle R, Monica Biernat, Scott Eidelman, and Debra J Palenske, "The Social and Personal Identities Scale: A Measure of the Differential Importance Ascribed to Social and Personal Self-Categorizations," *Self and Identity* 3, no. 2 (2004): 143–75, https://doi.org/10.1080/13576500342000103.

53. Russian supporters of the invasion cited as the justification the need to protect Russian-speaking people in Ukraine. See Anton Troianovski, Ivan Nechepurenko, and Valeriya Safronova, "Shaken at First, Many Russians Now Rally Behind Putin's Invasion," *New York Times*, April 1, 2022, https://www.nytimes.com/2022/04/01/world/europe/russia-putin-support-ukraine.html.

54. Björn Alexander Düben, "'There Is No Ukraine': Fact-Checking the Kremlin's Version of Ukrainian History," London School of Economics, Department of International History, blog, July 1, 2020, https://blogs.lse.ac.uk/lseih/2020/07/01/there-is-no-ukraine-fact-checking-the-kremlins-version-of-ukrainian-history/.

55. Steven Erlanger, "Putin's War on Ukraine Is About Ethnicity and Empire," *New York Times*, March 16, 2022, https://www.nytimes.com/2022/03/16/world/europe/putin-war-ukraine-recolonization.html.

56. This is why Anthony Marx asserts that "institutionalized exclusion may further consolidate subordinate identity and encourages self-interested mobilization and protest." Marx, *Making Race and Nation*, 6.

57. See Marx, *Making Race and Nation*, 19. ("In the absence of a self-conscious group, there is no collectivity that can interpret and act upon its situation.")

58. Jonathan Matthew Smucker, *Hegemony How-To: A Roadmap for Radicals* (Oakland, CA: AK Press, 2017), 90.

59. Janel D. Seagal, "Identity Among Members of Stigmatized Groups: A Double-Edged Sword," *Dissertation Abstracts International: Section B: The Sciences and Engineering* 62, 3-B (2001), 1647, https://psycnet.apa.org/record/2001-95018-197.

60. Viet Thanh Nguyen, "The Beautiful, Flawed Fiction of 'Asian-American,'" *New York Times*, May 31, 2021, https://www.nytimes.com/2021/05/31/opinion/culture/asian-american-AAPI-decolonization.html.

61. See Suzanne Nuyen, "Anti-Asian Attacks Rise During Pandemic. Read NPR's Stories on the Surge in Violence," NPR, March 17, 2021, https://www.npr.org/2021/03/17/978055571/anti-asian-attacks-rise-during-pandemic-read-nprs-stories-on-the-surge-in-violen; Sam Cabral, "Covid 'Hate Crimes' against Asian Americans on Rise," BBC News, May 21, 2021, https://www.bbc.com/news/world-us-canada-56218684.

62. Carol Hanisch, "The Personal Is Political," in *Notes from the Second Year: Women's Liberation*, ed. Shulamith Firestone and Anne Koedt (New York: Women's Liberation Movement, 1970), 76–77. See also Theresa Man Ling Lee, "Rethinking the Personal and the Political: Feminist Activism and Civic Engagement," *Hypatia* 22, no. 4 (2007): 165–68, https://www.jstor.org/stable/4640110.

63. Antonio Gramsci, *Selections from the Prison Notebooks of Antonio Gramsci*, ed. and trans. Quintin Hoare and Geoffrey Nowell Smith (New York: International), 511. This is the articulation of a common identity by creating a narrative and an identity based upon broadly shared problems.

64. Google Books Ngram Viewer for Negro, accessed August 10, 2022, https://rb.gy/rfgzpo. "The term 'Latino' also came into being in the 19th century. A shortening of the word *latinoamerico*, or 'Latin American,' it was coined as a variety of former Spanish colonies declared independence around the 1850s. The pan-national, pan-ethnic term was a nod toward the similarities of nations once owned by Spain." "For some, 'Latino' did away with the complexities of 'Hispanic,' and its lack of colonial ties increased its appeal. The term made its first appearance in the 2000 decennial census. But for others, it presented many of the same challenges, especially when used as a blanket term. Latinx, a gender-neutral version of 'Latino' that emerged in the 2000s, also has been met with criticism." From Erin Blakemore, "'Hispanic'? 'Latino'? Here's Where the Terms Come from," *National Geographic*, February 10, 2022, https://www.nationalgeographic.com/history/article/hispanic-latino-heres-where-terms-come-from. "'Latin America' came into wide use only in the middle of the twentieth century. Indigenous peoples inhabited the Americas for

thousands of years before the European conquest, and likely did not think of them-selves as part of a single geographic entity." From "An Overview of Latino and Latin American Identity," Getty Center, accessed August 10, 2022. https://www.getty .edu/news/an-overview-of-latino-and-latin-american-identity/. "As a proper noun, 'Latino' designates a resident of United States who is of Latin American descent. An adjective, it renders the noun that it modifies somehow pertinent to or associ-ated with such individuals. While the *Oxford English Dictionary* traces the use of the label back to the 1940s, it did not gain widespread currency until the 1980s. As Suzanne Oboler (1995) observes, 'Latino' emerged as a counter to 'Hispanic,' an um-brella term resented by many who into its fold as 'an artifact created and imposed by state administrative agencies.' Among other things, 'Hispanic' implicitly cleaned up the genealogy of . . ." From Phillip Serrato, "Latino/a," in *Keywords for Children's Literature*, ed. Philip Nel and Lissa Paul (New York: New York University Press, 2011), 133–37, http://www.jstor.org/stable/j.ctt9qg46g.32.

65. Edward R. Simmen and Richard F. Bauerle, "Chicano: Origin and Mean-ing," *American Speech* 44, no. 3 (1969): 225–30, https://doi.org/10.2307/454588; Mario T. Garcia, *The Chicano Movement: Perspectives from the Twenty-First Cen-tury* (New York: Routledge, 2014), https://doi.org/10.4324/9780203489130; Leo Guerra Tezcatlipoca, "Gripe: 'We're Chicanos—Not Latinos or Hispanics,'" *Los Angeles Times*, November 22, 1993, https://www.latimes.com/archives/la-xpm-1993 -11-22-me-59558-story.html.

66. Simmen and Bauerle, "Chicano," 225–26; Tezcatlipoca, "We're Chicanos." To many, the adoption of the term *Chicano* was an act of self-determination that radically rejected mainstream culture of both Mexico and the United States. In-spired by the Cuban Revolution and the civil rights movement in the United States, the Chicano movement that arose during the late 1960s fought to establish this new cultural identity and resist systemic oppression through radical labor and antiwar movements. Garcia, *The Chicano Movement*, 5, 8, 10–12. It should be noted that an-other term, *Xicana*, has been proposed as an alternative to *Chicano*. Joseph Flores, "From Chicano to Xicanx: A Brief History of a Political and Cultural Identity," Daily Dot, October 22, 2017, https://www.dailydot.com/irl/xicano/.

67. Terry Blas, "'Latinx' Is Growing in Popularity. I Made a Comic to Help You Understand Why," Vox, updated October 15, 2019, https://www.vox.com/ the-highlight/2019/10/15/20914347/latin-latina-latino-latinx-means. "Activists in Argentina have offered Latine as a non-Anglicized gender-neutral option which actually works in Spanish. Other accepted gender-neutral terms include Latin and Latin American. These alternatives prove that Latinx is simply not neces-sary." From Samantha Schmidt, "Teens in Argentina Are Leading the Charge for a Gender-Neutral Language," *Washington Post,* December 5, 2019, https://www

.washingtonpost.com/dc-md-va/2019/12/05/teens-argentina-are-leading-charge
-gender-neutral-language/; Learning Network, "For Most Latinos, Latinx Does
Not Mark the Spot," *New York Times*, June 15, 2021, https://www.nytimes.com/
2021/06/15/learning/for-most-latinos-latinx-does-not-mark-the-spot.html.

68. Latino Rebels, "During His Bill Maher Interview Friday Night, Here's
What Sen. Alex Padilla Said About the Use of LATINX," *Latino Rebels* (blog),
April 10, 2021, https://www.latinorebels.com/2021/04/10/padillalatinx/.

69. "Ask Smithsonian," *Smithsonian*, September 2022, https://www
.smithsonianmag.com/smithsonian-institution/why-can-we-see-moon-during-the
-day-180980568/.

70. Latino Rebels, "During His Bill Maher Interview Friday Night."

71. Latino Rebels, "Pew Study: 23% of US Latinos Aware of LATINX Term, but
Just 3% Use Term," *Latino Rebels* (blog), August 11, 2020, https://www.latinorebels
.com/2020/08/11/pewstudylatinx/. See also, Luis Noe-Bustamante, Lauren Mora,
and Mark Hugo Lopez, "About One-in-Four U.S. Hispanics Have Heard of
Latinx, but Just 3% Use It: Young Hispanic Women among the Most Likely to Use
the Term," Pew Research Center, August 11, 2020, pewresearch.org/hispanic/2020/
08/11/about-one-in-four-u-s-hispanics-have-heard-of-latinx-but-just-3-use-it/.

72. Erin Blakemore, "From LGBT to LGBTQIA+: The Evolving Recognition of
Identity," *National Geographic*, October 19, 2021, https://www.nationalgeographic
.com/history/article/from-lgbt-to-lgbtqia-the-evolving-recognition-of-identity.
Even though it is a conflation of both gender and sexual orientation identities. Trans
is a gender identity, while lesbian, gay, and bisexual are sexual orientation identities.

73. Lindo Bacon, *Radical Belonging: How to Survive and Thrive in an Unjust
World (While Transforming It for the Better)* (Dallas: BenBella Books, 2020), 160.

74. Solomon, *Far from the Tree,* 19.

75. On this point, and the cultural differences between "queer" culture and gay
or lesbian culture, see Andrew Sullivan, "Religion and the Decline of Democracy,"
The Weekly Dish—Andrew Sullivan (blog), April 2, 2021, https://andrewsullivan
.substack.com/p/religion-and-the-decline-of-democracy.

76. Merrill Perlman, "How the Word 'Queer' Was Adopted by the LGBTQ
Community," *Columbia Journalism Review*, January 22, 2019, https://www.cjr.org/
language_corner/queer.php.

77. Perlman, "How the Word 'Queer' Was Adopted."

78. "Sexuality and Queer Studies Program," Brandeis University, https://www
.brandeis.edu/sexuality-queer/.

79. "queer: terminology," NLGJA: The Association of LGBTQ Journalists,
https://www.nlgja.org/stylebook/queer/. Notably, Charles Blow says he prefers
"Gay" to "Queer" for this reason. Charles M. Blow, "My Journey to Pride," *New*

York Times, June 6, 2021, https://www.nytimes.com/2021/06/06/opinion/lgbtq -pride-month.html.

80. Ernie Suggs, "Black Doll, White Doll, and Racial Shame That's Nothing to Play With," *Atlanta Journal-Constitution*, February 1, 2019, https://www.ajc .com/news/mamie-and-kenneth-clark-doll-test-challenged-attitudes-segregation/ gGknWIaYpKa1Yh9Oqs6hjL/.

81. Tilly defines "social boundaries" as those which "interrupt, divide, circum-scribe, or segregate distributions of populations or activity within social fields." Andrew Abbott, "Things of Boundaries," *Social Research* 62, no. 4 (1995): 857, 882, quoted in Charles Tilly, *Identities, Boundaries and Social Ties* (Oxfordshire, United Kingdom: Taylor & Francis, 2015), 133. Tilly has a more complex definition, which he provides: "any contiguous zone of contrasting density, rapid transition, or separa-tion between internally connected clusters of population and/or activity for which human participants create shared representations." Tilly, *Identities*, 134.

82. Douglas S. Massey, *Categorically Unequal: The American Stratification System* (New York: Russell Sage Foundation, 2007), 1–27.

83. Charles Tilly, *Collective Violence, Contentious Politics, and Social Change: A Charles Tilly Reader*, ed. Ernesto Castañeda and Cathy Schneider (Oxfordshire, United Kingdom: Taylor & Francis, 2017), 328.

84. The mechanisms that Tilly proposes and points toward that constitute or precipitate boundary change include: 1) encounter—when members of two separate groups begin interacting in the same social space, 2) imposition—when authorities draw lines that did not exist, such as distinguishing citizens from non-citizens, 3) borrowing—when people creating a new organization emulate distinc-tions used elsewhere, 4) conversation—a wider range of interactions among social sites, 5) incentive shifts—where participants in boundary processes receive rewards or penalties that affect their behavior within or across the zone, 6) inscription-erasure—where social relations on either side of the boundary become more sharply differentiated, or are erased, 7) activation-deactivation—where a boundary becomes more or less salient, 8) site transfer—where a boundary shifts the location of people or sites on one side to another—as when people "pass" for another race or religiously convert. Tilly, "Social Boundary Mechanisms," in *Collective Violence*, 326–41. To the best of our knowledge, Tilly never formally validated them with empirical proof.

85. Tilly, *Collective Violence*, 336.

86. Tilly, *Collective Violence*, 173.

87. Williams Jr., *Savage Anxieties*, 1, 78, 220. "Aristotle used the idea of the savage to show us how human beings can reach the highest stage of perfection in an imperially minded civilization; they simply make slaves of the primitive and

uncivilized barbarians they can find to serve the needs and desires of a higher form of civilization's privileged leisure class of ruling aristocrats." (78)

88. This was the mistake that Justice Lewis Powell made in *Regents of the University of California v. Bakke* (1978), when he called the United States a "nation of minorities." Ian F. Haney Lopez, "A Nation of Minorities: Race, Ethnicity, and Reactionary Colorblindness," *Stanford Law Review* 59, no. 4 (April 2010): 985, https://www.jstor.org/stable/40040347.

89. Tim Jacoby and Nassima Neggaz, "Sectarianism in Iraq: The Role of the Coalition Provisional Authority," *Critical Studies on Terrorism* 11, no. 3 (2008): 478–500, https://doi.org/10.1080/17539153.2018.1487178. For more background and context, see Daniel Byman, "An Autopsy of the Iraq Debacle: Policy Failure or Bridge Too Far?" *Security Studies* 17, no. 4 (2008): 599–643, https://doi.org/10.1080/09636410802507974; and James Dobbins et al., "Occupying Iraq: A History of the Coalition Provisional Authority", RAND National Security Research Division, 2009, https://www.rand.org/content/dam/rand/pubs/monographs/2009/RAND_MG847.pdf.

90. See Richard Morrock, "Heritage of Strife: The Effects of Colonialist 'Divide and Rule' Strategy upon the Colonized Peoples," *Science & Society* 37, no. 2 (Summer 1973): 129–51, which describes how "[m]embers of different tribes were often forcibly segregated . . . as was the case in the Belgian Congo, or in South Africa today." Morrock later describes how "the colonial power sometimes openly supported a tribalist political party, such as Moise Tshombe's Conakat in the Congo or the Barotse-land separatists in Zambia" and continues: "the British had each of the three main Nigerian tribes convinced that they were the favorites of the colonial power; the Hausas because of their feudal traditions; the Ibos because of their success in business and high level of education; and the Yorubas because of their Protestantism and their democratic election of chiefs" (132).

91. More's refusal has been venerated as a difficult but notable example of moral conscience in the Oscar-winning film *A Man for All Seasons* and the novels and BBC series *Wolf Hall*. *A Man for All Seasons*, directed by Fred Zinnemann (Highland Films, 1966); Hilary Mantel, *Wolf Hall* (Fourth Estate, 2009); Peter Kominsky, "Wolf Hall: Why I Was Lost in Admiration for Anne Boleyn," *BBC Blogs*, January 27, 2015, https://www.bbc.co.uk/blogs/tv/entries/9212c447-0fc5-4815-955f-8ed20490666d.

92. Steve Martinot, *The Rule of Racialization: Class, Identity, Governance* (Philadelphia: Temple University Press, 2003): 54–57, 138.

93. Loving v. Virginia, 388 U.S. 1 (1967).

94. Yanick St. Jean, "Let People Speak for Themselves: Interracial Unions and the General Social Survey," *Journal of Black Studies* 28, no. 3 (1998): 398–414, https://doi.org/10.1177/002193479802800308.

95. Williams Jr., *Savage Anxieties*, 148.

96. Jennifer D. Keene, "Wilson and Race Relations," in *A Companion to Woodrow Wilson*, ed. Ross A. Kennedy (Hoboken, NJ: Wiley, 2013), 138–39.

97. Omi and Winant, *Racial Formation*, 106.

98. Tilly, *Identities, Boundaries and Social Ties*, 209.

99. Tilly, *Identities, Boundaries and Social Ties*, 59.

100. Aliya Saperstein, Jessica M. Kizer, and Andrew M. Penner, "Making the Most of Multiple Measures: Disentangling the Effects of Different Dimensions of Race in Survey Research," *American Behavioral Scientist* 60, no. 4 (April 2016): 519–37, https://doi.org/10.1177%2F0002764215613399.

101. Kwame Anthony Appiah, *The Lies That Bind: Rethinking Identity* (New York: Liveright, 2018), 18.

102. Satta Sarmah, "Is Obama Black Enough?" *Columbia Journalism Review*, February 15, 2007, https://archives.cjr.org/politics/is_obama_black_enough.php.

103. Jonathan Alter, *The Center Holds: Obama and His Enemies* (New York: Simon & Schuster, 2014), 69.

104. Martha Augoustinos and Stephanie De Garis, "'Too Black or Not Black Enough': Social Identity Complexity in the Political Rhetoric of Barack Obama," *European Journal of Journal Psychology* 42, no. 5 (2012): 564–77, https://psycnet .apa.org/doi/10.1002/ejsp.1868.

105. Tom Postmes, Alexander Haslam, and Roderick I. Swaab, "Social Influence in Small Groups: An Interactive Model of Social Identity Formation," *European Review of Social Psychology* 16, no. 1 (2005): 1–42, https://doi.org/10.1080/ 10463280440000062.

106. Dickson D. Bruce Jr., "W. E. B. Du Bois and the Idea of Double Consciousness," *American Literature* 64, no. 2 (June 1992): 299–309, https://doi.org/10.2307/ 2927837.

107. Daniel G. Renfrow, "A Cartography of Passing in Everyday Life," *Symbolic Interaction* 27, no. 4 (2011): 485–506, https://doi.org/10.1525/si.2004.27.4.485. Renfrow defines passing as "cultural performances in which individuals perceived to have a somewhat threatening identity present themselves or are categorized by others as persons they are not."

108. Allyson Hobbs, *A Chosen Exile: A History of Racial Passing in American Life* (Cambridge, MA: Harvard University Press, 2016), 8.

109. Morris and Ze'evi, *Thirty-Year Genocide*.

110. See Kwame Anthony Appiah, "Is It OK to Use Money Raised for a Child's Cancer Care on a Car?" *New York Times*, April 13, 2021, https://www.nytimes.com/ 2021/04/13/magazine/crowdfund-ethics.html. (Describing the case of a cisgender woman in a monogamous thirty-plus-year marriage with a cisgender straight man, but who does not identify as straight.)

111. Neelam Bohra and Michael Levenson, "Montana Restricts Changes to Birth Certificates for Transgender People," *New York Times*, September 13, 2022, https://www.nytimes.com/2022/09/13/us/montana-gender-birth-certificates.html; "Gender Affirming Health Program," UCSF Health, accessed October 25, 2022, https://www.ucsfhealth.org/clinics/gender-affirming-health-program; "Fact Sheet on U.S. Department of Education Policy Letter on Transgender Students," National Center for Transgender Equality, August 15, 2016, https://transequality.org/sites/default/files/ED-DCL-Fact-Sheet.pdf.

112. Alex Marzano-Lesnevich, "How Do I Define My Gender if No One Is Watching Me?" *New York Times*, April 2, 2021, https://www.nytimes.com/2021/04/02/opinion/transgender-nonbinary-pandemic-transition-.html   (Describing how the social pandemic led to more gender experimentation and less peer policing.)

113. Tilly, *Identities*, 63.

114. Ashley Fantz, Ray Sanchez, Faith Karimi, and Dana Ford, "NAACP Leader Resigns; Accused of Lying about Race," CNN, June 15, 2015, https://www.cnn.com/2015/06/15/us/washington-rachel-dolezal-naacp/index.html.

115. john a. powell, "Racing into the Future," HuffPost, December 31, 2015, updated December 6, 2017, https://www.huffpost.com/entry/racing-into-the-future_b_8900296.

116. Daniel Schorn, "Transcript Excerpt: Sen. Barack Obama," CBS News, February 11, 2007, https://www.cbsnews.com/news/transcript-excerpt-sen-barack-obama/.

117. Andrew Sullivan, "The End of Gay Culture," *New Republic*, October 24, 2005, https://newrepublic.com/article/61118/the-end-gay-culture; Carolyn D'Cruz, "Commemorating Homosexual: Rethinking Experience and the Disaffected through the Legacies of the Gay Liberation Movement," *Sexualities* 17, no. 3 (2014): 291–309, https://doi.org/10.1177/1363460713516784; Steven Seidman and Chet Meeks, "The Politics of Authenticity: Civic Individualism and the Cultural Roots of Gay Normalization," *Cultural Sociology* 5, no. 4 (2011): 519–36, https://doi.org/10.1177/1749975511401272; "Letters: Should Gay People Seek to Be Seen as 'Normal'?" *New York Times*, June 29, 2023, https://www.nytimes.com/2023/06/29/opinion/letters/gay-lgbtq.html.

118. Solomon, *Far from the Tree*, 7–19.

119. Charles Horton Cooley, *Human Nature and the Social Order* (New York: Scribner, 1902).

120. Kwame Anthony Appiah, "My Child's Egg Donor Is Latin American. Does That Make Him Latino?" *New York Times*, April 6, 2021, https://www.nytimes.com/2021/04/06/magazine/egg-donor-latin-american.html.

121. Appiah, "My Child's Egg Donor."

122. Tilly, *Identities, Boundaries and Social Ties,* 6.

123. Tilly, *Identities, Boundaries and Social Ties,* 59.

124. Paul Starr, "Social Categories and Claims in the Liberal State," in *How Classification Works,* ed. Mary Douglas and David Hull (Edinburgh: Edinburgh University Press, 1992), 169, quoted in Marx, *Making Race and Nation,* 5.

125. Andrea Plaid and Christopher Macdonald-Dennis, "'BIPOC' Isn't Doing What You Think It's Doing," *Newsweek,* April 9, 2021, https://www.newsweek .com/bipoc-isnt-doing-what-you-think-its-doing-opinion-1582494.

126. Plaid and MacDonald-Dennis, "'BIPOC' Isn't Doing What You Think It's Doing."

127. Muzafer Sherif, *Experimental Study of Positive and Negative Intergroup Attitudes Between Experimentally Produced Groups: Robbers Cave Study* (Norman: University of Oklahoma, 1954); Partha Dasgupta and Sanjeev Goyal, "Narrow Identities," *Journal of Institutional and Theoretical Economics* 175, no. 3 (2019): 395–419.

128. Dasgupta and Goyal, "Narrow Identities."

129. William James, *The Principles of Psychology* (London: Macmillan, 1890).

130. Kristy vanMarle, "Brainy Babies: Can Babies Count?," *Psychology Today,* January 4, 2011, https://www.psychologytoday.com/us/blog/babies-do-the-math/ 201101/brainy-babies.

131. Rebecca Rosen, "Pareidolia: A Bizarre Bug of the Human Mind Emerges in Computers," *Atlantic,* August 7, 2012, https://www.theatlantic.com/technology/ archive/2012/08/pareidolia-a-bizarre-bug-of-the-human-mind-emerges-in -computers/260760/.

132. Linda Krieger, "The Content of Our Categories: A Cognitive Bias Approach to Discrimination and Equal Employment Opportunity," *Stanford Law Review* 47, no. 6 (1995): 1188, https://doi.org/10.2307/1229191.

133. See Aliya Saperstein, "Capturing Complexity in the United States: Which Aspects of Race Matter and When?" *Ethnic and Racial Studies* 35, no. 8 (2011): 1484–1502, https://doi.org/10.1080/01419870.2011.607504. See also Jonathan B. Freeman, Andrew M. Penner, Aliya Saperstein, Matthias Scheutz, and Nalini Ambady, "Looking the Part: Social Status Cues Shape Race Perception," *PLoS ONE* 6, no. 9 (2011): e25107, https://doi.org/10.1371/journal.pone.0025107.

134. Andrew Noymer, Andrew M. Penner, and Aliya Saperstein, "Cause of Death Affects Racial Classification on Death Certificates," *PLOS ONE* 6, no. 1 (2011): e15812, https://doi.org/10.1371/journal.pone.0015812.

135. Daniel Kahneman, *Thinking, Fast and Slow* (New York: Farrar, Straus & Giroux, 2011); Cheryl Staats et al., *State of the Science: Implicit Bias Review* (Columbus: Ohio State University Kirwan Institute for the Study of Race and Ethnicity,

2017), https://kirwaninstitute.osu.edu/sites/default/files/pdf/2017-implicit-bias-review.pdf; Rachel Godsil et al., *The Science of Equality*, vol. 1: *Addressing Implicit Bias, Racial Anxiety, and Stereotype Threat in Education and Health Care*, Perception Institute, 2014, https://equity.ucla.edu/wp-content/uploads/2016/11/Science-of-Equality-Vol.-1-Perception-Institute-2014.pdf; Anthony Greenwald and Linda Hamilton Krieger, "Implicit Bias: Scientific Foundations," *California Law Review* 94, no. 4 (2006), https://doi.org/10.2307/20439056.

136. Anthony Greenwald, Debbie McGhee, and Jordan Schwartz, "Measuring Individual Differences in Implicit Cognition: The Implicit Association Test," *Journal of Personality and Social Psychology* 74, no. 6 (1998): 1464–80, https://doi.org/10.1037/0022-3514.74.6.1464.

137. Herbert Blumer, "Race Prejudice as a Sense of Group Position," *Pacific Sociological Review* 1, no. 1 (1958): 3–7, https://doi.org/10.2307/1388607; Lawrence D. Bobo, "Prejudice as Group Position: Microfoundations of a Sociological Approach to Racism and Race Relations," *Journal of Social Issues* 55, no. 3 (1999): 445–72, https://doi.org/10.1111/0022-4537.00127.

138. Blumer, "Race Prejudice."

139. Cecilia L. Ridgeway, "Why Status Matters for Inequality," *American Sociological Review* 79, no. 1 (2013): 1–16, https://www.asanet.org/sites/default/files/savvy/journals/ASR/Feb14ASRFeature.pdf.

140. Rémi Korman, "The Tutsi Body in the 1994 Genocide: Ideology, Physical Destruction, and Memory," in *Destruction and Human Remains: Disposal and Concealment in Genocide and Mass Violence*, ed. Élisabeth Anstett and Jean-Marc Dreyfus (Manchester, United Kingdom: Manchester University Press, 2014): 226–42, http://www.jstor.org/stable/j.ctt1wn0s3n.14.

141. William C. Wohlforth and David C. Kang, "Hypotheses on Status Competition," paper presented at the 2009 Annual Meeting of the American Political Science Association, Toronto, ; W. David Marx, *Status and Culture: How Our Desire for Social Rank Creates Taste, Identity, Art, Fashion, and Constant Change* (New York: Viking, 2022). https://www.researchgate.net/publication/228147044_Hypotheses_on_Status_Competition.

142. Jim Sidanius and Felicia Pratto, *Social Dominance: An Intergroup Theory of Social Hierarchy and Oppression* (Cambridge: Cambridge University Press, 1999). This does not mean, however, that all social hierarchies necessarily result in othering. As we noted in Chapter 2, social status hierarchies can arise without categorical social group othering.

143. Andrew Cockburn, "Iraq's Oppressed Majority," *Smithsonian*, December 2003, https://www.smithsonianmag.com/history/iraqs-oppressed-majority-95250996/.

144. Declan Walsh, "Eritrean Troops Continue to Commit Atrocities in Tigray, U.N. Says," *New York Times*, April 15, 2021, updated June 29, 2021, https://www.nytimes.com/2021/04/15/world/africa/ethiopia-eritrea-tigray.html; Kenneth Roth, "Ethiopia's Invisible Ethnic Cleansing: The World Can't Afford to Ignore Tigray," Human Rights Watch, June 16, 2022, https://www.hrw.org/news/2022/06/16/ethiopias-invisible-ethnic-cleansing.

145. Sikhulekile Duma, "The Danger of Zuma's Zulu Nationalism," *Mail & Guardian*, July 8, 2021, https://mg.co.za/opinion/2021-07-08-the-danger-of-zumas -zulu-nationalism/.

146. Alexander H. Stephens. "Cornerstone Speech," speech presented in Savannah, GA, March 21, 1861, https://www.battlefields.org/learn/primary-sources/cornerstone-speech.

147. Marx, *Making Race and Nation*, 11–13.

148. Cabinet Office of the Prime Minister, "Speech by Prime Minister Viktor Orbán at the 31st Bálványos Summer Free University and Student Camp," July 23, 2022, https://miniszterelnok.hu/speech-by-prime-minister-viktor-orban-at -the-31st-balvanyos-summer-free-university-and-student-camp/.

149. Murtaza Hussain, "On Hindutva: Reading History and V.S. Naipaul," April 26, 2023, accessed July 6, 2023, https://mazmhussain.substack.com/p/on -hindutva.

150. Abhrajyoti Chakraborty, "India's Leading Documentary Filmmaker Has a Warning," *New York Times*, December 1, 2020, https://www.nytimes.com/2020/12/01/magazine/india-documentary-anand-patwardhan.html.

151. Constitution of the Democratic Socialist Republic of Sri Lanka, Chapter II, Article 9, 1978, https://www.srilankalaw.lk/constitution-of-the-democratic -socialist-republic-of-sri-lanka.html.

152. Rohini Mohan, "Sri Lanka's Violent Buddhists," *New York Times*, January 2, 2015, https://www.nytimes.com/2015/01/03/opinion/sri-lankas-violent -buddhists.html.

153. Laurence Piper, "Nationalism without a Nation: The Rise and Fall of Zulu Nationalism in South Africa's Transition to Democracy, 1975–99," *Nations and Nationalism* 8, no. 1 (2002): 73–94, https://doi.org/10.1111/1469-8219.00039.

154. Duma, "The Danger of Zuma's Zulu Nationalism."

155. Haunani-Kay Trask, "Feminism and Indigenous Hawaiian Nationalism," *Signs* 21, no. 4 (1996): 906–16, http://www.jstor.org/stable/3175028.

156. Associated Press, "Native Hawaiians Seek to Restore Monarchy," *Denver Post*, June 19, 2008, updated May 7, 2016, https://www.denverpost.com/2008/06/19/native-hawaiians-seek-to-restore-monarchy/.

157. Paul Shore, "Theology and the Development of the European Confessional State," in *The Oxford Handbook of Modern Theology, 1600–1800*, ed. Ulrich Lehner et al. (Oxford: Oxford University Press, 2016), https://doi.org/10.1093/oxfordhb/9780199937943.013.19.

158. "Basic Law of Governance," Embassy of the Kingdom of Saudi Arabia, https://www.saudiembassy.net/basic-law-governance.

159. John Fea, "No Surprise That 32% of Americans Want a Christian Constitutional Amendment," First Things, April 9, 2013, https://www.firstthings.com/blogs/firstthoughts/2013/04/no-surprise-that-of-americans-want-a-christian-constitutional-amendment.

160. Juan J. Linz, "Church and State in Spain from the Civil War to the Return of Democracy," *Daedalus* 120, no. 3 (1991): 159–78, http://www.jstor.org/stable/20025392.

161. Steven Menashi, "Ethnonationalism and Liberal Democracy," *University of Pennsylvania Journal of International Law* 32, no. 1 (2010): 62–63, https://ssrn.com/abstract=1592560.

162. Zack Beauchamp, "What Is Zionism?" Vox, May 14, 2018, https://www.vox.com/2018/11/20/18080010/zionism-israel-palestine.

163. "Israel's Jewish Nation-State Law," Adalah, December 20, 2020, https://www.adalah.org/en/content/view/9569.

164. Diana Buttu, "The Myth of Coexistence in Israel," *New York Times*, May 25, 2021, https://www.nytimes.com/2021/05/25/opinion/israel-palestinian-citizens-racism-discrimination.html.

165. Judith Shulevitz, "Why Are American Jews Falling Out of Love with Israel?" *New York Times*, September 24, 2019, https://www.nytimes.com/2019/09/24/books/review/we-stand-divided-daniel-gordis.html, citing Menashi, "Ethnonationalism and Liberal Democracy," 57 (arguing that such national forms are common and not at all harmful).

166. Shulevitz, "Why Are American Jews Falling Out of Love with Israel?"

167. See Orlando Patterson, *Freedom*, vol. 1, *Freedom in the Making of Western Culture* (New York: Basic Books, 1991).

CHAPTER 4

1. "EU Referendum: UK Votes to Leave the EU," BBC News, June 23, 2016, https://www.bbc.co.uk/news/politics/eu_referendum/results.

2. Sir John Curtice, "How Young and Old Would Vote on Brexit Now," BBC News, August 10, 2018, https://www.bbc.com/news/uk-politics-45098550.

3. John Curtice, "Brexit: Behind the Referendum," *Political Insight* 7, no. 2 (2016): 4–7, https://doi.org/10.1177/2041905816666122.

4. Curtice, "Brexit."

5. Peter Walker, "Poorer Voters' Worries on Immigration Fueled Brexit Vote, Study Finds," *Guardian*, December 15, 2016, accessed November 20, 2017, https://www.theguardian.com/politics/2016/dec/15/poorer-voters-worries-immigration-fuelled-brexit-vote-study-finds; Matthew Goodwin and Oliver Heath, "The 2016 Referendum, Brexit and the Left Behind: An Aggregate-Level Analysis of the Result," *Political Quarterly* 87, no. 3 (2016): 323–32, www.matthewjgoodwin.org/uploads/6/4/0/2/64026337/political_quarterly_version_1_9.pdf.

6. Simon Goodman, "'Take Back Control of Our Borders': The Role of Arguments about Controlling Immigration in the Brexit Debate," *Yearbook of the Institute of East-Central Europe* 15, no. 3 (2017): 35–53.

7. Miqdaad Versi, "Brexit Has Given Voice to Racism—and Too Many Are Complicit," *Guardian*, June 27, 2016, accessed November 18, 2017, https://www.theguardian.com/commentisfree/2016/jun/27/brexit-racism-eu-referendum-racist-incidents-politicians-media; Viren Swami et al., "To Brexit or Not to Brexit: The Roles of Islamophobia, Conspiracist Beliefs, and Integrated Threat in Voting Intentions for the United Kingdom European Union Membership Referendum," *British Journal of Psychology* 109, no.1 (2017): 156–79, accessed November 20, 2017, https://doi.org/10.1111/bjop.12252.

8. Mark D'Arcy, "Nigel Farage: The Story of 'Mr Brexit,'" BBC News, November 29, 2019, https://www.bbc.com/news/election-2019-50565543.

9. "Growth and Opportunity Project," Republican National Committee, 2013, http://s3.documentcloud.org/documents/623664/republican-national-committees-growth-and.pdf.

10. "Growth and Opportunity Project," 6.

11. Ben Smith and Byron Tau, "Birtherism: Where It All Began," *Politico*, April 22, 2011, last modified April 24, 2011, https://www.politico.com/story/2011/04/birtherism-where-it-all-began-053563.

12. Adam Serwer, "Birtherism of a Nation," *Atlantic*, May 13, 2020, https://www.theatlantic.com/ideas/archive/2020/05/birtherism-and-trump/610978/.

13. Casey Sullivan, "Could Obama Sue Donald Trump Over 'Birther' Conspiracy?" Bloomberg Law, September 20, 2016, https://news.bloomberglaw.com/business-and-practice/could-obama-sue-donald-trump-over-birther-conspiracy.

14. "Full Text: Donald Trump Announces a Presidential Bid," *Washington Post*, June 16, 2015, https://www.washingtonpost.com/news/post-politics/wp/2015/06/16/full-text-donald-trump-announces-a-presidential-bid/.

15. Jenna Johnson, "Trump Calls for 'Total and Complete Shutdown of Muslims Entering the United States,'" *Washington Post*, December 7, 2015, https://www.washingtonpost.com/news/post-politics/wp/2015/12/07/donald-trump-calls-for

-total-and-complete-shutdown-of-muslims-entering-the-united-states/?utm_term
=.bb74e86b5e03.

16. Johnson, "Trump Calls."

17. Joshua Clark, *What Didn't Happen? Breaking Down the Results of the
2016 Presidential Election* (Berkeley, CA: Othering & Belonging Institute, 2017),
https://belonging.berkeley.edu/new-report-maps-change-and-continuity-2016
-voting-trends.

18. *Atlantic*, "'Hail Trump!': Richard Spencer Speech Excerpts," YouTube, November 21, 2016, video, 3:07, https://www.youtube.com/watch?v=106-bi3jlxk.

19. Daniel Lombroso and Yoni Appelbaum, "'Hail Trump!': White Nationalists
Salute the President-Elect," *Atlantic*, November 21, 2016, https://www.theatlantic
.com/politics/archive/2016/11/richard-spencer-speech-npi/508379/.

20. Abigail Tracy, "Trump Responds to Amorous Neo-nazi Supporters: Nothing to See Here," *Vanity Fair*, November 22, 2016, https://www.vanityfair.com/
news/2016/11/donald-trump-national-policy-institute-response.

21. William Cummings, "'I Am a Nationalist': Trump's Embrace of Controversial Label Sparks Uproar," *USA Today*, October 24, 2018; last modified November
12, 2018, https://www.usatoday.com/story/news/politics/2018/10/24/trump-says
-hes-nationalist-what-means-why-its-controversial/1748521002/.

22. Jenna Johnson and Karen Tumulty, "Trump Cites Andrew Jackson as His
Hero—and a Reflection of Himself," *Washington Post*, March 15, 2017, https://
www.washingtonpost.com/politics/trump-cites-andrew-jackson-as-his-hero--and
-a-reflection-of-himself/2017/03/15/4da8dc8c-0995-11e7-a15f-a58d4a988474_story
.html.

23. "Pat Buchanan for President 1996 Campaign Brochure: Reclaiming the
American Dream," 4president.org, http://www.4president.org/brochures/1996/
patbuchanan1996brochure.htm.

24. Richard L. Berke, "Buchanan a Narrow Victor over Dole in New Hampshire," *New York Times*, February 21, 1996, https://www.nytimes.com/1996/02/21/
us/politics-the-overview-buchanan-a-narrow-victor-over-dole-in-new-hampshire
.html.

25. Samara Freemark and Joe Richman, "'Segregation Forever': A Fiery Pledge
Forgiven, but Not Forgotten," NPR, January 10, 2013, https://www.npr.org/2013/
01/14/169080969/segregation-forever-a-fiery-pledge-forgiven-but-not-forgotten.

26. Walter Rugaber, "Wallace Off the Critical List; Sweeps Primary in Michigan and Wins Handily in Maryland," *New York Times*, May 17, 1972, https://www
.nytimes.com/1972/05/17/archives/wallace-off-the-critical-list-sweeps-primary-in
-michigan-and-wins.html.

27. Hunter S. Thompson, *Fear and Loathing on the Campaign Trail '72* (New York: Simon & Schuster, 2012), 137.

28. Thompson, *Fear and Loathing*, 166.

29. David French, "The Rage and Joy of MAGA America," *New York Times*, July 6, 2023, https://www.nytimes.com/2023/07/06/opinion/maga-america-trump .html.

30. James Fenimore Cooper, *The American Democrat* (Cooperstown, NY: H. & E. Phinney, 1838), 99–100, quoted in Larry Tye, *Demagogue: The Life and Long Shadow of Senator Joe McCarthy* (New York: HMH Books, 2020), 125.

31. Cooper, *The American Democrat*, 99–100.

32. Michael Signer, *Demagogue: The Fight to Save Democracy from Its Worst Enemies* (New York: Palgrave Macmillan, 2009): 40–51; W. Robert Connor, "A Vacuum at the Center: How a Demagogue Resembles a Typhoon, and Why It Matters to the Future of the Republic," *American Scholar*, March 5, 2018, https:// theamericanscholar.org/a-vacuum-at-the-center/.

33. "The Federalist Papers: No. 1," Avalon Project, http://avalon.law.yale.edu/ 18th_century/fed01.asp.

34. Reinhard H. Luthin, *American Demagogues: Twentieth Century* (Boston: Beacon Press, 1954).

35. Comer Vann Woodward, "Tom Watson and the Negro in Agrarian Politics," *Journal of Southern History* 4, no. 1 (1938): 14–33, https://doi.org/10.2307/2191851; Reinhard H. Luthin, "Flowering of the Southern Demagogue," *American Scholar* 20, no. 2 (1951): 185–95, http://www.jstor.org/stable/41205392; Charles Crowe, "Tom Watson, Populists, and Blacks Reconsidered," *Journal of Negro History* 55, no. 2 (1970): 99–116, https://doi.org/10.2307/2716444.

36. Woodward, "Tom Watson and the Negro," 26–30; Michael Goldfield, *The Color of Politics: Race and the Mainsprings of American Politics* (New York: New Press, 1997), 163.

37. Dennis Kearney, President, and H. L. Knight, Secretary, "Appeal from California. The Chinese Invasion. Workingmen's Address," *Indianapolis Times*, February 28 1878, quoted in Dennis Kearney "'Our Misery and Despair': Kearney Blasts Chinese Immigration," History Matters, http://historymatters.gmu.edu/d/5046/.

38. Chris Carlsson, "The Workingmen's Party & the Denis Kearney Agitation," Found SF, 1995, https://www.foundsf.org/index.php?title=The_Workingmen%E2 %80%99s_Party_%26_The_Denis_Kearney_Agitation.

39. Andrew Gyory, *Closing the Gate: Race, Politics, and the Chinese Exclusion Act* (Chapel Hill: University of North Carolina Press, 1998), 130–34.

40. Chinese Exclusion Act, Pub. L. 47–126, 22 Stat. 58 (1882) (repealed 1943).

41. Eva Horn and Joel Golb, "Work on Charisma: Writing Hitler's Biography," *New German Critique*, no. 114 (2011): 95–114, https://www.jstor.org/stable/41288117.

42. Mark Mazower, *The Dark Continent* (New York: Knopf, 1999), 97–102.

43. Mark Mazower, *Hitler's Empire: How the Nazis Ruled Europe* (New York: Penguin Books, 2009).

44. Katie Rogers, Lara Jakes, and Ana Swanson. "Trump Defends Using 'Chinese Virus' Label, Ignoring Growing Criticism," *New York Times*, March 18, 2020, https://www.nytimes.com/2020/03/18/us/politics/china-virus.html.

45. Laura Kurtzman, "Trump's 'Chinese Virus' Tweet Linked to Rise of Anti-Asian Hashtags on Twitter," UCSF News, March 18, 2021, https://www.ucsf.edu/news/2021/03/420081/trumps-chinese-virus-tweet-linked-rise-anti-asian-hashtags-twitter.

46. "Hitler's Antisemitism. Why Did He Hate the Jews?" Anne Frank House, accessed November 9, 2022, https://www.annefrank.org/en/anne-frank/go-in-depth/why-did-hitler-hate-jews/.

47. David Broder, "The Future Is Italy, and It's Bleak," *New York Times,* July 22, 2022, https://www.nytimes.com/2022/07/22/opinion/italy-draghi-meloni-government.html.

48. "Philippines: 'If You Are Poor, You Are Killed': Extrajudicial Killings in the Philippines' 'War on Drugs,'" Amnesty International, January 31, 2017, https://www.amnesty.org/en/documents/asa35/5517/2017/en/; "'License to Kill': Philippine Police Killings in Duterte's 'War on Drugs,'" Human Rights Watch, March 2, 2017, https://www.hrw.org/report/2017/03/02/license-kill/philippine-police-killings-dutertes-war-drugs.

49. Lilliana Mason, Julie Wronski, and John V. Kane, "Activating Animus: The Uniquely Social Roots of Trump Support," *American Political Science Review* 115, no. 4 (2021): 1508–16, https://doi.org/10.1017/S0003055421000563. See also Thomas B. Edsall, "Trump's Cult of Animosity Shows No Sign of Letting Up," *New York Times*, July 7, 2021, https://www.nytimes.com/2021/07/07/opinion/trump-gop.html.

50. Douglas Kierdorf, "Getting to Know the Know-Nothings," *Boston Globe*, January 10, 2016, https://www.bostonglobe.com/ideas/2016/01/10/getting-know-know-nothings/yAojakXKkiauKCAzsf4WAL/story.html?outputType=amp.

51. Brian Kelly, "Gathering Antipathy: Irish Immigrants and Race in America's Age of Emancipation," in *Rethinking the Irish Diaspora: After the Gathering*, ed. Johanne Devlin Trew and Michael Pierse (London: Palgrave Macmillan, 2018), 157–85.

52. Bryan Le Beau, "'Saving the West from the Pope': Anti-Catholic Propaganda and the Settlement of the Mississippi River Valley," *American Studies* 32, no. 1 (1991): 101–14, https://journals.ku.edu/amsj/article/view/2895.

53. Ronald Hayduk, *Democracy for All: Restoring Immigrant Voting Rights in the United States* (New York: Routledge, 2006), 23.

54. Alex Travelli and Hari Kumar, "Under Hindu Nationalist Leaders, Sectarian Violence Flares in India," *New York Times*, August 1, 2023, https://www.nytimes.com/2023/08/01/world/asia/india-hindu-muslim-violence.html; Debasish Roy Chowdhury, "India Is on the Brink," *New York Times*, August 9, 2023, https://www.nytimes.com/2023/08/09/opinion/india-modi-conflict-zone.html; Sushant Singh, "Why Modi Can't Make India a Great Power," *Foreign Affairs*, September 4, 2023, https://www.foreignaffairs.com/india/why-modi-cant-make-india-great-power.

55. "Religion in India: Tolerance and Segregation," Pew Research Center, June 29, 2021, https://www.pewforum.org/2021/06/29/religion-in-india-tolerance-and-segregation/.

56. Rama Lakshmi, "Indians Invented Planes 7,000 Years Ago—and Other Startling Claims at the Science Congress," *Washington Post*, January 4, 2015, https://www.washingtonpost.com/news/worldviews/wp/2015/01/04/indians-invented-planes-7000-years-ago-and-other-startling-claims-at-the-science-congress/. See also Ayeshea Perera, "Cows to Planes: Indian Ministers Who Rewrote Scientific History," BBC News, September 22, 2017, https://www.bbc.com/news/world-asia-india-41344136.

57. Rupam Jain and Tom Lasseter, "By Rewriting History, Hindu Nationalists Aim to Assert Their Dominance over India," Reuters, March 6, 2018, https://www.reuters.com/investigates/special-report/india-modi-culture/.

58. Erin Blakemore, "How Two Centuries of Slave Revolts Shaped American History," *National Geographic*, November 8, 2019, https://www.nationalgeographic.com/history/article/two-centuries-slave-rebellions-shaped-american-history.

59. Daniel A. Smith, Matthew DeSantis, and Jason Kassel, "Was Rove Right? Evangelicals and the Impact of Gay Marriage in the 2004 Election," 5th Annual State Politics and Policy Conference, Michigan State University, East Lansing, May 12–14, 2005, https://www.researchgate.net/publication/241880947_Was_Rove_Right_Evangelicals_and_the_Impact_of_Gay_Marriage_in_the_2004_Election.

60. Daniel A. Smith, Matthew DeSantis, and Jason Kassel, "Same-Sex Marriage Ballot Measures and the 2004 Presidential Election," *State & Local Government Review* 38, no. 2 (2006): 78–91.

61. Doug Criss, "This Is the 30-Year-Old Willie Horton Ad Everybody Is Talking about Today," CNN, November 1, 2018, https://www.cnn.com/2018/11/01/politics/willie-horton-ad-1988-explainer-trnd/index.html; Rachel Withers, "George H.W. Bush's 'Willie Horton' Ad Will Always Be the Reference Point for Dog-Whistle Racism," Vox, December 1, 2018, https://www.vox.com/2018/12/1/18121221/george-hw-bush-willie-horton-dog-whistle-politics.

62. Neither Bush was a demagogue in the classical sense, but they were not above employing demagoguery to serve their campaigns. In the critical South Carolina Republican primary in 2000, the George W. Bush campaign, under Karl Rove, notoriously circulated phone calls to primary voters insinuating that rival John McCain's adoptive daughter was an illegitimate Black love child. Ann Banks, "Dirty Tricks, South Carolina and John McCain," *Nation*, January 14, 2008, https://www.thenation.com/article/archive/dirty-tricks-south-carolina-and-john-mccain/.

63. Amartya Sen, *Identity and Violence: The Illusion of Destiny* (New York: Norton, 2006).

64. Erlanger, "Putin's War on Ukraine."

65. Du Bois, *Black Reconstruction in America*, 700.

66. Log Cabin Republicans, "About Us," accessed August 18, 2022, http://logcabin.org/about-us/.

67. Frances Kai-Hwa Wang, "How Violence against Asian Americans Has Grown and How to Stop It, according to Activists," *PBS NewsHour*, April 11, 2022, https://www.pbs.org/newshour/nation/a-year-after-atlanta-and-indianapolis-shootings-targeting-asian-americans-activists-say-we-cant-lose-momentum.

68. Ashley Jardina, *White Identity Politics* (Cambridge: Cambridge University Press, 2019), https://doi.org/10.1017/9781108645157.

69. Justin Khoo, "Code Words in Political Discourse," *Philosophical Topics* 45, no. 2 (2017): 33–64, https://www.jstor.org/stable/26529437.

70. Robert M. Sapolsky, *Behave: The Biology of Humans at Our Best and Worst* (New York: Penguin Books, 2017).

"Why and How We Act with Robert Sapolsky: In Conversation with Dacher Keltner," Conversations on Science, City Arts & Lectures, May 22, 2017, https://www.cityarts.net/event/why-and-how-we-act/.

71. Robert Shanafelt, "The Nature of Flag Power: How Flags Entail Dominance, Subordination, and Social Solidarity," *Politics and the Life Sciences* 27, no. 2 (2008): 13–27.

72. Joshua Hammer, "The Race to Save Ukraine's Sacred Art," *Smithsonian*, July 2022, https://www.smithsonianmag.com/arts-culture/the-race-to-save-ukraines-sacred-art-180980019/.

73. Mugambi Jouet, "Guns, Identity, and Nationhood," *Palgrave Communications* 5, 138 (2019), https://doi.org/10.1057/s41599-019-0349-z; Dylan Matthews, "How Gun Ownership Became a Powerful Political Identity," Vox, updated May 25, 2022, https://www.vox.com/2018/2/27/17029680/gun-owner-nra-mass-shooting -political-identity-political-science.

74. Engel v. Vitale, 370 U.S. 421 (1962).

75. "JFK's Address to Protestant Ministers," NPR, December 5, 2007, https:// www.npr.org/templates/story/story.php?storyId=16920600.

76. John Huntington, "The Kennedy Speech That Stoked the Rise of the Christian Right," *Politico Magazine*, March 8, 2022, https://www.politico.com/news/ magazine/2020/03/08/the-kennedy-speech-that-stoked-the-rise-of-the-christian -right-123369.

77. See Jeffrey Toobin, *The Nine: Inside the Secret World of the Supreme Court* (New York: Anchor, 2008), 86–98 (emphasizing the role of religious cases in the Supreme Court's docket).

78. George Stephanopoulos, "Rick Santorum: JFK's 1960 Speech Made Me Want to Throw Up," ABC News, February 26, 2012, http://abcnews.go.com/ blogs/politics/2012/02/rick-santorum-jfks-1960-speech-made-me-want-to -throw-up.

79. "The Congress: Hunting Time," *Time*, May 24, 1954, https://content.time .com/time/subscriber/article/0,33009,823381,00.html.

80. Act of June 14, 1954, ch. 297, 68 Stat. 249, also found at 4 U.S.C. § 4.

81. Katharine Batlan, "One Nation Under Christ: US Christian Amendment Attempts and Competing Visions for America in the 1940s and 1950s," *Journal of Church and State* 61, no. 4 (2019): 658–79, https://doi.org/10.1093/jcs/csz029.

82. Janell Ross, "Obama Revives His 'Cling to Guns or Religion' Analysis—for Donald Trump Supporters," *Washington Post*, December 21, 2015, https://www .washingtonpost.com/news/the-fix/wp/2015/12/21/obama-dusts-off-his-cling-to -guns-or-religion-idea-for-donald-trump/.

83. Portions of this section were previously published in blog form. Stephen Menendian, "Understanding 'Replacement Theory,'" *Berkeley Blog*, July 26, 2022, https://blogs.berkeley.edu/2022/07/26/understanding-replacement-theory/.

84. Saad Z. Nagi, "Status Profile and Reactions to Status Threats," *American Sociological Review* 28, no. 3 (1963): 440–43, https://doi.org/10.2307/2090355.

85. This is a feature of an influential theory known as Social Identity Theory, created by Henri Tajfel and John Turner. See "An Integrative Theory of Intergroup Conflict," in W. G. Austin and S. Worchel, eds., *The Social Psychology of Intergroup Relations* (Monterey, CA: Brooks/Cole, 1979), 33–47.

86. Glick and Fiske, "An Ambivalent Alliance," 113. ("For example, a sexist man might initially place a woman in whom he is romantically interested on a pedestal but abruptly change his views when she rejects him, reclassifying her from 'babe' to 'bitch.'") And, presumably, this would produce a corresponding shift in the quadrant location in the SCM, from perhaps pitied to despised.

87. As one commentator notes regarding Matthew Hale, a notorious seventeenth-century jurist briefly discussed in the supplementary chapter, "A central tenet of Hale's legal philosophy was that giving women legally enforceable rights over their own bodies was a threat to men's freedom." Amanda Taub, "The 17th-Century Judge at the Heart of Today's Women's Rights Rulings," *New York Times*, May 19, 2022, https://www.nytimes.com/2022/05/19/world/asia/abortion-lord-matthew-hale.html.

88. Thomas B. Edsall, "The Resentment That Never Sleeps," *New York Times*, December 9, 2020, https://www.nytimes.com/2020/12/09/opinion/trump-social-status-resentment.html; Barbara Ehrenreich, *Fear of Falling: The Inner Life of the Middle Class* (New York: Twelve, 2020).

89. Diana C. Mutz, "Status Threat, Not Economic Hardship, Explains the 2016 Presidential Vote," *PNAS*, March 26, 2018, https://www.pnas.org/content/pnas/115/19/e4330.full.pdf; Niraj Chokshi, "Trump Voters Driven by Fear of Losing Status, Not Economic Anxiety, Study Finds," *New York Times*, April 24, 2018, https://www.nytimes.com/2018/04/24/us/politics/trump-economic-anxiety.html; Olga Khazan, "People Voted for Trump Because They Were Anxious, Not Poor," *Atlantic*, April 23, 2018, https://www.theatlantic.com/science/archive/2018/04/existential-anxiety-not-poverty-motivates-trump-support/558674/; Daniel Cox, Rachel Lienesch, and Robert P. Jones, "Beyond Economics: Fears of Cultural Displacement Pushed the White Working Class to Trump," PRRI, May 9, 2017, https://www.prri.org/research/white-working-class-attitudes-economy-trade-immigration-election-donald-trump/.

90. Nicholas Carnes and Noam Lupu, "It's Time to Bust the Myth: Most Trump Voters Were Not Working Class," *Washington Post*, June 5, 2017, https://www.washingtonpost.com/news/monkey-cage/wp/2017/06/05/its-time-to-bust-the-myth-most-trump-voters-were-not-working-class; Thomas Ogorzalek, Luisa Godinez Puig, and Spencer Piston, "White Trump Voters Are Richer than They Appear," *Washington Post*, November 12, 2019, https://www.washingtonpost.com/politics/2019/11/13/white-trump-voters-are-richer-than-they-appear/.

91. Francis Fukuyama, *Identity: The Demand for Dignity and the Politics of Resentment* (New York: Farrar, Straus & Giroux, 2018), 85, citing Samuel Huntington, *Who Are We? The Challenges to America's National Identity* (New York: Simon & Schuster, 2004).

92. Fukuyama, *Identity*, 85, citing Huntington, *Who Are We?*

93. Ian Haney López, *Dog Whistle Politics: How Coded Racial Appeals Have Reinvented Racism and Wrecked the Middle Class* (Oxford: Oxford University Press, 2013), 27.

94. Mary Anne Franks, *The Cult of the Constitution* (Stanford, CA: Stanford University Press, 2019), 23.

95. Renegade Media, "Torch Lit March Charlottesville Virginia 2017," YouTube, 2017, https://www.youtube.com/watch?v=8KYifYzjKlc.

96. "Charlottesville: Who Was Victim Heather Heyer?" BBC News, August 14, 2017, https://www.bbc.com/news/world-us-canada-40924922.

97. Dan Merica, "Trump Condemns 'Hatred, Bigotry and Violence on Many Sides' in Charlottesville," CNN, video, 1:25, August 13, 2017, https://www.cnn.com/2017/08/12/politics/trump-statement-alt-right-protests/index.html.

98. Steven Nelson, "White Nationalist Richard Spencer Thanks Trump for 'Defending the Truth' on Charlottesville," *Washington Examiner*, August 15, 2017, http://www.washingtonexaminer.com/white-nationalist-richard-spencer-thanks-trump-for-defending-the-truth-on-charlottesville/article/2631630.

99. David Nakamura, "Trump Denounces KKK, Neo-Nazis as 'Repugnant' as He Seeks to Quell Criticism of His Response to Charlottesville," *Washington Post*, video, 2:24, August 14, 2017, https://www.washingtonpost.com/news/post-politics/wp/2017/08/14/trump-denounces-kkk-neo-nazis-as-justice-department-launches-civil-rights-probe-into-charlottesville-death/.

100. Julie Pace and Jonathan Lemire, "Trump Blames 'Both Sides' for Violence at Charlottesville Rally," PBS, video, 4:04, August 15, 2017, https://www.pbs.org/newshour/politics/trump-blames-sides-violence-charlottesville-rally.

101. Eric Bradner, "Donald Trump Defends Charlottesville Responses, Omits Reference to 'Many Sides,'" CNN, August 22, 2017, last modified August 23, 2017, https://www.cnn.com/2017/08/22/politics/trump-phoenix-rally/index.html.

102. Shelly Tan, Youjin Shin, and Danielle Rindler, "How One of America's Ugliest Days Unraveled inside and Outside the Capitol," *Washington Post*, January 9, 2021, https://www.washingtonpost.com/nation/interactive/2021/capitol-insurrection-visual-timeline/.

103. Radio Diaries, "'Segregation Forever': A Fiery Pledge Forgiven, but Not Forgotten," NPR, January 10, 2013, https://www.npr.org/2013/01/14/169080969/segregation-forever-a-fiery-pledge-forgiven-but-not-forgotten; "Mississippi Burning," FBI, accessed August 18, 2022, https://www.fbi.gov/history/famous-cases/mississippi-burning.

104. Facing History and Ourselves, "Confronting Apartheid," in *Growing Resitance Meets Growing Repression*, accessed August 20, 2022. https://www.facinghistory.org/confronting-apartheid/chapter-3/introduction.

105. Noah Kim and John Greenberg, "The Difference in Police Response to the Black Lives Matter Protests and the Capitol Assault," Poynter Institute, January 11, 2021, https://www.poynter.org/fact-checking/2021/the-difference-in-police -response-to-the-black-lives-matter-protests-and-the-capitol-assault/; Rachel Chason and Samantha Schmidt, "The Freedom to Assemble in Two Acts: Lafayette Square, Capitol Rallies Met Starkly Different Policing Response," *Washington Post*, January 14, 2021, https://www.washingtonpost.com/dc-md-va/interactive/2021/blm-protest -capitol-riot-police-comparison/.

106. Noam Gidron and Peter A. Hall, "Populism as a Problem of Social Integration," *Comparative Political Studies* 53, no. 7 (2019): 1027–59, https://journals .sagepub.com/doi/abs/10.1177/0010414019879947.

107. Michael Bang Petersen, Mathias Osmundsen, and Alexander Bor, "Beyond Populism: The Psychology of Status-Seeking and Extreme Political Discontent," in *The Psychology of Populism: The Tribal Challenge to Liberal Democracy*, ed. Joseph Paul Forgas, William Crano, and Klaus Fiedler (New York: Routledge, 2021), 62–77. Although this behavior or its evident effects are often described as "populism," these authors take pains to distinguish this "extreme discontent" from populism.

108. Graham Allison, "Destined for War: Can China and the United States Escape Thucydides's Trap?" *Atlantic*, September 24, 2015, https://www.theatlantic .com/international/archive/2015/09/united-states-china-war-thucydides-trap/ 406756/.

109. Ronald Brownstein, "The Racist 'Replacement Theory' Has it All Backward," CNN, April 23, 2021, https://www.cnn.com/2021/04/23/politics/race -immigration-replacement-theory-demographics/index.html.

110. Aaron Blake, "The GOP's Gradual Descent into 'Replacement Theory' and 'Nativist Dog Whistles,'" *Washington Post*, April 17, 2021, https://www .washingtonpost.com/politics/2021/04/17/gops-gradual-descent-into-replacement -theory/.

111. Dustin Jones, "What Is the 'Great Replacement' and How Is It Tied to the Buffalo Shooting Suspect?" NPR, May 16, 2022, https://www.npr.org/2022/05/16/ 1099034094/what-is-the-great-replacement-theory.

112. Frances Robles, "Dylann Roof Photos and a Manifesto Are Posted on Website," *New York Times*, June 20, 2015, https://www.nytimes.com/2015/06/21/us/ dylann-storm-roof-photos-website-charleston-church-shooting.html.

113. Paul Gill, John Horgan, and Paige Deckert, *Tracing the Motivations and Antecedent Behaviors of Lone-Actor Terrorism: A Routine Activity Analysis of Five Lone-Actor Terrorist Events* (University Park, PA: International Center for the Study of Terrorism, 2012), 25, accessed January 13, 2021, https://www.dhs.gov/

sites/default/files/publications/OPSR_TP_ARC-Lone-Actor-Routine-Activity-Analysis-Report_Aug2012-508.pdf.

114. Anders Behring Breivik, *2083—A European Declaration of Independence* (Estonia, Vettazedition Ou, 2011).

115. Norimitsu Onishi, "In France, a Racist Conspiracy Theory Edges into the Mainstream," *New York Times*, February 15, 2022, https://www.nytimes.com/2022/02/15/world/europe/france-elections-pecresse-great-replacement.html.

116. Norimitsu Onishi, "The Man Behind a Toxic Slogan Promoting White Supremacy," *New York Times*, September 20, 2019, https://www.nytimes.com/2019/09/20/world/europe/renaud-camus-great-replacement.html.

117. Philip Bump, "Tucker Carlson's Toxic 'Replacement' Rhetoric Gets Picked Up in the House," *Washington Post*, April 14, 2021, https://www.washingtonpost.com/politics/2021/04/14/tucker-carlsons-toxic-replacement-rhetoric-gets-picked-up-house/.

118. Blake, "The GOP's Gradual Descent."

119. Ryan Bort, "Quiz: Can You Tell the Difference Between Tucker Carlson and an Admitted White Supremacist?" *Rolling Stone*, September 23, 2021, https://www.rollingstone.com/politics/politics-news/tucker-carlson-great-replacement-white-supremacy-1231248/.

120. David Brody, "Trump: 'This Will Be the Last Election That the Republicans Have a Chance of Winning,'" CBN News, September 9, 2016, https://www1.cbn.com/thebrodyfile/archive/2016/09/09/brody-file-exclusive-donald-trump-says-this-will-be-the-last-election-that-the-republicans-have-a-chance-of-winning.

121. The Print, "Muslims Want to Take over India, I Stand by My Statement: BJP MP Parvesh Verma," YouTube, 2020, https://www.youtube.com/watch?v=kdnItfoxp9U; Mujib Mashal, Suhasini Raj, and Hari Kumar, "As Officials Look Away, Hate Speech in India Nears Dangerous Levels," *New York Times*, February 8, 2022, https://www.nytimes.com/2022/02/08/world/asia/india-hate-speech-muslims.html. ("As he sees it, India's Muslims—who account for 15 percent of the population—will turn the country into a Muslim state within a decade.")

122. "'The Great Replacement:' An Explainer," Anti-Defamation League, April 19, 2021, https://www.adl.org/resources/backgrounders/the-great-replacement-an-explainer.

123. Vivian Yee, "Europe Pushed Tunisia to Keep Migrants Away. The Result Is Harsh," *New York Times*, July 20, 2023, https://www.nytimes.com/2023/07/20/world/africa/tunisia-african-migrants.html.

124. Exodus 1:9–11 (New International Version), https://www.biblegateway.com/passage/?search=Exodus%201&version=NIV.

125. Francis Fukuyama calls this the "politics of resentment" in his book *Identity*. He names practitioners such as Donald Trump and Viktor Orbán. Fukuyama, *Identity*, 7, 9.

126. Choe Sang-Hun, "The New Political Cry in South Korea: 'Out with Man Haters,'" *New York Times*, January 1, 2022, https://www.nytimes.com/2022/01/01/world/asia/south-korea-men-anti-feminists.html.

127. Laura Bicker, "Why Misogyny Is at the Heart of South Korea's Presidential Elections," BBC News, March 8, 2022, https://www.bbc.com/news/world-asia-60643446.

128. Hinton, *America on Fire*, 80.

129. Arlie Russell Hochschild, *Strangers in Their Own Land: Anger and Mourning on the American Right* (New York: New Press, 2016). This book describes the feelings of a dominant group being displaced from its power, privileges, and prerogatives.

130. "Santelli's Tea Party Rant," CNBC, filmed February 19, 2009, published February 6, 2015, video, 0:38, https://www.cnbc.com/video/2015/02/06/santellis-tea-party-rant-february-19-2009.html.

131. Theda Skocpol and Vanessa Williamson, *The Tea Party and the Remaking of Republican Conservatism* (New York: Oxford University Press, 2016); Charles Homans, "How 'Stop the Steal' Captured the American Right," *New York Times*, July 19, 2022, https://www.nytimes.com/2022/07/19/magazine/stop-the-steal.html.

132. Olga Khazan, "How White Supremacists Use Victimhood to Recruit," *Atlantic*, August 15, 2017, https://www.theatlantic.com/science/archive/2017/08/the-worlds-worst-support-group/536850/. Another example is how Hindu monks in India are aggrieved by the foundation of the state, after Partition, as a secular state. Mashal, Raj, and Kumar, "Hate Speech in India."

133. Eve Fairbanks, "When Racial Progress Comes for White Liberals," *Atlantic*, July 19, 2022, https://www.theatlantic.com/ideas/archive/2022/07/south-africa-apartheid-white-afrikaners-the-inheritors/670554/.

134. Tom Magliozzi, *Car Talk*, NPR, n.d.; Harari, *Sapiens*, 382. This paradox also helps explain why discontent among marginalized groups may be *greater* after significant political and policy successes: those successes raise expectations while the failure to fully realize those expectations generates discontentment. See, e.g., Kerner Commission, *Report of the National Advisory Commission on Civil Disorders*, which covered massive national uprisings by Black Americans in the *wake* of the civil rights movement's many legislative successes.

135. Thomas B. Edsall, "Status Anxiety Is Blowing Wind into Trump's Sails," *New York Times*, February 9, 2022, https://www.nytimes.com/2022/02/09/

opinion/trump-status-anxiety.html (citing "The Geography of Desperation in America: Labor Force Participation, Mobility Trends, Place, and Well-being," 2019).

136. Andrés Rodríguez-Pose, "The Rise of Populism and the Revenge of the Places That Don't Matter," *LSE Public Policy Review* 1, no. 1 (2020), https://doi.org/10.31389/lseppr.4.

137. Pankaj Mishra, *Age of Anger* (New York: Farrar, Straus & Giroux, 2017), 343.

138. Diana C. Mutz, "Status Threat, Not Economic Hardship, Explains the 2016 Presidential Vote," *PNAS*, March 26, 2018, https://www.pnas.org/content/pnas/115/19/e4330.full.pdf. ("Thus far, the limited studies of the 2016 election have been rooted in the popular belief among political scientists that campaigns do not change public opinion so much as 'activate' or 'prime' certain considerations over others. In other words, by making some issues more salient than others, campaigns increase the extent to which those particular issue opinions are used by voters when choosing a candidate.")

139. One of us presented this metaphor in an interview with a campus reporter: Amrita Bhasin, "Capitol Riots: A Broader Symbol of Ethno-Nationalism across the Globe," *Daily Californian*, January 28, 2021, https://www.dailycal.org/2021/01/28/capitol-riots-a-broader-symbol-of-ethno-nationalism-across-the-globe/.

140. "The Southern Manifesto and 'Massive Resistance' to Brown," NAACP Legal Defense and Educational Fund, https://www.naacpldf.org/ldf-celebrates-60th-anniversary-brown-v-board-education/southern-manifesto-massive-resistance-brown/.

141. Stanley Jeyaraja Tambiah, *Sri Lanka: Ethnic Fratricide and the Dismantling of Democracy* (Chicago: University of Chicago Press, 1986), 92.

142. Max Fisher and Amanda Taub, "'Overrun,' 'Outbred,' 'Replaced': Why Ethnic Majorities Lash Out Over False Fears," *New York Times*, April 30, 2019, https://www.nytimes.com/2019/04/30/world/asia/sri-lanka-populism-ethnic-tensions.html.

143. Marc Mulholland, *Northern Ireland at the Crossroads: Ulster Unionism in the O'Neill Years, 1960–69* (London: Macmillan, 2000), 8.

144. Megan Specia and Ed O'Loughlin, "Catholics Outnumber Protestants in Northern Ireland for the First Time," *New York Times*, September 22, 2022, https://www.nytimes.com/2022/09/22/world/europe/northern-ireland-census-catholics-protestants.html.

145. Mark 12:17.

146. Mary Beard, *S.P.Q.R.: A History of Ancient Rome* (New York: Liveright, 2015), 16–17.

147. "Severus: Rome's First African Emperor," Sky History, https://www.history
.co.uk/article/severus-rome's-first-african-emperor.

148. Karen Barkey and George Gavrilis, "The Ottoman Millet System: Non-Territorial Autonomy and Its Contemporary Legacy," *Ethnopolitics* 15, no. 1 (2016): 24–42, https://www.tandfonline.com/doi/full/10.1080/17449057.2015.1101845.

149. Paul Miller-Melamed and Claire Morelon, "What the Hapsburg Empire Got Right," *New York Times*, September 10, 2019, https://www.nytimes.com/2019/09/10/opinion/hapsburg-empire-austria-world-war-1.html.

150. Gregory O. Hall, "The Politics of Autocracy: Serbia under Slobodan Milosevic," *East European Quarterly* 33, no. 2 (1999): 233–49. ("Worsening economic and social problems further divided Yugoslavs along ethnic and regional lines, and contributed to increasing popular disenchantment with the post-Tito communist leadership . . . the use of nationalism and populist politics were essential ingredients in Milosevic's ascension to power in Serbia.")

151. Anton Troianovski and Carlotta Gall, "After War Between Armenia and Azerbaijan, Peace Sees Winners and Losers Swap Places," *New York Times*, November 16, 2020, https://www.nytimes.com/2020/11/15/world/europe/azerbaijan-armenia-nagorno-karabakh.html.

152. William A. Pelz, "Economic Collapse and the Rise of Fascism, 1920–33," in *A People's History of Modern Europe* (London: Pluto Press, 2016), 128.

153. "Aftermath of World War I and the Rise of Nazism, 1918–1933," United States Holocaust Memorial Museum, n.d., https://www.ushmm.org/learn/holocaust/path-to-nazi-genocide/chapter-1/aftermath-of-world-war-i-and-the-rise-of-nazism-1918-1933.

154. David Brooks, "This Is Why Putin Can't Back Down," *New York Times*, March 10, 2022, https://www.nytimes.com/2022/03/10/opinion/putin-ukraine-russia-identity.html.

155. Robinson Meyer, "Donald Trump Is the First Demagogue of the Anthropocene," *Atlantic*, October 19, 2016, https://www.theatlantic.com/science/archive/2016/10/trump-the-first-demagogue-of-the-anthropocene/504134/, citing Jürgen Scheffran et al., "Climate Change and Violent Conflict," *Science* 333, no. 2083 (2012): 869–71.

156. Francis Fukuyama, "A Country of Their Own: Liberalism Needs the Nation," *Foreign Affairs*, June 2022, https://www.foreignaffairs.com/articles/ukraine/2022-04-01/francis-fukuyama-liberalism-country.

157. Mishra, *Age of Anger*, 5.

158. Mishra, *Age of Anger*, 9.

159. Katie Benner and Eileen Sullivan, "Top Law Enforcement Officials Say the Biggest Domestic Terror Threat Comes from White Supremacists," *New York*

Times, May 12, 2021, https://www.nytimes.com/2021/05/12/us/politics/domestic
-terror-white-supremacists.html.

160. "Global Trends 2040: A More Contested World," National Intelligence
Council, March 2021, https://www.dni.gov/files/ODNI/documents/assessments/
GlobalTrends_2040.pdf.

161. "Global Trends 2040," 73.

162. Murtaza Hussain, "On Hindutva," April 25, 2023, https://mazmhussain
.substack.com/p/on-hindutva.

163. Harari, *Sapiens*, 138.

CHAPTER 5

1. "Racial Disparities Dashboard," Othering and Belonging Institute, June 7,
2023, https://belonging.berkeley.edu/racial-disparities-dashboard.

2. Jesse Bedayn, "Targeted Universalism: A Solution for Inequality?" Cal Matters, February 3, 2022, https://calmatters.org/california-divide/2022/02/targeted
-universalism-racial-inequality/.

3. For a recent account, see Anne Gardiner Perkins, *Yale Needs Women: How
the First Group of Girls Rewrote the Rules of an Ivy League Giant* (Naperville, IL:
Sourcebooks, 2019).

4. Claire Cain Miller, "'A Very Unwelcome Feeling': The First Women at Yale
Look Back," *New York Times*, October 30, 2019, https://www.nytimes.com/2019/
10/30/upshot/yale-first-women-discrimination.html.

5. Dahlia Lithwick, "Sonia Sotomayor, Outsider," Slate, September 4, 2015,
https://slate.com/news-and-politics/2015/09/sonia-sotomayor-conversation-at
-notre-dame-first-latina-doesnt-feel-like-she-belongs-on-supreme-court.html.

6. john a. powell, "Righting the Law: Seeking a Humane Voice," *West Virginia
University Law Review* 96, no. 2 (1994): 333, https://researchrepository.wvu.edu/
wvlr/vol96/iss2/7.

7. john a. powell, "Transformative Action: A Strategy for Ending Racial Hierarchy and Achieving True Democracy," in *Beyond Racism: Race and Inequality in
Brazil, South Africa, and the United States*, ed. Charles Hamilton, Lynn Huntley,
Neville Alexander, Antonio Sérgio Alfredo Guimarães, and Wilmot James (Boulder, CO: Lynne Rienner, 2001).

8. Cleve R. Wootsen Jr., "A Black Yale Student Fell Asleep in Her Dorm's
Common Room. A White Student Called Police," *Washington Post*, May 11, 2018,
https://www.washingtonpost.com/news/grade-point/wp/2018/05/10/a-black
-yale-student-fell-asleep-in-her-dorms-common-room-a-white-student-called
-police/.

9. "I, Too, Am Harvard," March 7, 2014, https://itooamharvard.tumblr.com/.

10. Justin Phillips, "An Oakland Lake Became a Symbol of Black Resilience. Then the Neighbors Complained," *San Francisco Chronicle*, May 22, 2021, https://www.sfchronicle.com/local/justinphillips/article/An-Oakland-lake-became-a-symbol-of-Black-16194668.php.

11. Erin Baldassari, "'BBQing While Black' Festival Draws Huge Crowd to Oakland's Lake Merritt," *East Bay Times*, May 20, 2018, https://www.eastbaytimes.com/2018/05/20/bbqing-while-black-festival-draws-hundreds-to-oaklands-lake-merritt/.

12. Emily Stewart, "Two Black Men Were Arrested in a Philadelphia Starbucks for Doing Nothing," *Vox*, April 15, 2018, https://www.vox.com/identities/2018/4/14/17238494/what-happened-at-starbucks-black-men-arrested-philadelphia.

13. Martha Tesema, "Everything You Need to Know about Alison Ettel, aka 'Permit Patty,'" *Mashable*, June 24, 2018, https://mashable.com/article/permit-patty-oakland.

14. Joyce He and Sarah Kaplan "The Debate About Quotas," Gender and the Economy, October 26, 2017, https://www.gendereconomy.org/the-debate-about-quotas/. ("Evidence from the Norwegian experience suggests that few female board members who had been beneficiaries of the quotas reported feeling stigmatized or isolated. This was in part because with a 40% quota, women achieved a critical mass on every board. At 40% representation, a group is no longer marginalized.")

15. Nguyen, "The Fiction of 'Asian-American.'"

16. Santokh Anant, "The Need to Belong," *Canada's Mental Health* 14, no. 2 (1966): 21–27; Bonnie Hagerty, Judith Lynch-Sauer, Kathleen Patusky, Maria Bouwsema, and Peggy Collier, "Sense of Belonging: A Vital Mental Health Concept," *Archives of Psychiatric Nursing* 6, no. 3 (1992): 172–77, https://doi.org/10.1016/0883-9417(92)90028-H.

17. Some scholars, for example, have focused on the relational and spatial elements of belonging. See, e.g., Eva Youkhana, "A Conceptual Shift in Studies of Belonging and the Politics of Belonging," *Social Inclusion* 3, no. 4 (2015), https://doi.org/10.17645/si.v3i4.150; Marco Antonsich, "Searching for Belonging—An Analytical Framework," *Geography Compass* 4, no. 6 (2010), https://doi.org/10.1111/j.1749-8198.2009.00317.x.

18. See, e.g., Gretchen Rubin, *The Happiness Project* (New York: HarperCollins, 2018); Joachim Weimann, Andreas Knabe, and Ronnie Schöb, *Measuring Happiness: The Economics of Cuisine* (Cambridge, MA: MIT Press, 2016); Misha Gajewski, "Turns Out We Don't Really Know How to Measure Happiness," *Forbes*, December 9, 2020, https://www.forbes.com/sites/mishagajewski/2020/12/09/turns-out-we-dont-really-know-how-to-measure-happiness/?sh=31de2e535fdd. Note that just because something is hard to define, that doesn't mean it can't be measured, or

that a measuring system can't be employed to evaluate it. Utilitarianism and efficiency metrics are based on measures of happiness and well-being.

19. Bonnie Hagerty and Kathleen Patusky, "Developing a Measure of Sense of Belonging," *Nursing Research* 44, no. 1 (1995): 9–13, https://doi.org/10.1097/00006199-199501000-00003.

20. See, e.g., Social Connectedness Scale (SCS), Richard M. Lee, and Steven B. Robbins, "Measuring Belongingness: The Social Connectedness and the Social Assurance Scales," *Journal of Counseling Psychology* 42, no. 2 (1995): 232–41, https://doi.org/10.1037/0022-0167.42.2.232; General Belongingness Scale (GBS), Glenn P. Malone, David R. Pillow, and Augustine Osman, "The General Belongingness Scale (GBS): Assessing Achieved Belongingness," *Personality and Individual Differences* 52, no. 3 (2012): 311–16, https://doi.org/10.1016/j.paid.2011.10.027; Challenged Sense of Belonging Scale (CSBC), Lukas M. Fuchs, Jannes Jacobsen, Lena Walther, et al., "The Challenged Sense of Belonging Scale (CSBS)—A Validation Study in English, Arabic, and Farsi/Dari among Refugees and Asylum Seekers in Germany," *Measurement Instruments for the Social Sciences* 3, no. 3 (2021), https://doi.org/10.1186/s42409-021-00021-y. There are others but these are some of the more prominent among the various scales.

21. See, e.g., Center for Talent Innovation, "The Power of Belonging: What It Is and Why It Matters in Today's Workplace," Coqual, 2020; "Defining and Measuring Belonging at UCSF—Belonging Index," Learning & Organization Development (L&OD) Employee Engagement, 2020, https://devlearning.ucsf.edu/belonging-index.

22. In many cases, it is possible that such conditions may be highly correlated with the sense or experience of belonging. If so, we would feel confident in identifying them as definitional elements, even if their presence does not suffice to create belonging. Unfortunately, we are unaware of any study or effort that has attempted to identify the material conditions of belonging in this way.

23. Karen Barad, *Meeting the Universe Halfway: Quantum Physics and the Entanglement of Matter and Meaning* (Durham, NC: Duke University Press, 2006).

24. James Moore, "What Is the Sense of Agency and Why Does it Matter?," *Frontiers in Psychology* 7, no. 1272 (2016), https://www.ncbi.nlm.nih.gov/pmc/articles/PMC5002400/.

25. To help us understand this concept in practice, we designed and recruited an "artist in residence," filled first by Christine Wong Yap, to explore this concept. She interviewed dozens of people in the Bay Area, and held workshops in community based organizations. After reviewing her interviews, Christine surfaced fifteen distinct elements that recurred. Christine Wong Yap, *100 Stories of Belonging in the S.F. Bay Area* (Berkeley, CA: Haas Institute for a Fair and Inclusive Society, 2019).

26. For a powerful account of this element, see Charles Taylor, "The Politics of Recognition," in *Multiculturalism: Examining the Politics of Recognition*, ed. Amy Guttman (Princeton, NJ: Princeton University Press, 1994), 25–73. We recognized that "visibility" is ableist language, which is why we emphasize "recognition" in this element.

27. Moore, "What Is the Sense of Agency?"

28. Albert O. Hirschman, *Exit, Voice, and Loyalty: Responses to Decline in Firms, Organizations, and States* (Cambridge, MA: Harvard University Press, 1970); Stacy Ulbig, "Voice Is Not Enough: The Importance of Influence in Political Trust and Policy Assessments," *Public Opinion Quarterly* 72, no. 3 (2008): 523–39, https://www.jstor.org/stable/25167645.

29. James Baldwin and Sol Stein, *Native Sons: A Friendship That Created One of the Greatest Works of the 20th Century: Notes of a Native Son* (New York: Ballantine Books, 2004), 96–97.

30. We acknowledge that this view puts us at odds with many mainstream psychologists studying belonging, where the consensus appears to be that belonging is ultimately subjective. We admit it has a large subjective component, but nonetheless assert the above noted objective preconditions.

31. A. H. Maslow, "A Theory of Human," *Psychological Review*, no. 50 (1943): 370–96, https://scholar.google.com/scholar_url?url=http://eksis.ditpsmk.net/uploads/book/file/FAB7C886-3C74-4FE5-8645-341019EF8E8F/_Maslow__a_Theory_of_Human_Motivation_BookFi.org_.pdf&hl=en&sa=X&ei=yiPiYb79JYvoyATgzL_ABw&scisig=AAGBfm2c7ZJcLlvR7FNM19TARLe2J81G5g&oi=scholarr.

32. Walzer, "Citizenship"; john a. powell, "The Needs of Members in a Legitimate Democratic State," *Santa Clara Law Review* 44, no. 4 (2004), http://digitalcommons.law.scu.edu/lawreview/vol44/iss4/2; john a. powell, "Poverty and Race Through a Belonging Lens," *Policy Matters* 1, no. 5 (2012), https://www.law.berkeley.edu/files/PolicyMatters_powell_V4.pdf.

33. Orlando Patterson, *Slavery and Social Death: A Comparative Study* (Cambridge, MA: Harvard University Press, 1982).

34. See, e.g., Robert J. Taormina and Jennifer H. Gao, "Maslow and the Motivation Hierarchy: Measuring Satisfaction of the Needs," *American Journal of Psychology* 126, no. 2 (2013): 158, https://doi-org.libproxy.berkeley.edu/10.5406/amerjpsyc.126.2.0155; Tracy Bower, "Missing Your People: Why Belonging Is So Important and How to Create It," *Forbes*, January 10, 2021, https://www.forbes.com/sites/tracybrower/2021/01/10/missing-your-people-why-belonging-is-so-important-and-how-to-create-it/?sh=3a97d4de7c43. In fact, this need may extend beyond the human species to primates and other mammals.

35. Kirsten Weir, "The Lasting Impact of Neglect," *Monitor on Psychology* 45, no. 6 (2014): 36, https://www.apa.org/monitor/2014/06/neglect.

36. Diana Lang et al., "René Spitz: The Effects of Emotional Deprivation," accessed November 9, 2022, https://iastate.pressbooks.pub/parentingfamilydiversity/chapter/spitz/.

37. Bruce D. Perry and Maia Szalavitz, *Born for Love: Why Empathy Is Essential—and Endangered* (New York: Harper, 2011), 52–54.

38. Rachel Bachner-Melman and Richard P. Ebstein, "The Role of Oxytocin and Vasopressin in Emotional and Social Behaviors," in *Handbook of Clinical Neurology* 124, ed. Eric Fliers, Johannes A. Romijn, and Márta Korbonits (Cambride, MA: Elsevier, 2014), 53–68, https://doi-org.libproxy.berkeley.edu/10.1016/B978-0-444-59602-4.00004-6.

39. Katie Hafner, "Researchers Confront an Epidemic of Loneliness," *New York Times*, September 5, 2016, https://www.nytimes.com/2016/09/06/health/lonliness-aging-health-effects.html.

40. "Loneliness and Social Isolation Linked to Serious Health Conditions," Centers for Disease Control and Prevention, https://www.cdc.gov/aging/publications/features/lonely-older-adults.html.

41. Nicole K. Valtorta, Mona Kanaan, Simon Gilbody, Sara Ronzi, and Barbara Hanratty, "Loneliness and Social Isolation as Risk Factors for Coronary Heart Disease and Stroke: Systematic Review and Meta-Analysis of Longitudinal Observational Studies," *Heart* 102 (2016): 1009–16, https://heart.bmj.com/content/102/13/1009.

42. "Loneliness and Social Isolation Linked to Serious Health Conditions," Centers for Disease Control and Prevention, n.d., https://www.cdc.gov/aging/publications/features/lonely-older-adults.html.

43. "What Are the Effects of Solitary Confinement on Health?" *Medical News Today*, https://www.medicalnewstoday.com/articles/solitary-confinement-effects#summary.

44. Tiana Herring, "The Research Is Clear: Solitary Confinement Causes Long-Lasting Harm," Prison Policy Initiative, December 8, 2020, https://www.prisonpolicy.org/blog/2020/12/08/solitary_symposium/.

45. Sebastian Junger, *Tribe: On Homecoming and Belonging* (New York: Simon & Schuster, 2016), 89.

46. See, e.g., Center for Talent Innovation, "The Power of Belonging: What It Is and Why It Matters in Today's Workplace (Key Findings)," Coqual, 2020.

47. Nichole Argo and Hammad Sheikh, *The Belonging Barometer: The State of Belonging in America*, Over Zero, 2023, https://www.projectoverzero.org/media-and-publications/belongingbarometer. (Disclosure: we were advisors and expert reviewers on this project.)

48. Argo and Sheikh, *The Belonging Barometer*, vi.

49. Office of the Assistant Secretary for Health, "New Surgeon General Advisory Raises Alarm about the Devastating Impact of the Epidemic of Loneliness and

Isolation in the United States," May 3, 2023, https://www.hhs.gov/about/news/ 2023/05/03/new-surgeon-general-advisory-raises-alarm-about-devastating-impact -epidemic-loneliness-isolation-united-states.html. See also his contemporaneous op-ed: Vivek H. Murthy, "Surgeon General: We Have Become a Lonely Nation. It's Time to Fix That," *New York Times*, April 30, 2023, https://www.nytimes.com/ 2023/04/30/opinion/loneliness-epidemic-america.html.

50. Kim Samuel, "How Do We Tackle an Epidemic of Loneliness and Foster a Sense of Belonging?" *Independent*, May 7, 2023, https://www.independent.co .uk/voices/minister-loneliness-stuart-andrew-health-epidemic-b2334312.html.

51. Fukuyama, *Identity*, 16–24; David Brooks, "All Politics Is Thymotic," *New York Times*, March 19, 2006, https://www.nytimes.com/2006/03/19/opinion/ all-politics-is-thymotic.html; David Brooks, "Globalization Is Over. The Global Culture Wars Have Begun," *New York Times*, April 8, 2022, https://www.nytimes .com/2022/04/08/opinion/globalization-global-culture-war.html.

52. See e.g., Marx, *Status and Culture;* Michelle Goldberg, "The Book That Explains Our Cultural Stagnation," New York Times, August 29, 2022, https://www .nytimes.com/2022/08/29/opinion/status-culture-book.html.

53. Brooks, "All Politics Is Thymotic." This dynamic is remarkably similar to the dynamics described in Chapters 2 and 3, regarding identity affiliation, group positionality, and identity threats.

54. Hannah Arendt, *The Origins of Totalitarianism* (New York: Schocken Books, 1951), 173; Samantha Rose Hill, "Not Belonging to the World," *Lapham's Quarterly*, October 14, 2021, https://www.laphamsquarterly.org/roundtable/not -belonging-world.

55. Arendt, *The Origins of Totalitarianism*, 84.

56. Emine Battal, "Dying and/or Killing for the Faith: New Religious Movements and Violence," *Insan & Toplum* 6, no. 1 (June 2016): 7–22, https://doi.org/dx .doi.org/10.12658/human.society.6.11.M0143.

57. Amy Chua, *Political Tribes: Group Instinct and the Fate of Nations* (New York: Penguin Press, 2018), 109.

58. Morgane Rousselet et al., "Cult Membership: What Factors Contribute to Joining or Leaving?" *Psychiatry Research* 257 (2017): 27–33, https://doi.org/10.1016/ j.psychres.2017.07.018.

59. Rukmini Callimachi and Catherine Porter, "2 American Wives of ISIS Militants Want to Return Home," *New York Times*, February 19, 2019, https://www .nytimes.com/2019/02/19/us/islamic-state-american-women.html.

60. Les Picker, "Where Are ISIS's Foreign Fighters Coming From?" National Bureau of Economic Research, *Digest*, no. 6 (2016): 6, https://www.nber.org/ digest/jun16/where-are-isiss-foreign-fighters-coming.

61. Caitlin Gibson, "'Do You Have White Teenage Sons? Listen Up.' How White Supremacists Are Recruiting Boys Online," *Washington Post*, September 17, 2019, https://www.washingtonpost.com/lifestyle/on-parenting/do-you-have-white-teenage-sons-listen-up-how-white-supremacists-are-recruiting-boys-online/2019/09/17/f081e806-d3d5-11e9-9343-40db57cf6abd_story.html; Kevin Roose, "The Making of a YouTube Radical," *New York Times*, June 8, 2019, https://www.nytimes.com/interactive/2019/06/08/technology/youtube-radical.html.

62. Joanna Schroeder, "Racists Are Recruiting. Watch Your White Sons," *New York Times*, October 12, 2019, https://www.nytimes.com/2019/10/12/opinion/sunday/white-supremacist-recruitment.html.

63. David French, "The Rage and Joy of MAGA America," *New York Times*, July 6, 2023, https://www.nytimes.com/2023/07/06/opinion/maga-america-trump.html.

64. Smucker, *Hegemony How-To*, 38.

65. Smucker, *Hegemony How-To*, 98–99.

66. Michael Ignatieff, *Blood and Belonging: Journeys into the New Nationalism* (New York: Farrar, Straus & Giroux, 1993).

67. Harari, *Sapiens*, 26–27.

68. Harari, *Sapiens*, 22–24.

69. In fact, Benedict Anderson claims that this ability to construct an imagined community is distinctly modern. Benedict Anderson, *Imagined Communities: Reflections on the Origin and Spread of Nationalism* (Brooklyn, NY: Verso Books, 1983).

70. Theresa M. Duello, Shawna Rivedal, Colton Wickland, and Annika Weller, "Race and Genetics versus 'Race' in Genetics: A Systematic Review of the Use of African Ancestry in Genetic Studies," *Evolution, Medicine, and Public Health* 9, no. 1 (2021): 232–45, https://doi.org/10.1093/emph/eoab018.

71. Yoram Hazony, *The Virtue of Nationalism* (New York: Basic Books, 2018).

72. Kevin M. F. Platt, "The Profound Irony of Canceling Everything Russian," *New York Times*, April 22, 2022, https://www.nytimes.com/2022/04/22/opinion/russian-artists-culture-boycotts.html.

73. Samuel Huntington, *The Clash of Civilizations and the Remaking of World Order* (New York: Simon & Schuster, 1996).

74. Huntington, *The Clash of Civilizations*.

75. Falk, *Stigma*.

76. "Abandoning the Stigma of Leprosy," editorial, *Lancet* 393, no. 10170 (2019), https://doi.org/10.1016/S0140-6736(19)30164-3.

77. Amin Maalouf, *In the Name of Identity: Violence and the Need to Belong*, trans. Barbara Bray (New York: Penguin Books, 2001), 87–88.

78. Maalouf, *In the Name of Identity*, 89–90. Francis Fukuyama makes a very similar set of observations. Fukuyama, *Identity*, 68–69.

79. Ezra Klein, "The Enemies of Liberalism Are Showing Us What It Really Means," *New York Times*, April 3, 2022, https://www.nytimes.com/2022/04/03/opinion/putin-ukraine-liberalism.html.

80. Fukuyama, "A Country of Their Own."

81. Matthew Rose, *A World after Liberalism: Philosophers of the Radical Right* (New Haven, CT: Yale University Press, 2021).

82. Aja Romano, "A History of 'Wokeness,'" Vox, October 9, 2020, https://www.vox.com/culture/21437879/stay-woke-wokeness-history-origin-evolution-controversy.

83. Wes Carpenter, *Woke Religion: Unmasking the False Gospel of Social Justice* (Greenville, SC: Ambassador International, 2021); John McWhorter, *Woke Racism: How a New Religion Has Betrayed Black America* (New York: Portfolio, 2021).

84. Tyler Cowen, "Why Wokeism Will Rule the World," Bloomberg, September 19, 2021, https://www.bloomberg.com/opinion/articles/2021-09-19/woke-movement-is-global-and-america-should-be-mostly-proud.

85. Sidanius and Pratto, *Social Dominance*. Sidanius and Pratto appear similarly motivated to propound a theory that can broadly account for the many expressions of social group inequality observed in the world. Although some scholars claim that this particular theory has been falsified (on some grounds we agree with), it is not our aim to discredit any particular theory here. John C. Turner and Katherine J. Reynolds, "Why Social Dominance Theory Has Been Falsified," *British Journal of Social Psychology* 42 (2003): 199–206, https://doi.org/10.1348/014466603322127184. Rather, we hope to bring these scholars and perspectives into a conversation aimed at a similar set of goals, of how to build a world with less social group inequality and more belonging.

86. Huntington makes a version of this argument in another book, *Who Are We?*, examining certain cultural elements that he claims define American identity.

87. Sara Grossman, "In Discussion with Christine Wong Yap," Othering & Belonging Institute, April 10, 2019, https://belonging.berkeley.edu/blog-responding-racial-demagoguery.

88. Paul Tough, "Who Gets to Graduate?" *New York Times*, May 15, 2014, https://www.nytimes.com/2014/05/18/magazine/who-gets-to-graduate.html.

89. David Yeager et al., "A National Experiment Reveals Where a Growth Mindset Improves Achievement," *Nature* 573 (2019): 364–69, https://doi.org/10.1038/s41586-019-1466-y; "A Growth Mindset Intervention Can Change Students' Grades if School Culture Is Supportive," *UT News*, August 7, 2019, https://news

.utexas.edu/2019/08/07/a-growth-mindset-intervention-can-change-students
-grades-if-school-culture-is-supportive/.

90. Geoffrey Cohen, *Belonging: The Science of Creating Connection and Bridging Divides* (New York: Norton, 2022), 175–82.

91. Evelyn Hu-DeHart, "The History, Development and Future of Ethnic Studies," *Phi Delta Kappa* 75, no. 1 (1993): 50–54, https://www.jstor.org/stable/20405023.

92. Sidanius and Pratto, *Social Dominance*, 39.

93. Hirschman, *Exit, Voice, and Loyalty*.

94. Yuval Levin, *A Time to Build: From Family and Community to Congress and the Campus, How Recommitting to Our Institutions Can Revive the American Dream* (New York: Basic Books, 2020), 15.

95. Robert Putnam, *Bowling Alone: The Collapse and Revival of American Community* (New York: Simon & Schuester, 2000). See also Alexandra Hudson, "Bowling Alone at Twenty," *National Affairs*, Fall 2020, https://www.nationalaffairs.com/publications/detail/bowling-alone-at-twenty.

96. Levin, *A Time to Build*, 17.

97. Levin notes the ambiguity in the term *institutions*, but ultimately defines them as "durable forms of common law . . . frameworks and structures of what we do together." He notes that some institutions are organizations, but others, like the family or marriage, are not. Levin, *A Time to Build*, 17.

98. Levin, *A Time to Build*, 20.

99. Adrienne Clarkson, *Belonging: The Paradox of Citizenship* (Toronto: House of Anansi Press, 2014), 4–5, 168–71.

100. "The Role of Education," Thomas Jefferson's Monticello, accessed March 5, 2023, https://www.monticello.org/the-art-of-citizenship/the-role-of-education/#:~:text=A%20Closer%20Look-,The%20Idea,partially%20achieved%20his%20larger%20goals; John Dewey, *Democracy and Education: An Introduction to the Philosophy of Education* (1916; repr., Gorham, ME: Myers Education Press, 2018).

101. Brown v. Bd. of Educ., 347 U.S. 483, 493.

102. Gordon S. Wood, *Power and Liberty: Constitutionalism in the American Revolution* (Oxford: Oxford University Press, 2021).

103. See, e.g., Robert H. Nelson, "Homeowners Associations in Historical Perspective," *Public Administration Review* 71, no. 4 (2011): 546–49; Michael Williams, *Neighborhood Organizations: Seeds of a New Urban Life* (Westport, CT: Greenwood Press, 1985); Hugh Hawkins, *Banding Together: The Rise of National Associations in American Higher Education* (Baltimore: Johns Hopkins University Press, 1992).

104. Ghassan Hage, *White Nation: Fantasies of White Supremacy in a Multicultural Society* (Annandale, Australia: Pluto Press, 1998), 108.

105. "National Service: An Idea Whose Time Has Come," *New York Times*, May 14, 2020, https://www.nytimes.com/2020/05/14/opinion/letters/coronavirus -national-service.html.

106. Thomas F. Pettigrew, "Intergroup Contact Theory," *Annual Review of Psychology* 49, no. 1 (1998): 65–85, https://doi.org/10.1146/annurev.psych.49.1.65. See generally Gordon W. Allport, *The Nature of Prejudice* (Boston: Addison-Wesley, 1954); Thomas F. Pettigrew and L. R. Tropp, "A Meta-Analytic Test of Intergroup Contact Theory," *Journal of Personality and Social Psychology* 90, no. 5 (2006): 751–83, https://doi.apa.org/doiLanding?doi=10.1037/0022-3514.90.5.751; Tania Singer, "Empathy and Compassion," *Current Biology* 24, no. 18 (2014), https://doi.org/10 .1016/j.cub.2014.06.054.

107. Norimitsu Onishi and Constant Méheut, "In France's Military, Muslims Find a Tolerance That Is Elusive Elsewhere," *New York Times,* June 26, 2021, https:// www.nytimes.com/2021/06/26/world/europe/in-frances-military-muslims-find-a -tolerance-that-is-elusive-elsewhere.html.

108. Onishi and Méheut, "Muslims Find a Tolerance."

109. Onishi and Méheut, "Muslims Find a Tolerance."

110. Catherine Kim, "Pete Buttigieg Calls for Expanding National Service," Vox, July 3, 2019, https://www.vox.com/2019/7/3/20680963/pete-buttigieg-expand -national-service.

111. David Brooks, "We Need National Service. Now," *New York Times*, May 7, 2020, https://www.nytimes.com/2020/05/07/opinion/national-service -americorps-coronavirus.html.

112. "Should Young Americans Be Required to Give a Year of Service?" editorial, *New York Times*, May 1, 2021, https://www.nytimes.com/2021/05/01/opinion/ us-national-service-draft.html.

113. Jay Caspian Kang, "The Case for Mandatory National Service," *New York Times*, August 4, 2022, https://www.nytimes.com/2022/08/04/opinion/ mandatory-national-service.html.

114. "The African American Odyssey: A Quest for Full Citizenship," Library of Congress, accessed July 7, 2023, https://www.loc.gov/exhibits/african-american -odyssey/civil-rights-era.html; Tom W. Smith and Paul B. Sheatsley, *American Attitudes toward Race Relations*, National Opinion Research Center, University of Chicago, 1984, 50.

115. Andrew R. Flores, *National Trends in Public Opinion on LGBT Rights in the United States*, Williams Institute, UCLA School of Law, 2014, 5–7; Obergefell

v. Hodges, 576 U.S 644 (2015) (ruling that same-sex couples enjoy equal right to marriage under the Constitution).

116. Nora McGreevy, "The ADA Was a Monumental Achievement 30 Years Ago, but the Fight for Equal Rights Continues," *Smithsonian*, July 24, 2020, https://www.smithsonianmag.com/history/history-30-years-since-signing-americans-disabilities-act-180975409/.

117. Joseph Shapiro, "In Helping Those with Disabilities, ADA Improves Access for All," NPR, July 24, 2015, https://www.npr.org/2015/07/24/423230927/-a-gift-to-the-non-disabled-at-25-the-ada-improves-access-for-all.

118. Shapiro, "In Helping Those with Disabilities."

119. "Section 7(r) of the Fair Labor Standards Act—Break Time for Nursing Mothers Provision," U.S. Department of Labor, accessed on January 5, 2021, https://www.dol.gov/agencies/whd/nursing-mothers/law.

120. Religious Freedom Restoration Act of 1993, Pub. L. 103–141, 107 Stat. 1488 (1993); Voting Rights Act of 1965, Sec. 4, Pub. L. 89–110, 79 Stat. 437 (1965).

121. Joe Carter, "5 Facts About the Religious Freedom Restoration Act," Ethics & Religious Liberty Commission, January 18, 2018, https://erlc.com/resource-library/articles/5-facts-about-the-religious-freedom-restoration-act/.

122. Voting Rights Act of 1965, 52 U.S.C. § 5 (1965).

123. "The John Lewis Voting Rights Advancement Act," Brennan Center for Justice, December 22, 2021, https://www.brennancenter.org/our-work/research-reports/john-lewis-voting-rights-advancement-act.

124. john a. powell and Rachel Heydemann, "On Bridging: Evidence and Guidance from Real-World Cases," Othering and Belonging Institute, August 19, 2020, https://belonging.berkeley.edu/on-bridging.

125. "Listening as a Political De-Polarizer," editorial, *Christian Science Monitor*, July 12, 2022, https://www.csmonitor.com/Commentary/the-monitors-view/2022/0712/Listening-as-a-political-de-polarizer.

126. Irwin Gratz, "In New Book, a Progressive Maine Lawmaker Urges Democrats to Pay More Attention to Rural Voters," Maine Public Radio, May 4, 2022, https://www.mainepublic.org/politics/2022-05-04/in-new-book-a-progressive-maine-lawmaker-urges-democrats-to-pay-more-attention-to-rural-voters.

127. Emma Green, "Jimmy Carter Makes One Final Push to End Racism," *Atlantic*, May 31, 2016, https://www.theatlantic.com/politics/archive/2016/05/jimmy-carter-makes-one-final-push-to-end-racism/484859/.

128. Mark Wingfield, "New Baptist Covenant Shifts Gears to Convene, Connect and Communicate," Baptist News, February 22, 2022, https://baptistnews.com/article/new-baptist-covenant-shifts-gears-to-convene-connect-and-communicate/.

129. D. Amari Jackson, "The Lasting Legacy of the 1992 Watts Gang Truce," Atlanta Black Star, April 29, 2017, https://atlantablackstar.com/2017/04/29/lasting-legacy-1992-watts-gang-truce/.

130. Paul S. Adler and Seok-Woo Kwon, "Social Capital: Prospects for a New Concept," *Academy of Management Review* 27, no. 1 (2002): 17–40, https://doi.org/10.2307/4134367.

CHAPTER 6

1. See Bruno Bauer, *The Jewish Question* (Braunschweig, 1843); Karl Marx, "On the Jewish Question," Paris, 1844.

2. john a. powell, Stephen Menendian, and Wendy Ake, *Targeted Universalism: Policy and Practice* (Berkeley, CA: Haas Institute for a Fair and Inclusive Society, 2019), https://belonging.berkeley.edu/sites/default/files/targeted_universalism_primer.pdf?file=1&force=1.

3. Jerrold E. Siegel, *The Idea of the Self: Thought and Experience in Western Europe since the Seventeenth Century* (New York: Cambridge University Press, 2005).

4. René Descartes, *Discourse on the Method: Of Rightly Conducting One's Reason and of Seeking Truth in the Sciences*, trans. John Veitch (Chicago: Open Court, 1910), 35.

5. john a. powell and Stephen Menendian, "Remaking Law: Moving Beyond Enlightenment Jurisprudence," *Saint Louis University Law Journal* 54, no. 4 (2010), https://scholarship.law.slu.edu/lj/vol54/iss4/3.

6. René Descartes, *Meditations on First Philosophy* (Oxford: Oxford University Press, 2008); Lisa Shapiro, "Cartesian Selves," in *Descartes' Meditations: A Critical Guide*, ed. Karen Detlefsen (Cambridge: Cambridge University Press, 2012), 226–42, https://doi.org/10.1017/CBO9781139030731.017.

7. Descartes, *Discourse on the Method*, 43, 66.

8. Ernst Cassirer, *The Philosophy of the Enlightenment* (Princeton, NJ: Princeton University Press, 1951), 154–57, 163, 252.

9. John Scott, "Rational Choice Theory," in *Understanding Contemporary Society: Theories of the Present* (Sage, 2000), https://www.sisd.net/cms/lib/TX01001452/Centricity/Domain/170/Rational%20Choice%20Theory%20Reading.pdf; Jonathan Levin and Paul Milgrom, "Introduction to Choice Theory," 2004, https://web.stanford.edu/~jdlevin/Econ%20202/Choice%20Theory.pdf; Melanie Lockert, "Rational Choice Theory: A School of Thought That Predicts Economic and Social Behaviors," *Business Insider*, December 1, 2021, https://www.businessinsider.com/rational-choice-theory. Although it should be noted than many recent innovations and developments in economics are based on challenge to these assumptions, like

the field of behavioral economics. See Daniel Kahneman, *Thinking, Fast and Slow* (New York: Farrar, Straus & Giroux, 2011).

10. See William Sweet and Paul Groarke, "Bentham, Jeremy: Classical School," in *Encyclopedia of Criminological Theory* (Thousand Oaks, CA: Sage, 2010), 89–95, https://study.sagepub.com/system/files/Bentham%2C_Jeremy_-_Classical _School.pdf, which describes Jeremy Bentham, the English utilitarian philosopher's stance on morality, the law, and punishment based on the idea that individual actors make rational choices based on anticipated pleasure and pain. See also Scott, "Rational Choice Theory."

11. Fukuyama, *Identity*, 28.

12. Fukuyama, *Identity*, 33.

13. John Locke, *An Essay Concerning Human Understanding: Book II: Ideas* (1690; repr., Canada: Early Modern Texts, last updated 2007), 18, https://www .earlymoderntexts.com/assets/pdfs/locke1690book2.pdf.

14. Rosi Braidotti, *The Posthuman* (Cambridge, UK; Malden, MA: Polity Press, 2013), 24. Judith Butler has also observed a similar gendered dichotomy running through Western philosophical thought. "In the philosophical tradition that begins with Plato and continues through Descartes, Husserl, and Sartre, the ontological distinction between soul (consciousness, mind) and body invariably supports relations of political and psychic subordination and hierarchy. . . .The cultural associations of mind with masculinity and body with femininity are well documented within the field of philosophy and feminism." Butler, *Gender Trouble*, 16.

15. ST §27.

16. Imani Perry, "Seafaring, Sovereignty, and the Self: Of Patriarchy and the Conditions of Modernity," in *Vexy Thing: On Gender and Liberation* (Durham, NC: Duke University Press, 2018), 14–41, https://doi.org/10.1215/9781478002277.

17. Genevieve Lloyd, "The Man of Reason," *Metaphilosophy* 10, no. 1 (1979): 23–24, http://www.jstor.org/stable/24435599.

18. Mark Tunick, "Tolerant Imperialism: John Stuart Mill's Defense of British Rule in India," *Review of Politics* 68, no. 4 (2006): 586–611, https://www.jstor.org/ stable/20452826.

19. See, e.g., Tunick, "Tolerant Imperialism."

20. Justin D. Levinson, "SuperBias: The Collision of Behavioral Economics and Implicit Social Cognition," *Akron Law Review* 45, no. 3 (2012), https://ideaexchange .uakron.edu/akronlawreview/vol45/iss3/4.

21. This is a subject we have developed more fully elsewhere. See powell and Menendian, "Remaking Law."

22. George Herbert Mead, *Mind, Self, and Society from the Standpoint of a Social Behaviorist* (Chicago: University of Chicago Press, 1934), 140.

23. Fukuyama, *Identity*, 56.

24. Charles Taylor, *Sources of the Self: The Making of the Modern Identity* (Cambridge, MA: Harvard University Press, 1989).

25. Roberto Mangabeira Unger, *The Self Awakened: Pragmatism Unbound* (Cambridge, MA: Harvard University Press, 2009).

26. Immanuel Kant, *Groundwork of the Metaphysics of Morals*, trans. Mary Gregor and Jens Timmermann (1785; repr., Cambridge: Cambridge University Press, 2011).

27. And, as we will see, this recognition occurs internally as well.

28. Marilynn B. Brewer, "The Social Self: On Being the Same and Different at the Same Time," *Personality and Psychology Bulletin* 17, no. 5 (1991): 475–82, https://doi.org/10.1177/0146167291175001. Brewer has also developed a theory that helps explain how humans balance the need to belong with the need for differentiation, which she calls "optimal distinctiveness theory." "Optimal Distinctiveness Theory," Psychology, http://psychology.iresearchnet.com/social-psychology/social-psychology-theories/optimal-distinctiveness-theory/.

29. Aydan Gülerce, "Selfing *as, with*, and *without* Othering: Dialogical (im)possibilities with Dialogical Self Theory," *Culture & Psychology* 20, no. 2 (2014): 244–55.

30. George Herbert Mead, "The Self and the Organism," in *Mind, Self, and Society*, 135–44.

31. john a. powell, "The Multiple Self: Exploring between and beyond Modernity and Postmodernity," *Minnesota Law Review* 81 (1997): 1481–1520, https://scholarship.law.umn.edu/mlr/1669.

32. powell, "The Multiple Self."

33. Louise Vanden Poel and Dirk Hermans, "Narrative Coherence and Identity: Associations with Psychological Well-Being and Internalizing Symptoms," *Frontiers in Psychology* 10 (2019), https://doi.org/10.3389/fpsyg.2019.01171; Lotte van Doeselaar, Andrik I. Becht, Theo A. Klimstra, and Wim H. J. Meeus, "A Review and Integration of Three Key Components of Identity Development: Distinctiveness, Coherence, and Continuity," *European Psychologist* 23, no. 4 (2018), https://doi.org/10.1027/1016-9040/a000334.

34. Kimberly Rogers and Kaitlin Boyle, "Identity Coherence, Social Stress, and Well-Being," paper presented at Modeling Social Interactions: New Directions in Affect Control Theory, Hanover, NH, 2017. Our "selves" do not always agree or hold the same values or perspective. There is potential inner conflict.

35. Marchese, "Jerrod Carmichael."

36. Smucker, *Hegemony How-To*, 37.

37. Smucker, *Hegemony How-To*, 75.

38. See also Fathali M. Moghaddam, *Mutual Radicalization: How Groups and Nations Drive Each Other to Extremes* (Washington, DC: American Psychological Association, 2018), 31–32.

39. Thomas B. Edsall, "We're Staring at Our Phones, Full of Rage for 'the Other Side,'" *New York Times*, June 15, 2022, https://www.nytimes.com/2022/06/15/opinion/social-media-polarization-democracy.html.

40. Jay Van Bavel and Packer, *The Power of Us*, 192 (describing a revealing exercise by Jackson Katz on the salience of gender identity due to differential risks).

41. Ismail Muhammad, "Maggie Nelson Wants to Redefine 'Freedom,'" *New York Times Magazine*, September 2, 2021, https://www.nytimes.com/2021/09/02/magazine/maggie-nelson-on-freedom.html.

42. Jonathan Smucker also calls this "encapsulation." See Smucker, *Hegemony How-To*, 79.

43. powell and Heydemann, "On Bridging."

44. Chimamanda Ngozi Adichie, "The Danger of a Single Story," filmed 2009, TED video, https://www.ted.com/talks/chimamanda_ngozi_adichie_the_danger_of_a_single_story?language=en.

45. Maalouf, *In the Name of Identity*, 30.

46. The "twenty statement task" makes this evident in practice, which we noted in a previous endnote. See Van Bavel and Packer, *The Power of Us*, 22.

47. "Malcolm X Pleased by Whites' Attitude on Trip to Mecca," *New York Times*, May 8, 1964, https://www.nytimes.com/1964/05/08/archives/malcolm-x-pleased-by-whites-attitude-on-trip-to-mecca.html.

48. Van Bavel and Packer, *The Power of Us*, 19, 160 (describing studies in which new identities had observed effects).

49. Van Bavel and Packer, *The Power of Us*, 22, citing Stephen D. Reicher et al., "Core Disgust Is Attenuated by Ingroup Relations," *PNAS* 113, no. 10 (2016): 2631–35, https://doi.org/10.1073/pnas.1517027113.

50. Van Bavel and Packer, *The Power of Us*, 22.

51. McWhorter, *Words on the Move*, 3.

52. McWhorter, *Words on the Move*, 3.

53. See, for example, Serrato, "Latino/a."

54. powell and Menendian, "Remaking Law," 1113.

55. Bruno Latour, *Down to Earth: Politics in the New Climatic Regime* (Cambridge: Polity Press, 2018).

56. Marshall Sahlins, *What Kinship Is—and Is Not* (Chicago: University of Chicago Press, 2013), 28.

57. Sahlins, *What Kinship Is*, 18–20. See also Joel Robbins, "On Kinship and Comparison, Intersubjectivity and Mutuality of Being," *HAU: Journal of Ethnographic Theory* 12, no. 2 (2013): 309–16, https://doi.org/10.14318/hau3.2.022.

58. Siddhartha Deb, "'They Are Manufacturing Foreigners': How India Disenfranchises Muslims," *New York Times*, September 15, 2021, https://www.nytimes.com/2021/09/15/magazine/india-assam-muslims.html. ("Much of the anxiety among the Assamese springs from that time.") This episode is described in more detail in the supplementary chapter.

59. Dan T. Carter, "The Anatomy of Fear: The Christmas Day Insurrection Scare of 1865," *Journal of Southern History* 42, no. 3 (1976): 345–64, https://doi.org/10.2307/2207156.

60. Helen Mirren, "We're All in this Together," speech, Tulane University, May 20, 2017, *Time*, https://time.com/4787502/helen-mirren-speech-tulane-university-commencement-graduation-2017/.

61. Maalouf, *In the Name of Identity*, 139–40.

62. Maalouf, *In the Name of Identity*, 140.

63. Fukuyama, *Identity*, 141.

64. Hilal Isler, "James Baldwin Might Have Been Most at Home in Istanbul," Lit Hub, March 29, 2019, https://lithub.com/james-baldwin-might-have-been-most-at-home-in-istanbul/.

65. David Brooks, "The Nuclear Family Was a Mistake," *Atlantic*, March 2020, https://www.theatlantic.com/magazine/archive/2020/03/the-nuclear-family-was-a-mistake/605536/.

66. Kath Weston, *Families We Choose: Lesbians, Gays, Kinship* (New York: Columbia University Press, 1997), 108.

67. Solomon, *Far from the Tree*, 45.

68. Robert Putnam and Shaylyn Garrett, *The Upswing: How America Came Together a Century Ago and How We Can Do It Again* (New York: Simon & Schuster, 2020), 20.

69. Robert Putnam, "E Pluribus Unum: Diversity and Community in the Twenty-first Century: The 2006 Johan Skytte Prize Lecture," *Scandinavian Political Studies* 30, no. 2 (2007): 163–64, https://doi.org/10.1111/j.1467-9477.2007.00176.x.

70. Francis Fukuyama claims that "the apparent ethnic homogeneity of China, where more than 90 percent of the population are said to be Han Chinese, was the product of a lengthy cultural and biological assimilation of minority populations over three millennia." Fukuyama, *Identity*, 141.

71. Sunil Khilnani, *The Idea of India* (New York: Farrar, Straus & Giroux, 1997).

72. Rima Regas, "Transcript: James Baldwin Debates William F. Buckley (1965)," *Blog #42*, June 7, 2015, https://www.rimaregas.com/2015/06/07/transcript -james-baldwin-debates-william-f-buckley-1965-blog42/.

73. Smucker, *Hegemony How-To*, 63.

74. Moghaddam, *Mutual Radicalization*, 33–34.

75. Smucker, *Hegemony How-To*, 88.

76. Bill Bishop, *The Big Sort: Why the Clustering of Like-Minded America Is Tearing Us Apart* (Boston: Houghton Mifflin, 2008), 67.

77. Marx, *Status and Culture*; Cecilia L. Ridgeway, *Status: Why Is It Everywhere? Why Does It Matter?* (New York: Russell Sage Foundation, 2019).

78. Smucker, *Hegemony How-To*, 92.

79. However, a few political scientists claim that both bonding *and* bridging social capital is associated with support for the National Socialist Party in 1930s Germany, in other words, with Nazism. See Shanker Satyanath, Nico Voigtländer, and Hans-Joachim Voth, "Bowling for Fascism: Social Capital and the Rise of the Nazi Party," *UBS Center Working Paper Series* 7 (June 2014), https://www.zora .uzh.ch/id/eprint/97265/1/ubscenterwp007.pdf.

80. Kristin Garrity and Emily Crnkovich, "From Bigotry to Ban: The Ideological Origins and Devastating Harms of the Muslim and African Bans," *Southern California Interdisciplinary Law Journal* 29 (2020): 571–89, https://gould.usc.edu/ why/students/orgs/ilj/assets/docs/29-4-Garrity-Crnkovich.pdf.

81. Roxane Gay, "Cops Don't Belong at Pride," *New York Times*, May 29, 2021, https://www.nytimes.com/2021/05/29/opinion/culture/lgbtq-police-pride-parade .html.

82. Mark Van Streefkerk, "Why Pride Organizers Are Banning Cops," Mashable, June 20, 2021, https://mashable.com/article/pride-police-ban.

83. John Leland, "Pride Said Gay Cops Aren't Welcome. Then Came the Backlash," *New York Times*, May 28, 2021, https://www.nytimes.com/2021/05/28/ nyregion/lgbtq-pride-parade-reclaim-heritage.html.

84. Shant Shahrigian, "NYPD Should Be Allows to March in Pride Parade: Mayor de Blasio," *Daily News*, May 17, 2021, https://www.nydailynews.com/news/ politics/new-york-elections-government/ny-nyc-de-blasio-nypd-pride-parade -20210517-fjmb2zmxkzcdhjxp4koifnixky-story.html; Jonathan Capehart, "Opinion: Let LGBTQ Cops March in New York City's Pride Parade," *Washington Post*, May 23, 2021, https://www.washingtonpost.com/opinions/2021/05/23/lgbtq -police-nyc-pride-parade/.

85. "The Debate Between W. E. B. Du Bois and Booker T. Washington," *Frontline*, n.d., https://www.pbs.org/wgbh/frontline/article/debate-w-e-b-du-bois-and -booker-t-washington/.

86. Raya Jalabi and Michael Georgy, "Kurdish City Gassed by Saddam Hopes Referendum Heralds Better Days," Reuters, September 24, 2017, https://www .reuters.com/article/us-mideast-crisis-kurds-referendum-halab/kurdish-city -gassed-by-saddam-hopes-referendum-heralds-better-days-idUSKCN1BZ0AT.

87. Menashi, "Ethnonationalism and Liberal Democracy," 57–123. ("Israel emerged as a response, not a precursor, to liberal universalism.")

88. For an account of how two or more groups can simultaneously polarize society in a vicious cycle, see Moghaddam, *Mutual Radicalization*, 207–8.

89. "(1966) Stokely Carmichael, 'Black Power,'" Blackpast, July 13, 2010, https:// www.blackpast.org/african-american-history/speeches-african-american-history/ 1966-stokely-carmichael-black-power/.

90. *King in the Wilderness*, directed by Peter Kunhardt (2018; New York: HBO, 2018).

91. Ryan Grim, "Meltdowns Have Brought Progressive Advocacy Groups to a Standstill at a Critical Moment in World History," The Intercept, June 13, 2022, https://theintercept.com/2022/06/13/progressive-organizing-infighting-callout -culture/. One notable example of this was the infighting of the Women's March. Asma Khalid, "Women's March Divisions Offer Lessons for Democrats on Managing a Big Tent," NPR, January 17, 2019, https://www.npr.org/2019/01/17/ 685289036/womens-march-divisions-offer-lessons-for-democrats-on-managing-a -big-tent.

92. See Lindo Bacon's account in Bacon, *Radical Belonging*.

93. Paul Harrison, Ian Everall, and J. Catalan, "Is Homosexual Behaviour Hardwired? Sexual Orientation and Brain Structure," *Psychological Medicine* 24, no. 4 (1994): 811–16, https://doi.org/10.1017/S0033291700028919.

94. As has already been observed. See Eric Kaufmann, *Whiteshift: Populism, Immigration and the Future of White Majorities* (London: Penguin Random House UK, 2018).

95. Charles Homans, "How 'Stop the Steal' Captured the American Right," *New York Times*, July 19, 2022, https://www.nytimes.com/2022/07/19/magazine/ stop-the-steal.html.

96. James Baldwin, *The Devil Finds Work* (1976; repr., New York: Vintage Books, 2011), 64.

97. Robin DiAngelo, *White Fragility: Why It's So Hard for White People to Talk About Racism* (Boston: Beacon Press, 2018).

98. Geoffrey Skelley, "Just How Many Obama 2012-Trump 2016 Voters Were There?" University of Virginia Center for Politics, June 1, 2017, https:// centerforpolitics.org/crystalball/articles/just-how-many-obama-2012-trump-2016 -voters-were-there/; Zack Beauchamp, "A New Study Reveals the Real Reason

Obama Voters Switched to Trump," Vox, October 16, 2018, https://www.vox.com/policy-and-politics/2018/10/16/17980820/trump-obama-2016-race-racism-class-economy-2018-midterm.

99. Walt Whitman, "Song of Myself," in *Leaves of Grass* (Champaign, IL: Project Gutenberg, 1988).

100. Fukuyama, *Identity*, 56.

101. Fukuyama, *Identity*, 64–65, citing Ferdinand Tönnies, *Community and Society*, trans. Charles P. Loomis (Mineola, NY: Dover, 2002).

102. Omi and Winant, *Racial Formation*, 36–37.

103. Partha Dasgupta and Sanjeev Goyal, "Narrow Identities," *Journal of Institutional and Theoretical Economics* 175, no. 3 (2019): 395–419, http://www.econ.cam.ac.uk/people-files/faculty/sg472/wp18/narrowidentity6.pdf.

104. Fukuyama, *Identity*, 165–166.

105. Megan Specia, "Northern Ireland's Marching Season Begins in a Fraught Year for Unionists," *New York Times*, July 13, 2021, https://www.nytimes.com/2021/07/13/world/europe/northern-ireland-march-brexit.html; Patrick Kingsley and Hiba Yazbek, "Israelis March Through Jerusalem, Raising Tensions in a Divided City," New York Times, May 18, 2023, https://www.nytimes.com/2023/05/18/world/middleeast/israel-march-jerusalem-day.html. These kinds of parades are viewed as expressions of dominance by members of marginalized groups.

106. George Orwell, "Notes on Nationalism," *Polemic*, October 1945, https://www.orwellfoundation.com/the-orwell-foundation/orwell/essays-and-other-works/notes-on-nationalism/.

107. Appiah, *The Lies That Bind*, 35.

108. Chua, *Political Tribes*, 11.

109. Brooks, "Nuclear Family Was a Mistake."

110. Brooks, "Nuclear Family Was a Mistake."

111. Brooks, "Nuclear Family Was a Mistake."

112. Carol Ashby, "Adoption in the Roman Empire," *Life in the Roman Empire*, https://carolashby.com/adoption-in-the-roman-empire/.

113. Lesley Adkins and Roy Adkins, *Handbook to Life in Ancient Rome* (New York: Facts on File, 2004), 20; John H. Corbett, "The Succession Policy of Augustus," *Latomus* 33, no. 1 (1974): 89, https://www.jstor.org/stable/41528932.

114. J. A. Crook, *Law and Life of Rome, 90 BC.–A.D. 212* (Ithaca, NY: Cornell University Press, 1967), 111; Beryl Rawson, "The Roman Family" and "Children in the Roman *Familia*," in *The Family in Ancient Rome: New Perspectives*, ed. Beryl Rawson (London: Routledge, 1992), 12, 218; Neil W. Bernstein, "Adoptees and Exposed Children in Roman Declamation: Commodification, Luxury, and the Threat of Violence," *Classical Philology* 104, no. 3 (2009): 331–53, https://doi.org/10.1086/650144.

115. Antony Blinken, "X Gender Marker Available on U.S. Passports Starting April 11," U.S. Department of State, March 31, 2022, https://www.state.gov/x-gender-marker-available-on-u-s-passports-starting-april-11/.

116. Cade Hildreth, "What Are Your Facebook Gender Options? Facebook's Infinite Genders," March 8, 2021, https://cadehildreth.com/facebook-gender-options/; Russell Goldman, "Here's a List of 58 Gender Options for Facebook Users," ABC News, February 13, 2014, https://abcnews.go.com/blogs/headlines/2014/02/heres-a-list-of-58-gender-options-for-facebook-users.

117. Kristen L. Eckstrand, Henry Ng, and Jennifer Potter, "Affirmative and Responsible Health Care for People with Nonconforming Gender Identities and Expressions," *American Medical Association Journal of Ethics* 18, no. 11 (2016).

118. Jeffrey M. Jones, "LGBT Identification in U.S. Ticks Up to 7.1%," Gallup, February 17, 2022, https://news.gallup.com/poll/389792/lgbt-identification-ticks-up.aspx.

119. Philip Bump, "America's Increased Acceptance of Gay People Isn't about Schools," *Washington Post*, April 7, 2022, https://www.washingtonpost.com/politics/2022/04/07/americas-increased-acceptance-gay-people-isnt-about-schools/.

120. Rod Dreher, "No Families, No Children, No Future," *American Conservative*, October 22, 2020, https://www.theamericanconservative.com/no-families-no-children-no-future-lgbt-30-percent-carle-c-zimmerman/.

121. Ross Douthat, "How to Make Sense of the New L.G.B.T.Q. Culture War," *New York Times*, April 13, 2022, https://www.nytimes.com/2022/04/13/opinion/transgender-culture-war.html.

122. Eric Kaufmann, *Born This Way? The Rise of LGBT as a Social and Political Identity*, Center for the Study of Partisanship and Ideology, 2022, https://www.cspicenter.com/p/born-this-way-the-rise-of-lgbt-as-a-social-and-political-identity.

123. Mark Lilla, "The End of Identity Liberalism," *New York Times*, November 18, 2016, https://www.nytimes.com/2016/11/20/opinion/sunday/the-end-of-identity-liberalism.html.

124. Fukuyama, *Identity*, 163–64.

125. Fukuyama claims that "identity politics thus engenders its own dynamic, by which societies divide themselves into smaller and smaller groups by virtue of their particular 'lived experience' of victimization." Fukuyama, *Identity*, 165.

126. Sarmah, "Is Obama Black Enough?".

127. Ashley Fantz et al., "NAACP Leader Resigns; Accused of Lying about Race," CNN, June 15, 2015, https://www.cnn.com/2015/06/15/us/washington-rachel-dolezal-naacp/index.html.

128. Prizmi Tripathi, "Where Are Rachel Dolezal's Children Now?" Cinema-holic, May 5, 2020, https://thecinemaholic.com/rachel-dolezal-kids/.

129. Chris McGreal, "Rachel Dolezal: 'I Wasn't Identifying as Black to Upset People. I Was Being Me,'" *Guardian*, December 13, 2015, https://www.theguardian.com/us-news/2015/dec/13/rachel-dolezal-i-wasnt-identifying-as-black-to-upset-people-i-was-being-me.

130. McGreal, "Rachel Dolezal."

131. Diana Ohlbaum, "In Defense of Rachel Dolezal," *The Hill*, June 23, 2015, https://thehill.com/blogs/pundits-blog/uncategorized/245795-in-defense-of-rachel-dolezal?rl=1.

132. "Teaching Moments from the 'Hypatia' Controversy," *Inside Higher Ed*, June 29, 2017, https://www.insidehighered.com/views/2017/06/30/instructor-analyzes-how-discuss-hypatia-controversy-her-grad-students-essay.

133. James Baldwin, "On Being White . . . and Other Lies," *Essence*, April 1984, https://s3.amazonaws.com/omeka-net/20357/archive/files/2097825d00ddeobob54a3f7829f62045.PDF?AWSAccessKeyId=AKIAI3ATG3OSQLO5HGKA&Expires=1673481600&Signature=lgIk4Cjk%2FGMF8%2Fc2O1PcorlGAHA%3D.

134. Peter Aldhous, "She Was a 'Twitter Warrior' Fighting Sexual Harassment in Science. Some Say She Threatened the Movement," BuzzFeed News, August 29, 2020, https://www.buzzfeednews.com/article/peteraldhous/bethann-mclaughlin-metoostem-harassment-activism; Scott Jaschik, "Berkeley Professor Admits That She's White," *Inside Higher Ed*, May 8, 2023, https://www.insidehighered.com/news/faculty-issues/diversity-equity/2023/05/08/berkeley-professor-admits-shes-white; Vimal Patel, "Prominent Scholar Who Claimed to Be Native American Resigns," *New York Times*, August 27, 2023, https://www.nytimes.com/2023/08/27/us/uc-riverside-andrea-smith-resigns.html.

135. Jessica A. Krug, "The Truth, and the Anti-Black Violence of my Lies," Medium, September 3, 2020, https://medium.com/@jessakrug/the-truth-and-the-anti-black-violence-of-my-lies-9a9621401f85.

136. Roxane Gay, "I Think This Apology Is BS," Twitter post, September 3, 2020, https://web.archive.org/web/20201228013134/https://twitter.com/rgay/status/1301590075046723584.

137. Boris Kachka, "Author Jess Row: There Are Others Like Dolezal," Vulture, June 17, 2015, https://www.vulture.com/2015/06/author-jess-row-there-are-others-like-dolezal.html.

138. Such a concern brings us back to the earlier debate on "queerness" as an oppositional identity formation. For a critique of how this debate may impact gay and lesbian persons, see Andrew Sullivan, "The Queers Versus the Homosexuals," *The Weekly Dish*, May 19, 2023, https://andrewsullivan.substack.com/p/the-queers-versus-the-homosexuals.

CHAPTER 7

1. "Global Trends 2040," 80.

2. "Global Trends 2040," 80. This report, discussed in Chapter 3, outlines five scenarios for the world around 2040, many of which reflect these problems.

3. Recall, from Chapter 3, Viktor Orbán's 2022 speech on racial mixing. Cabinet Office of the Prime Minister, "Speech by Prime Minister Viktor Orbán"; Rick Noack, "Hungary's Viktor Orban Faces Outrage after Saying Europeans Shouldn't Become 'Mixed Race,'" *Washington Post*, July 27, 2022, https://www .washingtonpost.com/world/2022/07/27/viktor-orban-mixed-race-cpac/.

4. Harari, *Sapiens*, 21.

5. Elizabeth Kolbert, "Sleeping with the Enemy," *New Yorker*, August 8, 2011, https://www.newyorker.com/magazine/2011/08/15/sleeping-with-the-enemy.

6. We acknowledge Harari is building on the insights of other scholars, sociologists, anthropologists, and evolutionary psychologists, among others, who have emphasized the importance of collective cooperation to the success of our species. But we credit Harari for synthesizing these findings with a recognition of the role of narrative as the mechanism for facilitating this cooperation.

7. Joseph Campbell makes the assertion that myth is often more "real" than fact. And the mind science is beginning to teach us that the unconscious is more attentive and sensitive to stories and narrative than facts or data. Joseph Campbell, *The Power of Myth* (New York: Perennial Library, 1990), 11.

8. Joan Didion, *The White Album* (New York: Simon & Schuster, 1979), 8.

9. Malcolm Gladwell, "Revisionist Revisited: Extras from the Little Mermaid Series," in *Revisionist History*, podcast, 26:00, https://podcasts.apple.com/ us/podcast/revisionist-revisited-extras-from-the-little-mermaid/id1119389968?i= 1000534789436; Angus Fletcher, *Wonderworks: The 25 Most Powerful Inventions in the History of Literature* (New York: Simon & Schuster, 2021).

10. Harari, *Sapiens*, 31.

11. Harari, *Sapiens*, 108.

12. See Benjy Singer, "Does the Holocaust Still Shape Our Jewish Identity?" *Jerusalem Post*, February 18, 2020, https://www.jpost.com/diaspora/antisemitism/ does-the-holocaust-still-shape-our-jewish-identity-617923. See also Shaul Magid, "The Holocaust and Jewish Identity in America: Memory, the Unique, and the Universal," *Jewish Social Studies* 18, no. 2 (2012): 100–35; and "Jewish Identity and Belief," Pew Research Center, May 11, 2020, https://www.pewforum.org/2021/05/ 11/jewish-identity-and-belief/. ("Most Jewish adults say that remembering the Holocaust, leading a moral and ethical life, working for justice and equality in society, and being intellectually curious are 'essential' to what it means to them to be Jewish.")

13. "Rethinking Race: The Sociology of American Indian Identity," *University of Minnesota Sociology* (blog), August 6, 2019, https://cla.umn.edu/sociology/story/rethinking-race-sociology-american-indian-identity.

14. Timothy Egan, "America Is Getting Meaner," *New York Times*, June 25, 2021, https://www.nytimes.com/2021/06/25/opinion/trump-jan-6-america.html.

15. Theodore Allen observes that one of the ways people are dominated and controlled is by erasing or rewriting their history. Theodore Allen, *The Invention of the White Race* (New York: Verso Books, 1994).

16. Andrew Sullivan and Francis Fukuyama, "Francis Fukuyama on Liberalism's Crisis," May 27, 2022, in *The Dishcast with Andrew Sullivan*, podcast, 1:04:06, see 10:43–11:00, https://podcasts.apple.com/us/podcast/francis-fukuyama-on-liberalisms-crisis/id1536984072?i=1000564233633.

17. Lakshmi, "Indians Invented Planes 7000 Years Ago."

18. Joshua Hammer, "Bosnia on the Brink," *New York Times*, June 14, 2022, https://www.nytimes.com/2022/06/14/magazine/bosnia-genocide-pyramids.html.

19. Siddhartha Deb, "Those Mythological Men and Their Sacred, Supersonic Flying Temples," *New Republic*, May 14, 2015, https://newrepublic.com/article/121792/those-mythological-men-and-their-sacred-supersonic-flying-temples.

20. Teresa Watanabe, "Doubting the Story of Exodus," *Los Angeles Times*, April 13, 2001, https://www.latimes.com/archives/la-xpm-2001-apr-13-mn-50481-story.html.

21. Watanabe, "Doubting Exodus."

22. Jason Stanley (@jasonintrator), "From How Fascism Works, the Ten Pillars of Fascism," Twitter thread, September 25, 2022, https://web.archive.org/web/20220927022523/https://twitter.com/jasonintrator/status/1574183535602274304.

23. Johan Norberg, "Why We Can't Stop Longing for the Good Old Days," *Wall Street Journal*, December 26, 2020, https://www.wsj.com/articles/why-we-cant-stop-longing-for-the-good-old-days-11608958860.

24. Williams Jr., *Savage Anxieties*, 42.

25. Williams Jr., *Savage Anxieties*, 47, 133.

26. Norberg, "Longing for the Good Old Days."

27. Ian Daniel Stewart, "The "Golden Age" Fallacy," Ian Daniel Stewart, June 16, 2017, https://iandanielstewart.com/2017/06/16/the-golden-age-fallacy/#:~:text=%E2%80%9CGood%20old%20days%E2%80%9D%20is%20a,called%20the%20Golden%20Age%20Fallacy.

28. Anton Troianovski, Valerie Hopkins, Marc Santora, and Michael Schwirtz, "How the Kremlin Is Forcing Ukrainians to Adopt Russian Life," *New York Times*, July 30, 2022, https://www.nytimes.com/2022/07/30/world/europe/russia

-occupation-ukraine-kherson.html ("Mr. Putin has referred to Kherson and other parts of Ukraine's southeast as Novorossiya, or New Russia—the region's name after it was conquered by Catherine the Great in the 18th century and became part of the Russian Empire. In recent years, nostalgia in the region for the Soviet past and skepticism of the pro-Western government in Kyiv still lingered among older generations, even as the region was forging a new Ukrainian identity.")

29. Jane Burbank, "The Grand Theory Driving Putin to War," *New York Times*, March 22, 2022, https://www.nytimes.com/2022/03/22/opinion/russia-ukraine -putin-eurasianism.html.

30. Andrew Higgins, "Bound by a Sense of Victimhood, Serbia Sticks with Russia," *New York Times*, March 30, 2022, https://www.nytimes.com/2022/03/30/ world/europe/ukraine-serbia-russia.html.

31. Roger Cohen, "The Limits of a Europe Whole and Free," *New York Times*, February 22, 2022, https://www.nytimes.com/2022/02/22/world/europe/russia -putin-ukraine-europe-cold-war-nato.html.

32. Bryant Park, "Tibetan Sovereignty Has a Long, Disputed History," NPR, April 11, 2008, https://www.npr.org/2008/04/11/89552004/tibetan-sovereignty -has-a-long-disputed-history; Peter Hessler, "Tibet Through Chinese Eyes," *Atlantic*, February 1999, https://www.theatlantic.com/magazine/archive/1999/02/tibet -through-chinese-eyes/306395/.

33. Kevin M. F. Platt, "The Profound Irony of Canceling Everything Russian," *New York Times*, April 22, 2022, https://www.nytimes.com/2022/04/22/opinion/ russian-artists-culture-boycotts.html ("The idea of discrete national cultures, conducted in distinct languages and associated with states and their 'proper territories'—French culture in France, German culture in Germany—is associated with the rising tide of ethnic nationalist ideology of the 19th century. Even then, this idea didn't correspond to reality. The forces of migration—as well as the more destructive means of war, conquest and colonialism—have insured the mingling of people, languages and cultures throughout history. Borders between territories associated with one or another language or ethnic group have shifted over and over again, and so have the cultures they created.")

34. R. R. Palmer, *The Age of Democratic Revolution*, 2 vols. (Princeton, NJ: Princeton University Press, 1959), 282.

35. Wall Street Journal Editorial Board, "Beijing's Memory Control in Hong Kong," *Wall Street Journal*, November 9, 2021, https://www.wsj.com/articles/ beijing-hong-kong-ccp-june-4-tiananmen-square-jimmy-lai-gwyneth-ho-chow -hang-tung-11636305695.

36. Brooks, "Why Putin Can't Back Down."

37. Maalouf, *In the Name of Identity*, 124.

38. John F. Kennedy, "Address at Rice University on the Nation's Space Effort," JFK Library, September 12, 1962, https://www.jfklibrary.org/learn/about-jfk/historic-speeches/address-at-rice-university-on-the-nations-space-effort.

39. Van Bavel and Packer, *The Power of Us*, 240.

40. Mary Robinson "Address by the President, Mary Robinson, on the Occasion of Her Inauguration as President of Ireland," December 3, 1990, President of Ireland Media Library, transcript, https://president.ie/en/media-library/speeches/address-by-the-president-mary-robinson-on-the-occasion-of-her-inauguration.

41. Bret Stephens, "This Is a Moment for America to Believe in Itself Again," *New York Times*, February 22, 2022, https://www.nytimes.com/2022/02/22/opinion/ukraine-russia-us-war.html.

42. Hannah Gadsby, *Hannah Gadsby: Nanette* (Australia: Netflix, 2018).

43. Hoffer, *The True Believer*, 89.

44. Karim Sadjadpour, "What the U.S. Gets Wrong About Iran," *New York Times*, August 12, 2022, https://www.nytimes.com/2022/08/12/opinion/iran-america-nuclear-policy.html.

45. Malcolm Gladwell, "Little Mermaid Part 2: The Fairytale Twist," July 29, 2021, in *Revisionist History*, podcast, 37:28, https://www.pushkin.fm/podcasts/revisionist-history/little-mermaid-part-2-the-fairytale-twist.

46. Roxanne Roberts and Travis M. Andrews, "The Love Affair between Jeff Bezos and 'Star Trek,'" *Seattle Times*, October 13, 2021, https://www.seattletimes.com/entertainment/the-love-affair-between-jeff-bezos-and-star-trek/.

47. See, e.g., Octavia E. Butler, *Parable of the Sower* (New York: Four Walls Eight Windows, 1993); Octavia E. Butler, *Fledgling* (Jane Langton, 2005); Octavia E. Butler, *Kindred* (Boston: Beacon Press, 1979).

48. Karl Anthony Simpson Jr., "Michael B. Jordan Believes Killmonger Is Not a Villain," Game Rant, January 2, 2022, https://gamerant.com/michael-b-jordan-believes-killmonger-not-villain-black-panther/.

49. Gadsby, *Nanette*.

50. Ta-Nehisi Coates and Nikole Hannah-Jones, interview by Ezra Klein, "Transcript: Ezra Klein Interviews Ta-Nehisi Coates and Nikole Hannah-Jones," *New York Times*, https://www.nytimes.com/2021/07/30/podcasts/transcript-ezra-klein-interviews-ta-nehisi-coates-and-nikole-hannah-jones.html.

51. For a wonderful example of how creative storytellers retold Disney's *The Little Mermaid* in a way that dissolved the categorical boundary between the heroes and villains, listen to Malcolm Gladwell, "Little Mermaid Part 3: Honestly Ever After," August 2, 2021, in *Revisionist History*, podcast, https://www.pushkin.fm/podcasts/revisionist-history/little-mermaid-part-3-honestly-ever-after.

52. American Psychological Association, *APA Guidelines for Psychological Practice with Boys and Men* (Washington, DC: American Psychological Association, 2018), 2–3, https://www.apa.org/about/policy/boys-men-practice-guidelines.pdf.; Jared Yates Sexton, "Donald Trump's Toxic Masculinity," *New York Times*, October 13, 2016, https://www.nytimes.com/2016/10/13/opinion/donald-trumps-toxic -masculinity.html; Monika Frąckowiak-Sochańska, "Men and Social Trauma of Covid-19 Pandemic: The Maladaptiveness of Toxic Masculinity," *Society Register* 5, no. 1 (2021): 73–94, https://doi.org/10.14746/sr.2021.5.1.04; Sam de Boise, "Editorial: Is Masculinity Toxic?," *NORMA* 14, no. 3 (2019): 147–51, https://doi.org/10 .1080/18902138.2019.1654742.

53. Rachel Weeks, "How the Workplace Has Changed Since the 'Mad Men' Era," LinkedIn, May 1, 2015, https://www.linkedin.com/pulse/how-workplace-has -changed-since-mad-men-era-rachel-weeks/?trk=mp-reader-card.

54. Richard Reeves, *Of Boys and Men: Why the Modern Male Is Struggling, Why It Matters, and What to Do about it* (Washington, DC: Brookings Institution Press, 2022); Josh Hawley, *Manhood: The Masculine Virtues America Needs* (Washington, DC: Regnery, 2023).

55. French, "The Rage and Joy of MAGA America."

56. Coates and Hannah-Jones, interview by Klein, "Ezra Klein Interviews Ta-Nehisi Coates and Nikole Hannah-Jones." ("I want to pick up on one of the fears you identified in the article, which is, I think, a lot of the bills going through particularly Republican legislatures right now are basically playing on the fear of white parents, many white parents, that their kids are going to get taught your nation is racist, you're racist by virtue of being white, by being part of whiteness, and like it ends there, right? It's like all right, have a good summer everybody. To use a term used a minute ago Ta-Nehisi, what is the question of what this means? So OK you're learning in history class at your nation is deeply checkered, that important parts of the roots of the tree are not just complicated but immoral, immoral in a way nobody really denies now, and that that's part of the tree, you can't separate off, and that there is certain kinds of power and status and privilege that flows through even until today.")

57. See, for example, 1776 Unites (website), Woodson Center, https://1776unites .org/.

58. Coates and Hannah-Jones, interview by Klein, "Ezra Klein Interviews Ta-Nehisi Coates and Nikole Hannah-Jones."

59. Maalouf, *In the Name of Identity*, 28. And he continues: "And these killers will commit the most dreadful atrocities in the belief that they are right to do so and deserve the admiration of their fellows in this world and the next."

60. Peter Beinart, "Is Biden's Foreign Policy Team the Best of 'the Blob'?" *New York Times*, June 2, 2022, https://www.nytimes.com/2022/06/02/opinion/biden-the-blob-china-us.html.

61. See Moghaddam, *Mutual Radicalization*, 207–8.

62. Livingstone Smith, *Less Than Human*, 269.

63. Jeremy Suri, "History Is Clear. America's Military Is Way Too Big," *New York Times*, August 30, 2021, https://www.nytimes.com/2021/08/30/opinion/american-military-afghanistan.html ("This military hegemony has brought more defeats than victories and undermined democratic values at home and abroad.")

64. Stuart Hall, "Cultural Identity and Diaspora," chap. 13 in *Stuart Hall: Selected Writings on Race and Difference*, ed. Paul Gilroy and Ruth Wilson Gilmore (Durham, NC: Duke University Press, 2021), 260.

65. Gretchen Livingston and Anna Brown, "Public Views on Intermarriage," Pew Research Center, May 18, 2017, https://www.pewresearch.org/social-trends/2017/05/18/2-public-views-on-intermarriage/. (There are also differences in the types of intermarriage that may suggest relative group marginality. For example, white-Black intermarriage is much lower than white-Asian intermarriage.)

66. Gretchen Livingston and Anna Brown, "Trends and Patterns in Intermarriage," Pew Research Center, May 18, 2017, https://www.pewresearch.org/social-trends/2017/05/18/1-trends-and-patterns-in-intermarriage/.

67. Jay Readey, "The Coming Integration," *DePaul Journal for Social Justice* 7, no. 1 (2013): 15–53, https://via.library.depaul.edu/cgi/viewcontent.cgi?article=1002&context=jsj.

68. Kim Parker, Juliana Menasce Horowitz, Rich Morin, and Mark Hugo Lopez, "Multiracial in America: Proud, Diverse and Growing in Numbers," Pew Research Center, June 11, 2015, https://www.pewresearch.org/social-trends/2015/06/11/multiracial-in-america/.

69. Stephen Menendian, Samir Gambhir, and Chih-Wei Hsu, "Roots of Structural Racism: The 2020 Census Update," Othering & Belonging Institute, October 11, 2021, https://belonging.berkeley.edu/roots-structural-racism-2020 (132 percent increase).

70. Kaufmann, *Whiteshift*, 237.

71. Nisha Chittal, "The Kamala Harris Identity Debate Shows How America Still Struggles to Talk about Multiracial People," Vox, January 20, 2021, https://www.vox.com/identities/2020/8/14/21366307/kamala-harris-black-south-asian-indian-identity.

72. "Fact Check: Kamala Harris Did Not Switch from Identifying as Indian-American to Black," Reuters, August 21, 2020, https://www.reuters.com/article/uk

-fact-check-harris-did-not-switch-raci/fact-check-kamala-harris-did-not-%20switch-from-identifying-as-indian-american-to-black-idUSKBN25H1RC.

73. Ronald R. Sundstrom, "Kamala Harris, Multiracial Identity, and the Fantasy of a Post-Racial America," Vox, January 20, 2021, https://www.vox.com/first-person/22230854/kamala-harris-inauguration-mixed-race-biracial.

74. Jens Manuel Krogstad, "Hawaii Is Home to the Nation's Largest Share of Multiracial Americans," Pew Research Center, June 17, 2015, https://www.pewresearch.org/fact-tank/2015/06/17/hawaii-is-home-to-the-nations-largest-share-of-multiracial-americans/; "Nearly a Quarter of Hawaii's Population Is Multiracial," Pew Research Center, June 16, 2015, https://www.pewresearch.org/fact-tank/2015/06/17/hawaii-is-home-to-the-nations-largest-share-of-multiracial-americans/ft_15-06-11_multiracestate_310px/.

75. Moises Velasquez-Manoff, "Want to Be Less Racist? Move to Hawaii," New York Times, June 28, 2019, https://www.nytimes.com/2019/06/28/opinion/sunday/racism-hawaii.html.

76. Velasquez-Manoff, "Want to Be Less Racist?"

77. Lilia Moritz Schwarcz, "Not Black, Not White: Just the Opposite. Culture, Race and National Identity in Brazil," working paper 47, Centre for Brazilian Studies, University of Oxford, 2003, 26–30, citing "Brazil National Household Sample Survey 1976," Brazilian Institute of Geography and Statistics (IBGE).

78. Ian Haney López, "Racial Futures" in White by Law 10th Anniversary Edition: The Legal Construction of Race (New York: New York University Press, 2006), 145–47.

79. Yang Jie, Stephanie Yang, and Asa Fitch, "The World Relies on One Chip Maker in Taiwan, Leaving Everyone Vulnerable," Wall Street Journal, June 19, 2021, https://www.wsj.com/articles/the-world-relies-on-one-chip-maker-in-taiwan-leaving-everyone-vulnerable-11624075400; Yimou Lee, Norihiko Shirouzu, and David Lague, "T-Day: The Battle for Taiwan," Reuters, December 27, 2021, https://www.reuters.com/investigates/special-report/taiwan-china-chips/.

80. Rothkopf, Power, Inc.

81. Sarah Paynter, "Inside Tom Brady's $26M Homes and $140M Real Estate Side Hustle," New York Post, February 8, 2021, https://nypost.com/article/tom-brady-houses-photos/.

82. Hazony, Virtue of Nationalism. See also Kaufmann, Whiteshift, 31–32, 65, 105 (describing these people as "ethno-traditional nationalists").

83. Alberto Mingardi, "The Virtue of Nationalism by Yormam Hazony," Cato Journal 38, no. 3 (2018): 741–47, https://www.cato.org/cato-journal/fall-2018/virtue-nationalism-yoram-hazony.

84. There is more than one kind of globalization or form that it can take. Some would be more supporting of belonging than others. See Latour, *Down to Earth*, and john a. powell and S. P. Udayakumar, "Race, Poverty, and Globalization," in *Challenges to Equality: Poverty and Race in America*, ed. Chester Hartman (New York: Routledge, 2015).

85. Farhad Manjoo, "What If Humans Just Can't Get Along Anymore?" *New York Times*, August 4, 2021, https://www.nytimes.com/2021/08/04/opinion/technology-internet-cooperation.html.

86. Bongani Ngqulunga, "The Changing Face of Zulu Nationalism: The Transformation of Mangosuthu Buthelezi's Politics and Public Image," *Politikon* 47, no. 3 (July 2, 2020): 287–304, https://doi.org/10.1080/02589346.2020.1795992.

87. It is not only the case that Mandela pushed a vision that many of his contemporary countrymen opposed. South Africans today remain deeply divided on this vision. As a seventeen-year old South African told the *New York Times*, "He didn't revolt against white people. . . . I would have taken revenge." Lyndsey Chutel, "Mandela Goes from Hero to Scapegoat as South Africa Struggles," *New York Times*, July 18, 2023, https://www.nytimes.com/2023/07/18/world/africa/nelson-mandela-day-south-africa.html.

88. Nelson Mandela, "Inaugural Speech," presented in Pretoria, South Africa, May 10, 1994, https://www.africa.upenn.edu/Articles_Gen/Inaugural_Speech_17984.html. The term *rainbow nation* was first coined by Archbishop Desmond Tutu, as he called for racial reconciliation in post-apartheid South Africa. Mark Gevisser, "Remembering the Real Desmond Tutu, 1931–2021," *Nation*, December 31, 2021, https://www.thenation.com/article/world/desmond-tutu-south-africa/.

89. The symbol of the rainbow "aided the post-election euphoria as it captured the aura that swept through the nation in the early years of South Africa's democracy" and emphasized the diversity, multiculturalism, and patriotism of the new South African democracy. Mfaniseni Sihlongonyane, "Ideologies, Discourses and Vectors of African Urbanism in the Making of South African Cities," in *The Contested Idea of South Africa* (Milton, MA: Taylor & Francis, 2021).

90. B. G. Bhosale, "Indian Nationalism: Gandhi vis-a-vis Tilak and Savarkar," *Indian Journal of Political Science* 70, no. 2 (2009): 419–27, http://www.jstor.org/stable/42743906.

91. B. R. Nanda, "Gandhi and the Partition of India," in *Gandhi and His Critics*, ed. B. R. Nanda (New Delhi: Oxford University Press, 1997), 77–97, https://doi.org/10.1093/acprof:oso/9780195633634.003.0011.

92. Ramu Bhagwat, "When Gandhi Suggested That Jinnah Be Made PM . . . ," *Times of India*, December 23, 2015, https://timesofindia.indiatimes.com/city/

nagpur/when-gandhi-suggested-that-jinnah-be-made-pm/articleshow/50289468
.cms.

93. Manash Firaq Bhattacharjee, "Gandhi's Last Fast in the City of the Dead,"
The Wire, October 2, 2017, https://thewire.in/communalism/gandhis-last-fast-city
-dead; Ramachandra Guha, "Gandhi's Last (and Greatest) Fast," *Hindustan Times*,
September 8, 2018, https://www.hindustantimes.com/india-news/gandhi-s-last
-and-greatest-fast/story-wpfoNL3LgsWUegv7uVTopL.html.

94. Yasmin Khan, "Performing Peace: Gandhi's Assassination as a Critical
Moment in the Consolidation of the Nehruvian State," in *From Subjects to Citizens: Society and the Everyday State in India and Pakistan, 1947–1970*, ed. Taylor
C. Sherman, William Gould, and Sarah Ansari (New York: Cambridge University Press 2014), 64, https://search.ebscohost.com/login.aspx?direct=true&db=
e000xna&AN=761524&site=ehost-live&scope=site.

95. Ariel Sophia Bardi, "India's Hindu Nationalists Still Feed Off Partition's
Wounds," *Foreign Policy*, August 14, 2018, https://foreignpolicy.com/2018/08/14/
indias-hindu-nationalists-still-feed-off-partitions-wounds/; Manu Bhagavan, "The
Hindutva Underground: Hindu Nationalism and the Indian National Congress in
Late Colonial and Early Post-Colonial India," *Economic and Political Weekly* 43,
no. 37 (September 13, 2008): 39–48.

96. Appiah, *The Lies That Bind*, 93.

97. Appiah, *The Lies That Bind*, 93.

98. Appiah, *The Lies That Bind*, 96.

99. Sedition Act, 3(e), Republic of Singapore, 1948, revised 1985, https://sso.agc
.gov.sg/Act-Rev/SA1948/Published/20130831?DocDate=19870330.

100. Kwame Anthony Appiah, "Crazy Rich Identities," *Atlantic*, August 25,
2018, https://www.theatlantic.com/ideas/archive/2018/08/singapore/568567/.

101. "Diplomacy Ends a War: The Dayton Accords," National Museum of
American Diplomacy, accessed June 13, 2023, https://diplomacy.state.gov/online
-exhibits/diplomacy-ends-a-war-the-dayton-accords/.

102. Here is a UN Security Council press release describing the process from
1999: "Three-Member Presidency of Bosnia and Herzegovina Briefs Security Council, Announces 'New York Declaration,'" United Nations Meeting Coverage and
Press Releases, November 15, 1999, https://www.un.org/press/en/1999/19991115
.sc6755.doc.html; "Bosnia Peace Implementation Council: Declaration of the
Bosnia Peace Implementation Council," *International Legal Materials* 38, no. 2
(March1999): 484–88, https://www.jstor.org/stable/20698893.

103. Charles Landow and Mohammed Aly Sergie, "The Northern Ireland Peace
Process," Council on Foreign Relations, last modified March 5, 2020, https://www
.cfr.org/backgrounder/northern-ireland-peace-process.

104. Specia and O'Loughlin, "Catholics Outnumber Protestants in Ireland."

105. "Lebanese President Proposes Ending Sectarian Quotas to Break Govt Deadlock," France24, September 21, 2020, https://www.france24.com/en/20200921-lebanese-president-proposes-ending-sectarian-quotas-to-break-govt-deadlock.

106. Maalouf, *In the Name of Identity*, 146.

107. Fukuyama, "A Country of Their Own."

108. See, e.g., Miller-Melamed and Morelon, "What the Hapsburg Empire Got Right."

109. Fukuyama, *Identity*, 143.

110. Julia Gelatt, "Schengen and the Free Movement of People Across Europe," Migration Policy Institute, October 1, 2005, https://www.migrationpolicy.org/article/schengen-and-free-movement-people-across-europe.

111. Stephanie Bergbauer, *Explaining European Identity Formation: Citizens' Attachment from Maastricht Treaty to Crisis* (Germany: Springer International, 2017), 31–34.

112. Erich Striessnig and Wolfgang Lutz, "Demographic Strengthening of European Identity," *Population and Development Review* 42, no. 2 (2016): 305–11, https://www.jstor.org/stable/44015640.

113. "History of the European Union 1945–59," European Union, https://european-union.europa.eu/principles-countries-history/history-eu/1945-59_en.

114. "About the African Union," African Union, accessed March 9, 2022, https://au.int/en/overview.

115. In fact, religious liberty is core to American freedoms and liberty. See discussion of Madison legislative efforts on behalf of religious freedom in Michael Meyersen, *Liberty's Blueprint: How Madison and Hamilton Wrote the Federalist Papers, Defined the Constitution, and Made Democracy Safe for the World* (New York: Basic Books, 2009), 43–44.

116. Russell Brand, "Brexit: What Were We Thinking?!" *New York Times*, December 7, 2020, https://www.nytimes.com/2020/12/07/opinion/brexit-britain-covid-labour.html.

117. Weave: The Social Fabric Project (website), accessed December 1, 2023, https://weavers.org/.

THE MECHANICS OF OTHERING

1. Tilly, *Identities, Boundaries and Social Ties*, 72.

2. Tilly, *Identities, Boundaries and Social Ties*, 72.

3. Curt Bartol and Anne Bartol, "Psychology of Violence and Intimidation," chap. 8 in *Introduction to Forensic Psychology*, 6th ed. (Thousand Oaks, CA: SAGE, 2021).

4. David Treuer, "'A Sadness I Can't Carry': The Story of the Drum," *New York Times Magazine*, August 31, 2021, https://www.nytimes.com/2021/08/31/magazine/ojibwe-big-drum.html. ("among them: Tecumseh's War (1811), the Creek War (1813–14), the First and Second and Third Seminole Wars (1817–18 and 1835–42 and 1855–58), the Arikara War (1823), the Winnebago War (1827), the Black Hawk War (1832), the Cayuse War (1847–55), the Apache Wars (1861–1900), the Puget Sound War (1855–56), the Rogue River Wars (1855–56), the Yakama War (1855–58), the Utah War (1857–58), the Navajo Wars (1848–68), the Paiute War (1860), the Yavapai Wars (1861–75), the Dakota War (1862), the Colorado War (1864–65), the Snake War (1864–68), the Powder River War (1865), Red Cloud's War (1865–68), the Comanche Campaign (1867–75), the Modoc War (1872–73), the Red River War (1874–75), the Great Sioux War (1876–77), the Buffalo Hunters' War (1877), the Nez Percé War (1877), the Bannock War (1878), the Cheyenne Campaign (1878), the Sheepeater War (1879), Victorio's War (1879–80), the White River Ute War (1879), the Pine Ridge Campaign (1890–91), the Yaqui Wars (1896–1918)"; History .com Editors, "American Indian Wars: Timeline," *History*, October 19, 2021, Last updated November 30, 2021, https://www.history.com/topics/colonial-america/american-indian-wars-timeline.

5. Jonathan Riley-Smith, *The Oxford History of the Crusades* (Oxford: Oxford University Press, 2002).

6. One estimate puts the death toll at 1 million. Steven Pinker, *The Better Angels of Our Nature: Why Violence Has Declined* (New York: Viking, 2011), 140.

7. Jonathan Phillips, *Holy Warriors: A Modern History of the Crusades* (New York: Random House, 2009), 26.

8. Robert Michael, "Crusades and Defamations," in *A History of Catholic Antisemitism* (New York: Palgrave Macmillan, 2008), 68; Pope Urban II, "The Speech of Urban II at the Council of Clermont, 1095," in *A Source Book for Medieval History: Selected Documents Illustrating the History of Europe in the Middle Age*, ed. Oliver J. Thatcher and Edgar Holmes McNeal (New York: Charles Scribner's Sons, 1905), 513–18, https://www.gutenberg.org/files/42707/42707-h/42707-h.htm#mh279.

9. Andrew A. Latham, "Theorizing the Crusades: Identity, Institutions, and Religious War in Medieval Latin Christendom," *International Studies Quarterly* 55, no. 1 (2011): 223–43.

10. Nico Voigtlaender and Hans-Joachim Voth, "Persecution Perpetuated: The Medieval Origins of Anti-Semitic Violence in Nazi Germany," *Quarterly Journal of Economics* 127, no. 3 (2012): 1339–92. ("Anti-Semitic attacks in Germany were not limited to the fourteenth and twentieth centuries; there were scattered pogroms as early as the eleventh century. . . . The first pogroms in our data set were recorded during the First Crusade in 1096 in communities along the Rhine.")

11. "Orlando Nightclub Shooting: How the Attack Unfolded," BBC, June 15, 2016, https://www.bbc.com/news/world-us-canada-36511778.

12. Trip Gabriel, Jack Healy, and Julie Turkewitz, "Pittsburgh Synagogue Massacre Suspect Was 'Pretty Much a Ghost,'" *New York Times*, October 28, 2018, https://www.nytimes.com/2018/10/28/us/pittsburgh-shooting-robert-bowers .html.

13. Tore Bjørgo and Jacob Aasland Ravndal, *Extreme-Right Violence and Terrorism: Concepts, Patterns, and Responses* (The Hague: International Centre for Counter-Terrorism, 2019), 13, accessed January 13, 2021, https://icct.nl/app/ uploads/2019/09/Extreme-Right-Violence-and-Terrorism-Concepts-Patterns-and -Responses.pdf.

14. Matt Zapotosky, "Charleston Church Shooter: 'I Would Like to Make it Crystal Clear, I Do Not Regret What I Did,'" *Washington Post,* January 4, 2017, https://www.washingtonpost.com/world/national-security/charleston-church -shooter-i-would-like-to-make-it-crystal-clear-i-do-not-regret-what-i-did/2017/01/ 04/05b0061e-d1da-11e6-a783-cd3fa950f2fd_story.html.

15. Patrick Kingsley and Boryana Dzhambazova, "Europe's Roma Already Faced Discrimination. The Pandemic Made It Worse," *New York Times*, July 6, 2020, https://www.nytimes.com/2020/07/06/world/europe/coronavirus-roma-bulgaria .html.

16. William G. Hartley, "Missouri's 1838 Extermination Order and the Mormons' Forced Removal to Illinois," *Mormon Historical Studies* 2, no. 1 (2001): 5–27. ("General Clark was implementing orders he had received from Missouri's Governor Lilburn W. Boggs, dated 27 October 1838, which stated: 'Your orders are, therefore, to hasten your operations with all possible speed. The Mormons must be treated as enemies, and must be exterminated or driven from the state if necessary for the public peace.'")

17. "Racial Terror Lynchings," Equal Justice Initiative, https://lynchinginamerica .eji.org/explore; "History of Lynchings," NAACP, https://www.naacp.org/history -of-lynchings/. The real figure may even be as many as 6,500. See also Michael S. Rosenwald, "At Least 2,000 More Black People Were Lynched by White Mobs Than Previously Reported, New Research Finds," *Washington Post*, June 16, 2020, https://www.washingtonpost.com/history/2020/06/16/lynchings-report-equal -justice-initiative-reconstruction-racial-terror/.

18. "Our Story," Matthew Shepard Foundation, https://www.matthewshepard .org/about-us/our-story/.

19. Julie Bindel, "The Truth Behind America's Most Famous Gay-Hate Murder," *Guardian*, October 26, 2014, https://www.theguardian.com/world/2014/oct/26/ the-truth-behind-americas-most-famous-gay-hate-murder-matthew-shepard.

20. "A National Epidemic: Fatal Anti-Transgender Violence in America in 2018," Human Rights Campaign, https://www.hrc.org/resources/a-national-epidemic -fatal-anti-transgender-violence-in-america-in-2018; Madeleine Carlisle, "Anti-Trans Violence and Rhetoric Reached Record Highs Across America in 2021," *Time*, December 30, 2021, https://time.com/6131444/2021-anti-trans-violence/.

21. Mariel Padilla and Neil Vigdor, "Transgender Woman Found Burned Beyond Recognition in Florida, Officials Say," *New York Times*, September 14, 2019, https://www.nytimes.com/2019/09/14/us/black-transgender-woman-bee -love-slater.html?module=inline.

22. "AMA Adopts New Policies on First Day of Voting at 2019 Annual Meeting," American Medical Association, June 10, 2019, https://www.ama-assn.org/ press-center/press-releases/ama-adopts-new-policies-first-day-voting-2019-annual -meeting.

23. Das Kumar and Bijeta Mohanty, "The Growing Concern around Violence against Women in India—Where Do We Stand?" *International Growth Centre* (blog), November 25, 2020, https://www.theigc.org/blog/the-growing-concern -around-violence-against-women-in-india-where-do-we-stand/.

24. Dewan, "India the Most Dangerous Country to Be a Woman."

25. Niharika Mandhana and Anjani Trivedi, "Indians Outraged over Rape on Moving Bus in New Delhi," *New York Times*, December 18, 2012, https://india .blogs.nytimes.com/2012/12/18/outrage-in-delhi-after-latest-gang-rape-case/.

26. Jim Yardley, "A Village Rape Shatters a Family, and India's Traditional Silence," *New York Times*, October 27, 2012, https://www.nytimes.com/2012/10/28/world/ asia/a-village-rape-shatters-a-family-and-indias-traditional-silence.html. This girl was also poor and Dalit, a marginalized caste identity discussed later in this section.

27. Suhasini Raj and Jeffrey Gettleman, "She Wanted to See Her Boyfriend. She May Have Been Beheaded for It," *New York Times*, January 11, 2019, https://www .nytimes.com/2019/01/11/world/asia/india-girl-beheading-honor-killing.html.

28. Wolfgang Behringer and Lyndal Roper had independently calculated the number as being between 50,000 and 60,000.

29. "Witch Trials in Early Modern Europe and New England," Berkeley Law video adapted from *Famous Trials and Their Legacy* exhibit, held August 14–September 20, 2008, https://www.law.berkeley.edu/research/the-robbins-collection/ exhibitions/witch-trials-in-early-modern-europe-and-new-england/.

30. James Hookway, "Women Executed as Witches Centuries Ago Are Pardoned in Catalonia," *Wall Street Journal*, January 27, 2022, https://www.wsj.com/articles/ hundreds-of-women-executed-as-witches-pardoned-in-catalonia-11643290230.

31. Caroline Davies, "Women Executed 300 Years Ago as Witches in Scotland Set to Receive Pardons," *Guardian*, December 19, 2021, https://www.theguardian

.com/uk-news/2021/dec/19/executed-witches-scotland-pardons-witchcraft-act; Maria Cramber, "Scotland Apologizes for History of Witchcraft Persecution," *New York Times*, March 9, 2022, https://www.nytimes.com/2022/03/09/world/europe/scotland-nicola-sturgeon-apologizes-witches.html.

32. Dobbs v. Jackson Women's Health Organization, 597 U.S. ___ (2022).

33. Ken Armstrong, "Draft Overturning Roe v. Wade Quotes Infamous Witch Trial Judge with Long-Discredited Ideas on Rape," ProPublica, May 6, 2022, https://www.propublica.org/article/abortion-roe-wade-alito-scotus-hale.

34. Tali Farhadian Weinstein, "Book Review: A Rape Trial, and a Legal Travesty. In 1793," *New York Times*, July 14, 2022, https://www.nytimes.com/2022/07/14/books/review/the-sewing-girls-tale-john-wood-sweet.html.

35. Amanda Taub, "The 17th-Century Judge at the Heart of Today's Women's Rights Rulings," *New York Times*, May 19, 2022, https://www.nytimes.com/2022/05/19/world/asia/abortion-lord-matthew-hale.html.

36. Morris and Ze'evi, *The Thirty-Year Genocide*, 450.

37. "Rwanda Genocide: 100 Days of Slaughter," BBC, April 4, 2019, https://www.bbc.com/news/world-africa-26875506.

38. James S. Amelang, *Parallel Histories: Muslims and Jews in Inquisitorial Spain* (Baton Rouge: Louisiana State University Press, 2013), 163.

39. Douglas Massey and Nancy A. Denton, *American Apartheid: Segregation and the Making of the Underclass* (Cambridge, MA: Harvard University Press, 1998), 33–34.

40. Richard Fausset and Neil Vigdor, "8 People Killed in Atlanta-Area Massage Parlor Shootings," *New York Times*, March 16, 2021, https://www.nytimes.com/2021/03/16/us/atlanta-shootings-massage-parlor.html.

41. Rebecca Onion, "Coverage of Bay Area Anti-Asian Violence Is Missing a Key Element," Slate, March 19, 2021, https://slate.com/news-and-politics/2021/03/anti-asian-violence-bay-area-history-black-communities-race.html.

42. Andrew Sullivan, "When the Narrative Replaces the News," *The Weekly Dish* (blog), April 2, 2021, https://andrewsullivan.substack.com/p/when-the-narrative-replaces-the-news.

43. David F. Krugler, *1919, The Year of Racial Violence: How African Americans Fought Back* (Cambridge: Cambridge University Press, 2014), 20–21, 298.

44. "The Great Migration," History, March 4, 2010, last modified January 16, 2020, http://www.history.com/topics/black-history/great-migration.

45. Laurie Ochoa, "'Watchmen' Revived It. But the History of the 1921 Tulsa Race Massacre was Nearly Lost," *Los Angeles Times*, October 27, 2019, https://www.latimes.com/entertainment-arts/story/2019-10-27/history-behind-the-tulsa-race-massacre-shown-in-watchmen.

46. Pradip Kumar Bose, "Social Mobility and Caste Violence: A Study of the Gujarat Riots," *Economic and Political Weekly* 16, no. 16 (1981): 713–16, https://www.jstor.org/stable/4369726?seq=1.

47. John R. Wood, "Reservations in Doubt: The Backlash Against Affirmative Action in Gujarat, India," *Pacific Affairs* 60, no. 3 (1987): 408–30.

48. Durga Sob, "Caste and Gender Discrimination Against Dalit Women in Nepal," Feminist Dalit Organization, quoted in Smita Narula et al., *Caste Discrimination: A Global Concern* (New York: Human Rights Watch, 2001), https://www.hrw.org/reports/2001/globalcaste/caste0801-03.htm.

49. Aishwarya Mohanty, "In Gujarat, Caste-Based Crimes Rise by 46% in 2 Years," *Indian Express*, November 28, 2019, https://indianexpress.com/article/india/in-gujarat-caste-based-crimes-rise-by-46-in-2-years/, Damayantee Dhar, "Caste Violence in Gujarat: Number of Rape and Atrocity Cases on Rise," NewsClick, August 1, 2019, https://www.newsclick.in/caste-violence-gujarat-number-rape-atrocity-cases-rise.

50. Øivind Fuglerud, *Life on the Outside: The Tamil Diaspora and Long-distance Nationalism* (London: Pluto Press, 1999), 32, quoted in Ahalya Balasunderam, "Gang-Related Violence Among Young People of the Tamil Refugee Diaspora In London," *Safer Communities* 8, no. 2 (2009): 34.

51. Samanth Subramanian, "Two Wealthy Sri Lankan Brothers Became Suicide Bombers. But Why?" *New York Times*, July 2, 2020, https://www.nytimes.com/2020/07/02/magazine/sri-lanka-brothers-bombing.html.

52. Amresh Gunasingham, "Sri Lanka Attacks: An Analysis of the Aftermath," *Counter Terrorist Trends and Analyses* 11, no. 6 (2019): 10; Subramanian, "Two Wealthy Sri Lankan Brothers Became Suicide Bombers."

53. See, e.g., Thomas Sowell, *Discrimination and Disparities* (London: Basic Books, 2019), 29–30. Sowell describes two types of discrimination. The first refers to the "ability to discern differences in the qualities of people and things," and the second, more common definition, refers to "treating people negatively, based on arbitrary aversions to individuals of a particular [group]."

54. Bonnie Kristian, "Ahmaud Arbery and the Racist History of Loitering Laws," *The Week*, May 7, 2020, https://theweek.com/articles/912977/ahmaud-arbery-racist-history-loitering-laws. See also Matt Taibbi, "The Man Who Couldn't Stand Up," chap. 3 in *The Divide: American Injustice in the Age of the Wealth Gap* (New York: Random House, 2014), 85–140.

55. Ronnie Dunn, "Measuring Racial Disparities in Traffic Ticketing within Large Urban Jurisdictions," *Public Performance & Management Review* 32, no. 4 (2009): 537–61, http://www.jstor.org/stable/40586772.

56. Aala Abdelgadir and Vasiliki Fouka, "Political Secularism and Muslim Integration in the West: Assessing the Effects of the French Headscarf Ban," *American*

Political Science Review 114, no. 3 (August 2020): 707–23; "French Senate Approves Burqa Ban," CNN, September 15, 2020, http://edition.cnn.com/2010/WORLD/europe/09/14/france.burqa.ban/?hpt=T1.

57. Roger Cohen, "As Final Vote Nears in France, a Debate over Islam and Head Scarves," *New York Times*, April 17, 2022, https://www.nytimes.com/2022/04/17/world/europe/france-islam-le-pen-head-scarf.html.

58. Voting Rights Act of 1965, Pub. L. 89–110, 79 Stat. 437, 52 USCS § 10302, ("If in a proceeding instituted by the Attorney General or an aggrieved person under any statute to enforce the voting guarantees of the fourteenth or fifteenth amendment in any State or political subdivision the court finds that a test or device has been used *for the purpose or with the effect* of denying or abridging the right of any citizen. . . ."); Civil Rights Act of 1964, Pub. L. 88–352, 78 Stat. 241 (1964), e.g., "It shall be unlawful employment practice for an employer to fail or refuse to hire or to discharge any individual, or to otherwise to discriminate against any individual with respect to his compensation, terms, conditions, or privileges of employment *because of* such individual's race, color, religion, sex, or national origin. . . ." Civil Rights Act, 105 Stat. 1071 (1991).

59. This is where critics of disparate impact laws, such as Thomas Sowell, get it wrong. They assume that the legislative intent behind antidiscrimination laws is simply to remove barriers to inclusion, but antidiscrimination laws are also aimed at changing attitudes by establishing new collective norms. In other words, legislation is not simply about translating the will of the community into enforceable regulations, but also about reorienting community values and establishing new norms as well. Sowell, *Discrimination and Disparities*, 52–57.

60. Loving v. Virginia, 388 U.S. 1 (1967).

61. Geneva Abdul and Sameer Yasir, "Police in India Make First Arrest under New Interfaith Marriage Law," *New York Times,* December 3, 2020, https://www.nytimes.com/2020/12/03/world/asia/india-muslims-interfaith-marriage-arrest.html.

62. Jonathan Evans and Nega Sahgal, "Key Findings about Religion in India," Pew Research Center, June 29, 2021, https://www.pewresearch.org/fact-tank/2021/06/29/key-findings-about-religion-in-india/.

63. Sameer Yasir, Emily Schmall, and Iqbal Kirmani, "She Said She Married for Love. Her Parents Called It Coercion," *New York Times,* July 20, 2021, https://www.nytimes.com/2021/07/20/world/india-interfaith-marriage.html.

64. Abdi Latif Dahir, "In Burundi, the Drum Is a Revered Symbol of Unity. But Only Men Can Play," *New York Times*, March 6, 2022, https://www.nytimes.com/2022/03/06/world/africa/burundi-drumming.html.

65. Rebecca M. Blank, "Tracing the Economic Impact of Cumulative Discrimination," *American Economic Review* 95, no. 2 (2005): 99–103, http://www.jstor.org/stable/4132798.

66. Linda Babcock and Sara Laschever, *Women Don't Ask: Negotiation and the Gender Divide* (Princeton, NJ: Princeton University Press, 2003), quoted in Andreas Leibbrandt and John A. List, "Do Women Avoid Salary Negotiations? Evidence from a Large-Scale Natural Field Experiment," *Management Science* 61, no. 9 (2015): 2016–24.

67. Lilly Ledbetter Fair Pay Act of 2009, Pub. L. No 111–2, 123 Stat. 5 (2009). See also Miranda Houchins, "This Day in History: Equal Pay Trailblazer Lilly Ledbetter Turns 77," The White House: President Barack Obama, April 14, 2015, https://obamawhitehouse.archives.gov/blog/2015/04/14/day-history-equal-pay -trailblazer-lilly-ledbetter-turns-77, and Lani Guinier, "Courting The People: Demosprudence and the Law/Politics Divide," *Harvard Law Review* 127, no. 1 (2013): 437–44.

68. David R. Verbeeten, "The American Jewish Congress and the Second Generation," in *The Politics of Nonassimilation: The American Jewish Left in the Twentieth Century* (Dekalb: Northern Illinois University Press, and Ithaca, NY: Cornell University Press, 2017), 67–122; Nancy Weiss Malkiel, "'Keep the Damned Women Out': The Struggle for Coeducation in the Ivy League, the Seven Sisters, Oxford, and Cambridge," *Proceedings of the American Philosophical Society* 161, no. 1 (2017): 31–37. Another citation on Yale: Dan A. Oren, *Joining the Club: A History of Jews and Yale* (New Haven, CT: Yale University Press, 1985), quoted in Abraham J. Karp, "Review: Joining the Club: A History of Jews and Yale," *Academe* 72, no. 5 (1986), 33–34.

69. Verbeeten, "The American Jewish Congress," 103.

70. Oren, *Joining the Club*, quoted in Karp, "Review: Joining the Club," 33.

71. Oren, *Joining the Club*, quoted in Karp, "Review: Joining the Club," 33.

72. *Can Saudi Arabia Reform Itself?* (Cairo and Brussels: International Crisis Group, 2004), 17, quoted in David Commins, *The Wahhabi Mission and Saudi Arabia* (New York: Tauris, 2006), 109, 203; Muharrem Hilmi Özev, "Saudi Society and the State: Ideational and Material Basis," *Arab Studies Quarterly* 39, no. 4 (2017): 1012.

73. Samia Abbass, "Saudi Arabian Women Campaign for the Right to Drive, 2007–2008," Global Nonviolent Action Database, published November 29, 2010, last modified June 6, 2011, https://nvdatabase.swarthmore.edu/content/saudi -arabian-women-campaign-right-drive-2007-2008; Rothna Begum, "The Brave Female Activists Who Fought to Lift Saudi Arabia's Driving Ban," Human Rights Watch, September 29, 2017, https://www.hrw.org/news/2017/09/29/brave-female -activists-who-fought-lift-saudi-arabias-driving-ban.

74. "Saudi Arabia's Ban on Women Driving Officially Ends," BBC, June 24, 2018, https://www.bbc.com/news/world-middle-east-44576795#.

75. Vivian Yee, "Saudi Activist Who Fought for Women's Right to Drive Is Sentenced to Prison," *New York Times*, December 28, 2020, https://www.nytimes.com/2020/12/28/world/middleeast/saudi-arabia-loujain-al-hathloul-sentence.html.

76. Farnaz Fassihi, "Protests Erupt in Iranian Cities after Woman's Death in Custody," *New York Times*, September 20, 2022, https://www.nytimes.com/2022/09/20/world/middleeast/iran-protests-mahsa-amini.html.

77. Michael Georgy, "Videos Showing Iranian Crackdown on Protesters Go Viral as Anger Grows," Reuters, November 2, 2022, https://www.reuters.com/world/middle-east/videos-showing-iranian-crackdown-protesters-go-viral-anger-grows-2022-11-02/.

78. "Iran: A Really Simple Guide to the Protests," BBC, October 26, 2022, https://www.bbc.com/news/world-middle-east-63240911.

79. Ben Hubbard and Vivian Yee, "Saudi Arabia Extends New Rights to Women in Blow to Oppressive System," *New York Times*, August 2, 2019, https://www.nytimes.com/2019/08/02/world/middleeast/saudi-arabia-guardianship.html.

80. Commins, *The Wahhabi Mission*, 203; Özev, "Saudi Society and the State," 1012; Kelly J. Shannon, "The First Gulf War and Saudi 'Gender Apartheid,'" in *U.S. Foreign Policy and Muslim Women's Human Rights* (Philadelphia: University of Pennsylvania Press, 2018), 79–97; Clarisa Bencomo and Christoph Wilcke, "Separating Image from Substance in Saudi Arabia," *Middle East Report*, no. 48 (2008): 3. See also Katie Paul, "Saudi Arabia Lifts Cinema Ban, Directors and Movie Chains Rejoice," Reuters, December 11, 2017, https://www.reuters.com/article/us-saudi-film/saudi-arabia-says-cinemas-will-be-allowed-from-early-2018-%20idUSKBN1E50N1?il=0,%20https://www.nytimes.com/2018/03/08/world/middleeast/no-dancing-no-swaying-saudi-%20concert.html; Nour Youssef, "No Dancing, No Swaying: Saudi Pop Concert Comes with Warning," *New York Times*, March 8, 2018, https://www.nytimes.com/2018/03/08/world/middleeast/no-dancing-no-swaying-saudi-concert.html; Jane Kinninmont, "End of Saudi Women Driving Ban Reflects Deep Changes in Society," BBC, September 27, 2017, https://www.bbc.com/news/world-middle-east-41412022.

81. Agence France-Presse, "Saudi Arabia: Woman Is Beheaded after Being Convicted of Witchcraft," *New York Times*, December 12, 2011, https://www.nytimes.com/2011/12/13/world/middleeast/saudi-arabia-woman-is-beheaded-after-being-convicted-of-witchcraft.html.

82. Donald Black, *The Behavior of Law* (New York: Academic Press, 1976), 2, 6.

83. Jacek Wiewiorowski, "Deformed Child in the Twelve Tables," in *Mater Familias, Scritti Romanistici per Maria Zabłocka* (Warsaw: Journal of Juristic Papyrology, 2016), 1157–76, https://www.academia.edu/29144967/Deformed_child_in_the_Twelve_Tables_in_Mater_Familias_Scritti_Romanistici_per_Maria

_Zab%C5%82ocka_A_cura_di_Zuzanna_Benincasa_Jakub_Urbanik_con
_la_collaborazione_di_Piotr_Niczyporuk_Maria_Nowak_Varsovia_2016_The
_Journal_of_Juristic_Papyrology_Supplement_XXXIX_pp_1157_1176.

84. An observation also made by Harari, *Sapiens*, 106–7.

85. Saad D. Abulhab, Section 203–205 in *The Law Code of Hammurabi: Transliterated and Literally Translated from its Early Classical Arabic Language* (CreateSpace, 2017).

86. Harari, *Sapiens*, 106–7.

87. Department of Defense, *Qualification Standards for Enlistment, Appointment, and Induction*, DOD Directive 1304.26 (Washington, DC: Department of Defense, 1993), https://queerartvisualculture.files.wordpress.com/2018/10/dadt.pdf.

88. David F. Burrelli, "Don't Ask, Don't Tell: The Law and Military Policy on Same-Sex Behavior," in *Don't Ask, Don't Tell: Background and Issues on Gays in the Military*, ed. Brandon A. Davis (Hauppauge, NY: Nova Science, 2010), 35.

89. Secretary of Defense Ash Carter, *Memorandum: Implementation Guidance for the Full Integration of Women in the Armed Forces* (Washington, DC: Department of Defense, 2015), https://dod.defense.gov/Portals/1/Documents/pubs/OSD014303-15.pdf.

90. Militia Act of 1792, ch. 36, § 1, 1 Stat. 424 (1795). ("Each and every free able-bodied white male citizen of the respective states, resident therein, who is or shall be of age of eighteen years . . . shall severally and respectively be enrolled in the militia.")

91. "Exhibit: 54th Massachusetts Infantry Regiment Casualty List," National Archives and Records Administration, October 1996, https://www.archives.gov/exhibits/american_originals/54thmass.html.

92. Margery Austin Turner, Rob Santos, Diane K. Levy, et al., "Housing Discrimination Against Racial and Ethnic Minorities 2012," U.S. Department of Housing and Urban Development, Office of Policy Development and Research, June 2013, https://www.huduser.gov/portal/publications/pdf/hud-514_hds2012.pdf.

93. Harry S. Truman, Executive Order, "Desegregation of the Armed Forces, Executive Order 9981 of July 26, 1948," Ourdocuments.gov, *https://www.ourdocuments.gov/doc.php?flash=false&doc=84*. See also: Farrell Evans, "Why Harry Truman Ended Segregation in the US Military in 1948," History, November 5, 2020, https://www.history.com/news/harry-truman-executive-order-9981-desegration-military-1948.

94. Menendian, Gambhir, and Gailes, "Roots of Structural Racism Project."

95. Paul Nolan, "Two Tribes: A Divided Northern Ireland," *Irish Times*, April 1, 2017, https://www.irishtimes.com/news/ireland/irish-news/two-tribes-a-divided-northern-ireland-1.3030921.

96. Stephen Menendian and Arthur Gailes, *Racial Segregation in the San Francisco Bay Area, Part 4: The Harmful Effects of Segregation* (Berkeley, CA: Othering and Belonging Institute, 2019), https://belonging.berkeley.edu/racial-segregation -san-francisco-bay-area-part-4.

97. Some examples include decreased academic performance, increased hostility toward one's own racial group or others, and increased homicide arrests. Robert L. Carter, "The Effects of Segregation and the Consequences of Desegregation: A Social Science Statement," *Journal of Negro Education* 22, no. 1 (1953): 68–76, https://doi.org/10.2307/2293629; Roslyn Arlin Mickelson and Damien Heath, "The Effects of Segregation on African American High School Seniors' Academic Achievement," *Journal of Negro Education* 68, no. 4 (1999): 566–86, https://doi .org/10.2307/2668155; Ben Feldmeyer, "The Effects of Racial/Ethnic Segregation on Latino and Black Homicide," *Sociological Quarterly* 51, no. 4 (2010): 600–23, https://www.jstor.org/stable/40927660.

98. See, e.g., Rucker Johnson's paper, finding that integration prompted better resource distributions. Rucker C. Johnson, "Long-Run Impacts of School Desegregation & School Quality on Adult Attainments," working paper, National Bureau of Economic Research, 2011, https://www.nber.org/papers/w16664.

99. Rowan Ricardo Phillips, "Justice for the Negro Leagues Will Mean More Than Just Stats," *New York Times*, September 7, 2021, https://www.nytimes.com/ 2021/03/23/magazine/negro-leagues-baseball-stats-mlb.html ("infrastructural in- equalities—borderline unplayable fields, for example, or poor night lighting").

100. Brown v. Bd. of Educ., 347 U.S. 483, 492.

101. United States v. Virginia, 518 U.S. 515 (1996).

102. Brown v. Bd. of Educ., 347 U.S. 494.

103. Adam Nagourney, "Once a Crucial Refuge, 'Gayborhoods' Lose L.G.B.T.Q. Residents in Major Cities," *New York Times*, July 3, 2022, https:// www.nytimes.com/2022/07/03/us/lgtbq-neighborhoods-nyc-houston.html ?referringSource=articleShare. It is interesting to note that some of the same dy- namics about segregation and political power debated in the racial context are also present in the concerns here, and voiced throughout this article. Specifically, the fear that integration will dilute the ability to elect politicians that will "represent" the social group.

104. Parents Involved in Community Schools v. Seattle School District No. 1, 551 U.S. 701 (2007), 40–41. Chief Justice John Roberts described school segrega- tion as discrimination, writing, "The way to stop discrimination on the basis of race is to stop discriminating on the basis of race."

105. Brian Teppen, "Social Closure: An Introduction and Some Broad Exam- ples," University Corporation for Atmospheric Research: Cooperative Programs

for the Advancement of Earth System Science, April 20, 2018, https://cpaess.ucar
.edu/gold-blogs/social-closure-introduction-and-some-broad-examples.

106. Paul Toews, "Mennonites in American Society: Modernity and the
Persistence of Religious Community," *Mennonite Quarterly Review* 63 (1989):
227–46, https://fpuscholarworks.fresno.edu/bitstream/handle/11418/585/Toews
-Modernity-MQR.pdf?sequence=1&isAllowed=y; Richard Kyle, "The Concept
and Practice of Separation from the World in Mennonite Brethren History," *Direction* 84, no. 1–2 (1984): 33–43, https://directionjournal.org/13/1/concept-and
-practice-of-separation-from.html.

107. Any egalitarian imperative to reduce intergroup disparities is, in those instances, outweighed by cultural imperatives.

108. Maria Cryson and Kyle Crowder, *Cycle of Segregation: Social Processes and
Residential Segregation* (New York: Russell Sage Foundation, 2017), 108. ("People
do not have knowledge of all residential options. In metropolitan areas, it is unlikely that people are aware of every possible option, and since it is difficult to move
into a neighborhood or community if you have never heard of it, understanding
community familiarity is an important foundation to understanding residential
choices. . . . From the vantage point of the perpetuation of segregation, what is of
great interest is whether there are racial differences in which communities get filtered out in this way.")

109. Roger Andersson, Sako Musterd, and George Galster, "Port-of-Entry Neighborhood and Its Effects on the Economic Success of Refugees in Sweden," *International Migration Review* 53, no. 3 (2018): https://doi.org/10.1177/0197918318781785.

110. Jan Lin, "Ethnic Enclaves," in *The Blackwell Encyclopedia of Sociology*, ed.
George Ritzer (Malden, MA: Blackwell, 2007), 1453. ("The enclaves of Asian and
Latino immigrants emerging since the 1960s are comparable to the enclaves of
Jewish and Italian immigrants at the turn of the twentieth century. They present
a route for economic and social mobility by promoting positive returns on human
capital for immigrants in the labor market.")

111. Carl H. Nightingale, *Segregation: A Global History of Divided Cities* (Chicago: University of Chicago Press, 2012), 39.

112. Michael Sullivan, "An Untouchable Subject? Indian Government Wants
Caste System off U.N. Agenda," NPR, August 29, 2001, https://legacy.npr.org/
programs/specials/racism/010828.caste.html.

113. Balla Satish, "Why This India Priest Carried an 'Untouchable' into a Temple,"
BBC, April 19, 2018, https://www.bbc.com/news/world-asia-india-43807951.

114. Harveer Dabas, "'Barred from Entering Temple,' Dalit Youth, 17, Argues
with 4 Upper Caste Men, Found Shot Dead in Amroha," *Times of India*, June 8,
2020, https://timesofindia.indiatimes.com/city/meerut/up-barred-from-entering

-temple-dalit-youth-17-argues-with-4-upper-caste-men-found-shot-dead-in
-amroha/articleshow/76267143.cms. This is an example of where segregation and
violence interact.

115. "Saudi Arabia Ends Gender Segregation in Restaurants," BBC News, December 9, 2019, https://www.bbc.com/news/world-middle-east-50708384.

116. "The Venetian Ghetto: Hidden Secrets," *Economist*, June 18, 2016, https://
www.economist.com/books-and-arts/2016/06/18/hidden-secrets.

117. Stephen H. Haliczer, "The Castilian Urban Patriciate and the Jewish Expulsions of 1480–92," *American Historical Review* 78, no. 1 (February 1973): 52.
("Finally, bowing to heavy pressure from the towns, the monarchy conceded a
general segregation law at the Cortes of Toledo. . . . Since social intercourse with
Jews was dangerous for all Christians, the Jews must live in an area as remote from
Christians as possible . . . the law imposed strict prohibition on Jewish ownership of
houses outside the new ghetto, and Jews were forbidden to sleep outside its confines
for even one night.")

118. Mary Ann Watt and Christopher Zinkowicz et al., "African American
Occupations in the 1900s," *Historical Review of Berks County* (2007), https://
www.berkshistory.org/multimedia/articles/african-american-occupations-in-the
-1900s/; Kate Bahn and Carmen Sanchez Cumming, "Factsheet: U.S. Occupational Segregation by Race, Ethnicity, and Gender," Washington Center for Equitable Growth, July 1, 2020, https://equitablegrowth.org/factsheet-u-s-occupational
-segregation-by-race-ethnicity-and-gender/.

119. John Gunther, *Inside U.S.A.* (New York: Harper, 1947), 680.

120. David W. Wong, Christopher D. Lloyd, and Ian G. Shuttleworth, *Social-
Spatial Segregation: Concepts, Processes and Outcomes* (Bristol, United Kingdom:
Policy Press, 2015), 215.

121. Frederick W. Boal, "Segregating and Mixing: Space and Residence in Bel-
fast," in Frederick W. Boal and J. Neville H. Douglas, *Integration and Division:
Geographical Perspectives on the Northern Ireland Problem* (London: Academic
Press, 1982), quoted in David W. Wong, Christopher D. Lloyd, and Ian G. Shuttle-
worth, *Social-Spatial Segregation: Concepts, Processes and Outcomes* (Bristol, United
Kingdom: Policy Press, 2015), 200.

122. Jonathan Bardon, *A History of Ulster* (Ulster, Ireland: Blackstaff Press,
1992), 716, quoted in David W. Wong, Christopher D. Lloyd, and Ian G. Shuttleworth, *Social-Spatial Segregation: Concepts, Processes and Outcomes* (Bristol, United
Kingdom: Policy Press, 2015), 200.

123. Richard Seymour, "The Last Gasp of Northern Ireland," *New York Times*,
November 12, 2018, https://www.nytimes.com/2018/11/02/opinion/northern
-ireland-brexit-unionism.html.

124. Richard Sander, Yana A. Kucheva, and Jonathan M. Zasloff, *Moving Toward Integration: The Past and Future of Fair Housing* (Cambridge, MA: Harvard University Press, 2018), 168.

125. Kerner Commission, "Report of the National Advisory Commission on Civil Disorders"; Hinton, *America on Fire*, 191.

126. Jonathan Laurence and Justine Vaisse, "Understanding Urban Riots in France," Brookings Institution, December 1, 2005, https://www.brookings.edu/articles/understanding-urban-riots-in-france/; Christina Horvath, "Riots or Revolts? The Legacy of the 2005 Uprising in French Banlieue Narratives," *Modern & Contemporary France* 26, no. 2 (2018): 193–206.

127. 392. George Packer, "The Other France," *New Yorker*, August 31, 2015, https://www.newyorker.com/magazine/2015/08/31/the-other-france.

128. Hanna Papanek, "Purdah: Separate Worlds and Symbolic Shelter," *Comparative Studies in Society and History* 15, no. 3 (June 1973): 289–325. ("Purdah, meaning curtain, is the word most commonly used for the system of secluding women and enforcing high standards of female modesty in much of South Asia. Purdah is an important part of the life experience of many South Asians, both Muslim and Hindu, and is a central feature of the social systems of the area.")

129. Pintu Paul, "Explaining the Links Between Purdah Practice, Womens' Autonomy, and Health Knowledge in India," in *Urban Health Risk and Resilience in Asian Cities*, ed. R. B. Singh, Bathula Sriganesh, and Subhash Anand (Singapore: Springer Nature, 2006), 111–26. ("Purdah is a crucial instrument of female seclusion, sex segregation, and subordination of women . . . it is found that large proportions of women are secluded from both private and public domain which may affect their participation in economic activities, education, and health outcomes.")

130. Helen Rawlings, "The Spanish Inquisition and the Converso Challenge (c. 1480–1525): A Question of Race, Religion, or Sociopolitical Ascendancy?" in *A Companion to Heresy Inquisitions*, ed. Donald Prudlo (Leiden, Netherlands: Brill, 2019), 173–97. (""The Spanish Inquisition, established by papal bull on 1 November 1478, was originally set up to deal with a specific group of individuals known as conversos—Jews who had converted to Christianity either voluntarily or under duress in the wake of rising anti-Semitic tensions in society . . . the brutal persecution of converso heresy, concentrated over the next five decades (1480–1525), was set to continue—against all expectations—at intermittent intervals of the following three centuries.")

131. Plessy v. Ferguson, 163 U.S. 537 (1896), 551.

132. Radha Kumar, "The Troubled History of Partition," *Foreign Affairs* 76, no. 1 (1997): 22–34. ("India's political leadership agreed to partition the country before the spread of large-scale conflict; the 1947 partition agreement between the

Indian National Congress and the Muslim League was intended partly to prevent the spread of communal riots from Bengal in eastern India to northwestern India, which was also to be divided. But the riots that followed in 1947–48 left more than a million people dead in six months and displaced upwards of 15 million.")

133. "FDR Orders 'Enemy Aliens' to Register," History, November 16, 2009, last modified January 13, 2020, https://www.history.com/this-day-in-history/roosevelt-ushers-in-japanese-american-internment.

134. Korematsu v. United States, 323 U.S. 214 (1944).

135. Commission on Wartime Relocation and Internment of Civilians, *Personal Justice Denied: Report of the Commission on Wartime Relocation and Internment of Civilians* (Seattle and London: University of Washington Press, 1997), 71, 459.

136. Where the Foreign Fighters in Iraq and Syria Are Coming From [map], 2015, "Iraqi Army Retakes Government Complex in Central Ramadi," last updated December 28, 2015, *New York Times*, http://www.nytimes.com/interactive/2014/06/12/world/middleeast/the-iraq-isis-conflict-in-maps-photos-and-video.html, accessed February 16, 2016.

137. "Biden: Split Iraq into 3 Different Regions," *USA Today*, May 1, 2006, accessed on May 30, 2016, http://usatoday30.usatoday.com/news/washington/2006-05-01-biden-iraq_x.htm.

138. Although the British proposal was more thoughtful, and envisioned a federated union of two majority-Muslim provinces and a Hindu-majority province. Barbara D. Metcalf and Thomas R. Metcalf, *A Concise History of India* (Cambridge: Cambridge University Press, 2002), 211–13.

139. Barbara Surk, "In a Divided Bosnia, Segregated Schools Persist," *New York Times*, December 1, 2018, https://www.nytimes.com/2018/12/01/world/europe/bosnia-schools-segregated-ethnic.html.

140. Johnson v. California, 543 U.S. 499 (2005).

141. Richard Rothstein, *The Color of Law: A Forgotten History of How Our Government Segregated America* (London: Liveright, 2017), 31.

142. City of Richmond v. J.A. Croson Co., 488 U.S. 469 (1989).

143. "The Foundations of Black Power," National Museum of African American History and Culture, accessed March 17, 2023, https://nmaahc.si.edu/explore/stories/foundations-black-power.

144. Robert A. Brown and Todd C. Shaw, "Separate Nations: Two Attitudinal Dimensions of Black Nationalism," *Journal of Politics* 64, no. 1 (2002): https://doi.org/10.1111/1468-2508.00116.

145. Charles M. Blow, *The Devil You Know: A Black Power Manifesto* (New York: Harper, 2021).

146. Derrick Bell, *Faces at the Bottom of the Well: The Permanence of Racism* (New York: Basic Books, 1992).

147. Kendi, *How to Be an Anti-Racist*, 176.

148. Brown v. Bd. of Educ., 347 U.S. 483, 494 (emphasis added).

149. Sandi Cole et al., "The Relationship of Special Education Placement and Student Academic Outcomes," *Journal of Special Education* 54, no. 4 (2021): 217–27, https://doi.org/10.1177/0022466920925033; Sandi Cole et al., "The Relationship Between Special Education Placement and High School Outcomes," *Journal of Special Education* 0 (2022), https://doi.org/10.1177/00224669221097945. (Results of this study show that students with disabilities who spent 80 percent or more of their time in a general education inclusive classroom did significantly better in both reading and math assessment than their peers who spent more time in separate special education classrooms.)

150. Rachel Blustain and the Hechinger Report, "Gifted Programs Worsen Inequality. Here's What Happens When Schools Try to Get Rid of Them," NBC News, October 14, 2020, https://www.nbcnews.com/news/education/gifted-programs-worsen-inequality-here-s-what-happens-when-schools-n1243147.

151. Hiba Yazbek, "In an Israeli Oasis, a Model for Peace, if Messy and Imperfect," *New York Times*, September 30, 2023, https://www.nytimes.com/2023/09/30/world/middleeast/israel-peace-oasis-village.html.

152. Rick Gladstone and Peter Robins, "The Ghosts of Northern Ireland's Troubles Are Back. What's Going On?" *New York Times*, April 12, 2021, https://www.nytimes.com/2021/04/12/world/europe/Northern-Ireland-Brexit-Covid-Troubles.html.

153. Gladstone and Robins, "The Ghosts of Northern Ireland's Troubles."

154. Gladstone and Robins, "The Ghosts of Northern Ireland's Troubles."

155. Gladstone and Robins, "The Ghosts of Northern Ireland's Troubles."

156. Raymond Russel, *Census 2011: Key Statistics at Northern Ireland and LGD level* (Northern Ireland Assembly, 2013) 8, accessed September 12, 2021, http://www.niassembly.gov.uk/globalassets/documents/raise/publications/2013/general/russell3013.pdf.

157. Ian Talbot and Gurharpal Singh, "The Partition of India," *Journal of Islamic Studies* 21, no. 3 (2010): 464–67, accessed September 12, 2021, https://doi.org/10.1093/jis/etq049.

158. Rounaq Jahan, "Bangladesh in 1972: Nation Building in a New State," *Asian Survey* 13, no. 2 (1973): 199–210, https://doi.org/10.2307/2642736; Iftekharul Bashar, "Unresolved Statelessness: The Case of Biharis in Bangladesh," *Journal of International Affairs* 10, no. 1–2 (2006): 87–116, https://www.researchgate.net/publication/319207496_Unresolved_Statelessness_The_Case_of_Biharis_in_Bangladesh.

159. Jyotindra Nath Dixit, "The Break-up of Pakistan," in *India-Pakistan in War and Peace* (New York: Routledge, 2002), 161–231; "Quebec Separatism," *Britannica*, accessed August 22, 2023, https://www.britannica.com/place/Canada/Quebec -separatism; Montserrat Guibernau, *Catalan Nationalism: Francoism, Transition, and Democracy* (New York: Routledge, 2004); J. H. Elliot, *Scots and Catalans: Union and Disunion* (New Haven, CT: Yale University Press, 2018).

160. Fukuyama, *Identity*, 147.

161. Thomas Erdbrink, "Rattled by Attacks, Many Belgians Still Want Nation Split in Two," *New York Times*, April 8, 2016, http://www.nytimes.com/2016/04/ 08/world/europe/rattled-by-outside-threats-many-belgians-still-want-nation-split -in-two.html.

162. Center for Preventative Action, "Civil War in South Sudan," Council on Foreign Relations, updated May 12, 2022, https://www.cfr.org/global-conflict -tracker/conflict/civil-war-south-sudan.

163. Jacey Fortin, "Power Struggles Stall South Sudan's Recovery from War," *New York Times*, May 30, 2016, http://www.nytimes.com/2016/05/31/world/africa/ south-sudan-struggles-to-collect-taxes-after-years-of-war.html.

164. Ezra Klein, "The Rest of the World Is Worried about America," *New York Times*, July 1, 2021, https://www.nytimes.com/2021/07/01/opinion/us-democracy -erosion.html.

165. Appiah, *The Lies That Bind*, 84.

166. Jane Arraf, "Syria's Kurds Wanted Autonomy. They Got an Endless War," *New York Times*, February 7, 2022, https://www.nytimes.com/2022/02/07/world/ middleeast/syria-kurds.html?referringSource=articleShare.

167. Fuat Dundar, "'Statisquo': British Use of Statistics in the Iraqi Kurdish Question (1919–1932)," Crown Papers, Brandeis University, 2012, https://www .brandeis.edu/crown/publications/papers/pdfs/cp7.pdf, 45, table 10.

168. Saskia Sassen, *Expulsions: Brutality and Complexity in the Global Economy* (Cambridge, MA: Harvard University Press, 2014), 15. See also 48: "One of the most brutal forms of expulsion is the eviction of people from their homes for failure to pay outstanding debt on their home. This is an especially devastating trend in Europe because there the evicted remain responsible for the full amount of their loan even after foreclosure."

169. "Spain Announces It Will Expel All Jews," History, November 12, 2019, https://www.history.com/this-day-in-history/spain-announces-it-will-expel-all -jews.

170. "Zurich, Switzerland," Jewish Virtual Library, https://www.jewish virtuallibrary.org/zurich-switzerland.

171. Perdue, "Legacy of Indian Removal."

172. Russell Thornton, "The Demography of the Trail of Tears Period: A New Estimate of Cherokee Population Losses," in *Cherokee Removal: Before And After*, ed. William J. Anderson (Athens: University of Georgia Press, 1991), 92–93, quoted in Amy H. Sturgis, *The Trail of Tears and Indian Removal* (Westport, CT: Greenwood, 2007), 2. See also Thornton, "The Demography of the Trail of Tears," 75–95, quotes in Sturgis, *The Trail of Tears*, 60: "Determining the cost of the Trail of Tears in human lives is a difficult proposition. In the first wave of relocation, soldiers had strong motivation to underreport deaths. (The original official number provided by the government was approximately four hundred.) When the Cherokees themselves had some control over the removal process, they were more concerned about keeping each other alive than with documenting each loss along the way, even if they had possessed the means. Traditional approximations suggest that some four thousand Cherokees died of hunger, exposure, dysentery, whooping cough, violence, and other factors during or because of the Trail of Tears. This figure may date from one single missionary's 1839 estimation, repeated and cited until it gained the credibility of fact; at any rate, recent scholarship suggests that the death toll figure of four thousand may represent only half of the actual Cherokee lives lost. Regardless of the exact statistics, though, removal exacted a terrible toll on the people of the Cherokee Nation."

173. Jeffrey Ostler, "Disease Has Never Been Just Disease for Native Americans," *Atlantic*, April 29, 2020, https://www.theatlantic.com/ideas/archive/2020/04/disease-has-never-been-just-disease-native-americans/610852/.

174. Ostler, "Disease Has Never Been Just Disease."

175. Jennifer Nez Denetdale, "Chairmen, Presidents and Princesses: The Navajo Nation, Gender and the Politics of Tradition," *Wicazo Sa Review* 21, no. 1 (2006): 9–28, quoted in Finley, "State Crime, Native Americans and COVID-19," 51.

176. Denetdale, "Chairmen, Presidents, and Princesses," 9–28.

177. Anton Troianovski, "For Nagorno-Karabakh's Dueling Sides, Living Together Is 'Impossible,'" *New York Times*, October 27, 2020, https://www.nytimes.com/2020/10/13/world/europe/armenia-azerbaijan-nagorno-karabakh.html.

178. Troianovski, "Nagorno-Karabakh's Dueling Sides."

179. One of us wrote about this as it was occurring: Stephen Menendian, "Blog: Can We All Belong? Reflections on the War in Nagorno-Karabakh," *Othering & Belonging Institute* (blog), November 5, 2020, https://belonging.berkeley.edu/blog-can-we-all-belong-reflections-war-nagorno-karabakh.

180. Troianovski and Gall, "After War Between Armenia and Azerbaijan."

181. powell, "The Needs of Members."

182. Michael Walzer, "Citizenship," in *Political Innovation and Conceptual Change*, ed. Terence Ball, Russell L. Hanson, and James Farr (Cambridge: Cambridge University Press, 1989), 211–19.

183. powell, "The Needs of Members" (arguing that membership is the most important good we distribute in the political community, and that in the modern nation-state, membership is denoted by citizenship).

184. Neville Morley, *The Roman Empire: Roots of Imperialism* (New York: Pluto Press, 2010), 50–51.

185. Andrew Helms, "The Limits of Citizenship in the Roman Empire," *National Geographic*, accessed November 9, 2022, https://www.nationalgeographic .org/activity/limits-citizenship-roman-empire/.

186. Marx, *Making Race and Nation*, 5.

187. Frederick Douglass, "Should the Negro Enlist in the Union Army?" speech, National Hall, Philadelphia, July 6, 1863). ("Once let the black man get upon his person the brass letter, U.S., let him get an eagle on his button, and a musket on his shoulder and bullets in his pocket, there is no power on earth that can deny he has earned the right to citizenship.")

188. Jami L. Bryan, "Fighting for Respect: African-American Soldiers in WWI," National Museum of the United States Army, https://armyhistory.org/fighting-for -respect-african-american-soldiers-in-wwi/.

189. Du Bois ultimately soured on the war after learning how badly Black servicemen were treated, although he was so initially enthusiastic that he solicited his readers to send him stories for inclusion in what he had planned to be the ultimate history of Black service in the Great War and even sought to discover if he could get support as a booster for the War Department. Chad L. Williams, *The Wounded World: W. E. B. Du Bois and the First World War* (New York: Farrar, Straus and Giroux, 2023); Matthew Delmont, "W.E.B. Du Bois and the Legacy — and Betrayal — of Black Soldiers," *New York Times*, April 4, 2023, https://www.nytimes.com/2023/04/04/ books/review/chad-williams-the-wounded-world.html.

190. John Gunther, *Inside U.S.A.* (New York: Harper, 1947), 687.

191. Suhasini Raj and Jeffrey Gettleman, "A Mass Citizenship Check in India Leaves 2 Million People in Limbo," *New York Times*, August 31, 2019, https://www .nytimes.com/2019/08/31/world/asia/india-muslim-citizen-list.html; Jeffrey Gettleman and Hari Kumar, "India Plans Big Detention Camps for Migrants. Muslims Are Afraid," *New York Times*, August 17, 2019, https://www.nytimes.com/2019/08/ 17/world/asia/india-muslims-narendra-modi.html; Vidhi Doshi, "India Cast Millions of Muslims as Illegal Immigrants. Their Legal Battles Are Just Beginning," *Washington Post*, August 17, 2018, https://www.washingtonpost.com/world/asia _pacific/india-cast-millions-of-muslims-as-illegal-immigrants-their-legal-battles -are-just-beginning/2018/08/16/ce8438ca-8f80-11e8-ae59-01880eac5f1d_story.html ?utm_term=.4beed3b94837.

192. "Life Upended for Those Left off Indian Citizenship List," Arab News, September 2, 2018, https://www.arabnews.com/node/1365531/world.

193. Deb, "They Are Manufacturing Foreigners"; Harrison Akins, "Factsheet on the Citizenship (Amendment) Act in India," U.S. Commission on International Religious Freedom, February 2020, https://www.uscirf.gov/sites/default/files/2020%20Legislation%20Factsheet%20-%20India_0_0.pdf.

194. Deb, "They Are Manufacturing Foreigners."

195. The discriminatory motives are made even clearer by an amending law, the 2019 Citizenship Amendment Act, which allowed Hindu, Christian, Jain, Buddhist, Sikh, and Paris migrants to claim citizenship. The only major religious group excluded were Muslims. Roy Anupama, *Citizenship Regimes, Law, and Belonging: The CAA and NCR* (Oxford: Oxford University Press, 2022), 83–162; Deb, "They Are Manufacturing Foreigners."

196. Doshi, "India Cast Millions of Muslims."

197. Makiko Kimura, *The Nellie Massacre of 1983: Agency of Rioters* (New Delhi: SAGE, 2013), 1; Nooriya Jamil, "Nellie Massacre, 1983: A Hate Crime Against Muslims," Muslim Memo, August 12, 2016, https://muslimmemo.com/nellie-massacre/.

198. Jonathan M. Katz, "In Exile," *New York Times*, January 13, 2016, https://www.nytimes.com/2016/01/17/magazine/haitians-in-exile-in-the-dominican-republic.html.

199. Jonathan M. Katz, "What Happened When a Nation Erased Birthright Citizenship," *Atlantic*, November 12, 2018, https://www.theatlantic.com/ideas/archive/2018/11/dominican-republic-erased-birthright-citizenship/575527/.

200. Christina M. Cerna, "Judgment TC/0168/13 (Const. Ct. Dom. Rep.) & Statement of the Inter-American Commission on Human Rights on Judgment TC/0168/13," *International Legal Materials* 53, no. 4 (2014): 662–726, https://doi.org/10.5305/intelegamate.53.4.0662. See Rachel Nolan, "Displaced in the D.R.," *Harper's Magazine*, May 2015, https://harpers.org/archive/2015/05/displaced-in-the-d-r/?single=1.

201. Amanda Taub, "Dominican Republic Strips Thousands of Black Residents of Citizenship, May Now Expel Them," Vox, June 18, 2015, https://www.vox.com/2015/6/18/8802587/dominican-republic-haitian-deportation.

202. Leah Libresco, "The Dominican Republic's Revocation of Citizenship Creates 200,000 Stateless People," FiveThirtyEight, June 17, 2015, https://fivethirtyeight.com/features/the-dominican-republics-revocation-of-citizenship-creates-200000-stateless-people/.

203. Katz, "In Exile."

204. Taub, "Dominican Republic Strips Citizenship."

205. Katz, "In Exile."

206. Katz, "When a Nation Erased Birthright Citizenship."

207. "Poll Shows Large Swaths of Israeli Youth Hate Arabs, Back Revoking Citizenship," *Times of Israel*, February 19, 2021, https://www.timesofisrael.com/poll-shows-large-swaths-of-israeli-youth-hate-arabs-back-revoking-citizenship/.

208. Garrett Epps, "The Citizenship Clause Means What It Says," *Atlantic*, October 30, 2018, https://www.theatlantic.com/ideas/archive/2018/10/birthright-citizenship-constitution/574381/.

209. Naturalization Act of 1790, Pub. L. no. 1–3, 1 Stat. 103 (1790), https://govtrackus.s3.amazonaws.com/legislink/pdf/stat/1/STATUTE-1-Pg103.pdf. "Any Alien, being a free white person, who shall have resided within the limits and under the jurisdiction of the United States for the term of two years, may be admitted to become a citizen thereof."

210. john a. powell and Stephen Menendian, "Little Rock and the Legacy of Dred Scott," *St. Louis University Law Journal* 52, no. 4 (2008): 1159; Henry L. Chambers Jr., "Slavery, Free Blacks and Citizenship," *Rutgers Law Journal* 43 (2013): 487–88.

211. Dred Scott v. Sandford, 60 U.S. 393.

212. Ed O'Loughlin, "In Ireland, Bid to Restore Birthright Citizenship Gains Ground," *New York Times*, November 24, 2018, https://www.nytimes.com/2018/11/24/world/europe/ireland-birthright-citizenship.html.

213. Julie Hirschfeld Davis, "President Wants to Use Executive Order to End Birthright Citizenship," *New York Times*, October 30, 2018, https://www.nytimes.com/2018/10/30/us/politics/trump-birthright-citizenship.html.

214. Dara Lind, "Denaturalization, Explained: How Trump Can Strip Immigrants of Their Citizenship," Vox, July 18, 2018, https://www.vox.com/2018/7/18/17561538/denaturalization-citizenship-task-force-janus.

215. "Muslim Travel Ban," *Immigration History*, accessed December 1, 2023, https://immigrationhistory.org/item/muslim-travel-ban/.

216. "Le Pen's Plan to Legalise Discrimination against Foreigners in France—Including Dual Nationals," The Local, April 19, 2022, https://www.thelocal.fr/20220419/le-pens-plan-to-legalise-discrimination-against-foreigners-in-france-including-dual-nationals/.

217. Portions of this section have been previously published as a blog. Stephen Menendian, "From Tulsa, Texas, to Turkey: The Price of Denial," *Berkeley Blog*, June 1, 2021, https://blogs.berkeley.edu/2021/06/01/from-tulsa-texas-to-turkey-the-price-of-denial/.

218. Christine Hauser, "'It Is Not Coming Down': San Francisco Defends 'Comfort Women' Statue as Japan Protests," *New York Times*, October 4, 2018, https://www.nytimes.com/2018/10/04/us/osaka-sf-comfort-women-statue.html.

219. Iris Chang, *The Rape of Nanking: The Forgotten Holocaust of World War II* (New York: Basic Books, 1997), 6237, quoted in Raleigh Morgan, "Chinese, Japanese, and United States Views of the Nanking Massacre: The Supreme Court Trial of Shiro Azuma," *American Journal of Chinese Studies* 9, no. 2 (2002): 237.

220. Murray Williamson, "The Meaning of World War II," *Joint Force Quarterly* (Summer 1995): 50–57, quoted in Raleigh Morgan, "Chinese, Japanese, and United States Views of the Nanking Massacre: The Supreme Court Trial of Shiro Azuma," *American Journal of Chinese Studies* 9, no. 2 (2002): 237; Erin Blakemore, "The Brutal History of Japan's 'Comfort Women,'" History, published February 20, 2018; last modified July 21, 2019, https://www.history.com/news/comfort-women-japan-military-brothels-korea.

221. Williamson, "Meaning of WWII"; Blakemore, "Brutal History of Comfort Women."

222. Deborah Lipstadt, *Denying the Holocaust* (New York: Free Press, 1993).

223. Mitch Landrieu, "How I Learned about the "Cult of the Lost Cause"," *Smithsonian Magazine*, March 12, 2018, https://www.smithsonianmag.com/history/how-i-learned-about-cult-lost-cause-180968426/; Michel Paradis, "The Lost Cause's Long Legacy," *Atlantic*, June 26, 2020, https://www.theatlantic.com/ideas/archive/2020/06/the-lost-causes-long-legacy/613288/.

224. Michael Bobelian, *Children of Armenia: A Forgotten Genocide and the Century-Long Struggle for Justice* (New York: Simon & Schuster, 2009), 29, 171; Hakob Chakrian, "The Armenian-Turkish Dialogue: A Brief Note," *Iran & the Caucasus* 5 (2001): 225.

225. Regents of the University of California v. Bakke, 438 U.S. 265, 292 (1978).

226. Morris and Ze'evi, *The Thirty-Year Genocide*, 367.

227. Shaun Walker, "Genocide Denial Gains Ground 25 years After Srebrenica Massacre," *Guardian*, July 10, 2020, https://www.theguardian.com/world/2020/jul/10/genocide-denial-gains-ground-25-years-after-srebrenica-massacre.

228. Nuria Martinez-Keel, "'A Conspiracy of Silence': Tulsa Race Massacre Was Absent from Schools for Generations," *Oklahoman*, May 26, 2021, https://www.oklahoman.com/story/news/education/2021/05/26/oklahoma-history-black-wall-street-left-out-public-schools-tulsa-massacre-education/4875340001/.

229. Nur Masalha, "Decolonizing Methodology, Reclaiming Memory: Palestinian Oral Histories and Memories of the Nakba," in *An Oral History of the*

Palestinian Nakba, ed. Nahla Abdo and Nur Masalha (London: Zed Books, 2018), 7.

230. Chakraborty, "India's Leading Documentary Filmmaker Has a Warning."

231. Nikolay Koposov, *Memory Laws, Memory Wars: The Politics of the Past in Europe and Russia* (Cambridge: Cambridge University Press, 2017), 1. ("The term 'memory laws' (lois mémorielles) was coined in France in the 2000s to refer to legislation that penalizes Holocaust negationalism or recognizes certain events as crimes against humanity while not prohibiting their denial. The invention of a new term shows that memory laws were widely perceived as a novelty that could not be adequately described within existing categories.")

232. Uladzislau Belavusau, "The Rise of Memory Laws in Poland," *Security and Human Rights* 29, no. 1–4 (2018): 36–54.

233. Timothy Snyder, "The War on History Is a War on Democracy, "*New York Times*, June 29, 2021, https://www.nytimes.com/2021/06/29/magazine/memory -laws.html.

234. Kaleigh Rogers and Mary Radcliffe, "Over 100 Anti-LGBTQ+ Laws Passed in the Last Five Years—Half of Them This Year," FiveThirtyEight, May 25, 2023, https://fivethirtyeight.com/features/anti-lgbtq-laws-red-states/.

235. Steve Scherer, "Pope Sparks Row with Turkey by Calling Armenian Massacre Genocide," Reuters, April 12, 2015, https://www.reuters.com/article/us-pope -armenia-genocide/pope-sparks-row-with-turkey-by-calling-armenian-massacre -genocide-idUSKBN0N307820150412.

236. Ann M. Simmons, "Biden's Recognition of Armenian Genocide Helps Healing of a Deep Wound," *Wall Street Journal*, April 26, 2021, https://www.wsj .com/articles/bidens-recognition-of-armenian-genocide-helps-healing-of-a-deep -wound-11619435877; "Erdogan Slams Biden's Recognition of Armenian 'Genocide,'" Al Jazeera, April 26, 2021, https://www.aljazeera.com/news/2021/4/26/ erdogan-slams-bidens-armenian-genocide-recognition.

237. Phillip Pan, "Turkey Rejects U.S. Use of Bases," *Washington Post*, March 2, 2003, https://www.washingtonpost.com/archive/politics/2003/03/02/turkey-rejects -us-use-of-bases/01e53587-6d0b-4b3a-bb48-f86f87a15d02/.

238. Taner Akçam, "Turkey and Armenia: Is There Any Other Solution Than Dialogue?" *Cultural Survival*, June 2003, https://www.culturalsurvival.org/publications/ cultural-survival-quarterly/turkey-and-armeniais-there-any-other-solution-dialogue. "A society based on a mentality that views the absence of the other as the condition for its own existence, and on a legal system created as the product of this mentality, cannot be democratic. A future respecting human dignity and honor cannot be established." Taner Akçam and Umit Kurt, *The Spirit of the Laws: The Plunder of Wealth in*

the Armenian Genocide (Oxford: Berghahn Books, 2015), 193. "If Turkey is to develop from an authoritarian, bureaucratic state into a standard Western democracy, it must come to terms with history and take a critical approach towards the problems surrounding its national identity. For this to occur, Turkish society must take an active role in opening a debate on the Armenian Genocide. . . . The dominance of the denial syndrome must be overcome and direct interaction between Turkish and Armenian societies must take place." Taner Akçam, *From Empire to Republic: Turkish Nationalism and the Armenian Genocide* (London: Zed Books, 2004), 9.

239. Sam Jones, "Spain Passes Law to Bring 'Justice' to Franco-Era Victims," *Guardian,* October 5, 2022, https://www.theguardian.com/world/2022/oct/05/spain-passes-law-to-bring-dignity-to-franco-era-victims.

240. Constant Méheut, "Spanish Vote Threatens Efforts to Recover Franco's Victims," *New York Times,* July 18, 2023, last updated July 20, 2023, https://www.nytimes.com/2023/07/18/world/europe/spain-franco-victims-recover.html.

241. See, e.g., Dictionary.com, s.v. "erasure," accessed October 28, 2021, https://www.dictionary.com/browse/erasure. "Exclusion of a minority group or group member from the historical record." This is similar to, but different from, the definition offered here, which refers to a different set of phenomena: Parul Sehgal, "Fighting 'Erasure,'" *New York Times Magazine,* February 2, 2016, https://www.nytimes.com/2016/02/07/magazine/the-painful-consequences-of-erasure.html. "'Erasure' refers to the practice of collective indifference that renders certain people and groups invisible. The word migrated out of the academy, where it alluded to the tendency of ideologies to dismiss inconvenient facts, and is increasingly used to describe how inconvenient people are dismissed, their history, pain, and achievements blotted out."

242. Chris Buckley and Austin Ramzy, "China Is Erasing Mosques and Precious Shrines in Xinjiang," *New York Times,* September 25, 2020, https://www.nytimes.com/interactive/2020/09/25/world/asia/xinjiang-china-religious-site.html.

243. Sameer Yasir and Hari Kumar, "Museum in India Celebrating Muslim Dynasty Gets a Hindu Overhaul," *New York Times,* September 15, 2020, https://www.nytimes.com/2020/09/15/world/asia/india-museum-muslims-hindus.html.

244. English has two words to describe structures built to commemorate facts, events, or people: *memorial* and *monument,* and they are sometimes used interchangeably. These terms lack the nuance to help us understand the distinctions between different forms. German, however, does have a wider range of terminology to help delineate between forms and purpose. Carol Schaeffer, "Hatred in Plain Sight," *Smithsonian Magazine,* October 2020, https://www.smithsonianmag.com/history/germany-nazism-medieval-anti-semitism-plain-sight-180975780/ (describing the different German words used to describe monuments and memorials and their distinctive meaning).

245. Sridevi Nambiar, "A Brief History of How Bombay Became Mumbai," *Culture Trip*, September 19, 2016, https://theculturetrip.com/asia/india/articles/the-history-of-how-bombay-became-mumbai-in-1-minute/.

246. Ibram X. Kendi, "The Heartbeat of Racism Is Denial," *New York Times*, January 13, 2018, https://www.nytimes.com/2018/01/13/opinion/sunday/heartbeat-of-racism-denial.html.

247. Susan Neiman, *Learning from the Germans: Race and the Memory of Evil* (New York: Farrar, Straus & Giroux, 2019), quoted in Deborah E. Lipstadt, "Slavery and the Holocaust: How Americans and Germans Cope with Past Evils," *New York Times*, August 27, 2019, https://www.nytimes.com/2019/08/27/books/review/learning-from-the-germans-susan-neiman.html.

248. *Honouring the Truth, Reconciling for the Future: Summary of the Final Report of the Truth and Reconciliation Commission of Canada* (Winnipeg, Canada: University of Manitoba National Centre for Truth and Reconciliation, 2015), 202–9, https://ehprnh2mwo3.exactdn.com/wp-content/uploads/2021/01/Executive_Summary_English_Web.pdf; Archbishop Desmond Tutu et al., *Truth and Reconciliation Commission of South Africa Report*, vol. 1 (Cape Town, South Africa: Truth and Reconciliation Commission, 1998), 16, 49, 107–10, https://www.justice.gov.za/trc/report/finalreport/Volume%201.pdf.

249. Reid J. Epstein and Lisa Lerer, "Democrats Are Determined to Pressure Biden to Investigate Trump," *New York Times*, January 9, 2021, https://www.nytimes.com/2021/01/09/us/politics/democrats-trump-crimes-prosecute.html.

250. "For the first time meticulous and thorough research was carried on in an effort to determine the truth rather than to prove a thesis," was how one historian described the impact of the Dunning school in the *American Historical Review* in 1940. The "truth," though, meant Dunning school historians of the Reconstruction era chronicling the White South as victimized by the corrupt and incompetent Black politicians and the North mistakenly forcing Reconstruction before quickly correcting itself and leaving the noble White South on its own wits. "All the forces that made for civilization were dominated by a mass of barbarous freedmen," William Archibald Dunning supposed in his 1907 classic, *Reconstruction: Political and Economic, 1865–1877* (New York: Harper, 1907), 212, quoted in Kendi, *Stamped from the Beginning*, 286. "Dunning trained a generation of influential southern historians who became department chairs and dominated the discipline of history for decades in the twentieth century. His most notable student was Georgia native Ulrich Bonnell Phillips. In *American Negro Slavery* (1918), along with eight more books and a duffel bag of articles, Phillips erased the truth of slavery as a highly lucrative enterprise dominated by planters who incessantly forced a resisting people to labor through terror, manipulation, and racist ideas. Instead he dreamed up an

unprofitable commerce dominated by benevolent, paternalistic planters civilizing and caring or a 'robust, amiable, obedient, and content' barbaric people. Phillips's pioneering use of plantation documents legitimated his racist dreams and made them seem like objective realities." Ulrich B. Phillips, *American Negro Slavery* (New York: Appleton, 1918), quoted in Kendi, *Stamped from the Beginning*, 287.

251. Matthew Wills, "Origins of the Confederate Lost Cause," JSTOR Daily, July 15, 2015, https://daily.jstor.org/origins-confederate-lost-cause/ ("At its heart, the Lost Cause was a 'mystique of chivalric Southern soldiers and the noble Confederate leadership embodied in Jefferson Davis' defending a way of life, state's rights, even the original American Revolution, against a rapacious Northern industrial machine. The actual reason for the Confederacy's existence, slavery and the power of a plantation economy based on it, didn't play a large role in the myth, although continued white dominance of political power and the associated denial of humanity to black Southerners was very much the point of it.")

252. "Combating Holocaust Denial: Origins of Holocaust Denial," United States Holocaust Memorial Museum, https://encyclopedia.ushmm.org/content/en/article/combating-holocaust-denial-origins-of-holocaust-denial.

253. This is captured to some extent in the 1976 documentary *The Memory of Justice*, directed by Marcel Ophüls (Paramount Pictures).

254. Schaeffer, "Hatred in Plain Sight."

255. "Holocaust Restitution: German Reparations," Jewish Virtual Library, https://www.jewishvirtuallibrary.org/german-holocaust-reparations.

256. In 1985. Jacob Mchangama, "First They Came for the Holocaust Deniers, and I Did Not Speak Out," *Foreign Policy*, October 2, 2016, https://foreignpolicy.com/2016/10/02/first-they-came-for-the-holocaust-deniers-and-i-did-not-speak-out/; Max Söllner, "The Story of Why Holocaust Denial Is a Crime in Germany," *SmarterGerman* (blog), August 24, 2016, https://smartergerman.com/blog/holocaust-denial-crime-germany/; "Holocaust Memorial," Berlin.de (official website of city of Berlin), last updated March 18, 2022, https://www.berlin.de/en/attractions-and-sights/3560249-3104052-holocaust-memorial.en.html.

257. Richard Brody, "The Inadequacy of Berlin's 'Memorial to the Murdered Jews of Europe,'" *New Yorker*, July 12, 2012, https://www.newyorker.com/culture/richard-brody/the-inadequacy-of-berlins-memorial-to-the-murdered-jews-of-europe.

258. Suyin Haynes, "Germany Has Officially Recognized Colonial-Era Atrocities in Namibia. But for Some, Reconciliation Is a Long Way Off," *Time*, May 28, 2021, https://time.com/6052493/germany-colonial-genocide/.

259. Shelleygan Petersen, "Namibia Announces Acceptance of German Genocide Offer," *Namibian*, June 4, 2021, https://www.namibian.com.na/211960/archive-read/Namibia-announces-acceptance-of-German-genocide-offer.

260. Kavena Hambira and Miriam Gleckman-Krut, "Germany Apologized for a Genocide. It's Nowhere Near Enough," *New York Times*, July 8, 2021, https://www.nytimes.com/2021/07/08/opinion/germany-genocide-herero-nama.html.

261. Mattie Kahn, "The German Model for America," Vox, October 5, 2020, https://www.vox.com/the-highlight/21405900/germany-holocaust-atonement-america-slavery-reparations.

262. Lisa Sun-Hee Park, "Assimilation," chap. 3 in *Keywords for Asian American Studies*, ed. Cathy J. Schlund-Vials, K. Scott Wong, and Linda Trinh Vo (New York: New York University Press, 2015), 14–17.

263. Matthew Frye Jacobsen, *Whiteness of a Different Color: European Immigrants and the Alchemy of Race* (Cambridge, MA: Harvard University Press, 1999), 241.

264. Chua, *Political Tribes*, 17, quoting Woodrow Wilson, "Address to Naturalized Citizens at Convention Hall, Philadelphia," May 10, 1915, American Presidency Project, University of California, Santa Barbara, transcript, https://www.presidency.ucsb.edu/documents/address-naturalized-citizens-convention-hall-philadelphia.

265. "'Kill the Indian, and Save the Man': Capt. Richard H. Pratt on the Education of Native Americans," History Matters, http://historymatters.gmu.edu/d/4929.

266. Rukmini Callimachi, "Lost Lives, Lost Culture: The Forgotten History of Indigenous Boarding Schools," *New York Times,* July 19, 2021, https://www.nytimes.com/2021/07/19/us/us-canada-indigenous-boarding-residential-schools.html; Ian Austen, "'Horrible History': Mass Grave of Indigenous Children Reported in Canada," *New York Times*, May 28, 2021, https://www.nytimes.com/2021/05/28/world/canada/kamloops-mass-grave-residential-schools.html.

267. "'Kill the Indian, Save the Man': An Introduction to the History of Boarding Schools," National Native American Boarding School Healing Coalition, August 3, 2020, https://boardingschoolhealing.org/kill-the-indian-save-the-man-an-introduction-to-the-history-of-boarding-schools/.

268. Motoko Rich and Hikari Hida, "Japan's Native Ainu Fight to Restore a Last Vestige of Their Identity," *New York Times*, July 2, 2023, https://www.nytimes.com/2023/07/02/world/asia/japan-ainu-fishing.html.

269. Chris Buckley, "China Is Detaining Muslims in Vast Numbers. The Goal: 'Transformation,'" *New York Times*, September 8, 2018, https://www.nytimes.com/2018/09/08/world/asia/china-uighur-muslim-detention-camp.html.

270. Austin Ramzy and Chris Buckley, "'Absolutely No Mercy': Leaked Files Expose How China Organized Mass Detentions of Muslims," *New York Times*, November 16, 2019, https://www.nytimes.com/interactive/2019/11/16/world/asia/china-xinjiang-documents.html.

271. Sarah A. Topol, "Her Uighur Parents Were Model Chinese Citizens. It Didn't Matter," *New York Times Magazine*, last modified June 22, 2021, https://www.nytimes.com/2020/01/29/magazine/uyghur-muslims-china.html.

272. Amy Qin, "China Targets Muslim Women in Push to Suppress Births in Xinjiang," *New York Times*, May 10, 2021, https://www.nytimes.com/2021/05/10/world/asia/china-xinjiang-women-births.html.

273. Edward Wong and Chris Buckley, "U.S. Says China's Repression of Uighurs is 'Genocide,'" *New York Times*, January 19, 2021, https://www.nytimes.com/2021/01/19/us/politics/trump-china-xinjiang.html.

Index

Bharatiya Janata Party (India), 101–2, 277, 303
Biden, Joseph, 114, 292, 311
bigotry, definition of, 23
birtherism, 93, 121
Black Lives Matter movement, 41, 48, 111, 112, 214
Black Panther (film), 236–37
Black Power movement, 200–201, 293
Blow, Charles, 293
boarding schools, 316–17
boundary work, 67–71, 81, 178, 264
breaking, 176, 188, 220; defensive breaking, 197–201, 294
Breed, London, 309
Bremer, L. Paul, 291–92
Brexit, 91–92, 120, 296
bridging, practice of, 174–77
Briggs Initiative, 104–5
Brooks, David, 125, 148, 170, 210
Brown, James, 52
Brown v. Board of Education, 52, 166, 294
Buchanan, Patrick, 94
Buckley, William F., Jr., 197
Burns, Daniel, 195
Bush, George H. W., 203
Bush, George W., 102–3, 108
Butler, Judith, 56
Butler, Octavia, 236
Buttigieg, Pete, 170

Calhoun, John C., 102
Campbell, Joseph, 223
Camus, Renaud, 114
Carlson, Tucker, 114
Carmichael, Jerrod, 46–47, 186
Carmichael, Stokely, 52, 200–201
Cartesian duality, 181–82, 184, 186, 194

categorical inequality, 19, 263, 264
categorical othering, 44–45
censorship, 229, 310–11
Charleston church shooting, 113, 266
Charlottesville Unite the Right rally, 111
Cherokee people, 299–300
Chinese Exclusion Act, 99
Chua, Amy, 209
citizenship, 301–8
Civil Rights Act of 1964, 205, 276
Civil Rights Act of 1968, 276
Clark, Kenneth, 66
Clarkson, Adrienne, 165
Cleon, 97
Clinton, Bill, 108
Clinton, Hillary, 92–93
Coates, Ta-Nehisi, 237
Cold War, 122–24, 155, 236, 254, 296–97, 300
Confederate flag and monuments, 107, 111–12, 312
conspiracy theories, 9, 110, 121; birtherism, 93, 121; replacement theory, 113–18
contact theory, 168–69
Cooper, James Fenimore, 96–97, 100
Covid-19 pandemic, 99–100, 105, 248
Cowen, Tyler, 159
cults, 149–50
cultural imperialism, 315–18

Dalit stigmatization and rights, 23, 26, 43, 45, 81, 83, 272, 286–87
Defense of Marriage Act, 103, 108
definition of, 263–64
dehumanization, 23–24, 161, 308–9
deindustrialization, 92, 94, 121
demagoguery and demagogues: contemporary examples of, 101–3;

Hall, Stuart, 243
Hamilton, Alexander, 98
Hannah-Jones, Nikole, 237
Harari, Yuval Noah, 128, 222–24, 234, 248
Harris, Kamala, 245
Hazony, Yoram, 154, 155
Heyer, Heather, 111
hierarchy of human needs, 145–46, 147
Hitler, Adolf, 99, 100, 120, 125, 126
Hochschild, Arlie Russell, 117–18
Hoffer, Eric, 59, 235
Holocaust denial, 309, 314–15
humanizing strategies, 161–62, 240–41
Huntington, Samuel, 155–56, 157
Hussain, Murtaza, 127

identity: biological and birth-based criteria for, 55, 210–11; classification and categorization of, 77–81; contested and reclaimed, 63–67; fluidity and multiplicity of, 209–14; group formations and, 59–63; labels and terminology of, 8–9, 63–66, 76–77; "passing" and, 72–73; social construction of, 56–59; vertical and horizontal, 43–45, 75–76, 195–96, 246, 287
identity dissonance, 189
identity politics, 3, 207, 213–14
identity threats, 103–5, 107–9, 112, 186–87, 203, 240
Immigration and Naturalization Act of 1965, 308
inclusion: backlash and, 116–17; belonging and, 134–38, 141–42, 144, 163, 169–74; critical mass and, 136; definition of, 10, 136;

"guest membership" and, 135, 163; inclusive policies, 134–35; sacred symbols and, 106
India, partition of, 131, 251, 296–97
institutional belongingness, 164–70
intergroup contact theory, 168–69
intersectionality, 25–26
intersubjectivity, 72, 74, 183–85, 193
Iraq war, 291–92
Irving, Kyrie, 47
Islamophobia, 3–4, 8, 17, 20, 27–28, 32, 92
Ivy League institutions, 132–36, 278–79, 288

Jackson, Andrew, 94, 97
James, William, 78–79
January 6 Capitol attack, 111, 112, 205
Japanese-Americans, internment of, 62, 291
Jefferson, Thomas, 165
"Jewish question/problem," 179, 219–20, 279
Johnson, Lyndon Baines, 205
Johnson, Ron, 114

Kant, Immanuel, 181, 184
Kearney, Denis, 98–99, 120
Kendi, Ibram X., 23, 313
Kennedy, John F., 107–8
King, Martin Luther, Jr., 52, 200–201, 233–34, 260
kinship, 50, 154, 195, 209–10
Klein, Ezra, 158, 237, 239
Know-Nothing movement, 101, 259, 261
Krug, Jessica, 217, 221
Ku Klux Klan, 94, 111